BOB MARLEY

THE UNTOLD STORY

Also by Chris Salewicz

The Pretenders

Paul McCartney: The Biography

Billy Bragg: Midnights in Moscow

Bob Marley: Songs of Freedom

Jimi Hendrix: The Ultimate Experience

Punk: The Illustrated History of a Music Revolution

Oliver Stone: The Making of His Movies

George Lucas: The Making of His Movies

Firefly: Noel Coward in Jamaica

Rude Boy: Once Upon a Time in Jamaica

Reggae Explosion: The Story of Jamaican Music

Mick & Keith

Redemption Song: The Ballad of Joe Strummer

Keep On Running: The Story of Island Records (editor)

BOB MARLEY

THE UNTOLD STORY

CHRIS SALEWICZ

ff Faber and Faber, Inc.
An affiliate of Farrar, Straus and Giroux
New York

Faber and Faber, Inc.
An affiliate of Farrar, Straus and Giroux
18 West 18th Street, New York 10011

Distributed in Canada by D&M Publishers, Inc.
Printed in the United States of America
Originally published in 2009 by HarperCollins Publishers, Great Britain
Published in the United States by Faber and Faber, Inc.
First American edition, 2010

PICTURE CREDITS:
In text: pp. 107, 219, 242, 251, 258, 276, 277, 316, 320, 331, 332 © Island Records.
Plate section: p. 16 © Adrian Boot/Camera Press London; pp. 3 (left), 4 (centre right), 5 (bottom left) © Adrian Boot/Retna; p. 9 (top) © Alan Messer/Rex Features; p. 13 (bottom right) © Anwar Hussein/Press Association; p. 3 (right) © AP/Press Association Images; pp. 6 (bottom right), 10 (top right) © Armando Gallo/Retna Ltd/Corbis; p. 14 (bottom) © Brian Rasic/Rex Features; pp. 4 (top), 13 (centre right), 14 (top right), 15 (bottom right) © David Corio; p. 4 (bottom right) © Dezo Hoffmann/Rex Features; p. 10 (bottom right) © Ebet Roberts/Redferns/Getty Images; pp. 6 (bottom left), 12 (top right) © Everett Collection/Rex Features; p. 9 (bottom) © Fikisha Cumbo/Retna Pictures; p. 12 (bottom right) © GAB Archive/Redferns/Getty Images; p. 13 (bottom centre) © Ian Dickson/Rex Features; p. 11 (top left) © Media Press/Rex Features; p. 5 (bottom right) © Michael Ochs Archives/Getty Images; p. 13 (top) © Michael Putland/Retna Pictures; p. 7 (bottom) © Peter Mazel/Sunshine/ Retna Pictures; p. 10 (bottom left) © Peter Mazel/Sunshine/Retna UK; p. 2 (bottom) © Peter Simon/Retna Ltd/Corbis; p. 15 (centre left) © Ray Fairall/AP/Press Association Images; p. 14 (centre left) © Rob Verhost/Redferns/Getty Images; p. 13 (centre left) © S&G Barratts/ Press Association; p. 15 (top) © Sipa Press/Rex Features; p. 11 (top right, centre right) © Toica/Sunshine/Retna UK; pp. 1, 10 (top left), 11 (bottom), 12 (left), 13 (bottom left), 14 (centre right) © UrbanImage.tv/56 Hope Road Music/Adrian Boot; pp. 4 (centre left), 8 (top left), 15 (centre right, bottom left) © UrbanImage.tv/Adrian Boot; pp. 2 (top), 6 (top left, top right), 8 (top right) © UrbanImage.tv/Lee Jaffe; p. 3 (bottom) © UrbanImage.tv/Nathalie Dellon; pp. 7 (top left), 8 (bottom) © UrbanImage.tv/Trax on Wax/Astley Chin; pp. 2 (centre left, centre right), 4 (bottom left), 5 (top), 7 (centre) ©UrbanImage.tv/Trax on Wax/Ossie Hamilton; p. 14 (top left) © Zuma Press/Eyevine.

Library of Congress Cataloging-in-Publication Data
Salewicz, Chris.
    Bob Marley : the untold story / Chris Salewicz.— 1st American ed.
      p. cm.
    Includes index.
    ISBN 978-0-86547-999-9 (hardcover : alk. paper)
    1. Marley, Bob.   2. Reggae musicians—Jamaica—Biography.   I. Title.

ML420.M3313 S35   2010
782.421646092—dc22
[B]
                                                                  2010002410

www.fsgbooks.com

1   3   5   7   9   10   8   6   4   2

For Dickie Jobson (14 November 1941 – 25 December 2008)
and Rob Partridge (2 June 1948 – 26 November 2008)

Contents

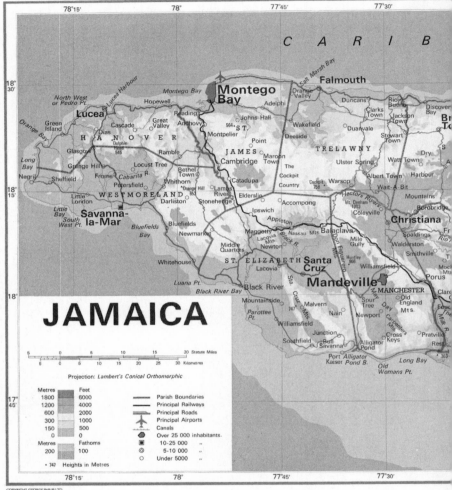

JAMAICA

```
5      0        5       10       15      20 Statute Miles
5   0   5   10   15   20   25   30 Kilometres
```

Projection: Lambert's Conical Orthomorphic

Metres	Feet
1800	6000
1200	4000
600	2000
300	1000
150	500
0	0
Metres	Fathoms
200	100

• 747   Heights in Metres

—— Parish Boundaries
—— Principal Railways
—— Principal Roads
✈ Principal Airports
—— Canals
⬡ Over 25 000 inhabitants
◼ 10-25 000 "
◎ 5-10 000 "
○ Under 5000 "

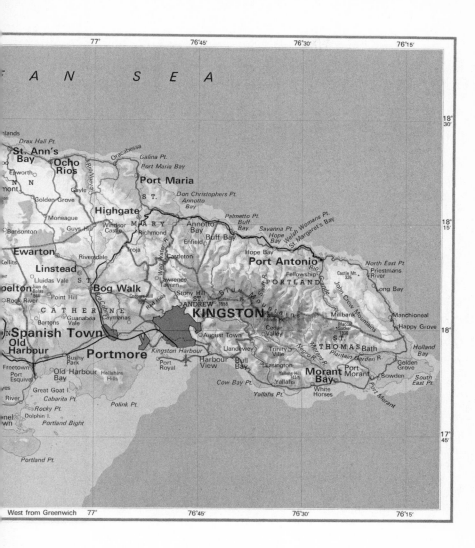

Acknowledgements

In the middle of the 1990s I found myself living in Jamaica for a couple of years. Almost every day I would hear fresh stories, of lesser or greater significance, about Bob Marley. One day, I sensed that, whilst there, I would write a full biography of the Tuff Gong; I had already written the text for *Songs of Freedom*, the book of Bob Marley photographs by Adrian Boot. Although certain improved sections of *Songs of Freedom*, and a section from my book *Rude Boy*, have been included in *Bob Marley: The Untold Story*, this book is the consequence of close to forty years of research into the fullness of the mystery of not only Bob Marley, but of Jamaican culture as a whole, including, naturally, the apparently odd religion of Rastafari.

Clearly, I must pay thanks to the assistance I have received from the people of Jamaica in the writing of this biography; and especially to all those who, over the years, have assisted my endeavours to comprehend the assorted complexities of these matters. Specifically, these have included Bob Marley himself; Peter Tosh; Bunny Wailer; Mrs Cedella Booker; Rita Marley; Cedella Marley; Ziggy Marley; Damian Marley; Judy Mowatt; Aston 'Family Man' Barrett; Junior Murvin; Al Anderson; Diane Jobson; Lee 'Scratch' Perry; Burning Spear; Prince Buster; Joseph Hill; Leonard Dillon; Alton Ellis; U Roy; I Roy; Dennis Brown; Chinna Smith; Gregory Isaacs; Dillinger; Trinity; Junior Marvin; Tapper Zukie; Ernest Ranglin; Johnny Moore; Jah Jerry; Sid Bucknor; Harry Johnson; Tony Washington; Linton Kwesi Johnson; Mrs Sonya Pottinger; Karl Pitterson; Augustus Pablo; Allan 'Skill' Cole; and many, many more.

I must also extend my most grateful appreciation to Chris Blackwell, Suzette Newman, Carl Bradshaw, Don Letts, and the late, great Dickie Jobson and his sister Diane Jobson. Similarly, it is impossible to overlook the contributions of the late Rob Partridge. Equally, I must offer unequivocal thanks to Brian Blevins, the then Island Records press officer who in 1972 turned me on to the music of the Wailers. The thoughts and work of Adrian Boot have proved inspirational, as have those of Vivien Goldman. I must give especial serious thanks to Roger Steffens and his priceless Bob Marley archive, as well as to Wayne Jobson and Lee Jaffe.

This book would not have existed without the exceptional work of several superb editors: Trevor Dolby, Natalie Jerome, Humphrey Price, Dan Bunyard, Sarah Lazin, and Sarah Day; and, as ever, I owe exceptional gratitude to my literary agent, Julian Alexander, and to Rose Lukas.

Hear Bob Marley and the Wailers

To hear a playlist of some of the music by Bob Marley and the Wailers discussed in these pages, specially compiled by the author, visit
www.bobmarleyuntold.com

Introduction

ME ONLY HAVE ONE AMBITION, Y'KNOW. I ONLY HAVE ONE THING I REALLY LIKE TO SEE HAPPEN. I LIKE TO SEE MANKIND LIVE TOGETHER – BLACK, WHITE, CHINESE, EVERYONE – THAT'S ALL.

In early 1978 I spent two months in Jamaica, researching its music and interviewing many key figures, having arrived there on the same reggae-fanatics' pilgrimage as John 'Johnny Rotten' Lydon and Don Letts, the Rastafarian film-maker. My first visit to the island was a life-changing experience, and I plunged into the land of magic realism that is Jamaica, an island that can be simultaneously heaven and hell. Almost exactly a year later, in February 1979, I flew to Kingston on my second visit to 'the fairest land that eyes have beheld', according to its discoverer, Christopher Columbus, who first sighted the 'isle of springs' in 1494. Arriving late in the evening, I took a taxi to Knutsford Boulevard in New Kingston and checked into the Sheraton Hotel.

Jet lag meant that I woke early the next morning. Seizing the time, I found myself in a taxi at around quarter to eight, chugging through the rush-hour traffic, rounding the corner by the stately Devon House, the former residence of the British governor, and into and up Hope Road. 'Bob Marley gets up early,' I had been advised.

Arriving at his headquarters of 56 Hope Road, trundling through the gates and disgorging myself from my Morris Oxford cab in front of the house, there was little sign of activity. On the wooden verandah to the right of the building was a group of what looked like tough ghetto youth, to whom I nodded greetings, searching in vain for any faces I recognised. In front of the Tuff Gong record shop to the right of the house was a woman who wore her dreadlocks tucked into a tam; she was sweeping the shop's steps with a besom broom that scurried around the floor-length hem of her skirt. A sno-cone spliff dangled from her mouth. Wandering over to her, I introduced myself, mentioning that I had been in Jamaica the previous year writing about reggae, showing her a copy of the main article I had written in the *NME*. She was extremely articulate, and I discovered that her name was Diane Jobson and that she was the inhouse lawyer for the Tuff Gong operation (over the years I was to get to know her well; and her brother Dickie, who directed the film *Countryman*, became a close pal).

Then a 5 Series BMW purred into the yard. Driven by a beautiful girl, it had – like many Jamaican cars – black-tinted windows and an Ethiopian flag fluttering in the breeze from an aerial on its left front wing. Out of it stepped Bob Marley. He greeted the ghetto youth, walked towards them, and began speaking with them. On his way over, he registered my presence. After a couple of minutes, I walked towards him. I introduced myself, and he shook hands with me with a smile, paying attention, I noticed, to the Animal Rights badge that by chance I was wearing on my red Fred Perry shirt; again, I explained I had been to Jamaica for the first time the previous year, and showed him the article. He seemed genuinely interested and began to read it. As he did so, like Bob Marley should have done, he handed me a spliff he had just finished rolling. Nervously, I took it and pulled away.

After a minute or two Diane came over. Gathering together the youth, she led them in the direction of a mini-bus parked in the shade that I had not previously noticed. Bob made his excuses – 'We have to go somewhere' – and walked over to the vehicle. Then, as he stepped into it, he turned. 'Come on, come with us.' He waved with a grin, climbing down out of the vehicle and holding the door open for me.

I hurried over. Ushering me into the mini-bus, Bob squeezed up next to me on one of its narrow two-person bench-seats, his leg resting against my own. I tried to disguise my feelings – a sense of great honour as well as slight apprehension that the herb I had smoked was beginning to kick in, suddenly seeming a million times stronger than anything I had ever smoked in London. I was starting to feel rather distanced from everything, which was possibly just as well. Bumping through the potholed backstreets of what I knew to be the affluent uptown suburb of Beverly Hills, I ventured to ask Bob, who was himself hitting on a spliff, where we were going. 'Gun Court,' he uttered, matter-of-factly.

I blinked, and tried quickly to recover myself. The Gun Court had a reputation that was fearsome. To all intents and purposes, the place was a concentration camp – certainly it had been built to look like one: gun towers, barbed-wire perimeters, visibly armed guards, a harsh, militaristic feel immediately apparent to all who drove past its location on South Camp Road. The Gun Court was a product of Michael Manley's Emergency Powers Act of 1975. Into it was dumped, for indefinite detention or execution after a summary trial, anyone in Jamaica found with any part of a gun. (In more recent times, it is said, the security forces adopt a more cost-effective and immediate solution: anyone in Jamaica found with any part of a gun, runs the myth, is executed on the spot – hence the almost daily newspaper reports of gunmen 'dying on the way to hospital' . . .) The previous year, when I had been in Kingston with Lydon, Letts, and co., the dreadlocked Rastafarian film-maker had been held at gunpoint by a Jamaica Defence Force soldier whilst filming the exterior of the Gun Court. At first the squaddie refused to believe Letts was British; only after being shown his UK passport did he let him walk away. What would have happened had he been Jamaican?

'Why are we going there?' I demanded of Bob, as casually as I could.

'To see about a youth them lock up – Michael Bernard,' he quietly replied.

Michael Bernard, I learned later, was a cause célèbre.

Having descended from the heights of Beverly Hills, a detour that had been taken to avoid morning traffic (like most of the rest of the world, and especially in Jamaica at that time, when cars and car parts were at a considerable premium, this was nothing compared to the almost permanent gridlock that Kingston was to become by the end of the century), we were soon pulling up outside the Gun Court's sinister compound.

At nine in the morning, beneath an already scorching tropical sun, the vision of the Gun Court was like a surreal dubbed-up inversion of one of the ugly, incongruous industrial-trading-estate-type buildings that litter much of Kingston's often quite cute sprawl.

At the sight of Bob emerging from the mini-bus, a door within the main gates opened for his party. We stepped through into the prison. After we stood for some time in the heat of the forecourt yard, an officer appeared. In hushed tones he spoke to Bob; I was unable to hear what passed between them, which was probably just as well – it being almost a year since I had last enjoyed a regular daily diet of patois, I was beginning to register I could comprehend only about half of what was being said around me.

Then we were led into the piss-stinking prison building itself. And through a number of locked, barred doors, and into the governor's broad office, like the study of a boarding-school headmaster, which was also the demeanour of the governor himself, a greying, late-middle-aged man who sat behind a sturdy desk by the window. We were seated on hard wooden chairs in a semicircle in front of him. I found myself directly to the right of Bob, who in turn was seated nearest to the governor. Through a door in the opposite wall arrived a slight man who appeared to be in his early twenties. He was shown to a chair. This was Michael Bernard, who had been sentenced for an alleged politically motivated shooting, one for which no one I met in Kingston believed him to be responsible.

Discussions now began, the essence of which concerned questions by Bob as to the possibilities of a retrial or of Bernard's release from prison. Bernard said virtually nothing, and almost all speech was confined to Bob and the governor. I asked a couple of questions, but when I interrupted a third time Bob wisely hushed me – I was starting to get into a slightly right-on stride here. Most of the dialogue, I noted, was conducted in timorous, highly reverent tones by all parties present, almost with a measure of deference, or perhaps simply hesitant nervousness. (Over the years I was to decide that it was the latter, noting that often Jamaicans called upon to speak publicly – whether rankin' politicians at barnstorming rallies, Rasta elders at revered Nyabinghi reasonings, Commissioner of Police Joe Williams in an interview I conducted with him, or crucial defence witnesses in the rarified, bewigged atmosphere of English courts – would present themselves with all the stumbling hesitancy and lack of rigorous logic of a very reluctant school-speechday orator. Yet in more lateral philosophical musings and reasonings, there are few individuals as fascinatingly, confidently loquacious as Jamaicans when it comes to conversational elliptical twists, stream-of-consciousness free-associations, and Barthes-like word de- and re-constructions.)

After twenty or so minutes, all talk seemed to grind to a halt. Afterwards I was left a little unclear as to what conclusions had been arrived at, if any. At first I worried that this was because initially I had been strug-gling with the effects of the herb, which seemed like a succession of psychic tidal-waves. Then later I realised that the purpose of this mission to the Gun Court was simply to show that Michael Bernard had not been forgotten.

Bidding farewell to the prisoner, wishing him luck, and thanking the governor for his time, we left his office, clanking out through the jail doors and into the biting sunlight. Soon we were back at 56 Hope Road, which by then had become a medina of all manner of activity. 'Stick around,' said Bob. I did. And on a bench in the shade of a mango tree round the back of the house promptly fell asleep for at least two hours from what was probably a combination of jet lag, the spliff, and some kind of delayed shock.

This visit to the Gun Court with Bob Marley was one of the great experiences of my life. I was in Jamaica for another three weeks or so. During that time I saw Bob several more times. I watched rehearsals at 56 Hope Road; saw Bob playing with some of his kids – the ones that had just released their first record as the Melody Makers; and found him with one of the most gorgeous women who had ever crossed my eyes (a different one from the car-driver at 56 Hope Road) at a Twelve Tribes Grounation (essentially, dances steeped in the mystique of Rastafari) one Saturday night on the edge of the hills. She turned out to be Cindy Breakspeare, Jamaica's former Miss World. I also interviewed Bob for an article: whilst doing so, I remember feeling a measure of guilt for taking up so much of his precious time – though I didn't realise then precisely quite how precious and finite it was. Part of the reason I thought this was because I felt Bob looked terribly tired and strained – it was only just over eighteen months later that he collapsed whilst jogging in Central Park with his friend Skill Cole, and was diagnosed as suffering from cancer.

It came as a deep, unpleasant shock just before midnight on 11 May 1981 to receive a phone call from Rob Partridge, who had so assiduously handled Bob's publicity for Island Records, to be told that Bob had lost his fight with cancer and passed on. (I had always believed that Bob would beat the disease . . .) Although I wrote his obituary for *NME*, it seemed my relationship with Bob and his music was only just beginning. In February 1983, I was back in Jamaica, writing a story for *The Face* about Island's release of the posthumous Bob Marley album *Confrontation*.

Again, jet lag caused me to wake early on the first morning I was there. This time I was staying just down the road from the former Sheraton, at the neighbouring Pegasus Hotel. Getting out of bed, I switched on the radio in my room. The Jamaican Broadcasting Corporation (JBC) seven o'clock news came on with its first story: 'Released from the Gun Court today is Michael Bernard . . .' Wow! Phew! *JAH RASTAFARI!!!* That Jamaica will get you every time. The island really *is* a land of magic realism, a physical, geographical place that is like a manifestation of the collective unconscious. Or is it that Bob Marley, as someone once suggested to me, is very active in psychic spheres and has a great sense of humour? Was this just something he'd laid on for me in the Cosmic Theme Park of the Island of Springs, I found myself wondering, with a certain vanity.

JAMAICA

The Caribbean island of Jamaica has had an impact on the rest of the world that is far greater than might be expected from a country with a population of under three million. Jamaica's history, in fact, shows that ever since its discovery by Christopher Columbus, it has had a disproportionate effect on the rest of the world.

In the seventeenth century, for example, Jamaica was the world centre of piracy. From its capital of Port Royal, buccaneers under the leadership of Captain Henry Morgan plundered the Spanish Main, bringing such riches to the island that it became as wealthy as any of Europe's leading trading centres; the pleasures such money brought earned Port

Royal the reputation of 'wickedest city in the world'. In 1692, four years after Morgan's death, Port Royal disappeared into the Caribbean in an earthquake. However, a piratic, rebellious spirit has been central to the attitude of Jamaicans ever since: this is clear in the lives of Nanny, the woman who led a successful slave revolt against the English in 1738; of Marcus Garvey, who in the 1920s became the first prophet of black self-determination and founded the Black Star shipping line, intended to transport descendants of slaves back to Africa; of Bob Marley, the Third World's first superstar, with his musical gospel of love and global unity.

Jamaica was known by its original settlers, the Arawak peoples, as the Island of Springs. It is in the omnipresent high country that resides Jamaica's unconscious: the primal Blue Mountains and hills are the repository of most of Jamaica's legends, a dreamlike landscape that furnishes ample material for an arcane mythology.

On the north side of the Blue Mountains, in the parish of Portland, one of the most beautiful parts of Jamaica, is Moore Town. It was to the safety of the impenetrable hills that bands of former slaves fled, after they were freed and armed by the Spanish, to harass the English when they seized the island in 1655. The Maroons, as they became known, founded a community and underground state that would fight a guerrilla war against the English settlers on and off for nearly eighty years.

When peace was eventually established, the Maroons were granted semi-autonomous territory both in Portland and Trelawny, to the west of the island. In Moore Town was buried the great Maroon queen, Nanny, who led her people in battles in which they defeated the English redcoats. Honoured today as a National Hero of Jamaica, Nanny's myth was so great that she was said to have the ability to catch musket-balls fired at her – in her 'pum-pum', according to some accounts.

Jamaica has always been tough. The Arawak peoples repulsed invasions by the cannibalistic Caribs who had taken over most of the neighbouring islands. Jamaica was an Arawak island when it was discovered in 1494. 'The fairest island that eyes have beheld; mountainous and the land seems to touch the sky,' wrote Columbus, although he may not have felt the same nine years later, on his fourth voyage to the New World. In St Ann's Bay, later the birthplace of Marcus Garvey, Columbus was driven ashore by a storm, and his rotting vessels filled with water almost up to their decks as they settled on the sand of the sea-bed.

Later placed into slavery by the Spaniards, the Arawaks were shockingly abused, and many committed suicide. Some were tortured to death in the name of sport. By 1655, when the English captured the island, the Arawaks had been completely wiped out.

Even after the 1692 earthquake, piracy remained such a powerful force in the region that a king's pardon was offered in 1717 to all who would give up the trade. Many did not accept these terms, and in November 1720 a naval sloop came across the vessel of the notorious pirate 'Calico Jack' Rackham anchored off Negril, in the west of Jamaica. Once the crew was overpowered – with ease: they were suffering from the effects of a rum party – two of the toughest members of Rackham's team were discovered to be women disguised as men: Anne Bonny and Mary Read, who each cheated the gallows through pregnancy.

Those Jamaican settlers who wished to trade legally could also make fortunes. Sugar, which had been brought to the New World by Columbus on the voyage during which he discovered Jamaica, was the most profitable crop that could be grown on the island, and it was because of their importance as sugar-producing islands that the British West Indies had far more political influence with the British government than all the thirteen American mainland colonies.

Sugar farming requires a significant labour force, and it was this that led to the large-scale importation of African slaves. For the remainder of the eighteenth century, the wealth of Jamaica was secured with the 1713 Treaty of Utrecht, which ended the War of the Spanish Succession: one of its terms was that Jamaica become the distribution centre for slaves for the entire New World. The first slaves shipped to the West Indies had been prisoners of war or criminals, purchased from African chiefs in exchange for European goods. With a much larger supply needed, raiding parties, often under the subterfuge of engaging in tribal wars, took place all along the west coast of Africa. The horrors of the middle passage had to be endured before the slaves were auctioned, £50 being the average price.

Although the money that could be earned was considerable compensation for the white settlers, life in Jamaica was often a worry. There were slave revolts and tropical diseases. War broke out frequently, and the island was then threatened with attack by the French or the Spanish – Horatio Nelson, when still a midshipman, was stationed on the island. Hurricanes, which invariably levelled the crop, were not infrequent; and earthquakes not unknown. In the late seventeenth century Kingston harbour was infested with crocodiles, but it should be said that in those days inhabitants of the entire south coast of the island always ran the risk of being devoured by them.

Despite such disadvantages, it has always been hard for Jamaica not to touch the hearts of visitors, with its spectacular, moody beauty. The island contains a far larger variety of vegetation and plantlife than almost anywhere in the world (as it is located near the centre of the Caribbean Sea, birds carrying seeds in their droppings fly to it from North, Central, and South America). Jamaica's British colonisers added to this wealth of vegetation, often whilst searching for fresh, cheap means of filling the bellies of its slaves. The now omnipresent mango, for example, was brought from West Africa, and it was on a journey across the Pacific to bring the first breadfruit plants to Jamaica that the mutiny on the *Bounty* took place.

Slavery was eventually abolished in 1838. From the 1860s, indentured labour from India and China was imported; the Indians brought with them their propensity for smoking ganja, itself an Indian word (interestingly, sometimes spelt 'gunjah'), as well as the plant's seeds. In the 1880s, a new period of prosperity began after a crop was found to replace sugarcane – the banana. In 1907, however, this new prosperity was partially unhinged by the devastating earthquake that destroyed much of Kingston. The economy recovered, and the next wave of financial problems occurred in the late 1930s, as the worldwide depression finally hit the island. A consequence of this was the founding of the two political parties, the Jamaica Labour Party (JLP) under Alexander Bustamante and the People's National Party (PNP) under Norman Manley, which would spearhead the path towards independence in 1962.

On 6 August 1962 Jamaica became an independent nation. The Union Jack was lowered and the green, gold, and black standard of Jamaica was raised. Three months previously, the JLP had won a twenty-six-seat majority and taken over the government under Prime Minister Bustamante. Paradox is one of the yardsticks of Jamaica, and it should be no surprise that the Jamaica Labour Party has always been far to the right of its main opposition, the People's National Party.

Beneath this facade of democracy, the life of the 'sufferah', downcast in his west Kingston ghetto tenement, was essentially unchanged. In some ways things were now more difficult. The jockeying for position created by self-government brought out the worst in people. Soon the MPs of each of the ghetto constituencies had surrounded themselves with gun-toting sycophants anxious to preserve their and their family's position. In part this was a spin-off from the gangs of enforcers that grew up around sound systems: back the wrong candidate in a Jamaican election and you can lose not only your means of livelihood, but also your home – and even your life. Political patronage is the ruling principle in Jamaica.

During the 1960s, Jamaican youth, who felt especially disenfranchised, sought refuge in the rude-boy movement, an extreme precursor of the teenage tribes surfacing throughout the world. Dressed in narrow-brimmed hats and the kind of mohair fabrics worn by American soul singers, rude boys were fond of stashing lethal 'ratchet' knives on their persons, and bloody gang fights were common. Independence for Jamaica coincided with the birth of its music business; in quick succession, ska, rock steady, and then reggae music were born, the records often being used as a kind of bush telegraph to broadcast news of some latest police oppression that the *Daily Gleaner* would not print.

In 1972, after ten years in power, the JLP was voted out of office. Michael Manley's People's National Party was to run Jamaica for the next eight years. Unfortunately, Manley's efforts to ally with other socialist Third World countries brought the wrath of the United States upon Jamaica, especially after the prime minister nationalised his country's bauxite industry, which provides the raw material for aluminium – and had been previously licensed to the Canadian conglomerate Alcan.

A policy of destabilisation began that turned Jamaica into a battleground, especially after Manley was returned to power in December 1976 in the subsequent election. Soon the country was almost bankrupt. Bob Marley played a part in attempting to restore peace, forcing Manley and his opposition rival, Edward Seaga, to shake hands publicly at the 1978 *One Love* Peace Concert in Kingston, and bringing opposing gunmen together. But the 1980 election, won by Edward Seaga, in power until 1989, was the bloodiest of them all.

In recent years, a measure of peace seems to have been brought to the island. A positive relationship with the nearby United States has been forged, and there is a previously unsurpassed national pride, following the Jamaican soccer team's qualification for the 1998 World Cup and an unprecedented run of successes at the 2008 Beijing Olympics.

Still, the story of Jamaica is that of an island that can be simultaneously heaven and hell – as indeed described in the Bob Marley song 'Time Will Tell', in its line 'Think you're in heaven but you're living in hell'; a country that could suffer the devastating economic bullying of the United States' Caribbean Basin Initiative during the 1970s but that now, against expectations, is experiencing economic growth and a resultant rise in self-esteem that lets it serve as a model for developing nations in the first years of the twenty-first century. And at least its inhabitants rarely forget that Jamaica is a land whose blessings are surely God-given.

Bob Marley is seen by the world as the personification of the rebellious island nation of Jamaica – not without considerable justification. For Bob Marley was a hero figure, in the classic mythological sense. From immensely humble beginnings, with his talent and religious belief his only weapons, the Jamaican recording artist applied himself with unstinting perseverance to spreading his prophetic musical message; he only departed this planet when he felt his vision of One World, One Love, which was inspired by his belief in Rastafarianism, was beginning in some quarters to be heard and felt. For example, in 1980, the European tour of Bob Marley and the Wailers played to the largest audiences a musical act had ever experienced there. And as much as the late Bob Marley continues to personify Jamaica, so he also embodied the soul of what the world knows as the odd, apparently paradoxical religion of Rastafari, the only faith uncritically accepted globally as an integral aspect of popular music.

Bob Marley's story is that of an archetype, which is why it continues to have such a powerful and ever-growing resonance: it embodies, among other themes, political repression, metaphysical and artistic insights, gangland warfare, and various periods in a mystical wilderness. It is no surprise that Bob Marley now enjoys an icon-like status more akin to that of the rebel myth of Che Guevara than to that of a pop star. And his audience continues to widen: to westerners, Bob's apocalyptic truths prove inspirational and life-changing; in the Third World, his impact is similar, except that it goes further. Not just amongst Jamaicans, but also amongst the Hopi people of New Mexico and the Maoris of New Zealand, in Indonesia, in India, even – especially – in those parts of West Africa from which slaves were plucked and taken to the New World, Bob Marley is seen as the Redeemer figure returning to lead this planet out of confusion. Some will come out and say it directly: that Bob Marley is the reincarnation of Jesus Christ long awaited by much of the world. In such an interpretation of his life, the cancer that killed Bob Marley is inevitably described as a modern version of the crucifixion.

Although the disease probably did have its origins in assorted injuries to his right foot, conspiracy theories still persist. Was Bob's body poisoned still further when going for medical check-ups in Babylonian cities, such as London, Miami, and New York? Were his hotel rooms or homes bombarded with cancer-inducing rays? Or, more simply, was Bob's system slowly poisoned by the lead from the bullet that remained in his body after the 1976 attempt on his life? (All of these were suggested to me by his mother as possible causes of her son's death.)

Prior to the US leg of the *Uprising* tour in the autumn of 1980, Bob Marley had been given a complete physical examination, allegedly passing with flying colours – though this is odd, as the musician was certainly in the latter stages of suffering from cancer. In Miami, before the tour kicked off, he played a game of football for America Jamaica United, against a team of Haitians, in which his fluid skills seemed unabated.

But yes, you think, the cancer probably was the consequence of the injuries to his foot. And then you remember that this was a time when the forces of darkness thought nothing of killing a woman such as Karen Silkwood, who was endeavouring to expose a nuclear risk. How much more must they have been threatened by a charismatic, alternative world leader who in widely accessible popular art was delivering warnings about the wickedness of the world's institutions?

Thanks to the tireless efforts of Timothy White, the author of *Catch a Fire*, the wonderful Bob Marley biography published in 1984, the extent of the CIA files on Bob has become widely known. Chris Blackwell, who signed Bob to his Island Records label, had personal experience of this. 'There are conspiracy theories with everything, especially out of Jamaica, because Jamaicans have such fertile imaginations. The only thing I will say is that I was brought in by the American ambassador in Jamaica to his office, and he said that they were keeping an eye on me, on what I was doing, because I was working with this guy who was capable of destabilising. They had their eye on him.'

Bob's end was very sad. After his collapse whilst jogging in New York's Central Park on 21 September 1980, he received radiation treatment at the city's Memorial Sloan-Kettering Cancer Center; his locks fell out, like a portent.

Even confronted by a future of such grim uncertainty, Bob Marley managed never to lose his wry view of life. Two weeks after his collapse, his death was being reported in the US media; he put out a statement in which his characteristic dry sense of humour was clearly still in evidence: 'They say that living in Manhattan is hell, but . . .'

With a similar attitude, he strove to make light of his illness to his children. Whilst he was being treated in New York, they flew up from Jamaica to see him at the Essex House hotel on Central Park South, where he habitually stayed when in Manhattan. 'He told us what was wrong with him,' said Cedella. 'His hair was gone. We were like, "Where's your hair?" He was making it to be such a big joke: "Oh, I'm Frankenstein." We said, "That's not funny."

'I knew Daddy had a bad toe, because I would have to clean it sometimes. But I just thought it was a bad toe. I didn't expect anything else but for maybe the nail to come off.'

By November 1980, the doctors at the Sloan-Kettering admitted they could do no more. A number of alternative cures were considered: the apricot kernel therapy attempted by the actor Steve McQueen; a spiritual cure by journeying to Ethiopia; a simple return home to Jamaica – though this plan was abandoned when the island was seen to be in the grip of the most violent general election it had ever known.

After the options had been weighed up, Bob travelled to Bavaria in West Germany, to the Sunshine House Cancer Clinic in Bad Wiessee. A holistic centre, it was run by the controversial Dr Josef Issels, a former SS officer. Issels only took on cases that had been proclaimed incurable, and he claimed a 20 per cent success rate.

The environment, however, was hostile and alien. The house of the dread who would never tour Babylon during the winter months was surrounded by thick snow. Bob would go to Issels's clinic for two hours of treatment each day then return to spend time with the several visitors who flew in to be with him – his mother, his wife, members of the Wailers, old friends. Much of his time was spent watching videotapes of soccer matches, particularly those played by the Brazilian team.

But Bob never stopped songwriting. He seemed to think he could make it. His weight went up and for a time he seemed in better spirits. But the sterile, picture-postcard atmosphere of Bad Wiessee hardly nurtured Bob's soul. 'It was a horrible place,' thought Chris Blackwell. 'It must have been very disorientating for him. He had virtually no hair, just scraggly bits, and was so thin: he must have weighed a hundred pounds or something like that. He looked terrible. But there was something . . . He was still so proud. He chatted for a bit. He was very strong somehow still.'

The atmosphere where he was staying was even worse: vicious psychological warfare was taking place between, as Mortimer Planner, the Rastafarian elder, described it, 'the Orthodox and Twelve Tribes factions'. It seems demeaning to everyone involved, including Bob, to describe this in further detail. Sufficient to heed Planner's words: 'A terrible misunderstanding has gone on. For *all* these people loved Bob.'

He developed a craving for plantain tarts, and it was arranged for a carton of them to be flown to him from Jamaica. Before they arrived, he decided he wanted to go home. He had had enough of Bad Wiessee. He knew what was going to happen. Bob Marley asked Chris Blackwell to rent him a plane. Blackwell said he would send one for him immediately. 'But even then, Bob hadn't lost his sense of humour,' smiled the Island Records boss. 'Bob always thought I was kinda cheap, so he said, "Don't send me one with propellers now."'

Accompanied by two doctors, Bob was flown across the Atlantic. He made it no further than Miami.

Judy Mowatt, one of the I-Threes, was at home on the morning of 11 May 1981. A little after 11.30 she heard a loud clap of thunder and saw lightning fork through a window of her house and flash on a picture of Bob on the wall. And Judy knew exactly what this foretold.

At a little after 11.30 a.m., in the Cedars of Lebanon hospital in Miami, Bob surrendered his soul to the Almighty Jah.

NATURAL MYSTIC

Although in later life the name of Bob Marley came to be considered as synonymous with Kingston's downtown ghetto of Trench Town, the singer was really a country boy, raised and reared in a backwoods part of Jamaica. There he would watch the ebb and flow of nature, observing animals and plants grow, paying especial attention to the timeless progress of trees; in his music there is often a sense of an association with the earth itself.

The 'garden parish' of St Ann in which he 'came up', as Jamaicans would say, is often considered the most beautiful part of Jamaica. And Nine Miles, where Nesta Robert Marley was born, is like a perfect microcosm of the north-central region of Jamaica in which it is located. Deep in the interior of the extraordinary lush landscape of St Ann, and not easily accessible, the rolling, feminine countryside around the hamlet of Nine Miles is like the heart, even the soul and mystery of the island. Located at 3,500 feet above sea-level, its height gives this land-locked region distinct climatic advantages: for example, it enjoys temperate weather, cooler and less oppressive than that of the marshy plains in the south of the island or the baking, concrete swelter of Kingston, the capital.

Cedella Malcolm, the mother of Bob Marley, was born on 23 July 1926; she shared the date, but not the year of birth, with a man whose very name ultimately would weave a life-changing spell over her: Ras Tafari, Emperor Haile Selassie I, Negus Negusti, King of Kings, Conquering Lion of the Tribe of Judah. Such an apparent coincidence should be no great surprise: the very air of Jamaica seems thick with great truths and inconceivable, magical mysteries. Obeah, an African diasporic word, a marriage of African animist and Catholic practices, had long been accepted by many as a norm. And in Jamaica – as in neighbouring Cuba and Haiti, where it is known as voodoo – it lived hand in hand with what often revealed itself to be a stringent, unforgiving form of Christianity.

This was the world in which Bob Marley's mother grew up. It was not surprising then that when Cedella Malcolm – whose name was familiarly shortened to 'Ciddy' – was eight years old, she saw Hubert Hall, a local practitioner of obeah, confess that he had caused the crash which had overturned her father's car when she was a toddler. On his deathbed the man struggled to save his soul by admitting the wickedness of his sins and transgressions. Lying on a board in Cedella's father's kitchen at Nine Miles, Hall's head seemed to dwarf his drawn, wretchedly suffering body: it was pure skin and bone, except for his feet, which had swollen up to almost the size of his skull. As he spoke, Cedella could see the fear and terror emanating in a kind of steam from his jaw, his lips skinning back from his teeth.

Driven by a bitterness and jealousy that gnawed away at him like a cancer, Hall had waited until Omeriah Malcolm's De Soto, a symbol of the family's prosperity, on that day piled up with relatives, purred along one of the only straight stretches on the endlessly winding, ever climbing road that clambers up through Nine Miles. As Cedella's father approached Eleven Miles, Hall summoned up his 'science', as obeah is also known, to flip the car over on its side. A truckdriver passing through Nine Miles called out the grim news: *Mr Malcolm's car overturn 'pon de bank and all de people dem dead dere!*

Omeriah's friends and relatives, the tiny Cedella clutched to the bosom of an aunt, hurried to the scene of the accident. Arriving there, they experienced a measure of relief; no one was dead, but there were some terrible injuries: the mother of one of Cedella's brothers – as befitted a man prosperous and powerful enough to be the local *custos* (a legally ordained arbitrator), her father had not restricted his love life to Cedella's mother, his wife Alberta, and he had over twenty children by various women – had had her hair burned off entirely by scalding water from the cracked radiator. Trapped in the wreckage, crumpled and crammed up on top of each other, were the other passengers, dreadfully burnt, or moaning from the pain of their broken bones and torn flesh. Sitting dazed by the side of the road, however, with only a slight cut to his face, was Cedella's father, balancing her little brother John on his knee: his inborn goodness had led God to protect Omeriah Malcolm.

Even as they were taking Hubert Hall's body on a stretcher up to the burial plot, little Ciddy was still mulling over the man's confession, her first direct experience of the force of obeah; the casualness of his wickedness caused her deep distress. Hall admitted he had been in league with others who had sought out his dark talent, urging him on to this terrible

act with no more lavish a bribe than a meal of goat's head, yam, and cho-
cho. But for most of the adults who had heard Hall's tormented words,
such wickedness unfortunately was commonplace. Her father, for example, had little doubt of their veracity; and of the way the obeahman had
distorted the 'natural mystic' that wafts on the breeze through Nine Miles
like one of God's greatest and most secret truths.

The Malcolms were the oldest, most respected family in the region of
Rhoden Hall, where Nine Miles is located, owning or renting a considerable amount of land and local properties. As the ownership of the
luxury De Soto motor car indicated, they were by no means impoverished. Although there was no electricity or running water in Nine Miles,
Ciddy's father owned one of the only Delco generators in the area.
Omeriah Malcolm would start it up on Sundays, so that his friends and
relatives could listen to his radio. For this enjoyment they would walk
from miles around. 'Sometimes we would hear a sermon from Kingston,
sometimes rumba music from Cuba,' said Ciddy.

Omeriah's father was Robert 'Uncle Day' Malcolm, who was descended from the Cromanty slaves shipped from the Gold Coast – what
is now Ghana – between 200 and 250 years previously: as tenant slaves,
the Malcolms had lived in this bush region long before slavery was abolished in 1838.

Cedella's grandmother, Katherine Malcolm, known as Yaya, lived
'down the bottom', away from the road over on the other side of a steep
hill. Her home was the family residence known as 'Big House', though it
consisted only of one room and a hall – but there were a number of
outhouses. Cedella had the impression that Yaya never slept. Every
morning, round about 3 or 4 a.m., the hour at which many Jamaican
countryfolk rise, Mr Malcolm would walk up the goat-path to his mother's

for his morning coffee. He would take with him – as would anyone who ventured up that way – a big log of wood to stoke up the fire that always blazed at Yaya's; in those days before matches became plentiful, anyone who needed fire would go up to see her and beg a blazing lump of wood. When Cedella's father returned home after an hour or so, he'd carry with him a covered quart tin full of coffee for the children's breakfast. Set up for the day, Omeriah would then leave for his various pieces of farmland. He was the biggest cultivator of coffee in the neighbourhood, taking it to market at Green Hill in his horse and cart before he bought first a Ford Model T and then the De Soto. But he would also grow pimento and bananas, making sure that every piece of land he worked had a plentiful supply of banana trees.

But Omeriah Malcolm's relative commercial success was not his only source of wealth. His father had carefully instructed him in the arcane arts brought to Jamaica by the Cromanty slaves. Omeriah proved to have an empathy and skill with these God-given positive forces; he was, to all intents and purposes, a magician, but one who dealt only with light and high matters; one of his closest friends was an eminent Jamaican 'scientist' so skilled he was said to be able simultaneously to write two letters of the alphabet with one hand. Omeriah Malcolm became what was known as a 'myalman', a healer and a bush doctor, and his understanding included the natural medicine and power in the individual plants, such as Tree of Life and Sink-a-Bible, which flourish in Jamaica. When she grew older, Cedella's father would confide in her about the many powerful spirits lodged in the neighbourhood of Nine Miles. It had always been so, he would say, and would puzzle why so many people there were ready to surrender themselves to the dark forces; why it would always be said that the place was a small garden but a bitter weed.

*   *   *

Ten years later, when Cedella Malcolm was pregnant with her son Nesta, her father or her grandmother would show her which herbs to take to ease any potential problems in the pregnancy; which blend of bush tea would ease high blood pressure or back-ache; which bush was the best cleanser for the coming baby's skin. Her father, in fact, was more nervous about this imminent birth than his daughter. Ciddy loved being pregnant, her already intriguing aura, one of a kind of infinite calm, heightened even further by a numinous glow as she felt the child growing within her. But her father would scold her. 'You runnin' around hearty, but you sicker than the rest of your sisters,' he would admonish. 'Take up your doctor book and read it instead of laughing and playing. Always remember,' he would add a piece of Jamaican folk wisdom about pregnancy, never failing to unnerve his daughter, 'you are between life and death until you give birth to that baby.'

'I was young. I didn't know any better. I was happy, everything was lovely. The pregnancy was great. Everything was nice.' Sometimes the unborn child would give a clue to one of the career options he would later consider: 'This baby kick like hell – like a footballer.' Cedella would even find it within her to be able to ignore those malicious souls in the neighbourhood who would audibly curse her as she passed, angry at her for having taken up with a white man.

For, two years previously, one Captain Norval Marley, a white Jamaican (although there are recent suggestions that, as with many 'white' Jamaicans, his blood bore more than a trace of a black lineage), had proudly ridden on his horse into Nine Miles. The man was employed by the colonial government: he was involved in yet another attempt by the authorities to persuade locals to farm or even settle in Jamaica's vast acres of uncultivated bush, the region around Nine Miles being this man Marley's particular terrain. At first he boarded in Yaya's Big House. Then one day he asked Omeriah if he could oversee the building of a small house for him to stay in: Omeriah complied, knocking up a wooden shack in a weekend. Marley was something of a ne'er-do-well, referred to by almost all those who knew him as 'the Captain' – even though it seemed there was scant justification for him to have been given such a rank. (It may have originated in a spell in the Nigerian police force after the First World War.)

It was in this tiny wooden house that Captain Marley, already in his sixties, began an affair with the foolish girl, then only seventeen: he would make little jokes with her about how their destinies were linked because of the way their surnames both began with the letters 'MA'. The relationship had a consequence that could be seen as virtually inevitable: Cedella was married to Captain Marley on a Friday in June 1944, not long after they had both learned of the pregnancy; the next day he left Nine Miles for Kingston, having bestowed legitimacy on his unborn child. Cedella was surprised, but protected by her youthful innocence from grief. Norval Marley had explained, after all, that he was becoming ill and needed to have an operation; his long days in the saddle had caused a hernia to develop. This was behind his move back to Kingston: for the sake of his health he was taking another, more humble job, as an overseer on the bridges being built to carry water into Kingston.

The pregnancy was problem-free. On the first Sunday of February 1945, Cedella Marley, as her marriage had caused her to be renamed, went as usual to church. The next day she hoped to fast, rejoice and give testimony in the church in the evening, as Elder Thomas encouraged his flock to do each Monday. But Cedella felt the first twinges of going into labour and remained at the property of her father, a vacant shop with two rooms attached, in which she had set up her bedroom. The next morning, Auntie Missus, as they called the great-aunt who doubled as local midwife, was called to Ciddy, who was starting to experience pain of a new and fearsome degree. Auntie Missus pointed at pictures of pretty women from magazines which Cedella had pasted up on her bedroom wall. 'All these women go through the same thing,' she reminded her. Auntie Missus had brought food – some yam, some sweet potato, some rice; by now the contractions were coming more powerfully, and Ciddy had to time each mouthful in between them.

The baby boy was born at around 2.30 on the Wednesday morning of 6 February 1945. He weighed 7 pounds 4 ounces; the afterbirth was taken and buried at the foot of one of Omeriah's coconut trees. The child was called Nesta Robert Marley. All three names came from the father. 'Robert' was in tribute to Norval's elder brother, a prominent cricket and tennis player. 'Nesta' was also suggested by Norval Marley: Ciddy had never heard the name before and she was concerned that people might mishear it as 'Lester'. She didn't know what it meant but in time she would discover it was 'messenger'. The child had been conceived in Yaya's Big House, and after the birth Cedella returned there to live with him.

Nesta was a healthy child. Running on the rock stone, 'him not have no time fe sick'; brought up on a country diet of fresh vegetables and fruit, the only inkling of a prickly digestion was the vomiting that would occur whenever he ate eggs. As the baby started to grow bigger, Cedella would from time to time feel a twinge of loneliness or sadness that she didn't hear more regularly from his father. Some help, some support, would have been nice, that was all. Even when he sent money – for a time four or five pounds would come most months, though it was by no means guaranteed – the envelope with the cash would be addressed to her father. As time went on, moreover, the money supply began to dwindle until Cedella hardly heard from her husband.

Still, Nesta was happy, running barefoot in the relatively car-free neighbourhood almost from when he could first walk. They would always say that Nesta loved to eat, and the boy was especially fond of his uncle Titus, who lived up by Yaya and always had plenty of surplus banana leaf or the spinach-like calaloo cooking on his stove. For a long time, Nesta's eyes were bigger than his stomach. It became a joke in the area how he would take up a piece of yam, swallow his first piece and almost immediately fall asleep: 'one piece just fill up his belly straightaway.'

Early on, there were signs that the child had been born with a poet's understanding of life, an asset in a land like Jamaica, where metaphysical curiosities are a fact of life. When he was around four or five, Cedella would hear stories from relatives and neighbours that Nesta had claimed to read their palm. But she took it for a joke. How could this little boy of hers possibly do something like that? Though she did feel slightly shaken when she first heard that what Nesta told people about their futures invariably came true. There was District Constable Black from Stern Hill, for example: he told Cedella how the child had read his hand and everything he said had come to pass. Then a woman who had also had her palm looked at by Nesta confirmed this, forcing his mother to accept this strange talent of her jolly, much loved son, one that went a considerable way to defining him as an obeahman. 'How he do things and prophesy things, he is not just by himself – he have higher powers, even from when he is a little boy,' said Cedella Booker, as she later became. 'The way I felt, the kind of vibes I get when Bob comes around . . . It's too honourable. I always look upon him with great respect: there is something inside telling me that he is not only a son – there is something greater in this man. Bob is of a small stature, but when I hear him talk, he talk big. When it comes to the feelings and reactions I get from Bob, it was always too spiritual to even mention or talk about. Even from when he was a small child coming up.'

If Nesta had read his own palm and perceived what was to be the pattern of his life, he never told his mother. When he was almost five, however, Omeriah received a visit from Norval. What Cedella should do, he suggested, was to give up Nesta for adoption by Norval's brother, the esteemed Robert, after whom he had been named. What was more, Cedella should guarantee that she would not attempt to see the boy any more. 'It's like he wouldn't be my child no more! I said, "No way."'

But then Norval came out to Nine Miles on another visit. He had had a different idea: what if the child were to come and stay with his father in Kingston for a time? He would pay for his education and let him benefit from all the opportunities and possibilities inherent in Norval's own large, affluent family, who owned Marley and Co., Jamaica's largest plant-hire company.

Cedella could see the advantages for her son in this. She felt she could go along with the plan. Nesta was duly delivered to her husband in Kingston. Hardly had the boy arrived, however, than he was taken downtown, to the house of a woman called Miss Grey. Norval Marley left his son with her, promising to return shortly. He never did.

All communication was then broken with the Malcolm family at Nine Miles. Cedella was deeply worried, fearing her son had been stolen from her – as indeed he had been. After almost a year, when Cedella had moved to Stepney, a village two or three miles past Nine Miles, a woman friend of hers went to Kingston to see her niece. The woman and her niece, who was called Merle, were together on the Spanish Town Road when they ran directly into Nesta. He had been sent to buy coal, he said, by the woman in whose house he was living. 'Ask my mother,' the boy continued, 'why she don't come look for me?' And he told the woman his address.

When Cedella's friend returned to Stepney that night she reported all that had happened. Nesta looked happy, she told Cedella: a little chubby, fat, healthy. A colossal sense of relief came over Cedella. 'I was so tickled pink, I was so happy when she told me.' But there was one problem: her friend had not had a pen or pencil with her. And she had forgotten the address where Nesta was living.

A solution was suggested – that Merle, the niece, might remember the address. Cedella wrote to her, and Merle replied straightaway that, although she couldn't remember the number of the building, she knew Nesta was living on Heywood Street, in a poor downtown neighbourhood. Heywood Street was a short street, she added, and told Cedella that if she came up to Kingston, Merle would help her look for the missing child.

Accompanied by another friend from Nine Miles, Cedella arrived in Kingston one evening. Meeting Merle as arranged, Cedella discovered Heywood Street to be off Orange Street, and filled with stores. All these businesses were closed, however. Outside the first building that she came to, Cedella saw a man sitting out on the pavement. 'I asked him,' she said, using the name by which her son's father called him, 'if he knew a little boy who lived round there by the name of Robert Marley?'

'Yeah mon,' the man replied, looking behind him. 'He was jus' here a minute ago.' Cedella's heart lifted, as it filled with happiness.

Then she followed the man's eyes. 'There he was, just on the corner, playing. Nesta just bust right round: when he see it was me him just ran and hugged me so. And he said, "Mummy, you fatty." I say, "Where you live?" He was very brisk, very bright. He say, "Right here. Her name is Mrs Grey: come and I'll introduce you to her."'

Mrs Grey was a heavyset woman. But she did not look at all well: she had lost almost all of her hair, and the skin peeled away in thin scales from both sides of her hands, one of the symptoms of 'sugar', as the widespread disease of diabetes is known in Jamaica; Mrs Grey also suffered from chronic high blood pressure. Robert, she told Cedella, had been her strength and guide, running errands for her, going to the market to fetch coal, as he had been on that day when he had been seen on the Spanish Town Road. He was going to school, Cedella discovered, though from what she heard it seemed as though his attendance was not regular. All the while, Mrs Grey said, she would find herself looking at Robert and wondering, 'What happen to your mother? How is it that your mother never come to see you?'

'I told her that I had to take him. And you could see how much she love him. She said she was going to miss him because he's her right hand, to do any little thing for her. But she know that he have to leave. Then Nesta and I just go home. And we come back and everybody was glad to see him at his school, everybody.'

Once Nesta was back at school, however, he started to become very thin, suffering an inexplicable weight loss, as the extra pounds he had put on in Kingston mysteriously peeled away. On the advice of his teacher, Cedella began to feed the boy with a daily diet of goat's milk. Whether it was that additional food supplement, or merely the healthier air and life he was living, he soon began not only to recover but to develop muscles and grow stronger and tougher, a country tough, that little-town-soft gone.

That was the only occasion on which Cedella could remember sickness coming near her son. Not long after he returned to Nine Miles, however, he suffered a physical injury, perhaps a portent of a future problem. Running along the road one day, he stepped with his right foot on some slivers and splinters of broken glass, the remnants of a bottle. At first not all the glass could be dug out from the sole, hard and tough from years of barefoot walking. Then the wound wouldn't heal up, pus seeping ceaselessly from it. When he tried to step on it, he would cry with pain, his foot going into involuntary spasms. Tears would well up in Cedella's eyes as she watched her young son hobble up the rocky path to Yaya's, trying to place his weight on the side of his foot. But it was not until several months had passed that his cousin Nathan, who was 13 years old, brought a potion, a yellow powder called Iodoform, from the chemist's in Claremont; mixing it with sour orange he baked a poultice which finally healed Nesta's foot. Nathan also made Nesta a guitar, constructed from bamboo and goatskin.

One more event of significance occurred shortly after Nesta returned from Kingston. When a woman asked him to read her palm, the boy shook his head. 'No,' said Nesta, 'I'm not reading no more hand: I'm singing now.'

'He had these two little sticks,' Cedella recalled. 'He started knocking them with his fists in this rhythmical way and singing this old Jamaican song:

Hey mister, won't you touch me potato,
Touch me yam, punking tomato?
All you do is King Love, King Love,
Ain't you tired of squeeze up, squeeze up?
Hey mister, won't you touch me potato,
Touch me yam, punking potato?

'And it just made the woman feel so good, and she gave him two or three pennies. That was the first time he talked about music.'

During this time, Nesta was a pupil at the Stepney All Age School, in which he had first been enrolled when he was four, before he went to Kingston. His mother had continued to live in Stepney when she brought him back from the capital. Cedella had set up a small grocery shop there, building most of it herself, carrying the mortar and grout. When it was set up Nesta would help her in it when he returned from school. Its stock was never more than the neighbourhood market would bear: bread, flour, rice, soft drinks, which she used to collect on a donkey carrying a hamper. One day as she was walking along the road, the donkey's rope held loosely in her hand, the animal reared up on its hind legs and ran down a hill, mashing up all the bottles it was carrying. Cedella cried and cried and cried, and was only somewhat mollified when people who had witnessed the incident assured her they had also seen the cause of it, a spirit that had come from Murray Mountain to frighten the beast. But it set Cedella to thinking: wasn't there perhaps an easier way of ensuring some small measure of prosperity for her and her pickney?

There was another new shopkeeper in the area: at Nine Miles, a man from Kingston called Mr Thaddius 'Toddy' Livingston had also opened up a small grocery shop. The man had a wife and a child, who had been christened Neville but was more popularly called Bunny. The boy had been born on 10 April 1947, and was also a pupil at Stepney All Age School. He and Bob became friends. Cedella, however, was only on nodding acquaintanceship with her business rival, Bunny's father. After a time, Mr Toddy sold up his business and moved back to Kingston, intending to open a rum bar.

Soon Cedella made a similar decision, and a relative bought her shop from her. She was now in her mid-twenties and becoming restless. Though she deeply loved her son, she felt her life was slipping away in Nine Miles. More and more, she had begun travelling to Kingston, taking jobs as a domestic help and leaving Nesta in the care of her father, Omeriah, who bore a deep love for the boy and was happy to care for him.

Omeriah Malcolm, a disciplinarian and a very hard worker, set Nesta Robert Marley to work chopping wood, caring for and milking the cows, grooming horses, mules, and donkeys and dressing their sores, chasing down goats, and feeding the pigs. To an extent Nesta ran free and wild. Unusually for a rural Jamaican family, little attention was paid to sending him to church – although a Christian, Omeriah Malcolm took an extremely free-thinking view of the necessity of regular church worship.

Years later, Bob would talk of his farmer grandfather as someone who had really cared for him, perhaps the only person who had really cared for him at that time – his mother's absences in Kingston rankled with him.

Inevitably, Nesta also began to absorb some of the arcane knowledge to which his grandfather was privy. Another relative, Clarence Malcolm, had been a celebrated Jamaican guitarist, playing in dancehalls during the 1940s. Learning of Nesta's interest in music, Clarence would spend time with the boy, letting him get the feel of his guitar. He was delighted when the boy won a pound for singing in a talent contest held at Fig Tree Corner on Fig Tree Road, on the way to the junction that leads to Stepney and Alderton. So began a pattern of older wise men taking a mentor-like role in the life of the essentially fatherless Nesta Robert Marley, a syndrome that would continue for all his time on earth.

From Nine Miles, Nesta would walk the two and a half miles to school at Stepney, dressed in the freshly pressed khaki shirt and pants that comprise the school uniform of Jamaican boys. The journey was not considered excessive – some children walked to the school from as far away as Prickle Pole, seven miles distant.

When he was ten, his teacher was a woman called Clarice Bushay; she taught most subjects to the sixty or so children in her overcrowded but well-disciplined class, which was divided only by a blackboard from the four or five other classes in the vast hall that formed the school. Away from his family circle, Nesta didn't reveal the cheerful countenance he presented in Nine Miles, where his wry and knowing smile was rarely absent.

Hidden behind a mask of timidity, his potential was not immediately apparent to Miss Bushay. When, however, she realised that this particular pupil required constant reassurance, needing always to be told that his work was satisfactory, he began to blossom. 'As he was shy, if he was not certain he was right, he wouldn't always try. In fact, he hated to get answers wrong, so sometimes you'd have to really draw the answer out of him. And then give him a clap – he liked that, the attention.'

She did, though, feel a need to temper the amount of concentration she could give him. 'Because he was light-skin, other children would become jealous of him getting so much of my time. I imagined he must have been very much a mother's pet, because he would only do well if you gave him large amounts of attention. But it was obvious he had a lot of potential.' The difficulties endured by Nesta Robert Marley because of his mixed-race heritage were representative of an archetypal Jamaican problem: since independence from colonial rule, the national motto has been 'Out of many, one people', but this aphorism masks a complex reality in which shadings of skin colour create prejudices on all sides. The truth was that, as a child, the future Bob Marley was a distinct outsider, the quintessential ugly duckling. Bob felt from the start that he wasn't wanted by either race, and he knew he had to survive, and become tough.

Even at Stepney All Age School, Nesta was confirmed in his extracurricular interests. After running down to the food vendors by the school gates at lunch-time to buy fried dumplings or banana, or fish fritters and lemonade, it would be football – with oranges or grapefruits used as balls – and music with which he busied himself for the rest of the break. But he was so soft-spoken when he sang – a further sign of an acute lack of self-confidence – that you would have to put your ear down almost to his mouth to hear that fine alto voice. Yet of all the children who attempted to construct guitars from sardine tins and bamboo, it would always be Nesta who contrived to have the best sound. 'He was very enterprising: you had to commend him on the guitars he made.'

He was a popular boy, with very many friends; very loving, but clearly needing to get back as much love as he gave out. 'When he came by you to your desk,' Miss Bushay noted, 'you knew he just wanted to be touched and held. It seemed like a natural thing with him – what he was used to. A loving boy, and really quite soft.' An obedient pupil, he deeply resented the occasion that he was flogged by the principal for the consistently late arrival at school by himself and the other children from Nine Miles. After the beating, falling back on his grandfather's secret world, he was heard to mutter dark threats about the power of a cowrie shell he possessed and what he planned to do with it to the principal.

Maths was Nesta's best subject, whilst his exceptionally retentive memory allowed him unfailing success in general knowledge. But Miss Bushay would have to encourage him to open reading books: she noticed that, although he'd read all his set texts, he wouldn't borrow further volumes, as did some of his classmates. 'He seemed to spend more time with this football business.'

One day, whilst she was in Kingston, his mother received a telegram from Nine Miles, telling her that Nesta had cut open his right knee and been taken to the doctor to have the wound stitched. When she next saw her son, he told her what had happened. Running from another boy at the back of a house, he had raced round a corner, directly into an open coffin. Startled, he had spun away, cutting his knee on a tree stump. 'I sometimes wonder,' said his mother, 'with his gift of second sight, did Nesta glimpse something that day in the gaping coffin that made him fly out of that back-yard in breakneck terror? What might he have seen that day?'

When Nesta was 11 years old, there was another accident. Playing in a stream to which his mother had forbidden him to go, he badly stubbed the big toe of his right foot, cutting it open. It was not until it became almost gangrenous that he told his mother, who then wrapped it in herbs to take down the inflammation and remove the poison. But from then on, that toe was always black.

* * *

Whilst his mother was in the capital, Nesta for a time was lodged with his aunt Amy, his mother's sister, who lived in the hamlet of Alderton, some eight miles from Ocho Rios, on the north coast. The aunt, Rita Marley later observed, was something of a 'slave-driver', a strict disciplinarian even by Jamaica's harsh standards. At five in the morning the boy would be woken up to do yard work: he would have to tie up and milk the goats and walk miles for fresh water before going to the local school, which he could see from his aunt's house. The only respite from his chores was the friendship of his cousin Sledger, Amy's son; the pair rebelled together against her regime, earning a reputation with Amy as troublemakers. One day Nesta's mother received a message: Nesta had run away from his aunt's, carrying his belongings, and made his way back to Nine Miles. In fact, he was fleeing punishment because he and Sledger had been left behind to make the Sunday 'yard' lunch but, clearly enthralled with their task, had then eaten up almost all of it before Amy returned from church.

However, Nesta's mother, Cedella, was also a naughty girl. One Sunday evening when Cedella was about to set off back to Kingston after a weekend with her family, she got a lift in the same car as Toddy Livingston, who had returned to Nine Miles to visit some friends. It was the first extensive period of time they had spent together and there was a strong mutual attraction. On their return to Kingston they started dating and, notwithstanding Toddy's married status, became lovers.

KINGSTON

As Amy was adamant that Nesta would not be accepted back at her home, Cedella decided that it was time for her 12-year-old son to come and live with her. Accordingly, she contacted her father, who two weeks later put the boy on a bus to Kingston. This hardly displeased Nesta, who had been unhappy with his strict aunt. Although the Jamaican capital was in 1957 a very different world from the rural runnings to which the boy had become accustomed, he had at least experienced city life when his father had whisked him off there seven years previously. At the corner of Beckford Street and Charles Street, close to the terminus for buses from the country, his mother had rented an upstairs room from a property-owning family called Faulkner. Living there, however, meant a problem for Nesta's education: there were no good schools in the neighbourhood. The difficulty was no less when Cedella and her son took short-term residence at other downtown addresses in Barrett Street, Oxford Street, and at 9 Regent Street, on one of whose corners Nesta's mother set up another small shop.

She needed the money as there were no free schools in the area. At first, Cedella, giving the address of her brother Gibson, had enrolled her son in a school close to his home, the Ebenezer government school near Nelson Road. But the journey was a chore for the boy, who would sometimes stay with his uncle Gibson, and the daily sixpenny bus-fare was half the amount it cost to feed him every week, so Cedella made the extreme decision that she would ensure that Nesta was educated privately: she had found one school nearby, the fee-paying Model school, a small establishment on Darling Street. The weekly rates were five shillings.

Although the boy's wry expression was beginning to cloak a sadness at the instability of his life, the teacher at his new school adored him. 'Where's Nesta?' she would demand as soon as she arrived for the morning. Now reading began to come to the fore for the boy, but only when it was linked to his copious knowledge of the Bible, the one text of which most Jamaicans have an in-depth knowledge. Like a typical youth from 'country', Nesta showed a deeply practical nature: when, unusually, Cedella fell into a rage and beat him soundly shortly before his thirteenth birthday after he had ruined a new pair of Bata shoes by playing football in them, he paid penance to her by cleaning their home and mending a broken kitchen table while she was at work. 'I sorry I mash up de shoes, Mamma,' he apologised.

Although by uptown standards the school fees were inexpensive, partly a reflection of the education provided, Cedella would have to hustle and scrape to find the money needed. 'But I never have to beg nobody or borrow from nobody. I could pay his fee, then save again to buy his shoes. I can't remember a time when I was so badly off that I couldn't find food for him. And he was not a child that demand this and demand that. Never have no problem with him: always obedient, would listen to me. Sometimes he get a little mad with me, but it never last fe time.'

The 'lost' year that Nesta had spent in Kingston had caused him subconsciously to absorb the moods and mores of the city. All the same, at first he was disoriented by being back in the capital. But he at least had the comfort of his now close friend Bunny Livingston not too far away. With an urgent need for expression, Bunny's soul also had music swirling away in it. Down on Russell Road, where Bunny lived with his parents, you would see Nesta with his little homemade guitar, trying to work up a tune with his friend. 'Bob wrote little songs, and then he and Bunny would sing them,' Cedella remembered. 'Sometimes I'd teach him a tune like "I'm Going to Lay My Sins down at the Riverside".' But Bunny would note the extent to which Nesta seemed timid, withdrawn, and sensitive, as though there was always something on his mind.

Cedella, meanwhile, was becoming more and more involved with Bunny's father, who would frequently come by and visit her. This would happen particularly when Nesta was playing and staying elsewhere, which was now not infrequent. Her son's secondary education was becoming a problem, especially after Cedella had moved to the newish housing scheme of Trench Town and decided that the boy should return to state education – even though the schools in this downtown, impoverished area of west Kingston were worryingly rough. For a time, Cedella fell back on her previous plan, lodging her son at her brother Gibson's home, farther uptown, in order to let him qualify for that better school up by Maxfield Avenue to which he now returned. A dual purpose was served here: her brother's girlfriend was able to care for Nesta and keep an eye on him when he came home at the end of the school day. Sometimes Cedella would pick the boy up in the evenings and take him down to Trench Town. Or if she was working in the neighbourhood, she would stay over at her brother's. Still, it wasn't too easy a life for either of them.

To all intents and purposes, Cedella was the mistress of Toddy, who now ran his rum bar near the bus terminal and worked on construction projects during the day, mainly on properties that he would buy, improve, and sell on. Toddy employed Cedella at the bar in the daytime, paying her two pounds ten shillings a week. He was a man of a certain means, and his rising status was cemented by his purchase of a Buick Skylark; but he also garnered a reputation as something of a bad man. The quirks of Toddy's personality, particularly his quick-tempered readiness to fight, meant that Cedella's love affair with him was not easy. His jealousy, for example, created a tension about the couple almost from the beginning. He would only have to hear that Cedella had had a conversation with another man and he would want to come and box him down. 'When a man is married they are always jealous of the woman they are with more than their own wife, because they know another man might come and take them. And that's how he was handling me. I would get frustrated and upset.'

The relationship, which for Cedella began to take on the features of a classic love-hate relationship, could only worsen; many times, Nesta would come into the family house to find his mother sitting crying at the kitchen table. 'Don't worry, Mummy, I love you,' he would attempt to console her, throwing his sinewy arms around her neck. He was extremely angry when, at almost 15 years of age, he saw his mother with a black eye, which Toddy had given her. 'When I grow big, Mamma, and become a man, I goin' lick dat man back inna him eye. You wait and see,' he promised.

Meanwhile, Cedella would hand herself over to the Lord's mercy: 'I would pray and wouldn't stop praying and asking God to take me out of that man's hands.'

Cedella's address was 19 Second Street, Trench Town; the area was so-called either because it had been built over a ditch that drained the city's sewage, or because of the name of a local builder on the project, a Mr Trench. Cedella took over the downstairs one-room concrete apartment from her elder brother Solomon, who was about to emigrate to England, quitting his job as a bus-driver. The rent was twelve shillings a month, whilst the upstairs apartments, which had two rooms, went for twenty-four shillings a month. In the evenings, Toddy was a frequent visitor, sometimes bringing Bunny with him.

Trench Town was a housing scheme built at the beginning of the 1950s, after the 1951 hurricane had destroyed the neighbourhood's squatter camps. These squatter camps, which had gradually been filling up west Kingston, had been built around the former Kingston refuse dump, from which the countryfolk and displaced city-dwellers who lived there would scavenge for whatever they could find. In the days of the 'plantocracy business', the area had been a sugar plantation, owned by the Lindos, one of the twenty-one families that are said to rule Jamaica, and the ances-tors of Chris Blackwell, who would some years hence play a highly signif-icant role in the life of Nesta Robert Marley. Later, the district that became Trench Town had developed as a spacious, largely white, middle-class housing area, verdant and fertile, home to macka and plum trees. Bang in its centre, the Ambassador Theatre hosted shows by such esteemed American artists as Louis Armstrong, at which the writer and performer Noël Coward was a regular attendee. But the encroaching squatter camps caused the middle classes to depart, selling up for what they could get.

For the country 'sufferahs' seeking employment, the area was not without its natural resources: west Kingston once had been a simple fishing village, and the fishing beach of Greenwich Farm was only a short walk away, providing a source of nutrition or income for anyone with a hook and line. If you had the nous to lash driftwood together into a raft on which to slide out to sea along the still, warm ocean shore, so much the better. The Zen task of fishing granted those who followed that occupation an honourable, respected role in the community. It had, after all, archetypal associations as an occupation of Jesus' disciples.

Trench Town, the core of the district, was in the hottest part of Kingston, almost untouched by the breezes from the Blue Mountains that wafted down to cool the city's more northerly, uptown reaches. But for the slum- and shantytown-dwellers who became lodged in it, Trench Town was considered a desirable place to live; the 'government yards' were composed of solidly constructed one- or two-storey concrete units built around a central courtyard that contained communal cooking facilities and a standpipe for water. Unhelpfully, Jamaica's colonial masters had seen fit to build Trench Town without any form of sewage system.

Alton Ellis, later to become one of Jamaica's most mellifluously beautiful – and, especially during the 1960s rock-steady era, most successful – vocalists, moved to the area as soon as the first stage of the building of the government yards had been completed: work began at Fifth Street and progressed to Seventh Street before the clearing of the 'Dungle' permitted the first four streets to be constructed. But there was a desperate insecurity about much of the influx of countryfolk into Kingston – those born in the city blamed them for the rise in crime figures. And Alton Ellis remembered how the entrenched lawlessness in the hearts of the shantytown dwellers soon surfaced, leading to the reputation that Trench Town developed as a haven of outlaw rejects, which later became a reality. Ellis and others, however, remembered it as initially being a 'peaceful, loving place'. 'When I went there,' recalled the singer, 'it was a new scheme, government-built for poor people.' Each apartment within the individual complexes had one or two bedrooms, in the communal yard there would be four toilets and bathrooms, and by each gate was planted a mango or pawpaw tree. 'But even though the place was nice,' he said, 'the poverty still existed. The poverty was so strong that you know what that would lead to.'

Near to Trench Town, in Jones Town, lived Ernest Ranglin, a professional jazz guitarist influenced by the likes of Charlie Christian and Django Reinhardt. Originally from a hamlet called Harry Watch in Manchester, Ranglin had been a teenage prodigy employed by prominent band leaders such as Eric Dean and Val Bennett, who from the end of the 1940s ran big, swinging dancehall bands in the American style. In Dean's orchestra Ranglin had shared the stage with another maestro, Don Drummond, who would later be considered one of the world's top jazz trombonists. Employed from 1958 as the staff guitar-player by JBC Radio, Ranglin was equally considered the Jamaican master of his particular instrument. Frequently, he would find himself in Trench Town, sometimes playing cricket with the local youth, including the Marley boy. 'Really, it was still a nice area. And even the parts that weren't, those kids didn't notice: when you're a child you only see the good things.'

Even before the 1951 hurricane had mashed down the zinc-and-packing-case residences of the shantytown, the region had a reputation as an area of outcasts. Specifically, the Trench Town environs had become one of the main homes in Kingston for the strange tribe of men known as Rastafarians, who had set up an encampment down by the Dungle in the early years of the Second World War. Although a few such men – like the trio of 'mountain lions', named after the Ethiopian guerrillas who swore not to cut their hair until Ethiopia was freed from Italian occupation – wore their hair long and uncombed, in the manner of Indian saddhus, most only had their faces framed by their matted beards. (It was not until the 1960s that 'locks' became common, partially because long hair had the effect – as it did elsewhere in that age – of unnerving the more conventionally coiffured populace. Briefly known as 'fearlocks', this soon mutated to the marginally less threatening 'dreadlocks'.) These primal figures, around whom the funky aroma of marijuana seemed permanently to float like an aura, could appear as archetypal and prophetic as a West African baobab tree or like the living, terrifying personification of a duppy, that most feared of dark spirits on the Island of Springs. It all depended on your point of view and upbringing.

Mortimer Planner (whose surname commonly mutated into 'Planno'), for example, was considered sufficiently elevated in the Rastafarian brethren to travel in 1961 to the Ethiopian capital of Addis Ababa to meet His Imperial Majesty Haile Selassie I, Conquering Lion of the Tribe of Judah; he had first moved to Trench Town in 1939. A very simple reason, he said, had drawn him there – the energy emanating from this part of Kingston: 'Trench Town is a spiritual power point.' Yet others in the area were not at all happy about the presence of these men with their curious belief that Haile Selassie was God. For example, a young woman called Rita Anderson, a worshipful member of the Church of God, would go out of her way to hurry across the road to avoid them; her parents had told her the truth about these people: that Rastafarians lived in the drainage gullies and carried parts of people they had murdered in their bags. No doubt it was such thinking that was the basis for the sporadic round-ups of Rastas – known at that time on the island as 'beardmen' – by the police, who would shove them into their trucks and cut off their locks.

In 1960, dynamite and assorted weapons were discovered at the Kingston home of Claudius Henry, a prominent Rastafarian who was a supporter of the Cuban revolutionary president Fidel Castro; Claudius Henry billed himself as the 'Repairer of the Breach' and had predicted repatriation to Africa would occur the previous 5 October, to this effect having sold hundreds of postcards that he claimed to be passports. The search of Henry's home was prompted by an incident involving his son Ronald; in company with other 'beardmen', Ronald had shot and killed two soldiers, for which the culprits were later hanged. At the time, Prime Minister Norman Manley delivered his thoughts to the nation on follow-ers of Rastafari: 'These people – and I am glad that it is only a small number of them – are the wicked enemies of our country. I ask you all to report any unusual or suspicious movements you may see pertaining to the Rastafarians.' Three years later, Rudolf Franklyn, a Rastaman who had been brutalised and imprisoned by police, took his revenge, murder-ing two people on the edge of the north-coast tourist town of Montego Bay. The next day, Good Friday, 12 April 1963, Norman Manley's succes-sor and cousin, Alexander Bustamante, sanctioned an attack by Jamaican security forces on Franklyn's Rasta encampment in Coral Gardens, near Montego Bay; Franklyn and several associates were shot dead and across the island police beat Rastafarians and shaved off their hair.

In the twenty-first century, dreadlocks are ubiquitous in many parts of the world – though often as a fashion statement rather than as an emblem of religious belief. This would seem to be missing the point for Jamaica's followers of Rastafari; after all, they are fully aware that, at this time of great change, humanity is living in the last days. Following the predic-tion of the Book of Revelation, upright dreads believe that only the righ-teous will move forward through the apocalypse into the new era: only 144,000 souls, those who have battled to save the world from the perpe-trators of the Babylonian greed and destruction that are all around and which are endeavouring to destroy both humanity's essential good and the environment in which positivity may flourish.

In the 1920s, the rhetorical fuel that would help bring about such fiery thinking was provided by Marcus Garvey, the colourful prophet of black self-determination. Garvey, who had been born in St Ann in 1887 and founded the United Negro Improvement Association, spoke to an audience at Madison Square Garden in New York of 'Ethiopia, Land of our Fathers', and proclaimed that 'negroes' believed in 'the God of Ethiopia, the everlasting God'. Most significantly, he delivered a pivotal pronouncement: 'Look to Africa, for the crowning of a Black King; He shall be the Redeemer.' (Later, there was some debate about this: was it Garvey who said these words? For an associate of his, the Reverend James Morris Webb, the author of *A Black Man Will be the Coming Universal King, Proven by Biblical History*, had spoken to the same effect at a meeting in 1924.)

In 1930, rising above aristocratic in-fighting which could have overshadowed that in a Medici court, Ras Tafari Makonnen, great-grandson of King Saheka Selassie of Shoa, was crowned Emperor of Ethiopia and given the name of Haile Selassie, King of Kings, Lord of Lords, Conquering Lion of the Tribe of Judah. Surely this was the fulfilment of Garvey's prophecy?

As they were elsewhere in the world, the 1930s were years of social unrest and upheaval in Jamaica. Labour unrest on the island in 1938 culminated in the vicious suppression of striking sugarcane workers on the Tate & Lyle estate at Frome in Westmoreland, in the west of Jamaica. Under the orders of Tate & Lyle, the estate's manager, a member of the Lindo family, met with six hundred plantation workers and dismissed out of hand their demands for wages of a minimum of four shillings a day, offering half that amount.

After hearing the addresses of assorted labour leaders, including Alexander Bustamante, then the leader of the new Jamaican labour movement, the workers attacked the Tate & Lyle offices and assaulted the European staff. Local police fixed bayonets and advanced on the employees: four strikers were killed, including an elderly woman who was bayoneted to death. Dozens were rounded up and jailed, including Bustamante.

Such labour and social unrest was a perfect context for the rise of a band of islanders who had divorced themselves mentally from a system in which such wrongs could be perpetrated. Though often cast as a religion of the dispossessed, there is an element of condescension in such an assessment of Jamaica's early followers of Rastafarianism. Denied is the intellectual, even existential, acuity and rigour of so many practitioners of the religion: the depth of biblical and historical knowledge displayed at a Rastafarian reasoning is impressive, as is the mental agility to perceive every semantic subtlety of the arguments propagated. The myriad contradictions that litter Rastafari assume the status of numinous truths when one recalls Carl Jung's assertion that 'all great truths must end in paradox.'

In the hills of eastern Jamaica, in the parish of St Thomas, which is traditionally associated with such mystical – and specifically Jamaican – strands of Christianity as kumina, pocomania, and revivalism, Rastafarian encampments sprang up; here a life of asceticism and artistry became. the armour of the religion's followers against Babylon. To the west, Leonard Howell, one of the island's chief propagators of the religion, also known as 'the Gong', founded the Pinnacle encampment in an abandoned hilltop estate between Kingston and Spanish Town, conveniently, when it came to growing plantations of marijuana, out of sight of the authorities. Eventually taking thirteen wives, Howell finally decided that it was not Haile Selassie who was Jah but himself. After his mountain eyrie was raided by police in 1954, he was thrown into a home for the mentally ill, and Pinnacle was closed down. The dreads from it spilled into the ghettoes of west Kingston. Shortly before and after independence in 1962, the violent incidents between Rastas and the police made headlines in the *Daily Gleaner*, but the number of His Majesty's follow-ers involved in such affairs was infinitesimal compared to the way the movement was burning its thoughts with the speed of a bush-fire into the popular psyche of Jamaica.

But it took the unceasing efforts of one man, who had come up in Kingston hearing the stream-of-consciousness orations of dreads in Back-a-Wall and the Dungle, to popularise and make universally known the apparently crazy idea that the emperor of Ethiopia could be the living deity.

That man, of course, was Bob Marley, who came to be seen as the personification of Rastafari. Without Bob Marley most of the world would never have learned of Jah Rastafari, or entered into any debate whatsoever about the possible divinity of Haile Selassie. In Jamaica, the image of His Imperial Majesty Haile Selassie I, King of Kings, Conquer-ing Lion of Judah is inescapable, accompanied as it invariably is by a soundtrack of the addictive hymns of praise to His divinity that make up most of the material of roots and conscious reggae – a music whose father, to all intents and purposes, was the fatherless Bob Marley, a man who never wrote an indifferent song and who united masses around the globe. Many of his brethren in the faith felt that this was the entire purpose of the blessing of the man's talent. Many others, however, believed that Bob was capable of this task because of his spiritual close-ness to His Majesty himself, on whose right-hand side he was more than adequately fitted to sit.

As yet, young Nesta Marley knew almost nothing about the Rastas' religion. He was simply getting through his schooldays, in a more perfunc-tory manner than perhaps his hardworking mother realised, anxious to get out into some form of adult life. However, his mother had moved him yet again: to St Aloysius Boys School, located at 74–76 Duke Street, on the corner of Sutton Street and Duke Street, run by Catholic sisters. Bob never really adapted to St Aloysius: ultimately, he would come to understand he had had almost no secondary education. With no permanent male role model to act as a guide, the transition from childhood to adolescence was even more awkward for him than for most teenagers. And in the evenings, his mother would not be around. On the corner of Beeston Street and Spanish Town Road, Cedella had started up a 'cold-supper shop', as they are known in Jamaica – curiously, as the food cold-supper shops offer is generally hot, fried, or cooked in a pot, sold next to the bottles of Red Stripe and rum that also characterise such institutions. Late one afternoon, whilst Cedella was working at her business, a rough-looking youth appeared in her shop. 'Lady, you have a son named Nesta?' he demanded. When Cedella asked why he wanted to know, the youth replied that Nesta had got a 'chop over his eye'. Worried, she went to search for her son, but he ran off when she caught a glimpse of him down by his school. When he eventually came up to see his mother at her shop, Nesta had a Band-Aid plastered above his eye. One of his friends, he said, had thrown a stone and caught his face, an everyday cause of blindness in developing countries. Nesta had run off when he'd seen his mother by the school, he said, in case she might have called the police on his friend.

There would be few more opportunities for such after-school pranks. When he was 15, Nesta came home one day from school carrying a large pile of textbooks. Cedella asked him why. The headteacher, he told his mother, had closed down the school and returned to live in the country. Although startled by the news, Cedella knew there was only one response: to get her son working, preferably at a trade. She was used to the sound of Nesta rehearsing music with his friends – specifically, Bunny Livingston and a friend from the neighbourhood, Desmond (Dekker) Dacre – but she had little faith that this would secure his future. By now, Cedella had bought a small restaurant, putting her sister Rose in charge of it. But one day Nesta came home and told his mother that the restaurant had been broken into and all its contents stolen. The boy and his mother decided to sleep the night in the premises in order that it be protected from further attacks, but left and went home after a friend pointed out that if the thieves returned they would almost certainly kill anyone they found there. Soon Cedella sold it to her brother John, who resolved the problem of night-time break-ins by turning the property into a twenty-four-hour business.

For Cedella's son there were too many unanswered questions, not the least those surrounding his parenthood. Why did he never see his father? Why had he been cursed with light skin, a clear indication of white blood flowing in his veins? It was a weapon for other youth when they wanted to taunt him for something. So much moving around from place to place, from home to home . . . As Nesta roamed Kingston, often playing truant, he would sometimes find himself in the area he spent time in during that year in the capital when he thought he had lost his mother for ever; and at those times he would feel an inexplicable chill run through him. Within him was a gnawing sense of unease, a fear of opening himself to others. He was no stranger to a feeling of tears of frustration and anger welling in his eyes. No wonder he veered between an appearance of shy timidity and that pure screwface mask that was the habitual shield of the ghetto youth. As he grew older, he often seemed to wear a permanent frown.

In Jamaica in the late 1950s, there was an undercurrent that suggested everything was up for grabs. People were redefining themselves, working out who they were with a new confidence. The increasingly uncertain, guilty and repressive hold of the British colonialists was about to be shaken off. Already there were whispers of independence being granted to the island, as, in the wake of the Second World War, it had begun to be around the world. New times were coming.

This sense of optimism was reflected in the music. Jamaicans had developed a taste for American R'n'B when US troops were based there during the Second World War. During the late 1940s, a number of big bands were formed – those of Eric Dean, who had employed both Don Drummond and Ernest Ranglin, and Val Bennett, for example. Jitter-bugging audiences would dance until dawn to tunes they drew from American artists such as Count Basie, Duke Ellington, and Glenn Miller.

By 1950, in the USA the big bands were being superseded by newer outfits: the feisty, optimistic new sounds of bop and rhythm and blues. In Jamaica, these new American popular-music forms were absorbed but in each case given a unique, local, stylistic twist.

There had always been a large traffic of Jamaicans to the United States, a country ever eager – as the United Kingdom was – for fresh supplies of manual workers to undertake the jobs disdained by its more successful citizens. Ambitious, musically inclined Jamaicans would return from the USA with piles of the hottest, most underground 78s; to conceal the tunes' identities, the labels would be scratched off before they were used by sound systems. Sound systems were like portable discos for giants: they would consist of up to thirty or forty speakers, each as large as a wardrobe, joined by a vast, intricate pattern of cables that seemed an organic growth from Jamaica's profusion of dangling liana vines. Music, which would sporadically and often eccentrically be commented on by the disc jockeys spinning the records, would thud out of them at a spine-shaking volume.

The sound-system dances took over Jamaica. Few people owned radios, and the only way to hear the latest rhythm and blues was to go to the big outdoor dances held at 'lawns' in locations such as Chocomo on Wellington Street and Jubilee on King Street. Setting up in 1950, Tom the

Great Sebastian was the first significant sound-system operator. He would 'toast' as a DJ on the microphone, also using Duke Vin (who in 1956 began the first 'system' in the United Kingdom) and Count Machuki, another legendary figure from the days of sound systems. Many believe Tom the Great Sebastian was the all-time giant of sound systems. 'He is the *man*,' said Prince Buster, who later ran his own system and became one of Jamaica's most innovative musicians. Goodies, Count Smith the Blues Blaster, Count Joe, and Sir Nick the Champ, among the leading contenders, never triumphed over Tom the Great Sebastian, as would be apparent at the dances billed as sound-system battles in which two or more systems would compete, each playing a record in turn. Tom would mash up the opposition with the uniqueness of his tunes, straight off the plane from the USA, and with the originality of his DJing and the sheer power of his equipment.

Although there was a clear ironical purpose in the taking up of aristocratic titles, it was also the only way non-white Jamaicans could possibly hope to aspire to such dizzy heights. Duke Reid the Trojan was also named after the Bedford Trojan truck he used to transport his equipment – the money for it came from the liquor stores owned by his family, an empire that began when his wife won the national lottery.

Reid, who had formerly been a policeman, was a contentious figure. Sporting a pair of revolvers in his belt, from which he would indiscriminately loose off shots, he was more inclined to destroy the opposition through violence than talent. To Duke Reid, who began operating a couple of years after Tom the Great Sebastian, may be attributed the genesis of much of the gangland-like behaviour that became a later feature of the Jamaican music business. Instead of mashing up the sound-system opposition by playing the heaviest, loudest tunes, he would simply charge into opposition dances with his gang, beating up people or stabbing them and destroying their equipment. And if that didn't work, Reid was always partial to resorting to a spot of obeah. Undoubtedly a colourful character, at dances Reid would even have gangs of tough, sexy women, controlled by a female lieutenant called Duddah, all dressed in the same uniforms. But he also had tons of boxes, tons of house of joy, as sound-system speakers were sometimes known.

Soon, however, there came a contender for Duke Reid's crown: the Sir Coxsone Downbeat sound system, which took its name from the Yorkshire cricketer Coxsone and was run by one Clement Seymour Dodd. Dodd had first earned his spurs as one of Reid's myriad helpers and his family was also in the liquor-store business. King Stitt and Machuki, two of Dodd's principal DJs, built the set; 'Brand-new – dig, daddy' was one of their great catchphrases. Another of the leading disc jockeys employed by Coxsone, as he became known, was Prince Buster, whose former occupation of boxer also ensured he was a sizable deterrent to the thugs run by Reid.

Although not always. By 1958, Prince Buster was running his open sound system; Reid and fifteen of his thugs went to a dance at the Chocomo Lawn on Wellington Street looking for him. Buster wasn't there: he was playing dice down on Charles Street. Hearing that Reid and his gang were up at Chocomo, Prince Buster hurried up there, and a man immediately pulled a knife on him. In the mêlée that followed, another of Reid's hoods split the back of Buster's skull open with a rock. Later, he and Reid became good friends: 'He became a nice man: he was just possessed by what was going on.'

Soon both Coxsone and Duke Reid began recording songs by local artists specifically for use on their respective systems. The law of supply and demand showed itself to be inescapable, and out of this – as well as Coxsone's realisation that American record companies such as Imperial and Modern didn't seem to notice when he blatantly pirated their material – was born the Jamaican recording industry.

* * *

The first two dances at which the Sir Coxsone Downbeat sound system played were in Trench Town; and the first of these was an event put on by Jimmy Tucker, a leading Jamaican vocalist.

The cauldron of Trench Town epitomised one of the great cultural truths about Jamaica – and other impoverished countries in the Third World, come to that: how those who have nothing – and therefore nothing to lose – have no fear of expressing their God-given talents. People whose earning potential sometimes seems to be literally nil have a pride and confidence in their innate abilities in arts and crafts – a pride and confidence that western educational and employment systems appear to conspire to kick out of those who pass through them. The pace of life in Jamaica, moreover, often seems to accord with the God-given rhythms of nature: rising with the sun, people are active early in the day until the sun goes down. Such a harnessing of man's soul to the day's natural process seems to allow free rein and progress to the creative forces that dance out from both the personal and collective unconscious.

Nesta Robert Marley would rise in the cool of first daylight, but long after sunset he could still be found, with or without his spar, Bunny, strumming his sardine-can guitar and trying out melodies and harmonies. Apart from football, it was his only solace, the only space where he could feel comfortable within his head. Later in life he would say, 'Sleep is for fools.'

Often he would feel alienated and ostracised in the city. With his mixed-race origins clearly visible in his facial skin, he was considered a white boy and was taunted for this; his complexion could bring out the worst in people: after all, why was this boy from 'country' living down in the ghetto and not uptown with all the other lightskin people? Being so consistently and miserably tested can bring the worst out in someone, destroying them; or it can assiduously and resolutely build their character. Such daily bullying ultimately created in Nesta his iron will, his overpowering self-confidence and self-esteem.

'Sometimes he'd come across the resistance of being half-caste,' said Rita Marley. 'There was a problem with his counterparts: having come through this white father caused such difficulties that he's want to kill himself and thinking, "Why am I this person? Why is my father white and not black like everybody else? What did I do wrong?"

'He was lost in that: not being able to have anyone to say, "It's not your fault, or that there's nothing wrong in being like you are." But that was the atmosphere he came up in that Trench Town environment where everybody is rough. He had to show them that although he didn't know his father, at least he knew there was a God and he knew what he was feeling.

'Bob had to put up with a lot of resistance. If he wasn't that strong in himself he wouldn't be what he became. He would be downtrodden and seen as another half-caste who would never make it.'

The still air of Trench Town was barely ever disturbed by traffic noise; from those rare yards that had a tenant sufficiently fortunate to possess a radio would sail the favourite new songs from the United States, fading in and out as they drifted down the Caribbean from New Orleans or Miami, or Nashville, the home of the enormously powerful Radio WALC. Especially popular was the ten-to-midnight show sponsored by White Rose Petroleum Jelly whose DJ was Hugh Jarrett, a vocalist with Elvis Presley's Jordanaires backing group, who were in need of employment in 1958 when Elvis went into the army. Enormously powerful, WALC could easily be tuned in to throughout the US eastern seaboard and far further south in to the Caribbean than Jamaica.

Nat King Cole, Billy Eckstine, Fats Domino, Brook Benton, Larry Williams, Louis Jordan, and white iconoclasts such as Elvis Presley and the milder Ricky Nelson all made a strong impression on Nesta; he also absorbed the omnipresent Trinidadian calypso and steel-band music that had been adopted by Jamaica almost as its own.

It was in Trench Town that Nesta Robert Marley was exposed for the first time to bebop and modern jazz – at first, however, 'mi couldn't understand it,' Bob later admitted. But in 1960, he began to take part in the evening music sessions held in his Third Street yard by Joe Higgs – and Joe Higgs loved jazz, especially hornsmen. He was one of the area's most famous residents, due to his role as one of Jamaica's first indigenous recording artists, as part of the Higgs and Wilson duo.

Joe Higgs, who had been born in 1940, had begun 'foolin' around on a guitar' in 1956, when he was 16. Perhaps pertinently, the guitar had belonged to a Rastaman. 'He used to allow me to play and I used to pick. I tried to combine notes in a freak manner 'cause I was just aware of harmony structure. I couldn't tell whether this was G or F or whatever on the guitar. I know that I was just forming and building songs. Then I'd take my time and make songs around those chords. That's the way I made most of my music.'

Another singer, Roy Wilson, lived on the same Trench Town street; they each used the rehearsal studio at Bim and Bam. Due to simple expediency, they ended up singing together as a duo at a talent contest, in which they came second. Higgs and Wilson, as they had become, were signed up by Edward Seaga, who later became Prime Minister, his only act at the time. Their first release in 1960 on his West Indies Records label (WIRL) was 'Oh Manny Oh'; this jumping boogie raced up the Jamaican charts from 43 to 3 before hitting the top spot for two weeks. 'Sold a lot!' said Joe Higgs. Their biggest record, however, was 'There's a Reward', recorded for Coxsone Dodd on his Wincox label. But when Higgs went to see Coxsone and asked for royalties, the sound-system boss took out a gun and beat his artist with it.

Joe Higgs was as conscious in his actions as in his lyrics; these included the unmentionable, radical subject of Rastafari – for publicly espousing the faith, which grew by quantum leaps amongst the ghetto sufferahs, he had been beaten up by the police and imprisoned during political riots in Trench Town in May 1959. This only strengthened him in his resolve. Higgs had himself learned music from his mother, who sang in a church choir; recalling how fortified he had been by the spiritual aspect of her teaching, Joe Higgs henceforth paid great attention to playing the part of both musical and moral tutor to those youth of the area with the ears to hear. The musical seminars he conducted could be rigorous affairs: especial attention would be paid to breath control and melody, as well as guitar lessons in which he would instruct his students in the art of writing lyrics that would carry clear ideas to the people. It was not all work: sometimes entire classes would voyage together the short distance to the end of Marcus Garvey Drive to swim at the beach known as Hot and Cold, an effect created on the water by an electrical power generator.

It was in Higgs's yard that Nesta had his first encounter with something that stilled his thoughts sufficiently for him to empathise with the lateral processes of jazz: the Jamaican natural resource with which he was later to become inextricably associated in the public mind. 'After a while I smoke some ganja, some herb, and get to understand it. Mi try to get into de mood whar de moon is blue and see de feelin' expressed. Joe Higgs 'elped me understands that music. 'E taught mi many t'ings.'

Another of the male role models who appeared consistently through the course of the fatherless Nesta's life, Joe Higgs assiduously coached the 15-year-old and his spar Bunny in the art of harmonising and he advised Bob to sing all the time, to strengthen his voice. At one of these sessions Bob and Bunny met Peter McIntosh, another youth wanting to try out as a vocalist, who lived in nearby West Road.

Unlike the more humble Bunny, this tall, gangly, and arrogant youth was older than Bob. He had been born Winston Hubert McIntosh on 19 October 1944 in the west of Jamaica, in the coastal hamlet of Bluefields, Westmoreland, to Alvera Coke and James McIntosh. His father had left his mother soon after the child was born. Taken into the care of an aunt, the first sixteen years of his life had been spent first in the pleasant coastal town of Savanna-la-Mar and then the rough section of west Kingston called Denham Town. In 1956, after his aunt died, he moved in with an uncle who lived in Trench Town. Lonely and isolated, the boy was consumed with an urgent need to make it as a musician. Unlike Bob and Bunny, however, whose guitar-playing had only developed perfunctorily as they concentrated on their vocal skills, Peter McIntosh was a competent guitarist, owning his own cheap acoustic model. As a boy he had piano lessons for two years, until his mother could no longer afford them.

Nesta and Bunny first encountered Peter when they literally walked into him as he rounded a Trench Town corner while he was playing his guitar and singing. Peter was especially fond of Stan Jones's much covered country-cowboy song '(Ghost) Riders in the Sky', with its 'yippey yi-yay' chorus, a simultaneous hit in 1949 for three separate artists, Burl Ives, Bing Crosby, and Vaughn Monroe – apocryphally, it was '(Ghost) Riders in the Sky' he was singing when he bumped into Nesta and Bunny. Falling into conversation with this relative newcomer to the area, they learned that Peter already had plenty of songs he had written: he had decided much earlier that his course of life would be as a singer. Peter had learned to play the guitar by observing a bushman in Savanna-la-Mar, who would play his instrument by the roadside or on the seashore. Every day, Peter would study the man's hands and watch where he placed them. After some time, he asked the bushman to hand him the guitar. He proceeded to perform a perfect rendition of a song the man had himself been playing. 'Who taught you to play like that?' asked the bushman. 'You did,' replied Peter. It was the older boy's skill on the instrument that inspired Nesta to pay serious attention to mastering the guitar. After a while he was thwarted in any further progress. Peter's battered instrument simply fell to pieces.

Another older friend of Nesta's in Trench Town was Vincent Ford, also known as Jack Tartar or, more usually, simply Tartar, which may also be spelled 'Tata'. Tartar had first come across the Marley boy when he was around 13 and Tartar was 17. A close bond had developed between the two: Tartar had worked as a chef at the Boys Town school, and then started up a little kitchen in his yard on First Street, which he and Nesta would refer to as 'the casbah'. As well as the ganja that fulfilled a crucial gap in the desperate economy of Trench Town, Tartar would sell dishes like calaloo and dumplings – at times when Nesta was entirely impoverished it would be at Tartar's that he would find free food. When Nesta made the decision to apply himself to the guitar, it was Tartar who would stay up all night with him, turning the 'leaves' of the *Teach Yourself Guitar* book Nesta had bought as he strummed the chords, peering at the diagrams of where to put his fingers in the light of a flickering oil lamp. In the mornings, their nostrils would be black from the lamp's fumes.

One day in her bar, Cedella found herself talking to a customer who told her of a welding business on South Camp Road that regularly took in apprentices. The next day Nesta secured himself a position there as an apprentice welder – when he started work as a trainee at the South Camp Road premises he discovered that his friend Desmond Dekker was already employed there: having already passed all his exams, Dekker now was beginning to learn underwater welding.

'I knew men who were doing welding for a livin', and I suggested that he go down to the shop and make himself an apprentice,' remembered

Cedella. 'He hated it. One day he was welding some steel and a piece of metal flew off and got stuck right in the white of his eye, and he had to go to the hospital to have it taken out. It caused him terrible pain; it even hurt for him to cry.' Peter Tosh was similarly employed, having been pushed into learning welding by his uncle; he was working at another firm, but Bob's accident gave Peter the excuse to back out of the trade.

That rogue sliver of metal that caused such agony to Nesta's eye had a greater significance. From now on, he told Tartar, there would be no more welding: only the guitar. Bob convinced his mother he could make a better living singing. By now, Bunny also had made a ghetto guitar, similar to the ones Nesta constructed, from a bamboo staff, electric cable wire, and a large sardine can. Then Peter Tosh, as the McIntosh boy was more readily known, brought along his battered acoustic guitar to play with them. '1961,' remembered Peter Tosh, 'the group came together.'

At the urging of Joe Higgs, they formed into a musical unit, coached by Higgs: the Teenagers contained the three youths, as well as a strong local singer called Junior Braithwaite. 'It was kinda difficult,' said Joe Higgs later, 'to get the group precise – and their sound – and to get the harmony structures. It took a couple years to get that perfect. I wanted each person to be a leader in his own right. I wanted them to be able to wail in their own rights.'

Nesta Marley, Bunny Livingston, and Peter Tosh were the only singers that Joe Higgs rehearsed in that manner. Although they would be beaten to this by the Maytals, who began performing in 1962, they were one of the first groups in Jamaica who were more than a duo; previously the island's charts had been dominated by pairs of singers – the Blues Busters, Alton and Eddie, Bunny and Scully, and – of course – Higgs and Wilson.

A close brethren of Joe Higgs, Alvin 'Franseeco' Patterson, later known simply as Seeco, instructed the Wailers, as the Teenagers would become known, in the philosophy of rhythm. Originally from St Ann,

Seeco was another professional musician now living in Trench Town. An accomplished hand drummer, he had worked with various of Jamaica's calypso groups, as well as having had involvement with the Jamaican musical form of mento. The burru style of drumming he played was an African rhythm of liberation welcoming the return of released prisoners of war; it had been co-opted into Rastafari's Nyabinghi style of inspirational chanting and drum rhythms. And it was this blend of devotion and rebellious fervour that formed the basis of the Wailers' understanding of rhythm.

Endeavouring to understand and master music was something which Nesta Marley never stopped doing. As soon as he rose in the morning he picked up his guitar, and would rarely be without it for the rest of the day and night, practising immensely hard. With Joe Higgs, the harmony master, Nesta, Bunny, and Peter would often practise and rehearse until five in the morning. Taking a break around 2:30 a.m., they would head over to Ma ChiChi, who sold oily fried-corn dumplings and what was said to be Jamaica's best soursop juice, so thick you had to tap the bottom of the bottle to get it out; Ma ChiChi only lit her pan at 2:30 a.m., when the dancehalls were closing down.

Other times in the early hours of the morning, the three youths would wander with Joe Higgs down to Back-a-Wall, then to Maypen Cemetery, then over to Hot and Cold. Singing all the time they walked, they would check out the responses to such songs they favoured as Little Antony and the Imperials' 'Tears on my Pillow', the Platters' 'My Prayer', Frankie Lymon's 'I'm Not a Juvenile Delinquent', and Gene Chandler's 'Duke of Earl', with Peter on the bass part. At other times, they would stand on corners or in parks trying out material, or call on such revered local figures as Brother Gifford, One Sam, or Sonny Flight to air their musical wares for them, wondering whether they could detect the trio's development.

Finally, they even acquired their first conventionally constructed and manufactured guitar. Around the corner of Ebenezer Street and Darling Lane, just off Spanish Town Road, in what is now Tivoli Gardens, was the Ebenezer Boys' Club, a local youth club. Discovering that the institution possessed its own badly mistreated guitar, hardly larger than a child's instrument, Bob appropriated it for the group.

It was Peter who could play guitar, and organ and piano, who worked with the instrument more than his two musical partners. One evening, they had been invited over to play in Greenwich Farm at the cold-supper shop of a man called Sheriff Brown, one of the area's main herbsmen. Late for their show, the three youths were running there, racing each other. Then Peter's foot collided with Bob's, and he tumbled. He was carrying the Ebenezer guitar and it was smashed beyond repair.

Almost immediately they acquired a far more satisfactory replacement. It was sold to them by a local man named Deacon, an intellectual, highly literate Rasta who was a cultural historian and had stored and recorded the history of Marcus Garvey. Noticing the guitar hanging on Deacon's wall, they made him an offer for it.

This guitar was full-sized and in good condition. Nicknaming the instrument 'Betsy', as Bo Diddley had christened his guitar, they added an electrical pick-up, and would use it either unamplified or with electricity. Five years later, in 1967, they were still using it on recordings.

It was now public knowledge in Trench Town that Nesta Marley, who was beginning to be known more as Bob, or Bobby or Robbie, was a musician of some sort. At that time, Pauline Morrison lived in the area and was a pupil at Kingston Senior School. Every afternoon she would make her way home from her lessons, usually with a large group of children from the same neighbourhood; they would walk from West Road to

Thirteenth Street, to Ninth Street and the Gully Bank and then across a bridge. At the end of a lane, she invariably would see Bob sitting under a broad, tall tree, accompanying himself on a homemade guitar as he sang songs of his own composition. Fifteen or twenty schoolchildren would be gathered all around. It was a regular fixture. 'We'd come from school and see this guy singing, singing, and we'd always sit around and watch and listen to him. After him finish we clap him, and after we'd go home.'

Bob seemed like a bird, remembered Pauline, 'like a young hatchling just coming up'. Later, as success started to make his songs familiar, she would recognise some of the tunes from those after-school perform-ances – he would certainly play, for example, an early version of 'Simmer Down'; those who knew Bob would always hear him singing that song from around the beginning of 1962. (On that long journey back from school, she and her companions would often have had another musical experience: in an entirely different neighbourhood, a young Jimmy Cliff could also be seen singing, planted under the boughs of an ackee tree.)

Although football was almost as much a love for Bob Marley as music, he occasionally would also be seen playing cricket, on that same gully bank Pauline would have had to pass over. Ernest Ranglin would see him knocking a ball about as he passed and sometimes join in for a few minutes. To Ranglin he always seemed a very well-brought-up boy, extremely polite and considerate.

As a youth who knew what he wanted in life, Bob was not caught up in the negative existence of the ghetto bad boy, those packs of adoles-cents who only desired to emulate and try to surpass the worst exploits of the slum gangs of the United States, glorified and glamorised in movies such as *West Side Story* that they would catch at the Carib cinema after sneaking in the exit door.

Bob certainly wasn't some pavement bully. Although, Pauline pointed out, 'if a guy come for him and trouble him, him can defend himself.' But even then he operated simultaneously on several levels. On the one hand, he was affable, open, eager to assist. 'He was a very easygoing person,' Pauline said. 'He was never rude or anything. Him never be aggressive. Him was always irie to me, even as a kid coming from school. And although I still get to know him and be around him, him never be rude.'

Then again he could be almost the definition of a loner. 'It was always the man and his guitar,' Pauline observed. 'But it was very rare you could just sit with him and be with him. Because he was a very moody person, the way I see him. Him is very moody. If people were sitting together with him, he would suddenly just get up and go somewhere else. Just to be by himself.'

In the end, Nesta knew, there was only one person he could rely on – himself – although he could expect the occasional unexpected intervention and assistance of others.

TRENCH TOWN ROCK

On 6 August 1962, Jamaica was granted independence from British colonial rule. A by-product of independence for Trench Town's population was that a sewage system was almost immediately installed. Two songs that year summed up the optimistic mood of an emergent nation: Lord Creator's 'Independent Jamaica' and 'Forward March' by Derrick Morgan. Morgan recorded for the Beverley's label, owned by a Chinese Jamaican businessman called Leslie Kong who ran Beverley's Record and Ice Cream Parlor (which also sold stationery) on the corner of North and Orange Streets in downtown Kingston. Upstairs, past the seated restaurant area, past the cigarette machine, was where Leslie Kong had his office. Kong had started the label after Morgan had sought finance for the recording of a tune called 'Dearest Beverley' which Jimmy Cliff had written, its title shrewdly bearing the same name as Kong's wife – hence the name of the recording venture. At one stage in 1961, Morgan had seven records in the Jamaican Top Ten; one of the reasons he recorded so prolifically was that Kong only made a flat payment of ten Jamaican dollars per tune. Morgan also, however, had a role as an unofficial talent scout for the Beverley's label.

In those days, Morgan would drink at a bar on Charles Street by the junction with Spanish Town Road – then known as Back-a-Wall, the area is now notorious as the JLP 'garrison community' of Tivoli Gardens.

On Charles Street lived a girlfriend of Morgan's called Pat Stewart. She was acquainted with an aunt of Nesta's, a 'brown woman', and when the youth visited her one time, Pat heard him sing. 'Bob can sing good, y'know, Derrick – why not try 'im?' she suggested.

'You really do singin', baas?' Morgan checked with him in February 1962. The answer came in the affirmative. 'Me seh well come over Beverley's nuh: mek me hear you. And 'im come up deh one day and I play the piano and 'im sing the tune "Judge Not".'

Two or three days later, Nesta turned up at Beverley's, accompanied by his friend Jimmy Cliff, who was already recording on the label. Morgan thought the youth's song was good but not great. And he was struck by the fact that Bob seemed to dance almost better than he sang when he auditioned the tune: ''im could DANCE.' Finding himself one night in Cedella's rum shop, Morgan complimented the boy's mother on her son's abilities. 'You have a son who's very talented,' he told her. 'He has a lot of potential.'

Jimmy Cliff, who lived by the bridge near Queen's Theatre, recalled a slightly different version of the genesis of the first recording by Bob Marley: 'Desmond came to me and I introduced him to Leslie Kong, and he got his song recorded. He then went and told Bob, "I know this youth called Jimmy Cliff, and he helped me to get my song recorded." He then brought Bob to me, and I introduced him to Leslie Kong. And Bob had his song recorded. So that was the first recordings, so it meant a lot. Your first song, it really means a lot.'

Leslie Kong was willing to take a chance. 'Alright,' he decreed, 'mi could try it now.' The next Saturday morning, Kong drove down to Trench Town and turned up on the doorstep at 19 Second Street, looking for Nesta. His mother told him her son had gone out. Leslie Kong was disappointed: he wanted to offer him a recording contract, he said. But when Nesta came home in the early evening, he had managed to run into Kong, signed the contract, and been paid the five pounds it specified. Generously, a precursor of his later attitude towards finances, the youth gave two pounds to his mother, ten shillings to his aunt Enid, and five shillings to a woman who was visiting from the country.

'Judge Not' and its B-side, 'Do You Still Love Me,' were recorded at Federal Studios the same month. Bob took Bunny along with him for moral support. 'Judge Not' was the joyous gallop of ska, a music at the time as fresh and unique as the nation of Jamaica itself, which the shrill, youthful voice of Bob Marley had as the backbeat to his first recorded work. But its celebratory sound could not conceal the biblical tone that was significantly present in his first release: chiding those who passed judgement on himself and his kind, he warns that 'While you talk about me / Someone else is judging you.' The song hardly sold at all and radio play was nonexistent; this was in contrast to the experience of Desmond Dekker, whose first song, 'Honour Your Father and Your Mother', was a hit.

Two months later, in April 1962, Bob recorded two other ska numbers, 'Terror' ('He who rules by terror do aggrievous wrongs / In hell I'll count his error / Let them hear my song') and 'One Cup of Coffee', which was put out as a 45, to little avail. 'One Cup of Coffee', a strange saga of separation and financial settlement, turned out to be based largely on a 1961 country song by the musician Claude Gray. The few listeners that the song garnered assumed it was the work of one 'Bobby Martell', the name listed on the label: Kong had renamed him with this kitsch moniker in much the same way as he had changed James Chambers's name to Jimmy Cliff. (Released in England on the new Island Records label, 'Judge Not' was credited to 'Robert Morley'.)

Leslie Kong was largely preoccupied with his new, big-selling vocal act, Jackie Opel, a Barbadian. And when the producer refused to give any more money to 'Bobby Martell' the relationship ended. It was said that, after an argument over Kong swindling him, Bob prophesied to the label owner, frightening him, that one day he would make plenty of money out of Bob but would never have the luxury of enjoying it. 'So Robert said to me,' said Desmond Dekker, '"Look, I'lla dig up." I said, "Where you goin'?" Him say, "Watch out. I'll leggo dis Chinaman y'unno. I'll go up a Coxsone. Yuh a come?" I said, "Well, I gotta wait and see before I make my move."'

Morgan, however, continued his association and friendship with Bob. The next year he emigrated to the United Kingdom. Kong promoted a pair of farewell shows for him, one at the Capri Theatre in May Penn in the middle of the island, and another in Montego Bay, and Derrick Morgan ensured that Bob was on each bill. Again, Morgan noted that Bob, perhaps through nervousness, had not balanced the energies of his performance especially well. At the Capri Theatre show, for example, 'when Bob go on stage he was dancin' more than he was singin' . . . An' 'im tired when 'im come back to the vocal, so me beg 'im and seh: "No, youth: when ya sing two verse you dance, an' then you go back to your other verse."'

At the Montego Bay venue, Bob performed as Morgan had suggested. But during 'One Cup of Coffee', his first song, he didn't receive the audience response either of them had expected. In fact, the typically volatile and expressive Jamaican crowd started to boo. 'The next song, 'im just get up and seh: "Judge not, before you judge yourself!" So the audience think a him mek that song immediately offa dem! And 'im tear dung the whole place with that tune: Judge not, before you judge yourself. When 'im reach a part there the audience 'ray and seh: Wait, this boy a bad, 'im a jus' mek a sound offa we, same time, yeah man, an' deh so 'im hit. That was the last time I see Bob fe a long while.'

Kingstonians, however, were able to see Bob Marley most weeks, at the Queen's Theatre, as part of the weekly Opportunity Knocks talent shows. These stage shows run by Vere Johns, before an audience of some 600 people, were broadcast on RJR, one of the island's two radio stations, and featured such guest artists as Higgs and Wilson, and Alton and Eddy. The best contending singer would win a guinea (£1.10, or $1.60), through the simple test of being brought back for the most encores – if the crowd took against you, you'd be booed off. Bob would steal these shows every time, hurrying away from the venue with his prize before other, less successful contenders could beg some of it away from him. He would sing 'Judge Not', and another song he had written, 'Fancy Curls' ('Last night your best friend was sick / Goodness gracious, another of your trick / Hey little girl with those fancy curls'). For a time Bob was even awarded the nickname 'Fancy Curls'.

The fact that the records released by Beverley's hadn't sold was, after the initial disappointment, irrelevant. Only 16 years old, Bob had been given the sign that he was perfectly justified in imagining that there could be some kind of musical future for him. To make the next step forward, he decided to make a serious go of it with his spars from Trench Town. Accordingly, the Teenagers became first the Wailing Rudeboys, and then the Wailing Wailers, before finally mutating into simply the Wailers.

One of the maxims of a man called Lee 'Scratch' Perry, who worked for Coxsone Dodd's sound system, was that every man has a name for a purpose. So it also was and is with groups. And the name 'The Wailers' didn't merely reflect some alleycat screech made by the trio. Whether consciously or unconsciously chosen, it spoke volumes about the deep miasma of anguish and lonely hurt all three, especially Nesta and Peter, had felt within their souls as youths coming up. Bob Marley's vocals sound sometimes as if he is literally crying. 'The word "wail" means to cry or to moan,' said Peter Tosh later. 'We were living in this so-called ghetto. No one to help them. We felt we were the only ones who could express the people's feelings through music, and because of that the people loved it. So we did it.'

Definitively ghetto sufferahs, the trio responded to music made by their American equivalents – Ray Charles, Sam Cooke, and the flawless harmonising of the Impressions, led by Curtis Mayfield and Jerry Butler. When the Impressions came to Jamaica in the early 1960s to play warmup dates before a US tour (the reason so many American acts played in Jamaica), all three Wailers went together to see them at the Carib Theatre, fighting to get up to the front row. The group's 'One Love' utilised sections of the Impressions' 'People Get Ready'. The Wailers also recorded versions of the Impressions' 'Another Dance', for Studio One, and 'Keep On Movin'', for Scratch Perry.

Looking at it with a clear vision, the future seemed to contain myriad musical possibilities. But without that hope, the reality of Bob's then existence could only have been seen as bitterly grim. He had no real source of income, and literally would have starved on occasions if it had not been for Tartar's kitchen.

A further set of complications was on its way. Bob's mother, Cedella, had become pregnant by Toddy, Bunny's father, giving birth to Pearl

Livingston early in 1962; Bob and Bunny were thereby linked even closer by their new half-sister. Bob, meanwhile, had had a passionate affair himself with a local girl, two years younger than he was. Her older brother, though, forbade the girl to carry on the relationship because of Bob's white blood, a recurring and consistent problem for him. The shock of being the victim of such racism, combined with Pearl taking much of the unstinting attention that Cedella had previously given her son, caused tensions within Bob and in the yard at 19 Second Street. But did her brother have another reason for objecting to his sister associating with Bob Marley? For on 22 May 1963, Cheryl Murray, a local girl, gave birth to Bob Marley's first child, Imani Carole, conceived when he was sixteen and about whom little is known.

It had taken the birth of Pearl to make Cedella realise precisely how hopeless her relationship was with the baby girl's father. To escape from this unprofitable union and to advance her life, she decided to move to the north-eastern United States, to Wilmington in Delaware, where there was yet another branch of the Malcolm family. She agonised over what to do with her son. But then it was decided that he would stay behind and wait for her to send for him and for Pearl.

Cedella's sister Enid moved into the home on Second Street to care for her nephew and niece. When Enid moved back to St Ann, however, Toddy Livingston took over the apartment. Although the residence theoretically remained as Bob's home, he was unhappy when Toddy moved in Ceciline, another of his baby-mothers. Bob turned up at 19 Second Street less and less frequently. Effectively, he found himself homeless, living for a time in west Kingston's various squatter camps. It was as though, yet again, he had been abandoned. To all intents and purposes, he was destitute. But then Tartar took him in and gave him a corner of the kitchen, in which he also slept. Bob's bed was the gambling table that Tartar would set up for reasons that were both social and financial: Bob would have to wait until the games had finished to reclaim his bed.

These were very hard times indeed. But in that strange way in which adversity can be turned to advantage, they also served to focus and hone Bob's art. There was no choice, no other way out. Bunny would come round, and – to a lesser extent – Peter and Junior Braithwaite, and they would sit around practising harmonies until they fell asleep. 'Me and Bunny used to be the harmony of the group, and we sang harmony like birds,' said Peter Tosh. 'We two sing harmony, sound like five. Bob Marley never sing harmony, no time.'

Junior Braithwaite had been born on 4 April 1949 on Third Street and West Road, in what became known as Rema, immediately to the east of Trench Town. Also living on Third Street was Joe Higgs; Roy Wilson, Higgs's partner in Higgs and Wilson, had been raised by Junior Braithwaite's grandmother. 'They used to rehearse in the back of our yard,' Junior Braithwaite said. 'So we as kids hang out around them.' The early Wailers, composed of Bob, Bunny, Peter, Junior Braithwaite, and a girl they would soon meet called Cherry Green was, according to Junior, 'just a singing group, a harmonising group. We had nothing to do with instruments.' In the early days of the group, other potential members had been briefly tried out: a couple of tenors, Barrington Sayles and Ricardo Scott, decided for themselves that their voices weren't really strong enough; meanwhile, 'P', the sister of Joe Brown, a rude boy from Second Street, would turn up at early rehearsals, but also came to the conclusion that her vocals were not sufficiently powerful.

Falling back on himself in these endless rehearsals, Bob found his confidence and ability growing almost by the day. To provide light for their sessions, another ghetto-dweller by the name of George Headley Robinson would gather brushwood from all about the area and lug it to Tartar's yard. Some thirteen years older than Bob, 'Georgie', as he was more commonly known, was a devoted believer in the talents of the youth and his musical companions. Georgie, who made his living as a fisherman, would try and instruct Bob in matters of Rastafari, constantly referring to one of the copies of the Bible that are omnipresent in Jamaica. 'But Bob,' Georgie said, 'was too young to reason with me.'

'Georgie would sit there shirtless all night,' Tartar recollected, 'tending the flames as they played.' When they awoke, after falling asleep exhausted from practicing, the fire would still be burning; straightaway Georgie would 'bwile up some porridge' or a kettle for some bush tea.

At around this time, unexpectedly, a turning point was reached. Alvin Patterson – Seeco the rhythm master – was acquainted with Clement Dodd, the sound-system man who had begun his own record label. He knew of the auditions that Coxsone would regularly hold on Sundays at Studio One, his new one-track studio on Brentford Road, to the north of Trench Town. In the summer of 1964, at the urging of Joe Higgs, Seeco took Bob and the rest of the group, including Beverley Kelso and another girl, called Cherry Green (named after the surname of her half-brother), over there one Sunday. Cherry Green's real name was Ermine Ortense Bramwell, but she gained the nickname Cherry from her skin's red hue.

Although Clement 'Coxsone' Dodd was not a musician himself, he had what Ernest Ranglin described as 'an extraordinary pair of ears'. He was also a wizard at contriving musical concepts. 'He was really the man, the man who came up with the ideas. But he couldn't play, so he would come and explain it to us. After explaining it, I always knew what the man wanted.'

One Sunday morning in 1959, the bass player Cluett 'Clue-J' Johnson and Ranglin had been requested by Coxsone in a surprisingly formal manner to meet him at the liquor store he ran in Love Lane. 'I need something to get away from this blues,' he told the two master musicians, bemoaning the manner in which Jamaican music was imitating contemporary American black music.

In the store's backyard, they sat down and worked out the recipe for a new sound; they sought a formula for a music that was distinctly Jamaican whilst retaining its roots in the R'n'B and popular jazz that beamed down into Jamaica from radio stations in the southern American states. Ska, the music that resulted from that Sunday-morning session, was a shuffle boogie rhythm of the type popularised by artists such as Louis Jordan and Erskine Hawkins; the unexpected emphasis on the offbeat only emphasised its addictive flavour. An apocryphal explanation of the galloping sound of ska was that this was a replication of the way music on those southern stations would fade in and out. Ranglin, however, has a simpler explanation: 'We just wanted it to sound like the theme music from one of those westerns that were on TV all the time in the late 1950s.' The term 'ska' was an abbreviation of 'skavoovee', a popular catchphrase of the time, a term of approval, for the use of which 'Clue-J' was famous. (Coxsone, for his part, addressed almost every man he encountered as 'Jackson', for which verbal eccentricity he was at least equally renowned: when he used the term 'Jackson', it frequently indicated disapproval, that the artist was not coming up to scratch.)

The next day, Coxsone went to the JBC Radio studios, which could be hired for recording, and started trying out examples of this new music to be tested on his sound system. The first ska record that was released, after it had received tumultuous acclaim at dances, was 'Easy Snappin'' by Theophilus Beckford. It featured the pianist Beckford on vocals, 'Clue-J' on bass, Ian Pearson on drums, Ken Richards on guitar, Roland Alphonso on tenor sax, and the trombonist Rico Rodriguez. The record was a big hit; its B-side was 'Silky', featuring Ernest Ranglin on his own composition.

'Easy Snappin'' was also the first tune Coxsone recorded at Federal Studio. When Federal bought equipment for a two-track, Coxsone bought its original one-track to install it in new premises, a former nightclub, he was taking over at 13 Brentford Road in the Crossroads area of Kingston. Along with the new studio, Coxsone also opened a liquor store within the building. After a time, Federal graduated to an eight-track machine, and Coxsone purchased its two-track.

It was to these new premises, which would form the base and basis of Clement Dodd's Studio One label, that Seeco took the Wailers. Listening to them in his studio's dusty yard, beneath the mango tree that was the location of these weekly auditions, Coxsone liked their sound and several of the songs they had written. But he didn't truly bite until they played their fifth tune: Bunny suggested 'Simmer Down', the song Bob had been playing around with for at least two years. Before Bob answered, Peter started playing it. They hadn't even sung a full verse before Coxsone declared, 'Okay, that one: come tomorrow and we'll record that one.'

'I was very impressed with them the first time,' remembered Coxsone. 'I was hoping to really get a kind of group with that team feel, young voices and things like that. But they need a lot of polishing.'

Bob Marley himself wasn't as enthused about 'Simmer Down' as Coxsone and the rest of the group: Coxsone knew it would work as a sound-system song, but Bob allegedly saw the tune, so old it had become part of his mental furniture, as a nursery-rhyme-type number – paradoxically, much of 'Simmer Down', as it had originally been conceived, is sound-system battle-talk. However, he would not let his personal opinion interfere with an opportunity to make another record.

Coxsone Dodd signed the Wailers as both performers and songwriters. They were offered his standard deal: a five-year contract for exclusive recording rights and management, and a guarantee of twenty pounds between them for every side.

The money on offer was so small that it hardly improved the group's financial position at all. Accordingly, for the entire time they would record with Coxsone Dodd, the Wailers would get by with that same routine of hustle-hustle-scrape employed by much of the local youth merely to keep existing. Going down to the beach and fishing with a rod and line, they would take what they caught to the market, exchanging the fish for other food; off the local trees they would pick mangoes, ackee, guinips, tambrines, and June-plums and sell them; they would also gather up any scrap metal or bottles, and regularly would trek over to the nearby dairy farm to pick up all the lead that came off the milk tins. Sponsored when necessary by his father, Bunny was more likely to have a few pence in his pockets. Peter was the only one with any sort of job, pressing clothes at a local dry-cleaner's run by a friend; he would care for the Wailers' stage outfits, and also their day-to-day clothes – they each had two pairs of pants and two shirts. Bob, meanwhile, would simply try to somehow get by.

When, within days, the first session took place, the sides chosen were not 'Simmer Down' but 'I'm Still Waiting' and 'It Hurts to Be Alone', engineered by Sid 'Siddie' Bucknor, Coxsone Dodd's cousin, who performed the same function on most of their Studio One work. Although Coxsone had marked out 'Simmer Down' for release as a single, he first wanted to establish interest in the Wailers by pushing another song to be promoted by his several sound system sets. 'They had songs that was all do-over material, early doo-wop stuff, so I instructed them to try and do some writing.' Out of an evening's work at Studio One, overseen by Coxsone and Ernest Ranglin, had come 'I'm Still Waiting' and 'It Hurts to Be Alone'. The first song was a beautiful Bob Marley original, even though the preamble of the vocal harmonies owed much to the Impressions. But when Bob delivered his breathtakingly sweet vocal solo, it bled from a tearful heart; suspended in a void of echoing pain, his voice felt as though it was recorded at a different, slowed-down speed from the rest of the track. 'It Hurts to Be Alone' was a Junior Braithwaite number, on which he sang lead. As Coxsone's house arranger, Ernest Ranglin oversaw the production of the pair of sides.

The instrumentation was basic: Lloyd Knibbs on drums, Lloyd Brevett on bass, and Jah Jerry Haines on guitar. Bob, noted Jah Jerry, was 'a nice boy, a nice young feller: not a rough guy, a polite guy'.

For once Ranglin didn't have to spice up the song with guitar over-dubs. 'You could see they had something in them. They were all very nice guys, but they seemed very young. And little too.' Braithwaite, in partic-ular, was very short, whilst both Bob and Bunny stood not much more than five foot four inches in height; by comparison, Peter Tosh, at six feet four, seemed to tower over the rest of the group. After Coxsone had pressed up three hundred copies of the two tunes, they were distributed to sound systems; the word came back that 'It Hurts to Be Alone' was going down well.

As soon as Coxsone heard this, he called the group back to the studio. But there had been changes of which no one had notified him. Junior Braithwaite wasn't with them: to Coxsone's surprise and initial chagrin he learned that Braithwaite was in the final stages of preparing to leave Jamaica for Chicago with his family. 'I only lead sung on "It Hurts to Be Alone",' said Junior. 'And that was the day, 28 August 1964, just before I flew out of Jamaica. Because they had to have me do a solo just before I left, and so it only took a few hours to learn this new tune, and one take. We were that tough, man.'

If Coxsone were to continue working with the group, the producer insisted, the Wailers required a clearly defined lead vocalist. After some discussion, it was decided that the task should fall to Bob Marley; Bunny and Peter were promised they would also get their share of lead vocals. Coxsone was encouraged in this decision by 'Simmer Down', the contract-winning song Bob had sung at the audition, which served a dual purpose: a warning to the newly emergent rude boys – that tribal grouping of cool, disaffected, and desperate youth – not to bring down the wrath of the law upon themselves; and a frustrated response to a letter from Bob's mother in the United States, fearful that her only son was becoming involved with bad company.

The full panoply of his label's finest ska musicians was summoned by Coxsone for the session. Yet again Ernest Ranglin arranged the tune, whilst Don Drummond, Jamaica's king of the trombone, added his deeply creative jazz parts. Drummond, who had played with Ranglin in the Eric Dean Orchestra, was the virtuoso of a group of musicians who shortly were to be working together, for a little over a year, under the name of the Skatalites, an ensemble that would in time become legendary. As well as Drummond, the group included Roland Alphonso and Tommy McCook, the group's leader, on tenor sax, Lester Sterling on alto sax, Johnny 'Dizzy' Moore on trumpet, Jah Jerry on guitar, Lloyd Nibbs on drums, Lloyd Brevitt on bass and Jackie Mittoo on keyboards, along with Theophilus Beckford and Clue-J Johnson.

Being part of this elite team was far more financially remunerative than being one of the accredited artists on the record label. Coxsone paid £2 a tune per musician, and frequently they would record twenty songs in a day. One bonanza day, Jah Jerry worked on fifty songs in an epic session at Beverley's. In 1964, this kind of money would have meant you were considered rich in the United Kingdom or even in the United States, let alone in impoverished Jamaica. Often hanging around at 13 Brentford Road was Jackie Opel, the Bajan vocal star, first pushed by Leslie Kong, and renowned for the rare six-octave range with which he would perform his soul tunes; his 'Cry Me a River' (aka 'You Gotta Cry') tune had sold a million copies in Jamaica, Britain, and the US, and it was said that Coxsone was anxious that he should not learn of this. (When in 1970

Jackie Opel was in a fatal car-crash on a highway in his native Barbados, there were some who attributed this to the effects of obeah.) Notwithstanding the financial imbalance between Studio One's session musicians and the Wailers, Jah Jerry could not help being struck by their extreme confidence on the 'Simmer Down' session. This was a mark, he was sure, of their regular, rigorous rehearsals.

The Wailers, noted Johnny Moore, trumpet player for the Skatalites, had first come along to Studio One 'more or less as the Impressions: they were dissuaded from going along that line, and influenced to go inside themselves, however silly or simple they feared what they found there might sound like. They were simply urged to try and cultivate their own thing. And it worked. Even at that age they knew what they wanted. From the time that they realised that trying to be the Impressions was not what they should be doing, they really checked themselves and got into it. You can hear it in the music.

'At the time they were young and vibrant, and you could see they were very good friends: they were very, very close to one another. They really did care about each other. I guess that's why they made a success of it as it was.

'Bob didn't necessarily seem like the leader. The thing was so closely knit, the sound, whatever they were trying to get at: that was the objective, the force of what they were trying to accomplish. Rather than worrying about you lead or me lead, everyone would put their shoulder and heave-ho. They seemed to realise that it's much easier to get things done that way.'

It was for professional reasons that Joe Higgs would accompany the group up from Trench Town to Studio One. 'Wailers weren't even conscious of sound when I started to deal with them. To hear that "Joe assisted with the Wailers" – this is foolishness. The Wailers weren't singers until I taught them. It took me years to teach Bob Marley what sound consciousness was about. It took me years to teach the Wailers. For example, they will be going to make a record and I would go with them and there is somebody making constant mistakes. I would just have to take his part to get the record finished in time.'

(Interestingly, at this time, Peter Tosh brought a potential singer called Leonard Dillon to Studio One. Although he would later form the Ethiopians with Aston Morrison and Stephen Taylor, Dillon recorded four tunes as a solo act for Coxsone Dodd, under the nom-de-disque of Jack Sparrow; he was backed on all of them by the voices of the Wailers, with the tunes arranged to an extent by Lee Perry but largely by Jackie Mittoo, the label's driving force from 1964 to 1969, its golden period. Mittoo worked as musical director, principal arranger and keyboard player, and his relaxed, cool style on his Hammond B3 organ would make him a legend. But, according to Dillon, who occasionally played trumpet with the Skatalites, the legend that Bob Marley became was not at that point the main thrust behind the Wailers. Instead, he said, he felt it was Bunny Livingston who was pushing the group along.)

Beverley Kelso was born on 14 April 1948, the third eldest of three sisters and four brothers, in Jones Town. But when she was three her family moved to 4 Fifth Street in Trench Town. The popular conception of Trench Town as an area of grinding poverty was not the place that Beverley knew: 'Trench Town people dressed to their best. I would say there wasn't poor people, because majority of Trench Town people go to high school, they're educated people.'

Also on Fifth Street lived Alton Ellis and his family: the entire neighbourhood would gather to watch him and his talented sister Hortense rehearse in their yard. Even at a young age, Beverley Kelso knew something of the art of singing. In the school choir at Denham Town primary school, she was the lead vocalist on the hymns they would perform at morning assembly. The then zenith of her vocal achievements was when she performed solo, singing 'I Waited for the Lord', at St Andrew Scots Kirk for Queen Elizabeth II on the 1954 visit to the island by the newly crowned British monarch. 'I was the first to sing. They didn't even wait until the song finished, they were just clapping. And then that made me sing for the better.'

To perform before Queen Elizabeth, Beverley needed to overcome her natural shyness. 'Sometimes we'd all just sit there on the side of the road and somebody would start to sing something. But I was a quiet one. I never bother. I just shut up and listen. But I loved the singing. But I was so shy. I'm still shy.'

Ten years after that regal performance, some friends of Beverley persuaded her to accompany them to Chocomo Lawn, the celebrated outdoor dancehall in Denham Town, west Kingston. (Although run in conjunction with Edward Seaga and the JLP, Chocomo's appeal overrode its political affiliation.) When she arrived there, they asked her to perform, suggesting she sing Patti LaBelle's 'Down the Aisle'. And the moment Beverley uttered the opening lines, 'the fence tear down,' the crowd pushing forward to see her: this made Beverley so nervous that she started the song all over again.

The next evening, after she had returned home from school, Beverley was cleaning the kitchen when there was a knock on the door. Bob Marley, who had seen her Chocomo Lawn performance, was standing there. 'I asked him, "You want somebody?" He said, "Yes, you." I said, "Me?" And he said, "Yeah, I'd like it if you'd sing a song with me." So I said, "Well, you'll have to ask my mother if you want me to sing with you. But my mother is not here now. She went to work."'

Beverley had never met Bob before. 'My first impression of him was ordinary. Ordinary. I didn't think of him as nobody special. But he was very polite. Never sad. Even that evening he was just smiling. He was just looking at me, like, oh, pretty girl. That's what I have in my mind.

'When he came back my mother was there. And he asked her and she said, "Yes, but you'll have to take care of her." He asked me if I could come and rehearse the same evening.'

Beverley knew where to go, the fourth yard on Second Street, because her family would buy bread from Sonny and Gertie Hibbert, who lived at 13 Second Street, across the road from a rehearsal yard at 14 Second Street. 'So I went up and when I went there Peter, Bunny, and Junior was sitting under a tree on a workbench. Bob wasn't there.'

Bob had gone off to collect their guitar. When he returned with it, he introduced Beverley to Peter, Bunny, and Junior. But, she emphasised, 'I didn't call him Bob and nobody in Trench Town called him Bob. He introduced himself to me as Lester.' One might assume this to be a misremembering of 'Nesta', precisely what had concerned the boy's mother when his father suggested the name. Yet Cherry Green also believed that Bob was called Lester: had he renamed himself with such a corruption of his original first name? Or is this simply an example of Jamaican word mutation, in which aural misunderstandings translate into such oral errors as Matthews Lane being pronounced as 'Mattress Lane'? It was only shortly afterwards that Rita Anderson first met him, and she insists he was known to all Trench Town as 'Robbie'. It is worth remembering that, in Jamaica, people are often known by several different names and nicknames – for example, 'Little' Lee 'Scratch' Perry, the 'Upsetter'.

At Beverley Kelso's evening encounter with 'Lester' and his fellow musicians, she immediately began to rehearse 'Simmer Down' with them. In rehearsal, 'Simmer Down' had seemed like some tough Jamaican variant of the protest 'message' songs newly popular in the United States. In the recording studio, however, it became positively transcendent. Popular songs with lines about the running bellies of nanny-goats? This song was not only very unusual, but also tied together by an extremely commercial set of hooks.

'Control your temper / Simmer down / The battle will get hotter / Simmer down,' declared Bob on what was one of his greatest songs. In the style unique to Coxsone's label, the voices are buried back in the mix, fighting to get out with the same ferocity with which they had tried to liberate themselves from the dead-end of the ghetto. Could the vocal sound have been a reflection of the studio conditions? On the 'Simmer Down' session, Bob Marley stood directly in front of the microphone, flanked on either side by Bunny and Peter, forming a half-circle, their faces almost touching. Coxsone himself engineered the recording on his portable one-track that he unplugged and took home at the end of the session.

Also providing backing vocals – though not on the earliest recording sessions – was Cherry Green. Cherry was born in Upper Trench Town on 22 August 1943, although the family soon moved to Jones Town. Green was her half-brother's surname, which she took when her father died in 1958, after which they moved to Second Street in Trench Town. Her father, a dentist, had been relatively affluent, and the family had a large radiogram in the house, ideal for listening every Saturday night to the latest hit tunes on Duke Reid's radio show – she would turn it up loud so that all the neighbours could hear. Her musical Trench Town neighbours included Lascelles Perkins, Alton Ellis and his sister Hortense, Jimmy Tucker, a group called the Schoolboys, which included 'Pipe' Matthews and 'Bread' MacDonald, later of the Wailing Souls, and the ubiquitous Higgs and Wilson.

At the Baptist Church Sunday School she would sing songs such as 'Let the Lord Be Seen in You', which she would later record with the Wailers for Coxsone Dodd. Yet it was in American popular music that lay her main musical love: 'Harry Belafonte, Nat King Cole, Duke Ellington, and all those kind of big-band people.'

One day Joe Higgs heard Cherry's voice, as she copied a recent American hit tune whilst she washed clothes in the yard. 'My voice was way up there and he stopped immediately. He said, "Cherry, that's you?" So I said, "Yeah." We used to listen to him and he would tell us little things,' she said.

Another figure in the area familiar to her was the Marley boy: 'All the little girls used to like him. Nice boy. He was funny. Cracking jokes. Teasing. He used to be shy, though.' She recalled a significant sobriquet that was given to him: 'We used to call him "Little White Boy", 'cause his hair was curly.' Rather than offering a judgement, the nickname seemed to be one of affection: contrary to the myth, Cherry does not believe that being a 'browning', as mixed-race individuals are frequently known in Jamaica, led the teenage Bob Marley to be picked on in any way. 'We was all kids. We grew up with all different people. There was two Chinese boy, they live in the Bronx now. They had a grocery shop there right in front of where they guys used to rehearse. Mr Lee's.'

But Cherry was struck by Bob's appearance, hardly that of a ragamuffin ghetto boy: Nesta and Bunny, she said, 'used to dress nice in the Fifth Avenue shoes and nice shirt.' Peter, she remembered, invariably would be with them: 'Peter come with his guitar. Peter was always feisty, he had an attitude. Bossy, mouthy, oh yes. Full of joke.' More than the other two, Peter came the closest to personifying high-spirited pushiness. Not once, for example, did Cherry recall Nesta getting into a fight; invariably she saw him out with Bunny: 'You always see both of them together. They were polite, well-mannered, intelligent. Like I said, we would just sit down and we would sing. Somebody try to do the bass, I think a guy named Barrington Sales. But he wasn't strong enough. Then Peter come. And Georgie. Bob would say, "No, mon, that's not your part." You know, so everybody would try to sing.'

Cherry remembered a favourite spot of theirs, by Third Street and West Road, where they would sit and sing on the pavement, 'by the Branch yard. It's like the JLP. It's a place, like a yard where they have meetings, and a youth club.' Singing with the three of them would be 'Cardo' – Ricardo Scott, who eventually moved to the USA, where he gained medical and law degrees.

Unfortunately, Cherry Green was unavailable for the first Coxsone Dodd sessions, having a regular well-paid seasonal job with Caribbean Preserving, providing money she needed to keep her 3-year-old daughter. Hence she was not available for the photographs of the line-up that featured Bob, Bunny, Peter, and Beverley Kelso. 'When Junior Braithwaite left, that's when I took his space,' she said. Cherry sang on the recordings of 'Amen', 'Lonesome Feelings', 'Maga Dog', and 'There She Goes'. But she also thought she sang on 'I Am Going Home' (which both Bunny and Coxsone believed was recorded in the first session).

Before studio sessions, all concerned paid assiduous attention to mastering their parts in outdoor rehearsals, lit by a kerosene lamp or a fire, or simply the rays of the moon. 'We rehearse and we rehearse, rehearse, until we know the song. And they would say, "Well, tomorrow we going up to the studio." So we all get ready, get dressed and we walked with each other, a long walk. It's nervous: a lot of people there. And we come back late in the night and we have to walk through this burying ground. 'Cause that's the shortest way.'

Cherry Green always felt that it was Junior Braithwaite who owned the finest voice of them all: 'Oh yes. He carried.' But as far as she was concerned, her singing excursions were only for fun – 'cause we didn't get pay for it. We didn't get nothing. He give us five pounds to buy a dress.' She and Beverley wore identical dresses for the only live show Cherry Green played with the Wailers, at the Sombrero, shortly after she had recorded the 'Maga Dog' tune with Peter Tosh. As time passed at Studio One, however, the two girls would gradually fall away from the group.

Before the instant popularity of 'Simmer Down' had time truly to translate into sales, Bob found himself onstage as lead singer for the first time at that show at the Sombrero Club in Kingston. At the helm of the Wailers, he steered the group to a performance that stole the event, assisted in great part by the crisp and clear sound that Count Machuki, who had started as a DJ with Coxsone's sound system, obtained for him at the mixing desk. The audience response was overwhelming, but the other artists on the show were *vex*. Both these acts recorded for Coxsone: did they sense a conspiracy?

Yet Beverley Kelso did not recall such a success translating into local reverence. 'Nobody did not bow down to us. Nobody didn't care who the Wailers was because Higgs and Wilson was already there singing. Hortense was singing, Bunny and Scully, Toots and the Maytals, Delroy Wilson, everybody was right there singing. People gathered to hear us sing but only because they were proud of us: when we would go to the studio people would just wave. The Wailers? It was just like ordinary people, you know.'

In those days, she said, none of them smoked – neither cigarettes nor herb. On the journey to Studio One, 'me and Junior is two little short ones, so we would stay in the back, hold each other's hand and walk and start talking our little talk. Bob would be pushing Bunny, Bunny would be pushing Bob and Peter, and they laugh and they clown and they tease each other. They would laugh at people. The little things that they talk, you just sit down and crack up. I'm telling you, you'd be around them you don't wanna move. I used to look up on them and they look up on me. With respect. They treat me like a sister and they treat me good.'

Almost as soon as it was in the shops, 'Simmer Down' went to number one in the Jamaican charts. This tune's subject of teenage crime was notice served that the Wailers were the ambassadors of the island's rebels, the rude boys. Yet the Wailers were never able to compete with the colossal popularity enjoyed in Jamaica by another three-piece male vocal trio, the Maytals, fronted by Toots Hibbert.

The subject matter of 'Simmer Down' made the Wailers stand out amongst their contemporaries. Up until then no one in Jamaican music had been expressing ghetto thinking. Even the seasoned ska musicians down at Studio One were impressed. 'The uniqueness of the sound they projected,' said Johnny Moore, 'was specifically local and really good. The subject matter was clean, and the lyrics were really educative. The statements might be a bit serious, but the way they projected it you could absorb what they were saying. There were some good lessons, we had to admit that.'

However, Beverley Kelso was surprised at the version of the song that was released. In fact, on it there was a vocal error by Peter Tosh, which seemed to appeal to Coxsone. 'We had a better cut than the release. We was singing when the musicians come in, but Peter comes in at the wrong point and says "simmer", and Coxsone said that's it, that was the one that he wanted. So, it was a mistake, but it was made into something that wasn't a mistake.'

New to the line-up, Beverley kept very much to herself at the session: 'They said I was shy. I don't think I was shy to sing, but after singing I wouldn't say a word. If you say something to me I would answer you. I would sing and Bob and Peter and Bunny would be one place with all the rest of the guys and I would be just by myself. I was an observer.' Unlike Leonard Dillon, Beverley confirmed that Bob appeared to be the acknowledged leader of the group. And that rigour was the middle name of their work ethic.

'It was like every day or every other day we would be in the studio. If we're not recording for ourselves, we were backing up other people because we have other people coming and singing. Like, for instance, if Tony Gregory or anybody in the studio want back-up we would just come in and harmonise. Everybody would just back up, either you back sing, clap, whatever you wanna do over there to back up everybody. So we was in the studio most of the time. We were like a family. And there were times when we didn't go home. We would be in the studio like two, three days.

'When Junior was leaving to go to America they were doing an album and for like, two, three days we would be in the studio. We didn't have place to sleep. We didn't even have no time to sleep. It was just fun in the studio. We would eat and would sit down and get a little nap. Sometimes I would run home and come right back. We have the privilege to go into that studio that most people they couldn't come in.'

Bob was also learning some good lessons himself. A number of the musicians he now began playing with at Studio One – Johnny Moore himself, for example – were dedicated and devout Rastafarians. For years, Bob's Bible had rarely been out of his sight. Now he began to be offered new, apocalyptic interpretations that would make his jaw drop with disbelief. Sometimes he would wander away from Studio One after a day's sessions in a mystified haze, as he struggled to process the biblical information and interpolations to which he had been made privy.

Bob's soul was being nourished. In addition, he now had sufficient funds to pay for the nutrition of his body: as well as having ordered gold lamé collarless suits – a kind of Beatle jacket version of the famous ensemble worn by Elvis Presley on the sleeve of *Elvis Gold Discs Volume 2* – for the three men in the group, Coxsone had also put them each on a weekly wage of £3.

'We all used to go to church to search, and knowing that we found reality and righteousness we relaxed,' recalled Peter Tosh. 'So when you saw us in the slick suits and things, we were just in the thing that was looked on as the thing at the time. So we just adjusted ourselves materially.'

'Simmer Down' was followed up by an official release for 'It Hurts to Be Alone', another hit; curiously, even though the song had been written and sung by Junior Braithwaite, the title could definitively sum up Bob's feelings about substantial chunks of his life. For the rest of 1964, the Wailing Wailers were rarely out of the Jamaican charts, with a string of tunes recorded at 13 Brentford Road: 'Lonesome Feeling', 'Mr Talkative', 'I Don't Need Your Love', 'Donna', and 'Wings of a Dove'. 'Mr Dodd' was not unhappy.

Coxsone became another father figure to Bob, and to a lesser extent, to Bunny and Peter. When he learned that Bob didn't have a home of his own, he did a deal with the youth. He would turn new artists over to Bob to find songs for them; Bob could then sit down with his guitar with them – with Delroy Wilson or Hortense Ellis, for example – and rehearse the tune. In return, Clement Dodd would let Bob Marley live at the studio, and sleep in a back room they'd use for auditions or rehearsals. Bob was unable to put his head down, however, until the sessions had ended, often late-late in the night. And when he did, he often found his sleep was strangely disturbed, as though perhaps there was someone else in the room with him.

The Wailing Wailers had become the roughneck archetype of the three-piece harmony group, a specifically Jamaican form of high popular art that was more usually burnished to a shining gloss. By such members of their peer group as the estimable Alton Ellis, the group was considered to be very strong indeed. 'They have a different sense of music than us, and we all love it. It wasn't so much dancehall. Bob's sound was always different: it mesmerised me from those times. His music always have a roots sense of direction. Not even just the words – I'm talking about the sound, the melody that him sing, the feel of the rhythm. Always a bit different.'

This sense was complemented in live performances. 'Bob was always this ragamuffin onstage. We – myself, people like John Holt in the Paragons – were more polished and act like the Americans. Him was a rebel: jump up and throw himself about onstage. The Wailers them just mad and free: just threw themselves in and out of the music, carefree and careless.'

Miming to their records, the Wailers would appear all over Jamaica at dances at which the Downbeat sound system would play. This was a regular Coxsone strategy. 'That's how we got them launched. With several other of my artists, we used to tour the country parts.' The Wailing Wailers made more hits: 'I Need You'; 'Dance With Me', a rewrite of the Drifters' 'On Broadway'; 'Another Dance'; and the 'Ten Commandments of Love', an extraordinary interpretation of the Moonglow's song. And there were more tunes that seemed like messages direct from Rude Boy Central: 'Rude Boy' itself, late in 1965; 'Rule Dem Rudie'; 'Jailhouse', another paean to rude boys, containing the lines 'Can't fight against the youth now / 'Cause it's wrong.' Small wonder that such tunes took off with Jamaica's teenagers, of whatever social origins.

Shortly before Christmas of 1964 the Wailers were at Studio One, recording a version of the standard 'White Christmas', using a two-track recorder. It was Peter Tosh's idea to change the lyrics so that they contained greater authenticity for citizens of the tropical Caribbean: 'I'm dreaming of a white Christmas, not like the ones I used to know.' At the same session they recorded 'I Left My Sins' and 'Sound the Trumpet' – on which Johnny Moore took the solo on the instrument.

Religious holidays, specifically Christmas and Easter, were always counter-balanced in Jamaica by temporal celebrations, with top acts playing several morning shows, and literally running between the various venues, as they could not risk relying on the tardy bus service: from the Ward Theatre show, the Wailers would hurry up Orange Street, and along Slipe Road, to the State Theatre; further up Slipe Road they would reach the Regal on Old Hope Road; and then they would rush to the Carib, at the top of Slipe Road in Crossroads Square.

Enormous sartorial efforts would be made by the audiences, many clad in top hats and white gloves, wearing pleated and frilled shirts and carrying walking canes – as though they were attending an evening at London's Café de Paris, rubbing shoulders with royalty.

The Wailers' first exposure to such shows came on Christmas Day of that year. In their first significant live performances since enjoying chart success – 'Simmer Down' alone had sold 80,000 copies – the group was determined to wipe the floor with any opposition. Accordingly, they had assiduously rehearsed for over six weeks; warming up on the local beach with a game of football, they would practise until their act was an explosion of choreographed gymnastics, each member adept at splits and snap-falls. Bob, for example, would take Bunny and throw him in the air, fall to the floor as Bunny performed a perfect pair of splits above him, then rise into a kneeling position as Bunny jumped over his back; tall Peter, meanwhile, would balance and bounce Bob and Bunny like rubber balls. And, onstage, all this would take place as they assumed their customary vocal positions at the microphones. Beverley Kelso, meanwhile, was left to dance on her own, off to one side of the stage.

Many of these shows were put on by Coxsone Dodd – the Ward Theatre event was always one of his promotions – while Victor 'Captain Daddy Glasses' Sampson, Tony Cobb, Ronnie Nasralla, and Clancy Eccles would also promote these morning concerts.

At the Palace Theatre event on 25 December 1964, also promoted by Coxsone Dodd, the Wailers were backed by the Skatalites. Bouncing onto the stage as though they were in the full gaze of the sun on their sandy rehearsal space, the Wailers leapt into their first number, inevitably, 'Simmer Down'. As the choreographed performance and heartfelt vocals of these new local heroes grabbed the audience's attention, Dodd stood at the side of the stage in awe: great secrecy had surrounded the Wailers' rehearsals for their Christmas Day shows, and he was thrilled by the sight of their routines. 'Simmer Down' was followed by 'I Don't Need Your Love', 'How Many Times?', a version of the Impressions' 'I'm Going Home', and 'Amen'. During the next number, 'It Hurts to Be Alone', in the middle of a guitar solo by the masterful Trinidadian Lynn Taitt, the electrical power for the entire building cut out, infuriating the audience.

The Palace was located in a district controlled by a don with whom Coxsone Dodd had had some bad run-ins. Known as Big Junior, his reputation had been considerably bolstered in 1962 when he had appeared as one of the Three Blind Mice, a trio of hitmen, in the opening sequence of *Dr. No*, the first James Bond film to be shot, set largely in Jamaica. Due to their previous history, Coxsone assumed that the power had been cut by Big Junior's gang to sabotage his promotion: after all, during the outage, a crew had rampaged through the packed crowd, snatching chains, bracelets, and wallets.

Hardly according with the season of good will, the audience raged on, yelling abuse and showering bottles like rain on the stage. In the dark, the Wailers nervously felt their way backstage, all of them squeezing into a single toilet together and hiding for at least an hour, feeling the storm of anger coming closer.

Suddenly the lights came back on: the loss of electricity had had nothing to do with Big Junior – the power-cut had been city-wide, and the don and his men were innocent of causing the outage. Eventually, the concert resumed. 'When the show started again,' said Beverley Kelso, clearly impressed by the boys' gymnastic efforts, 'Bob coming from one side like he was flying, Peter coming from one side like he was flying, flapping their arms, because they couldn't dance.' (Her assessment, of course, is markedly different from Derrick Morgan's view of Bob Marley as a superlative dancer.)

The riot, however, immediately enhanced the Wailers' reputation and legend. When they arrived later that day at the Ward Theatre, the crowd saw Bob and lifted him onto their shoulders.

After the riot, the Wailers wrote the song 'Hooligans' about Big Junior. Another song also emerged from that Christmas morning, written by Peter Tosh: 'Jumbie Jamboree', with its newsworthy line 'What a jumbie jamboree take place in the Palace' – 'jumbie', a word that was by then old-fashioned in Jamaica, was a synonym for 'duppy'. Both these songs, along with 'Diamond Baby' and 'Playboy', were recorded almost immediately, this time using a two-track recorder. (By now, Joe Higgs had established himself as a regular presence at Wailers sessions, sharpening up any harmonies he felt were too blunt. It was at one of these Studio One sessions that Coxsone, disagreeing with Joe, punched him in the eye, affecting his sight; it was always said that Coxsone, who had also kicked and punched his helper 'Little' Lee Perry, would wait until you turned away before he hit you.)

Although each of the Wailers had received a fee of only £7 for the Palace gig, Coxsone Dodd was so delighted with the ultimate success of this chaotic show that, immediately after they came offstage, he gave them all a bonus of £3 – and topped it up with another pound per person at the studio the next day.

By the time they came to play their second big-production live show, in Montego Bay, 'Mr Dodd' had decided to give Beverley Kelso £2 for a new dress; when Peter and Joe Higgs learned of this, they tried to get her to share the money with them. It is this dress she wears on the cover of the Wailers' Studio One recordings on the distinguished American reggae reissue label, Heartbeat Records. After driving all day to Montego Bay on the north coast for the show, they discovered that the venue had no sound system and no lights. Bob Marley attempted to calm the furious crowd, saying they would somehow perform all the same, but to no avail – they drove back to Kingston, exhausted. A further performance, again at Kingston's Sombrero Club, turned out to be a big success, however. 'That was great,' said Beverley Kelso.

Smaller-scale shows were played most Monday nights at the Jamaica Success Club on Wildman Street, about a quarter mile to the east of East Parade; this was a weekly residency for the Coxsone Sound. An indoor, roofed venue, which held at least three thousand people, the Success had a small stage, and the three frontline Wailers would huddle around a single microphone. Mind you, they would be playing only a couple of songs, generally the two sides of their latest release. And there would be half as many people dancing outside in the street as inside the venue. In fact, the ranking dancers, such as Persian the Cat and Harry T, would *only* dance outside, where they were certain of a large, dedicated audience. (Persian the Cat was a skinny, dark-brown Rastaman who would integrate his walking-stick, hat, and handkerchief into the moves he would 'originate' – the Tommy McCook instrumental 'Persian Cat' was written about him.) Another regular Saturday-night date for Dodd's sound system was at the Forester Hall.

Although their sound made them aural celebrities in any part of Jamaica with access to a radio or jukebox, in downtown Kingston the Wailers went largely unrecognised, passers-by refusing to marry the down-to-earth appearances of these youths with any concept of stardom. Those familiar with them, however, would hail them on the street, receiving a personal Wailers vocal performance in exchange for a beer and some small change. Sometimes they would sing in the evenings for

Sanghu, a drinksman who ran a small gambling house in the neighbour-hood. Babu Man, a local gangster with a fearsome reputation, would often ask them to sing for him. The Wailers were not unnerved by his reputation: Bunny's father enjoyed an even worse one, and the Wailers therefore always had a certain understood protection.

In 1965, the Wailers – as they simply had become known by now – delivered the spiritual counter-balance to such rude-boy militancy. 'One Love' was a distillation of the Rastafarian sentiments Bob had absorbed in his years in Trench Town; it contained the anthem-like essence of the message and philosophy of Rastafari: 'Let's join together and feel alright.' Later in the year, the group recorded 'Put It On', another anthem to self-determination. According to the Jamaican music critic Garth White, 'Put It On' was a pivotal recording: 'The religious, the romantic, and the sexual are all one – and yet nothing is overstated, one of the keys to Marley's music.' On 10 February 1966, 'Put It On' was played non-stop for over half an hour at the wedding of Bob Marley and Rita Anderson.

Alvarita Constantia Anderson had lived for most of her life at 18a Green-wich Park Road, off Lyndhurst Road in Trench Town. She was born in Cuba on 25 July 1946 to a Jamaican father and a Cuban mother, but whilst she was still a babe-in-arms her parents moved to Kingston. After her musician father and then her mother moved to England, she remained in the Jamaican capital with her aunt Viola and an uncle. She became a Sunday-school teacher in the Presbyterian church, but three evenings a week she also went to the more fundamentalist Church of God. Singing and getting the spirit like this was more than enjoyable to her. 'I thought it was amazing. The first time I went there I watched and thought, "This is sanctifying, this is holy." It came over me and I realised it was something for real that can take you away.'

Sometimes when she was out and about, she would see some of the local Rastafarians and feel very wary. She had been taught to be scared of them. But something about these wild men touched her heart. 'I would also feel sympathy for them. I'd think, "Oh poor people. I don't believe they are as bad as they say." Because you'd see them and they'd say, "One Love", and you would wonder how people saying that could deal with hate. Even though I was living in Trench Town, I was exposed to certain things above the normal living: I felt that these people were innocent, because of their innocency.'

Rita, to which her full name of Alvarita inevitably became abbreviated, had had a good high-school education. She had been training to be a nurse until a teenage love affair led to the birth of her daughter Sharon on 23 November 1964 – the child's father, Rita's boyfriend, had been sent to live in England by his parents to save all concerned from the shame of this illegitimate birth. 'Auntie', as Viola was largely known, contributed a great deal to the child's care. Rita, meanwhile, was wondering whether she should become a teacher. And then she met Bob Marley.

Rita already knew of Bob as part of the Wailers. To her, when she heard them on the radio, their sound was definitively modern. And, for some reason, it seemed to have a profound effect on her. Then she realised why: 'It sound like angels . . . So I say to myself, I shall be meeting these people one day.'

Studio One was north of Trench Town. Bob, Peter, and Bunny would pass through the Ghost Town area, along Greenwich Park Road where Rita lived, opposite Dovecot Cemetery, on their journey to Coxsone's recording yard. Standing at the gate, observing the world, Rita would see the trio, aware that it was these guys who were mashing up the charts with their hit tunes.

But Rita was not so impressed: to this strict 'churchical gal', they looked like 'rough little guys'. As an ambitious girl, getting away from

Trench Town was Rita's principal concern; and she had a musical group of her own, the Soulettes, which she had formed with her friend Marlene 'Precious' Gifford, a fellow pupil at Dunrobin School, and her male cousin Constantine 'Dream' Walker (the son of Vesta Anderson, a sister of Aunt Viola and a militantly political follower of Marcus Garvey). Dream would often also be at the gates of 18a Greenwich Park Road when the Wailers were walking past. 'It was always an event to watch them, because it was like a gang going up the road,' he said. 'Like pied pipers, because they would walk, and Peter would have his guitar in his hand, and kids and people start to follow them, because of the vibes the men moved with.' ('Dream' Walker, who developed a fine tenor voice and was a gifted guitarist, was born on 19 October 1951 – the same day, though not the same year, as Peter Tosh. He had acquired his sobriquet when the doctor informed his mother that she was pregnant. 'Oh, doctor, that's a dream,' she had said, not believing she, a woman in her thirties, could be expecting a child; in what could be seen as something of a proprietorial gesture, as is much of the propensity for bestowing nicknames in Jamaica, a friend of the Wailers called Fowlie renamed him 'Vision', a term common for dreaming amongst the thinking youth – especially followers of Rastafari – in Jamaica.)

The Soulettes, a name inspired by Motown's Marvelettes, copied hit tunes off the radio, often Motown material by the early Supremes, Martha and the Vandellas, or Mary Wells, singing most evenings under the plum tree in Rita's auntie's yard. Like so many Jamaican acts of the time they had first displayed their talents on Vere Johns's amateur-hour radio programme, on which they had performed 'What's Your Name?', an American R'n'B classic by Don and Juan. 'When we harmonied that,' said Dream/Vision Walker, 'it used to just knock people out, that sound just like the record.'

Although she initially had been unimpressed with the cut of the Wailers' collective jib, Rita decided that she should connect with these local stars – they clearly knew the runnings as to how to get records made. Waving to the three young men as they passed her house one evening, she received a response. As the other two members leaned on the cemetery wall, strumming guitars, Peter Tosh came over and introduced himself, addressing Rita as 'nice girl'.

Determined to grab this opportunity, the Soulettes decided to make the Wailers aware that they also were a vocal group. Rita resolved that she, Dream, and Marlene should try to sing for them, a blatant effort to move the Soulettes forward a stage. When the three young men passed 18a Greenwich Park Road the next day, they were serenaded by the three Soulette members performing 'What's Your Name?' from behind the fence of the yard – since her pregnancy Rita had been forbidden to venture beyond it to speak to men. But Peter and then 'Robbie', as she came to know him, stepped across the street to speak to her. It was Peter, however, who suggested that one day Rita and her two companions might want to come up to audition at Coxsone's studio.

Although this was precisely what she had been seeking, Rita was aware of the wiles of local men – especially those who considered themselves to be musicians – and took the offer with a pinch of salt. But she had an older male friend called Andy who was also close to Clement Dodd. When, not long after, he took Rita up to the studio on Brentford Road, all three of the main Wailers were there. But they adopted a distinctly distant air until Rita reminded Peter that she was the girl who they would see standing on Greenwich Park Road. The Soulettes' audition impressed Coxsone; moreover, the mixed-sex group was passed on to Bob for management and to find material for them.

If anything, Rita now realised, it was shyness that had been behind the offhand manner exhibited by the Wailers, and especially by Bob, towards her: their hit records had not gone to their heads, as she had initially suspected. Now she saw that staying on top of current music and being consistent, with hits one after another, was not easy. Especially when she discovered that though the Wailers were immensely popular, they were making virtually no money.

The first tune that the Soulettes worked on at Studio One was 'Roast Duck'. It was one of a number of 'rude' songs, the Jamaican genre of often humorously absurd, sexually explicit tunes that the studio helper Lee Perry was recording for Coxsone from the end of 1964. Although the record was popular, when the Soulettes backed Perry onstage – his first live appearance – at the Ward Theatre singing the tune, he was booed off. The Soulettes worked as backing vocalists on other songs that Perry was creating at the studio, including 'Please Don't Go', 'By Saint Peter', and 'Rub and Squeeze', another rude song, which used the same rhythm as 'Put It On'. (The Wailers themselves sang harmony on Perry's huge 1966 Jamaican hit 'Pussy Galore', which celebrated the talents of the woman character of that name in the film *Goldfinger*, the third James Bond movie; the rhythm track was an alternate take of the early Wailers tune 'Rude Boy Ska' – which Perry had helped arrange. On another, more important, song, 'Hand to Hand, Man to Man', a spiritual song rife with metaphor, he used the Wailers as backing vocalists, his first collaboration with the group, and a pointer to their future work together.)

Already signed to Studio One when the Wailers first arrived there was Norma Fraser. She was something of a superstar, her 1961 tune 'We'll Be Lovers', which she had recorded with Trinidad's Lord Creator, having been number one in Jamaica for over a year. Although she described Studio One as 'like the Motown label in America', and Coxsone Dodd as its 'mastermind', she also recalled that the relationship between Bob and Dodd was 'strained and strange because Mr Dodd just did not pay his artists for their work. Bob would have to fight him constantly, as we all did, to get him to acknowledge that he owed us money. I really liked Bob Marley because he was rather earthy, religious, and so very talented: I spoke to Bob constantly during his and my struggles with Mr Dodd's refusal to pay us for our work. Bob dealt with his frustrations during this period by being philosophical about the entire matter and by using spiritual quotations from the Bible to demonstrate how Mr Dodd would eventually succumb to karmic destruction.' She also claimed that when Rita first arrived at Dodd's studio, 'she could not sing at the time' – until Norma taught her.

Bob's responsibility towards Coxsone's new artists increased his work-load, as Rita saw from his assiduous efforts with the Soulettes. He rewrote Paul Anka's 1957 song 'I Love You, Baby' for them, and it became the trio's first release and hit, with Delroy Wilson singing backing vocals. Most of the songwriting for the Soulettes, noticed Rita, took place in the studio at the time they were recording. Bob's skills as a lyricist impressed her, especially his willingness to use himself as an archetype. 'Through using himself as an example, he was able to express what was happening in people's lives, especially when it came to identifying with the street people, the common people.'

Although it was always imbued with a conscious sensibility, Bob's approach to the acts under his care was like a Jamaican version of the Motown charm school. Rigour was the keynote. The example came always from himself, as he would insist on a disciplined approach to work. He would carry such an air of discipline that it would be impossible for the Soulettes not to be in the same studio without it rubbing off on them. A respectable, responsible public image should be presented at all times, he insisted to them – especially when Coxsone was around.

Such a stance made Rita and the two other members of the Soulettes initially very wary of their unsmiling tutor. He didn't seem too much fun. 'He was very firm about what we were about: if you come to the studio, you don't come to play; you're here to work. As long as Bob was there that discipline was established.'

Then Rita found that, if she did as he suggested, chinks of light quickly appeared in his seemingly impenetrable facade: 'You have to be prepared to meet him. Then when you do, you find that behind all of that he is the nicest person, like an angel.'

Rita had her own sense of reserve about her. 'When I met these guys I was not sure if this was where I wanted to be. They knew my upcoming – how I was brought up – and they could see how I was grown up different from the regular girl you could hit on easily. But then because them being the Wailing Wailers, I was proud to be among them. But I was also wary: what if my mother finds out?'

Rita was looking after her child full-time when she became involved with the Soulettes. The Wailers, however, had no idea that she was a mother. 'One day I was in the studio and my breasts got real hard with milk, and it started to come through my brassiere. Bob looked at me and said, "Oh, you have a baby!" Because I hadn't told anybody. I said, "Of course!" The other two said, "You didn't tell us." And then we all started to get closer. They were nice guys, and I began to feel strong from having them as my friends. I got more firmly into myself. This was when they started to tell me about Rastafari. How being a pretty black girl you mustn't do this, mustn't wear that, mustn't eat pork . . . All these things.'

To Rita's surprise, however, Bunny one day told her that Bob had claimed to be in love with her. From then on he would occasionally bring her short love letters from Bob. At first, Rita was not convinced – Bob had a rival. 'It didn't happen so fast. It took a time for me to decide whether it was Bob or Peter. Because I was liking Peter more, because he was more friendly and would chat and laugh, and Bob was too serious – Peter was more jovial.' Life around Peter Tosh, she was aware, seemed more like fun. Blessed with an alert, highly intelligent humour, of which his love of punning wordplay was only one aspect, he also brought with him an apparently endless element of drama. Arriving at the studio, he would tell stories of how he had been smoking a spliff during his walk there and been obliged to jump over a fence and run from the police. Although by now all three of the Wailers' front-line were consuming 'herb' whenever they could, even Bob and Bunny would be concerned about such deliberate acts of defiance by Peter as his tendency to fire up spliffs whilst travelling on buses with them. And he would frequently run the risk of a beating or worse from a woman's boyfriend because of his insistence on touching up any female who attracted him – even those walking down the street with their husband. On many Jamaican record releases by Peter his surname is spelt 'Touch'; although often hilarious misspellings are part of the everyday Jamaican experience, this was apparently not the case here: 'Touch' was a nickname of Peter Tosh that derived directly from his behaviour. 'Peter was very touchy,' said Rita. 'He would see you and hug you up and try to squeeze you.'

Serious 'Robbie' Marley, however, seemed a better long-term prospect for Rita: 'Bob was for the discipline, which impressed me very much.' She also noted that whenever Bob had any money he would turn up at the gate of 18a Greenwich Park Road bearing an offering of Cow & Gate baby formula, powdered milk. 'I found that concern to be very mature for a young man still in his teens. His interest in my baby made me feel proud instead of ashamed. I looked at him and thought, uh-oh, such a nice guy. And I got weak in the knees. Oh my God, I thought.'

Rita felt that Bob very evidently loved not only her but also her baby daughter, Sharon – unable to pronounce the name Robbie, the infant later addressed him as 'Bahu'. But he was not at all happy that she was continuing to correspond with her daughter's father in England; after finding Dream Walker with a letter that Rita had asked him to mail to the UK, Bob confiscated it and insisted Rita draw the relationship to a close.

It was some months before a sexual relationship began between Bob and Rita. They made love for the first time in Bob's old home of Tartar's kitchen, Tartar having discreetly absented himself for the evening. From then on, when they saw each other at night, Bob and Rita would frequently return to Tartar's: sometimes Tartar would take Rita home to Greenwich Park Road on the crossbar of his bicycle; sometimes he would lend it to Bob to carry her back. Bob told Rita that Bunny's father, Mr Toddy, had offered to let him live at his home but that he always felt like an outsider whenever he visited there. He was turning into a man, and the people there would still treat him as a boy, causing him considerable resentment.

However, there were perhaps larger problems connected with his residence at Studio One. That sense of unease he had often felt in the room he'd been given had intensified, until it had become thoroughly specific: he believed, he told Rita, that there was a duppy in the room. He felt, he said, as though somebody was trying physically to hold him down. Bwai, he would say, he can't sleep in the night because the thing just keep coming back to haunt him.

Rita decided to spend the night with him there, sharing his bed of an old door balanced on some bricks . . . and experienced precisely the same sensation. 'I felt as though someone came into the room and held me down. You'd try to get out of this grip and feel as though you were going into a trance: you couldn't speak; you couldn't talk; you couldn't see anything – you just felt the sensation. I wondered if it was something I'd smoked, but Bob said it happened to him every night.'

Realising that Bob couldn't stay there any longer, Rita offered a solution: Bob must come and stay with her at 18a Greenwich Park Road. All she had was a little room she shared with her cousin and baby Sharon, but at least Bob would be safe there from this duppy. The next night, Bob climbed into Rita's room through the window. But once he was tucked up in bed with her, her cousin, and baby Sharon, the girls began to giggle. Rita's auntie Viola – whom Bob was always nervous of because of her reputation as an obeahwoman – came into the room and turned on the light. Outraged at what she saw, she made Bob and her niece leave the house by the same method with which Bob had sneaked in: through the window. The couple passed a night under the stars.

The next morning, however, when Rita told Auntie Viola that she would leave the house for good if Bob wasn't permitted to stay there, her relative relented. Realising her niece was serious about this relationship, she took the line of least resistance: Viola agreed to build a shack by the side of the house in which the couple would be able to live.

What Rita did not know was that Bob's mother had remarried in the United States, to a Mr Edward Booker, an American. Ever since she had arrived in Wilmington, Delaware, Cedella Booker, as she was now known, had intended to bring Bob up there – when she left Jamaica she had assured him that this would take no more than three months. Now, three years later, at last she had her green card, giving her official residency in the US; accordingly, she had written to her son, telling him he should come and live with her, even if only for a short time. To help facilitate this, she flew down to Jamaica to guide Nesta through the bureaucratic formalities of obtaining a Jamaican passport. At the passport office in Kingston, Mrs Booker encountered unexpected opposition from the clerk over the name by which she had addressed her boy ever since he was born. Adamant that Nesta was a girl's name, which would be misunderstood in the United States, the man pedantically insisted on replacing it with Robert, his middle name, pointing out to Cedella and her son that it inevitably would be abbreviated to Bob. And so, by this twist of officious fate, did Bob Marley finally receive his name.

As to immediately packing his bag and flying off to the US, Bob was uncertain. He told his mother he was not yet ready to travel: his career

FULL NAMES (Surname)........MARLEY........Christain..ROBERT NESTA.

PASSPORT NUMBERS...........57778..................

WHERE PASSPORTS WERE ISSUED........KINGSTON....JAMAICA..........

DATE OF ISSUE.........21ST MARCH 1969.........

EXPIRY DATE..........5TH MARCH 1974........

DATE OF BIRTH.........6TH APRIL 1945........

PLACE OF BIRTH......RHODEN HALL...ST.ANN...JAMAICA.

NATIONALITY........JAMAICAN..........

HOME ADDRESS...........NINE MILES...BULL BAY P.A.........

TYPE OF PASSPORT.........JAMAICAN........

FATHERS FULL NAMES (Surname)......MARLEY......Christain....NORVAL.

FATHERS NATIONALITY.......JAMAICAN...........

MOTHERS FULL NAMES (Surname)......BOOKER.......Christain....CEDELLA

NATIONALITY..........JAMAICAN...........

DETAILS OF MUSICAL INSTRUMENTS PLAYED.........GUITAR..........

:...

SONG WRITING ABILITY.........Writer.Artist............

A work permit form filled in by Bob Marley for his first UK shows. Note a couple of curious dates: the reference to a passport issued in 1969, presumably a renewal of his 1966 document; and a birth date given as 6 April – not the day Bob was actually born, but more likely the day his mother actually got round to registering her son's birth.

as a musician was going well. Why should he risk losing it? Then, over the coming months, he realised the only thing he would be losing was his reputation. He had his wages of £3 a week from Coxsone, but otherwise Bob was still stony broke, and beginning to feel resentment about this. Before he had become so involved with Rita, he already had made the decision to move up to the States for a short time; he knew the experience would be important in his life.

Before Bob left for the United States, he met a local man called Dago, a draftsman who had spent time living there. Dago had fully accepted the faith of Rastafari, and discussed its principles at length with the young Bob Marley. When Bob questioned some of these matters, he would request Dago to show him as evidence the precise biblical reference points. 'I talked to him plenty before I leave. Him show me things. Some of the things when I asked him I said show it to me in the Bible, and he looked in the Bible and show me. I say Ah, this is not really a wrong.'

Bob had another decision to make. For the first time since he had fallen for the girl in Trench Town, Bob was truly in love. With that pattern of people being taken from him, his life had been full of loss. Now it seemed as though it was he who could be throwing away an important relationship, he couldn't believe that, if he didn't formalise his relationship with Rita, he wouldn't lose her to someone else whilst he was away. There seemed to be only one way out of this dilemma. He resolved to marry Rita, and in this he was encouraged by Coxsone Dodd, who felt it would give the youth some foundation to his life. (Later, Bob would resent Dodd for this advice.) Similarly, the most successful female artist on Studio One, Norma Fraser, adamantly encouraged Rita to exchange wedding vows with Bob.

As a sensitive soul – one of the reasons Bob had chosen her as his girlfriend – Rita was not unaware of the deep loneliness this young man had encountered in his life. She had seen the times when he lost confidence in himself. 'Who is me? A fockin' bloodcla'at white man pickney?' God is your father, Rita would remind him. 'This therapy of the Bible was what I had to use, and how colour is nothing: this father was just sent physically to bring you, but your real father is watching over you and he will never disown you.'

Rita deeply loved Bob. But when he asked her to marry him, she had to bring a level of humanitarian consideration into her decision to say yes. 'Bob had a lot of hurt. He was very sensitive – just born that way, and he just had to adapt to it. When I went off with Bob, it wasn't just love-love-love, in terms of falling in love and being head over heels in love with him. It was out of real sorrow for this guy. I'm saying to myself: "Shit, we have it bad, but this guy's having it worse, and I don't see why he should be having it this way."'

On 6 February 1966, Bob Marley turned 21. Four days later, on 10 February, at 11 a.m., he married Rita Anderson in the home of a friend, celebrating with a wedding breakfast of curried goat, rice, and green bananas. Neither Bunny nor Peter had been invited to the ceremony but, that evening, the Wailers were booked to play their largest concert yet, at Kingston's National Stadium. In the midst of the concert, a voice announced: 'Congratulations to Bob and Rita, who got married today!' 'Who told them?' wondered Bob.

Rita was about to take on her own share of pain: two days after Bob married her, he left Jamaica for Wilmington, Delaware. Returning from the airport, Rita went back home and cried. Later, she went to Studio One with Bunny, Peter, and her cousin Dream: she recorded a tune with the title 'I've Been Lonely'; composed by Fredrick Knight, it was later released on the Tuff Gong label, attributed to 'Rita and the Soulettes.'

Bob Marley's absence from his wife runs a close parallel with the manner in which his father had left his mother the day after they wedded.

On one hand, of course, he was simply following a pattern of Caribbean migrant behaviour in which males headed for the US, UK, or Canada to earn money for their families, intending to return soon, an intention often thwarted through economic realities. Unusually, Bob had already achieved considerable success at a very young age, and had a very specific reason – other than Rita – for going back. Yet you can't help but feel that here was a young man fleeing his early marriage, one that marked him out as extremely rare in downtown Kingston, where only one in ten live-in relationships bore the legal sanction of marriage. In the ensuing years, Bob Marley would develop his own perhaps convenient version of how the wedding came about. According to his mother, on the day he was to be married, an old woman from Greenwich Farm came up to him and kissed his hand. Later Bob learned that this woman had a reputation as a maddah, a powerful obeahwoman: he was not surprised – after she had kissed his hand, the next thing Bob Marley discovered was that he had married Rita Anderson. Although a state of shock is often the mental condition of those getting married, it seems strange that Bob claimed to recall nothing of the wedding ceremony.

In Wilmington, Cedella had heard rumours that her son was planning a wedding. He had written to her some months previously saying that he had a lovely new girlfriend, that she was pregnant, and that he intended to marry her. Cedella wrote back, advising him to seriously consider the big step on which he seemed to have set his mind. In fact, Rita had suffered a miscarriage; but this resulted only in a postponement of the date.

When Cedella picked Bob up at the airport in Philadelphia for the forty-mile drive to her home at 2313 Tatnall Street in Wilmington, he immediately told her that he was now married to Rita, even producing newspaper cuttings about the wedding – his relative poverty notwithstanding, he was nonetheless a local Kingstonian celebrity. 'He was madly, madly, madly in love with that girl . . . All his heart, his mind, his soul. He'd say to me, "Mama, if you would ever see her, you would love her. She is just a plain girl, and she walk on road." I asked someone what that means – and it's kind of knock-kneed. He loved those things about her.' Cedella noticed that local girls might call up for her son, but he would hand the phone to her, refusing to speak with them.

When Bob arrived from the airport at the house his mother shared with Edward, her American husband, he found it was an exact replication of the home he had dreamed of the previous night. In Wilmington, Bob at first tried to find work as a stevedore at the docks, but was rejected because of his slight build. One day whilst out searching for a job, the Jamaican youth failed to appreciate the severity of the cold that had descended upon the city and came close to suffering frostbite in his fingers. Eventually he found employment as a janitor at Wilmington's Dupont Hotel. Back at home, waiting to go to work, he would sit at the kitchen table or in the living-room, strumming his guitar, writing songs.

In Kingston, meanwhile, Rita continued with her own musical career. Bob's departure had confused her. 'Oh, is this what they call marriage?' she mused, puzzled. But Tartar would give her strength and motivation as she waited for Bob's return. 'He'll come back soon,' he would say to her. 'Don't worry, don't fret.'

Besides, Bob had left his new bride with an important task. Growing up amongst the rebellious thinkers of Trench Town and Studio One, Bob had extremely positive feelings about the philosophy of Rastafari. He believed in it sufficiently to lecture non-believers about its worth: Rita had benefited from his instruction, and in Wilmington he would admonish his mother for cooking bacon and other pork products. But he was still questing to penetrate to the heart of this mystery and he required further guidance.

On 21 April 1966, just over two months after Bob left Jamaica, an event of extraordinary significance was to occur for all followers of Rastafari. His Imperial Majesty Haile Selassie I, Emperor of Ethiopia, was due to arrive at Kingston Airport.

Bob had written to Rita: 'If possible, go and see for yourself.' She had required no urging. This could give the proof to her of what she needed to know.

So, with Vision and Precious, on that rainy April morning, Rita stepped out, heading eastwards to Windward Road, which leads in from the airport. From their vantage point, Rita Marley had what was perhaps the most profound of many remarkable, God-given experiences she would enjoy in her life.

Seated in Governor-General Clifford Campbell's purring official limousine, Haile Selassie was driven into Kingston. In the shadow of the vast cement works, a grim eyesore like a reminder of the hell of Jamaican heavy industry, Rita eased her way to the front of the hundreds of people around her on this section of the coastal Windward Road. She stood in the warm, light rain, waiting for Haile Selassie's car to come nearer. In the crush of the huge crowd, Rita was anxious. For she had made a secret decision: if somehow she saw the sign she was looking for, she would accept the divine status of Haile Selassie.

But as the Daimler limousine drew parallel with her, Rita's thoughts were not positive. 'How is it they are saying that this man is so great', she was idly pondering, 'when he looks so short, with his army hat over his head in such a way I can't even see his eyes. Then I thought, "What am I even thinking about? Jesus is a spirit."' At that exact moment, Haile Selassie raised his face: he looked directly into Rita's eyes and waved. 'And I looked into his hand, and there was the nail-print. It was a mark, and I could only identify that mark with the scriptures of history saying "When you see him, you will know him by the nail-print in his hands." So when I saw this, I said to myself that this could be true, this could be the man of whom it was said: before the year 2000, Christ will be a man walking on this earth.'

Vision Walker felt similarly awed: 'I just feel a power, like I see the power in this man. How he turned, like, to us, and just wave like that. That was the mystical thing. They were going by kind of fast, so that's why it touched us.'

Rita wrote to Bob and told him that what she had seen far surpassed anything she had expected. And that this thing seemed to be true.

What she had seen had shaken her to the foundation of her soul. She spent long days pondering and wondering about it. 'Then I stopped processing my hair, changed my diet, started to see my brother as a brother. I find I slide from that Christian thinking into recognising Haile Selassie, into recognising Africa, into recognising the Rasta philosophy of God and living their lifestyle, one that suits me more than this other one which seems so hypocritical. You realise it is the same as Christianity, but with maybe a little more freedom.'

As though he also were being offered proof of the veracity of this ostensibly confusing religion, Bob Marley had another dream whilst staying at his mother's American home. 'He said a short man wearing a khaki cloak and a mash-up mash-up hat had appeared to him in his vision,' remembered his mother. Her son told her that this man had come over to him, where he lay on the family couch, and placed a ring on Bob's finger. Mrs Booker's interpretation of the dream was that the man was Bob's father, coming to offer him something in recompense for his previous failures to do so. The explanation satisfied her son, seeming to give him a sense of instant well-being. Later, when the grandson of His Majesty Haile Selassie I gave her son a ring the Emperor had formerly worn himself, Cedella Booker would come to appreciate the accuracy of her analysis of this profoundly pivotal message from the unconscious of Bob Marley – and to appreciate that this figure was indeed her son's father.

Awed by what they had seen, heard and learned, the Wailers and Soulettes sought out elders who could offer them further information. In Trench Town there were assorted revered followers of Rastafari: Bongo Donald, for example, a man who already wore his hair in dreadlocks, who lived in the Ghost Town area, near Rita's aunt's home on Greenwich Park Road, on the way to Studio One. He passed on suitable salutary advice.

Also living in Trench Town at this time was Mortimer Planner (Planno). With a warm glow in his heart, he observed the sense of bewilderment and ultimately enlightenment which the Emperor's visit wrought in many of Jamaica's citizens. People, he saw, were wandering about the streets of the capital, visibly perplexed as they mused on these matters of profound spiritual and theological importance. So many people were asking themselves the same questions that Rita Marley had puzzled over: was this really the man who the Rastafarians claimed he was? The longer His Majesty remained in their midst, Planno noted, the more people started having different considerations about their lives and about the world.

Planno had moved to Trench Town in 1939. Although some claimed he had been born in Kingston, he was more likely to have been born, like Rita Marley, in Cuba, but in 1929, when he was three, his parents brought him to Jamaica. As an early convert to Rastafari, he was one of the founder members of Kingston's first Rastafarian encampment in the Dungle. His devout studies of all matters connected with the faith, coupled with his intellectual brilliance, established him as one of the elders of Rastafari.

He was part of the natural mystic within the orthodox Nyabinghi school, the branch of Rastafari that keeps the sovereignty of ancient, sacred African rhythms through hand-drumming. Planno had played drums all his life. Carrying these rhythms to recording studios, he would harmonise with whatever the other musicians had to offer.

After the construction of the government yards, he had become a tenant at 5 Fifth Street in Trench Town, where he established what he described as a 'Rastafari encampment'. Taking the name Brother Kumi and styling himself as a 'thoughtist', dispensing wisdom to both believers and non-believers of this eccentric religion, Planno was a founder of the Ethiopian Orthodox church in Jamaica; he was also the instigator of Rastafari's first universal grounation in Kingston. As befitted his profession of 'herbsman', such events coincided with copious consumption of 'the weed of wisdom'.

A man of great perception, Planno was consulted on all matters of serious import by the 'clean, poor people' of Trench Town, as he defined them; acknowledging the true nature of his neighbours was essential in attempting to arrive at any solution. 'They were not particularly law-abiding,' he noted. 'That was how the society have the people. That was one part of the people's predicament.'

When a deputation was gathered to travel to Ethiopia in 1961 to pay homage to His Majesty, it was considered right and proper that Mortimer Planner should be a member of this small, honoured group. Planno loved Ethiopia. To him the cradle of civilisation looked heavenly. In the unpolluted atmosphere of Addis Ababa, he breathed in the air and gazed in awe at the city's tall eucalyptus trees. Most inspiring of all, of course, was his visit to His Imperial Majesty Haile Selassie I. To call the forty-five minutes he spent with Him as divine is the most exact description possible.

It was Mortimer Planner, his Kodak Brownie camera dangling around his neck as though he were a tourist, who had ascended the steps of His Majesty's plane when it landed in Kingston to extend a welcome from the brotherhood of Rastafari. The mystic breeze that blew from this moment was to dominate the rest of his life. Gradually, it showed him, he believed, how to teach the world.

This understanding simmered as he travelled around the island of Jamaica with His Majesty on his three-day stay: on the journey to Montego Bay, and – in addition to the various state functions necessitated by his rank – to the special places he asked to visit, such as certain communities that had once welcomed Rasta but no longer extended a hand of greeting.

He noted that Haile Selassie was lodged at the official government residence of King's House, the only time that a person of that rank would be quartered there, which became a fact of deep significance to the island's Rastas. All His Majesty's movements were mystic, as far as Mortimer Planner was concerned.

Specifically, however, Planno paid heed to the parting words of advice left by Haile Selassie: *that international cooperation will quicken progress.* And Planno would pray that the people of the world could become receptive to such a simple truth.

Like his brethren, and even more so because of his own exalted position, Mortimer Planner believed that democracy had run its course: now was coming the time of theocracy, in which each person must bear their own responsibility for governing themselves, according to the laws of the ultimate power on high, which every man and woman knows, because it is inborn within them. Of the role of Rastafari in the time of change and world crisis that would lead up to the year 2000, Planno had no doubt. He had read it all in Revelation, the final, apocalyptic book of the Bible.

Rita flew to Delaware in August 1966. She and Bob fell into each other's arms – their separation had been difficult for both of them. Rita found that, much to his mother's chagrin, her husband's hair bore the first hints of becoming an Afro. Rita had much to tell him. For example, after seven or eight years of the same mutated boogie beat of ska dominating the music of Jamaica, it had begun to change: the bass line had started to break up, coming in shorter, more pronounced patterns of notes than it had for ska.

Rock steady was the new form – literally a steadier form of the beat. Its origins had a probably apocryphal explanation: that the unusually hot summer of 1966 rendered impossible the faster dance movements of ska. Languid and sensuous, rock steady sounded like trouble. It was little surprise that it had been taken up as *their* music by the rude boys – cooler than cool, hotter than hot. Several records vied for the title of the first rock-steady tune, amongst them Roy Shirley's 'Hold Them', Derrick Morgan's 'Tougher Than Tough', and Alton Ellis's 'Girl I've Got a Date'. The last tune was produced by Duke Reid; whatever the truth behind the various claims for having had the first rock-steady disc out of the traps, one fact was certain: Duke Reid seized the rock-steady moment with a sure grip that eluded his great rival Coxsone Dodd.

Although Coxsone was to enjoy the Wailers tune 'Rocking Steady' – which contained these Bob Marley lyrics: 'When first I heard rock steady / It thrilled me to the bone' – his studio had momentarily lost momentum. Within little more than a year, however, a trio of producers – Bunny Lee, Lee 'Scratch' Perry, and Osbourne 'King Tubby' Ruddock – were to have brought about a third change, into reggae music. In any case, the Wailers were about to quit the Coxsone stable for good.

What hit a sharper nerve in the soul of Bob Marley were Rita's stories about the visit of His Imperial Majesty. He noted the changes, characterised by the same sense of aura-like numinous bliss with which much of Kingston seemed to be afflicted, that had clearly descended upon her. His time in the United States, where, as well as his hotel work, he had taken waitering jobs and driven a fork-lift truck on the assembly line in a Chrysler plant, had been a crucial period of self-reflection. One chapter was over now, he knew.

When he returned to Kingston two months later, it was with two quite specific purposes. As far as his musical career was concerned, Bob Marley had resolved to set up his own record company, to be a self-financing musical artist. To this end, he had been both storing new songs and assiduously stashing away every cent that came his way, although that hoard only amounted to some US$700. His other main intention was to pursue his quest for knowledge about Rastafari. Little did he know that the two would become irrevocably interlinked.

Bob had already encountered Mortimer Planner in his day-to-day runnings in Trench Town. Now he was impelled actively to seek out this shaman of the ghetto. In his nervous request to Planner to provide him with instruction in the great truths of Rastafari, the singer's natural humility prevailed.

'Planner was someone we would listen to,' said Rita Marley. 'He was a community elder, someone who everyone would respect for what he stood for in the Rastafarian faith. And he used to sell herbs – that was his trade. And he would talk about Rastafari.

'He was respected in that sense of communicating with the people and being able to tell us what was happening in Africa. And he was a great reader, and a good psychologist: he had a lot of head, to survive in that type of community he had to be something of a psychologist.

'He had been into Rastafari for a long time. Because when we knew him, he was established into organisations like the World Federation and Rasta groups that went to Ethiopia and visited His Majesty. He had a great past in terms of what he used to do.

'Planner grew up that way: in the ghetto as a bad boy and come up tough and then found himself. Not bad in terms of doing wrong things.

But growing up in that kind of community he had no chance but to be tough.'

'Him learn so much from the experiences of people who suffer,' was Planner's explanation for the readiness with which Bob absorbed his teaching. 'Bob was taught in a Rasta university. And him understood well. Him a bright student.'

As Bob's 'mentor and tutor', as he described himself, Mortimer Planner took up and guided that profound but unformed sense within the musician. 'It had for long been coming to the conscious thought within his soul: *Serve Rastafari!* Understand how you have to hear it and see it and feel it to come free. How you have to let it pilot you and open your eyes and see within your life how you want to live.'

Planner's teaching took many forms. At his yard, all manner of local personalities would gather for instruction. These included Alton Ellis, Ken Boothe, Carlton Manning of Carlton and the Shoes, and Donald Manning of the Abyssinians. An Ethiopian scholar called Professor Efiam Isaac instructed those assembled in Amharic, the Ethiopian language, playing them tapes in Amharic and English. (One consequence of these lessons was the Abyssinians' celebrated reggae classic 'Satta Massa Ganna', which translates from Amharic as 'Give Thanks'.)

Planner explained to Bob the links between Egyptology and the Coptic Church, and went on to describe in intricate detail the symbolism at the heart of various international systems: such mysteries as the reason for the image of the Egyptian pyramid on the dollar note, and the true significance of the English Crown, and its relation to the Church of England and to that of Rome.

This was crucial, believed Planner, in helping Bob come to terms with who the Rastaman sage believed the young musician to be: the personification of a hybrid of the United States and Britain. 'His mother is a green-card American, and his father was British. So Bob come out a

British-American. And him have to move far from there to be the success-ful universal figure that him end up to be.'

Something had shifted within Bob's unconscious, at the very deepest level. It was as though he doubted the validity of the paeans to rude-boy culture formerly sung by the Wailers. Rastafari, he began to instruct the ratchet-knife wielders of Trench Town, was the only course. At this time, observed Planner, Bob had a strong influence on the youth in shaping them out of their rude-boy image. And Bob's own physical image now altered. Returning to Jamaica from Delaware, he began to grow his already bushy hair – to 'knot up', in the then contemporary local parlance – into what were now known as 'dreadlocks'. So did Rita. So did Bunny. Peter Tosh did not grow locks, but simply stopped visiting barbers – although he still combed his hair.

While Bob Marley was in the United States, Peter Tosh and Bunny Livingston remained in Jamaica, continuing to pursue their career. It is said that it was only now that Coxsone Dodd came to appreciate their talents. But they needed a further voice – who should they recruit? The answer was almost self-evident, staring them in the face: Constantine 'Dream' Walker, by now more commonly known as 'Vision' Walker, was enlisted. And Vision's work with Peter and Bunny signified a few months of considerable creative productivity – prior to this the two had always felt somewhat in the shadow of taskmaster Bob, the only one of the three Wailers who had had studio- and record-release experience before Studio One. (Like most other artists recording at Studio One, Vision Walker had also regularly been performing on other artists' songs. Classics on which he sang harmony vocals included Ken Boothe's 'The Train is Coming' and Bob Andy's 'I've Got to Go Back Home'.)

Given their heads, in an often overlooked rush of creativity, the group recorded some of the Wailers' greatest ever songs – amongst them Peter Tosh's signature statement of intent, 'The Toughest', as well as his first interpretation of the Smokey Robinson composition, a hit for the Temptations, 'Don't Look Back', with Bunny and Vision providing gorgeous falsetto harmonies. On the B-side of this reasonable-sized Jamaican hit was 'Dancing Shoes', on which Bunny took the lead. 'Let Him Go', 'Sunday Morning', and 'Rock Sweet Rock' were also recorded by this reconfigured edition of the Wailers; and they were joined by Rita Marley when they cut 'The Vow', a cover of an Aladdin Records tune by the Los Angeles doo-wop duo Gene and Eunice, already covered – again for Coxsone Dodd – by Jackie and Doreen in 1959. Meanwhile, Bunny recorded a tune called 'Dreamland', essentially a reworking of the 1962 Veejay song 'My Dream Island' by El Tempos, written by Al Johnson.

Unexpectedly, Peter also recorded an out-and-out rocker, 'Can't You See?', a pounding R'n'B-style tune that could have come from an American garage band of the same period or, just as likely, off an early Rolling Stones album – from the first time he heard them, Peter was a fan of the Stones' musical taste and this would in later years stand him in good stead. (In 1970, and then again in 1978, he would re-record the tune, on each of these occasions adding specifically Jamaican rhythms.)

Perhaps the most significant recording during this period was 'Rasta Shook Them Up', written by Peter Tosh and recorded in May 1966, a direct and self-explanatory response to the visit to Jamaica the previous month of Haile Selassie and its profound impact on Peter and Bunny, who as well as Rita and Vision had witnessed the event. This was the first song bearing the Wailers' name that mentioned Rastafari; it was also the first tune on which Peter expressed the character, both militant Black Power prophet and sensitive spiritual sage, that the world would come to know him as. 'Our father wept just to see where his children slept,' declared Peter in the song, which begins with a few words spoken by him in Amharic. All three of the then current Wailers sang on the song, as well as Rita and Norma Fraser, with further harmony provided by the Gaylads, a Studio One male vocal act. But it was Peter Tosh who first nailed the Wailers' red, gold, and green colours to the mast of Rastafari.

When Bob returned to Jamaica in November 1966 he explained his intentions to found the Wailers' own label, for which he had been assiduously stashing away his earnings whilst in Wilmington. The shack that Auntie Viola had built for Bob, Rita, and Sharon to live in at the side of 18a Greenwich Park Road would become by day the Wail'n' Soul'm record store, in honour of its two acts, the Wailers and the Soulettes; it was an attempt at democracy, and perhaps a peace offering to Rita to make up for his absence almost immediately after their wedding. Even though it hardly tripped off the tongue, Wail'n Soul'm was also to be the name of the Wailers' label.

Bob installed a counter window in their little home, as it reverted to by night. A first single was released, a rock-steady tune, 'Bend Down Low', recorded on time rented at Studio One. Produced by Bob and released on Wail'n Soul'm in late 1966, 'Bend Down Low' was the first record to come out on the label; 'Mellow Mood', the B-side, was one of Bob's finest ever songs. This single appeared with label art bearing four stars, and all subsequent releases had a green, gold, and black background.

These large-scale changes around and within Bob, this struggle to reassemble himself and state who he was only just beginning to realise he was, came not without considerable internal struggle. Towards the end of the year, he appeared to undergo something of a minor nervous breakdown. During this time, Bob Marley was unable or unwilling to speak to anyone other than Rita or Planno. If others attempted to speak to him, he would only reply through them. There was even a story that Bob had tried to hang himself in Planno's yard.

In Trench Town, unsurprisingly, this was the cause of considerable discussion. Everyone had a point of view: some believed Bob to be seriously mentally ill; others felt that downright despair was behind his behaviour; then there were those who perceived him to have plunged into a depressive malaise; whilst a more radical faction, with which Mortimer Planner aligned himself, believed that this withdrawal was motivated by a need for psychic self-protection which ultimately might lead to extended mental powers.

Whatever the cause, however, this syndrome vanished with the same speed with which it had begun. As well as becoming Bob's spiritual coach, Mortimer Planner began to take on the role of his business manager – in a country where there was virtually no music-business tradition or infrastructure, the task of management very often fell to the artist's closest friend. Planner backed Bob to the best of his abilities, although this help often consisted of little more than moral support. In an interview with Bob only days before he collapsed in Central Park, the prelude to his end, he seemed curiously dismissive of Planno: 'Mortimer Planner, you know, an influence, but I don't think him have an influence 'pon me.' By that time, however, plenty of polluted water had passed under the bridge.

NICE TIME

Born on 19 August 1940, Johnny Nash was a handsome Texan-born singer with a sweet, powerful voice; he had been a local child star, covering R'n'B hits of the day on the Houston television series *Matinee*. Signed to ABC Records in 1957, he hit the national American charts the following year with a cover of Doris Day's 'A Very Special Love', succeeding again the year after that with 'The Teen Commandments', recorded with similar teen prodigy Paul Anka, and George Hamilton IV. When his record label tried to sell him to the middle-of-the-road market, Johnny Nash moved into acting, appearing with Dennis Hopper in the acclaimed *Key Witness*. He continued to record, yet failed to chart with the saccharine material he was given. In 1965, however, he made the US R'n'B Top Five with the funkier 'Let's Move and Groove Together'. The tune also made the charts in Jamaica, where it was a big hit. With his new manager, Danny Sims, Johnny Nash travelled there in 1966 to play some live dates.

Danny Sims was the proprietor of Sapphire's, the first black midtown Manhattan supper club, off Times Square. He also promoted concerts by American artists throughout the Caribbean and South America, as well as having managed Paul Anka, a prolific songwriter. 'I had all the big show people coming in my restaurant; we were open twenty-four hours and I sold soul food. Sidney Poitier, Harry Belafonte, and Ossie Davis, all of the entertainers used to come in. Johnny Nash used to be one of my customers. He was a huge artist at ABC/Paramount on the Arthur Godfrey show, he came to me for management, we became partners and we started doing concerts in the Caribbean.' Sims discovered he could record music for the American market far more cheaply in Kingston. Sims and Nash, along with Arthur Jenkins, an American producer, accordingly formed JAD Records – after the initials of their first names – and all three moved to the island, sharing a house in the uptown area of Russell Heights.

But, according to Sims, there had been a very specific reason for the move to Jamaica: 'The first R'n'B record that I ever got Johnny Nash to do was "Let's Move and Groove Together". That record became number one in the R'n'B market. We did a commercial with the track and we put it on every station in the country. And do you know what they put on the commercial? They put "burn baby burn" and this record was number one in Chicago and Watts and so the FBI called me and said, "Danny, we finally got you, you are out of your mind, they are burning down Watts, they are burning down the cities." We got on a plane and moved to Jamaica. We thought we were going to get killed by the CIA and the FBI, for "inciting a riot", they called it. Detroit went down, Chicago went down,

LA went down, the country just went up in flames and we were right in the midst of that. Jamaica was a place to get away from the shooting.'

Some of Nash's songs began to develop a Jamaican sense. He was the first international artist to regularly co-opt Jamaican rhythms into his tunes, exemplified by the rock-steady feel of a big international hit he had with an interpretation of 'Cupid', the Sam Cooke tune. In 1968 he hit the US Top Ten with 'Hold Me Tight', recorded at Federal Studios in Kingston.

Many of the musicians Nash met in Jamaica were Rastafarians. To find out more about this baffling religion, Nash accompanied Neville Willoughby, a top Jamaican radio disc jockey who had family connections with the Texan's girlfriend, to west Kingston on 7 January 1968, the Ethiopian Christmas Day; taking place there was a ceremony at which the Nyabinghi rituals of drumming and chanting were enacted – a grounation. Present at this event was Mortimer Planner, and also Bob and Rita Marley. As the ganja chalice was passed around the blazing fire, Nash couldn't believe the number of beautiful, clearly commercial songs Bob Marley sang and had also written. Immediately he came home he told Danny Sims about them. 'Johnny came back and told me about this fantastic artist he'd seen,' remembered Sims. 'He said the songs were great, and he had invited him up to see me at my house in Russell Heights. Bob came up with Peter, and Rita, and Mortimer Planner. And Bob was at my house ever since. He took over my house when I went on the road, and often stayed there for the next two or three years.'

The musician then sent Planno along to negotiate a deal with the American. After Planno and Sims had had 'a few lickle rough talks', according to the Jamaican, the American ended up addressing the dread as 'chief', and an agreement was struck. Sims promised he would apply his best endeavours to breaking Bob both as a songwriter and as an artist in his own right – the Jamaican's ambition, he said, was to be 'a soul singer like Otis Redding'. Bob, Peter, and Rita would receive adequate royalties for their songwriting and a publishing deal for five years with Sims's company, Cayman Music; in addition, each of them would be put on a retainer of US$200 every fortnight. Ultimately, both as demos and completed studio songs, Bob and the Wailers would record 211 songs for Danny Sims. Bunny Livingston wasn't with the group at this point; at the time the contract was signed, he was in prison on a trumped-up charge, so he was not party to this arrangement. Although Planno had done the deal for each of them, Sims noted that it was only Bob who had an association with the elder: 'Mortimer Planner had the relationship with Bob Marley, not with Bunny and Peter. Bunny and Peter were really independent of that. But at the time I met them, I never saw anything between Peter and Bob and Bunny, except love. They had things between them, like brothers and sisters – that was always there. And they were just great friends.'

(Five days after Bob signed with Danny Sims he received a message from a man called Dickie Jobson, who had ridden down on his bicycle to Trench Town to try and find him. Could Bob please come and check him? was the message – he might be able to help in some way. Bob came up to see Dickie, who told him he had a close friend in the music business called Chris Blackwell, who ran Island Records. Dickie had heard Bob's recent music and had been very impressed and would Bob like to meet his friend? Unfortunately, Bob replied, he had just signed a deal with Danny Sims. But maybe another time.)

Considering the Wailers' relative success and status in Jamaica, Danny Sims had been shocked by the collective members' hand-to-mouth standard of living: 'They had no jobs. They had no way to earn money, except sell single records. There was no money. How low could they go? In Jamaica it was hot all year round, where you could go out and pick your food off the tree or you could have your garden, which they had, and could plant their food, and you could go out to sea and catch your fish.

That level in America would have been bad, that level in Jamaica wasn't too bad.'

Bob's visits to Russell Heights were not as simple as might be imagined. The Trench Town youth would experience serious discrimination when he headed to this affluent suburb. On several occasions, he and Peter Tosh, with whom he would cycle up there, were physically turned away from the area by police. When he did manage to make it to the prestigious property in which Danny Sims and Johnny Nash lived, the maid at first refused to serve Bob food, because she considered him too low-caste. Despite the distance between each house in this uptown district, neighbours would complain that their presence brought the area down, especially the herb-smoking clearly taking place – neither Johnny Nash nor Danny Sims had previously been consumers of marijuana, but they soon fell into this regular cultural practice. 'I don't think I've ever seen Peter when he didn't have a joint,' said Danny Sims. 'There's no such thing as Peter without a joint. Peter, Bunny, and Bob, Rita, all of them, even myself . . . It's just part of the environment. They smoked constantly. But so did everybody else. It's not unusual: you're in a hot climate, and it seems to just go right out of your body. It just seemed to me, when I was there, that everybody smoked weed.' Responding to the complaints of the uptight neighbours, the musicians would deliberately sit out on the lawn, writing and rehearsing songs, reasoning, and smoking.

The uptown Jamaican girls hanging out at the house could be similarly snobbish, snootily disappearing into the rear rooms at the arrival of these ghetto boys, a revealing symptom of the island's vicious class – and skin – consciousness. 'They smell,' one of these 'brownings' once complained, hardly even registering how light-skinned one of these visitors from the ghetto actually was. On one such visit, Bob Marley caught a brief glimpse of a young girl he would later come to know very well indeed: her name was Cindy Breakspeare.

With their regular tranches of cash, the Wailers finally and quite suddenly were raised out of their former grinding poverty. But their workload doubled: Sims was aware that the American R'n'B market would have no interest whatsoever in tunes with Jamaican terminology or subject matter – let alone references to Rastafari – and required broader-based love-songs, pop music's staple, which Bob and Peter began to provide. Yet they also continued to work on more localised material for release on Wail'n Soul'm – which at least they now had the money to get pressed up whenever necessary.

The preceding year had been a life-changing one for the Wailers. The year 1967 was hardly more than a few months old before Bob began to discover that there was more than one side to Mortimer Planner, as there is with so many people. Whilst the Wailers believed the revered Rastafarian leader to be a portal to profound spiritual insight, Planno himself seemed to consider the group as an entrée to music-scene fun and frolics. The Wailers wanted to learn arcane information about Rastafari, huddled over a chalice of ganja; Planno desired to drunkenly party with them in nightclubs and dancehalls, a world which they had already learned offered nothing. At one point, Planno had allegedly been eager to get Bob off with his daughter, and one evening he also took him to a whorehouse – which caused considerable conflict within the tempted Bob, already confused by his private discovery that his marriage to Rita had not assuaged his attraction to other women who passed through his life.

As one of downtown Kingston's leading herbsmen, Planno was also something of a don, with a crew that tended towards nefarious activities. When his efforts to persuade Bob to put on a potentially lucrative Wailers live show were rejected, he was said to have threatened him, obliging Bob to call up the supportive protection of a local gang of rough-necks, militant youth who were fans of the Wailers, known as the Vikings.

Bob realised he was in too deep and needed a way out. The near-breakdown he had suffered at the end of 1966 was caused in large part by a creative block – could it have been that the ceaseless exhausting changes of the previous year had overwhelmed his brain? Early in 1967, the Wailers went into the studio and recorded 'Nice Time', a song Bob had managed to write but whose lyrics precisely cried out his frame of mind: 'Long time mi don't have no nice time / Fe think about this and think about that'. 'Nice Time' was released in July of that year, as the B-side of another song, 'Hypocrites', and was in the Jamaican Top Ten during August and September. It was quickly followed by another hit, which in October reached number five, 'Stir It Up', a song that in time would become acknowledged as one of the greatest Bob Marley tunes ever; it was backed by 'This Train'.

Despite such ostensible success, something needed to shift. There was stress also at Auntie's house on Greenwich Park Road: Rita's older brother had become a policeman and was appalled at his sister and her apparently feckless husband for having adopted the faith of Rastafari – on one occasion he even hit her in an argument over this. And as though there hadn't been enough transformations of late, Bob had just learned that Rita was pregnant – when the baby was born, it would be given the 'Nice Time' title as a nickname.

In consequence of this, with Rita and her daughter, Sharon, Bob moved back to his birthplace of Nine Miles in St Ann, to farm some of the land Omeriah Malcolm had bequeathed to his mother after he passed away – the same week in 1963 that she had moved to the United States. The rest of the Wailers – Peter Tosh, Bunny Livingston, and also Vision Walker – accompanied them. (Even up in the bush at Nine Miles, however, Bob Marley was not free of Planno's wily schemes. When he sent some men up to St Ann to administer Bob a talking-to, locals were obliged to see them off.)

Peter almost immediately tired of this isolated life, with no tap-water, no toilet, no electricity, and a distinct lack of cute girls to touch up. At this time there was a very specific female he wanted to spend time with: Shirley Livingston, Bunny's younger sister, who would give birth on 19 June 1967 to Peter's first child, a son named Andrew. In addition to Bob and Bunny having become related through Pearl, the daughter born to Bob's mother and Bunny's father, now Peter had inserted himself into this collective bloodline, binding the three young musicians even more tightly.

Of all the Wailers, Peter had the greatest fondness for the latest technological trappings of the modern world – he would happily spend hours watching television, drawn to the device even more after the Wailers had appeared on several local shows in the period prior to their retreat to the country. And he had a need for electric light: Peter was by far the keenest reader of the three, his entire life amassing books wherever he travelled. Although he would make sporadic visits to Nine Miles, within a week he was back in Kingston, a move that placed him in demand as a session player, a trusted instrumentalist – mainly on keyboards rather than the guitar, on which he was becoming extremely adept – on sessions at Duke Reid's Treasure Isle studio.

Yet Peter's whims, needs, and desires aside, to all intents and purposes the group was in touch with the zeitgeist: that collective semi-hippy need to connect communally with the essence of the earth, more publicly expressed by the desire of the English group Traffic to 'get it together' in a cottage in rural Berkshire, and by the Band, who creatively isolated themselves in Woodstock in New York. Even though they may have had very exact reasons for this, the lengthening of the Wailers' hair accorded with the emergence of similar more hirsute appearances around the globe.

Both Bob Marley and Bunny Livingston felt utterly at home and at peace within themselves in the land in which they had grown up. Bob and Rita moved into the tiny wooden shack atop a steep rise in which he had first been raised with his mother, and which now had been given to him by his grandfather – '*My* yard,' as he would proprietorially refer to it. It was chilly at night, on account of its high altitude, and they would watch as clouds and fog drifted around, above and below them, sometimes passing literally through the door of their home. After repeatedly playing the Beatles' 'Eleanor Rigby' on a tinny, tiny portable cassette-machine he had purchased in America, Bob wrote 'Sun Is Shining' and, unsurprisingly, the bare bones of 'Misty Morning', which he finally brought to fullness when he was back in Delaware two years later.

It was an existence that epitomised what a decade later in Jamaica would became known as 'roots and culture', the roots in this case being somewhat literal. 'Bob wanted to go back to nature,' said Vision Walker. 'Find himself.' Together, they planted food – yams, potatoes, cabbage. 'I was there,' said Vision. 'Bob, Rita, Bunny was back and forth. We never used to stay in just one place: we used to stay, then leave and go back to town. But that's where he did plan to go for a certain time to get his head together.'

In the backyard of the tiny house on top of the hill was a large, felled pimento tree. Bob always had an axe stuck in it, ready for the chopping of chunks of wood as they were required for the cooking fire. In the little open-air kitchen its flames flickered undyingly, corn or cocoa, yam or sweet potato roasting. The tree served a further purpose: they would sit on it and rehearse – although the sun would shine down scorchingly on the other side of the building, this side was permanently in the shade, cool and comfortable. In the evenings, their rehearsals would be lit by kerosene lamps, but more by the fire's dancing flames, the background sparkle of fireflies offering a counterpoint.

Water was collected from 'Spring', down the bottom of the hill, in a crevice between two rocks. At times of drought, people would journey there from as far away as Seven Miles, carrying off water in pots, pails, and pans. When the sun rose, around five in the morning, the Wailers collective would head down there to bathe, Rita washing the one pair of underpants owned by her husband and letting them dry on the always warm rocks.

In the country, Bob Marley's creativity came back. Working on the land during the day, he and his fellows would return to their rehearsing and writing of an evening and further songs – 'Trouble on the Road Again' and 'Comma Comma' – were quickly completed.

Shortly, however, Bob Marley suffered an accident that was potentially extremely serious. Tilling the land one morning, barefoot as ever, he stepped with his right foot, the one with the black toe, on the razor-sharp blade of a hoe, almost slicing his foot in two. In agony, he dug deep into the earth, grabbing handfuls of dark soil, damp from the frequent rainfalls, and packed it around the bloody wound, then tore a strip of cloth from his shirt and tied it tightly around it. Then he continued to work on the land for the rest of the day. By the next morning, he was unable to walk. This was now the third time he had badly injured that foot. Were the seeds of something much worse now in place?

The wound took almost a month to heal, during which time he travelled everywhere on Nimble, an old donkey that belonged to the Malcolm family and was treated as much as a pet as a beast of burden. Bob would even feed Nimble vitamin supplements and bee pollen, religiously purchased on Rita's regular weekly trips to Kingston to oversee their business there: the record store at 18a Greenwich Park Road was still operating, run by local brethren. After a few months, it shifted location, to Crescent Road, off Waltham Park Road, but soon moved back again to Rita's auntie's. During this time, Wail'n Soul'm releases included 'Hurting Inside' and, on the B-side of a song called 'Funeral', Peter's prophetic tune 'Pound Get a Blow'. At the time he wrote and recorded it, the UK pound was relatively stable; almost as soon as the record was released, however, the pound's value took a nosedive, and the currency was devalued: 'Cost of living get high, pound get low'. Inevitably, the endlessly wry, almost Chaucerian figure of Peter Tosh claimed full responsibility for this financial downturn. The song, which had introductory brass from Johnny Moore and Tommy McCook, also contained an implicit criticism of the business practices of Coxsone Dodd, with whom the Wailers were now ceaselessly engaged in a verbal war (as in the lines: 'The money you did say you gonna give me / Pound get a blow.'). For having had the temerity to start up their own label, the Wailers worried established producers.

Meanwhile, Rita was pregnant with her husband's first child. On that initial four-hour bus ride to Nine Miles from the terminus in the Parade in downtown Kingston, the driver had been obliged to pull the bus over for her to vomit, as Rita was suffering from morning sickness in the early stages of her pregnancy.

'It was different for me, because I'd never been exposed to a country,' said Rita of the move to Nine Miles. 'I'd been in Kingston all my life. It was different: I had to carry water, collect wood to make the fire, and I had to sleep on a little, small bed on the dirt, because they didn't have flooring. But it was all out of love – I had decided to do so, and it didn't matter. I was going into the faith of Rastafari, and I was seeking to find an independent sort of self.

'Because Bob was already exposed to this lifestyle, it was a thrill for him to see me just living it. It was something he had decided he would do eventually – just be a farmer and stay in the country and live. So this was always his feeling: his need to go back into the open country, and just be himself.

'We did a lot of writing and singing there, sharing a lot of special times, special moments, when I was getting to know the other side of him more so than just being in the studio.

'We did things like "Chances Are", and a lot of his songs – sometimes Bob only write one verse today, and then when he gets into the studio he finds the chorus and the other verses. He'd try out stuff on me. Listen to this one, listen to that one. And look up into the sky and the air – a lot of inspiration coming from there.'

In Stepney, close to Nine Miles, there was a medical clinic to which Rita would regularly travel for check-ups. As someone who had trained to be a nurse, however, she began to feel some concern over its effectiveness, specifically over its approach to hygiene. Rita and Bob made a decision: a month before the baby was due, they would return to Kingston, to Auntie's – the difficulties with her brother would not recur, they were aware, as he had left Jamaica. Their daughter Cedella was born on 23 August 1967, in Kingston Public Hospital.

Bob decided that he and his family needed some help, this time in the form of a tractor to help plough the land at Nine Miles. He had rarely spoken of his absent father, who had died in 1955: 'There was nothing to talk about, really. How can you talk about someone you never know?' explained Rita. All the same, Bob made a great personal decision. With Rita beside him he went to uptown Kingston, to the offices of Marley and Co., his late father's family firm, to ask if he could borrow a tractor.

But, after Bob had introduced himself, his request was met with embarrassed bewilderment on the part of his father's two brothers whom he found there. 'Their attitude,' recalled Rita, 'was "Why you come to us? Yes, Norval might be your father, but he didn't leave anything here for you." And so we left very disappointed, very upset. That had been the only hope: let's go and check these people and see if we can get some help. Because we didn't have nothing, we didn't have anything.'

Early on in their stay at Nine Miles, another blow had occurred, this time one that affected the entire future of the Wailers: Bunny was busted for herb. Like the move to the country, in retrospect this can seem like another zeitgeist moment – pop stars suddenly becoming the targets of drug laws. That summer in England the Rolling Stones had been at the centre of a celebrated drug case, and John Lennon and George Harrison of the Beatles would also soon feel the full weight of the UK judiciary. The charge against Bunny was definitively trumped up. Was this a consequence, Bob wondered, of some of the rude-boy anthems released by the group? Or, more likely, of a disagreement at Studio One? After an argument had broken out between Peter Tosh, Bunny, and Coxsone, the label boss had called the police; when they arrived, Bunny had launched into a vitriolic tirade against the forces of law and order.

The facts of the bust were simple. Around the Wailers there was always plenty of herb, which was pretty much a way of life in Trench Town. One of the reasons many musicians preferred to work at Studio One rather than Treasure Isle was because Coxsone Dodd was not against the smoking of marijuana – the former policeman Duke Reid adamantly was. Also, both Planno and Tartar sold herb. Often the Wailers would leave Betsy, their collectively owned guitar, at Tartar's yard. One day in July 1967 Bunny had gone over there to pick up the instrument. Bunny had 9 pence in his pocket. Just as he was suggesting that they buy some lunch with it, Brother Sam, who was the caretaker of the park on First Street, came to buy a half-stick of herb from Puku, the youth who dealt ganja at Tartar's yard. At the same time, Bunny asked C-Lloydy, another brethren, to go to buy the food with his money. Whilst he did so, Bunny went with Puku to fetch the herb for Brother Sam from where it was stashed nearby.

By the time they returned, however, Brother Sam had temporarily gone elsewhere. Puku took out the half-stick and put the bag of weed from which he had taken it behind a curtain. Yet a jeepful of plainclothes police who were driving by on Collie Smith Drive had seen Puku go to his stash. C-Lloyd, Puku, and a man called Tom, another guitarist, were sitting with Bunny in Tartar's yard, playing on Betsy. Suddenly, Bunny saw three of the plainclothes cops enter the yard, each from different directions: they found not only the half-stick but also the main stash-bag. The policemen announced that everyone present would be jointly charged with possession of marijuana. Then they discovered that Puku was a juvenile and therefore could not be tried in the adult courts, so they let him go. Although Tom was initially charged, the case against him was ultimately withdrawn. And Bunny Livingston was left holding the metaphorical smoking gun.

In court, Bunny pleaded not guilty, insisting that the herb was not his. His defence was not believed and he was sentenced to eighteen months in prison. Although Bunny was permitted an appeal, the judge refused bail. Bunny spent two months in the anarchic, brutal hellhole of the General Penitentiary in downtown Kingston before his appeal was heard, in front of three judges. Bunny was asked how old he was. When he replied that he was twenty, one of the judges turned to the others: 'That's old enough to go to prison.'

Transferred from the General Penitentiary, Bunny Livingston was dispatched to the north to Richmond prison farm in St Mary, which held two hundred inmates. The food, bad though it was, was better for many of the prisoners than their habitual fare – at least in prison they ate three solid meals a day. Furthermore, in terms of treatment, Bunny received some dispensation: a good cricketer, his skills honed on the steeply graded slopes of Nine Miles and the rough pitches of Trench Town, he played on the St Mary's team, and he also received a measure of respect in prison because of who he was. In a suitable irony, he was able to stay stoned for the entire sentence – Crackie, the number-one ganja dealer in Jamaica, was also serving a sentence at Richmond, and his own high-quality product was being sold in the prison. Coolie Boy, another herbs-man, about whom Don Drummond had recorded a song, was also a fellow inmate. With time remitted for good behaviour, Bunny Livingston was released from Richmond in September 1968. When he emerged from jail, there were those who noted that he was more difficult and awkward than formerly. He seemed to have an outsized chip on his shoulder and some of those around him wondered what had happened to him in prison. It can't have helped that he had been completely excluded from the Danny Sims deal.

If the Wailers' retreat to the country had been in accord with a more general unconscious mood, a less-benign collective atmosphere was apparent the next year, epitomised by the riots in France in May 1968, the surge for freedom from Soviet rule in Czechoslovakia, and student demonstrations against the Vietnam War across the globe. For followers of the civil-rights movement, there was both a downside and an upside: in April that year, Martin Luther King had been assassinated in Memphis, Tennessee; and on 16 October 1968, the American athletes Tommie Smith and John Carlos won the 200-metre race at the Olympics in Mexico City, each making a Black Power salute as they received their medals, and to symbolise black poverty, the pair appeared on the podium with bare feet.

Jamaica was not exempt from this current of social ferment. Also on 16 October 1968, there took place what became known as 'the Walter Rodney riots'. Dr Walter Rodney, a Guyanese university lecturer teaching at the University of the West Indies in Kingston, was a friend of the poor, a hardline socialist and activist in the Black Power movement who had visited Cuba and the Soviet Union; during his time in Kingston he had proselytised against what he considered the ceaselessly self-seeking Caribbean middle-class. After attending a black writers' conference in Montreal in Canada earlier in October, he discovered that the JLP government had banned him from returning to the island: this edict was under the auspices of Prime Minister Hugh Shearer. On 16 October, university students demonstrated, taking over the campus and then marching on Shearer's official residence and the Jamaican parliament. Along the way, the students were joined by thousands more demonstrators; ugly riots broke out across Kingston, and a number of people were killed.

Peter Tosh, who had been seized by the Black Power mood sweeping down from the States as powerfully as he had been by the Afrocentricity of Rastafari, found himself on a number 19 bus, whose route led from Parade to Trench Town. As the vehicle purred slowly through masses of angry demonstrators, he was moved to action. Forcing the driver from his seat, Peter took the wheel – and drove the bus directly into the main display window of a department store, exhorting his fellow passengers to take whatever they wanted from the shop. With the bus crammed with stolen luxury items, Peter resumed his usurpation of the driver's role, delivering the vehicle to its Trench Town destination, where it was abandoned.

When the police learned who was responsible for this incident, a senior officer named Joe Williams sent a message into the ghetto, demanding that Peter Tosh report to his police station for questioning. Unsurprisingly, Peter ignored the order. Accordingly, some days later Joe Williams personally came down to Trench Town, searching for him. Finally, he came upon the Wailer in an alleyway, and pulled his gun on him. In a move he had observed on numerous occasions in Westerns screened at the Carib or Rialto cinemas, Peter simply grabbed Joe Williams and spun him around, leaping over a fence and running off before the policeman could recover himself. Not unsympathetic to the protesters' views on the day of the Walter Rodney demonstration, Williams did not attempt to pursue Peter Tosh, and there were no further repercussions. By the middle of the next decade, however, Joe Williams had been made Commissioner of Police in Jamaica. Although he may have had some understanding at the time of the incident, he did not forget Peter's revolutionary behaviour that day in October 1968.

Increasingly militant, Peter Tosh was evolving into the character he would come to represent a decade hence, something akin to a Malcolm X of the Caribbean. Bob Marley, meanwhile, would more closely resemble the figure of the murdered Martin Luther King, a man of peace and justice. 'More than Bob Marley, Peter Tosh was a revolutionary writer. And a very hardcore revolutionary. Bob Marley could be anything, but he wasn't hardcore,' said Danny Sims.

Towards the end of the year, Bob and his family returned to Kingston. Rather than moving back into 18a Greenwich Park Road, he, Rita, and baby Cedella took up residence in shared accommodation with Peter and Bunny in Regent Street, where he had lived with his mother soon after they moved to Kingston. The property into which they moved had formerly been a club and therefore possessed the appropriate facilities for group rehearsals. The Wailers worked on three more singles for the Wail'n Soul'm label. 'Thank You Lord' expressed the optimism felt by Bob and Rita, despite the financially hard times; the tune was backed by 'Nice Time', and the third was a song called 'Bus Dem Shut (Pyaka)', which was produced by Mortimer Planner and sold well: a 'pyaka', a word with African origins, is a hawkish person, and the song was a social comment on the situation in Jamaica at the time, as well as on the group's deteriorating relationship with Coxsone Dodd. The sound was rougher and tougher than the Studio One material had been; the feel was looser, freed up, though that was partially the effect of the slower rhythm of rock steady.

Vision Walker continued singing with the Wailers, and is featured on the very rarest of their songs, 'Selassie Is the Chapel', written especially for him by Mortimer Planner. According to Planno, the tune was recorded on 8 June 1968 at Kingston's JBC studios – although Bunny Livingston disputes this date, insisting that he played on the B-side, 'A Little Prayer', after he was released from prison in September. Only twenty-six copies of 'Selassie Is the Chapel' were pressed, twelve of which were later taken to Ethiopia by Bob's close friend the Jamaican football hero Allan 'Skill' Cole. 'Selassie Is the Chapel' was an adaptation of the American country-and-western song 'Crying in the Chapel', a hit in 1953 for Rex Allen, one of the last of the 'singing cowboys'. Although country music was forever popular in Jamaica, it is likely that the Wailers and Mortimer Planner were more familiar with the Elvis Presley version that had been a hit three years previously, in 1965.

Gathering together some of these songs, JAD Records released an album, in Canada only, entitled 'Bob, Rita, and Peter'. It failed to sell. 'That was the first release by them on JAD Records,' said Danny Sims. 'I was told I was crazy for putting it out and that the words needed an interpreter. But it was early times for them.'

'Danny spent a lot of money and time in working with us,' said Rita. 'Keeping us in the studio day after day and night after night at Federal Studios. It was owned by Ken Khouri. And before that there had been times when we would have to stay outside the gate, waiting to be seen by the Khouris just to get an audition. And we'd be told, "No, no, no, no, no: next week, next month." So getting in there with Johnny Nash and

Danny Sims was like a feeling of victory. And later we became the owners of it. So life is something else.'

It was whilst living in Regent Street that Bob, Peter, and Bunny began seriously playing football. Nearby were the three champion clubs in Jamaica: Railway, which was the number-one team, Boystown, and George's Kensington. Railway, based at the bottom of Darling Street, was blessed with Jack Murphy, one of the greatest goalkeepers ever known in Jamaica, a tough, roughhouse player. On practice grounds around the area, the Wailers would play with such top footballers. Eventually the Wailers formed their own team, the Soul Rebels, with Bunny as striker (or 'scorer', as the position is known in Jamaica), playing full-scale, keenly contested matches against these top sides, and participating in a local competition known as the Black Shield.

One day in 1969, Bob Marley met and befriended Antonio Gilbert when he called in on the Wailers' record store, which was now on Beeston Street. 'Gilly', to which his name was inevitably abbreviated, had been part of Jamaica's national football team. He was impressed with the rigour with which both Bob Marley and Bunny Livingston were prepared to train. Out at Bull Bay, there was always the promise of a nutritious meal, courtesy of a character called Gabby Dread. Gilly noted that Peter Tosh did not so often partake in their lengthy runs: 'Tosh was a serious character, and a physical man, into yoga. He exercised and trained differently from Bob. A little jogging here and there, swimming and all of that.'

Although he had enthusiastically played football ever since he was a small boy, in Kingston Bob Marley was at first scorned as a 'country' player, zealous but unorthodox and unsophisticated; he was even given the insulting nickname of 'Miss Marley' – he played, insisted these ghetto hard-men, like a girl. Obliged, therefore, to up his skills and training, after some time Bob would mete out his full wrath to anyone who dared to slight him, the player who by then, in a typical Jamaican twist of acceptance, had become 'Mister Marley'. It was during this time that Bob Marley first encountered Allan 'Skill' Cole. 'Skill', as for obvious reasons he was known throughout Jamaica, was a tall, well-built youth five or so years younger than Bob, a midfield football player of ferocious talent who had been the youngest team-member ever on the Jamaican national side; the team was managed by the father of John Barnes, the great English footballer who would later briefly take on his father's role. Skill Cole wore his hair in locks and professed allegiance to Rastafari, so it was unsurprising that he and Bob bonded, and that they became close friends.

As well as being a member of the national Jamaican squad, Skill Cole played for Boys Town, which was near Trench Town, and also for another team, Universal 11, against whom the Soul Rebels would have matches. Bunny Livingston had already encountered him when each was at senior school, playing in the inter-schools Manning Cup competition. Skill had been a pupil at Kingston's prestigious Kings College, but he had been expelled from 'KC' for dealing ganja. Clearly he and the Wailers were of like mind. Skill couldn't, however, dissuade Bob Marley from one of his country football habits: he had been so used to playing the game barefoot that he always felt more comfortable without boots – even when the other players wore football boots, he would tackle them in his bare feet. Playing football in this manner, the black toe on his right foot which he had injured in the Nine Miles stream – which now bore a visible scar from when he had sliced it with the hoe – would become bruised and battered, sometimes suppurating with pus.

The shop and label and – most significantly – the deal with Danny Sims brought independence. But it was hard work. Every time the Wailers came out with a new wax, the three members would personally take it round Kingston's record shops to feel the vibe, then Rita would go from store to store, usually on a bicycle, to sell it to them. Everyone in the record retail business knew about Rita the Rastawoman who sold records, aware that every time they saw her walk into their premises she would be bringing a new tune from the Wailers. Sometimes when she had a heavy load to deliver she would ask Bob to give her a hand. Partly to facilitate this, in 1968 Bob managed to pull the cash together to buy a second-hand Hillman Minx car, a consequence of the deal with Danny Sims, and a sign of a certain ambition. 'Bob had a car,' said the American, 'and if someone had a car in Jamaica in those days it was unusual. But if Bob had a car it was for Bob, Bunny, and Peter – for all of them, to help them, not just for him alone. This was a situation where all three of them were inseparable – from kids they were that way.'

Mortimer Planner and Bob, despite their serious conflicts the previous year, had reconciled – Planno had observed Danny Sims's efforts with Bob and the Wailers with considerable interest, and came to a positive conclusion: that Sims *loved* Bob and had only his best interests at heart. One day whilst out with him in the Hillman Minx, Bob let the revered dread drive. Surely the man who was heavy enough to ascend the steps of His Imperial Majesty's plane to greet Him could steer Bob's car through Kingston – even if he didn't have a full driving licence? When they were stopped by the police and this offence was discovered, the pair were imprisoned overnight.

As soon as he was released, Bob left Kingston and returned again to the country. Shortly before the family left the city, on 17 October 1968, the day after Peter Tosh had hijacked the bus during the Walter Rodney riots, Rita had given birth to his second child, David as his name read on his birth certificate, Ziggy as everyone called him. 'This was his first son, so there was much excitement: what shall we call him?' wondered Rita. 'I wanted David, because of how he was born at home in Trench Town:

I said, "This little boy must be David." And I also saw Bob as a great writer: sometimes I would even call him King David. His appearance sometimes is very royal when you look at him – and that was before fame, success, and money. And I also thought it was a good name to make a great son: because he was born so humble in a little house in Trench Town, on newspaper. We couldn't afford much. Auntie was the midwife: Bob was there helping to clean up blood. It was a special baby to us, a special thing in our life, even though Cedella was there already. But having a boy is important.

'And Bob said, "Well, this is Ziggy, man," because his foot was all turned. He said, "This is Ziggy, Ziggy." And I said, "What is this Ziggy?" And Bob said, "It's football!" – a name for, what they call it, dribbling. They used to call out to Bob, "Ziggy, Bob, Ziggy!" He was good at that, taking the ball and moving it up and down. And so Bob said, "This is Ziggy, this is Ziggy!" That's how Ziggy got that name.'

Loving his children, but also needing to absent himself from them to continue his work, Bob had often been spending nights at Danny Sims's uptown house and also at Planno's Fifth Street home. This did not go down well with Rita. By now she was becoming vexed over Bob's regular absences from home, sometimes for two or three days at a time. Although sometimes he was with other women – 'Bob was always a womaniser,' said Danny Sims – half the time Bob was merely off with his Rasta brethren, reasoning, making music, smoking herb, or simply hanging out. Rita angrily complained to Bob's mother that her husband had taken Cedella to a Rasta priest for baptism and that the man had blown ganja smoke in the infant's face.

But Bob's own psychic powers were still working actively for his family. One time he had spent the evening working at Coxsone's studio – which he had hired – and lay down to rest. Immediately he had a dream in which he saw a scorpion crawling towards the bed of Sharon, Rita's first child.

Bob hurried home and searched Sharon's room, finding a scorpion on the wall. Carrying the sleeping Sharon into another room, he came back into the bedroom and killed the lethal insect.

Yet in the manner of many young couples, especially those with very young children, the relationship between Bob and Rita became endlessly quarrelsome. 'Try to understand one anodder and not fuss so much. See one side and de odder. Look 'pon de odder point of view,' advised Bob's mother, suspecting her words would fall on deaf ears.

In early 1968 Danny Sims flew Bob Marley, Rita, and Peter Tosh to New York. Johnny Nash was about to record a new album and Sims wanted their input. Whilst in New York, Peter acquired assorted pedals and devices which greatly enhanced his guitar-playing, leading to the distinctive sound he developed, employed on all subsequent Wailers' recordings. Danny Sims also introduced Bob Marley to Jimmy Norman, a celebrated R'n'B songwriter and musician who had written the lyrics for 'Time Is on My Side', a US hit for the Rolling Stones, and played with Jimi Hendrix before the guitar-player left Greenwich Village for London. Having met Bob earlier in the day in Manhattan, Jimmy invited him and Rita over to his apartment in the Bronx that evening. 'He wasn't wearing dreadlocks at the time. He was just a regular cat and he loved rhythm and blues. All he wanted to talk about was music,' remembered Jimmy Norman. Jamming together that night, they played on three tunes written by Norman and Al Pyfrom, his songwriting partner – 'Falling in and out of Love', 'Stay with Me', and 'You Think I Have No Feelings' – and such Bob Marley songs as 'I'm Hurting Inside' and 'One Love'. (In 2004, a tape of this session was sold at Christie's in New York.) As Danny Sims had predicted, Bob Marley and Jimmy Norman clicked, and the American was invited to Kingston the following week to work on sessions with both the Wailers and Johnny Nash. Jimmy Norman ended up remaining in the Jamaican capital for the next seven months, staying at the house in Russell Heights.

He was not the only American to fly down to Kingston for these sessions at Dynamic Studios, produced by Johnny Nash and Arthur Jenkins – who was also an adept arranger, keyboards player, and percussionist. Danny Sims flew a number of top musicians to Jamaica to play sessions with the Wailers; amongst them was the great South African trumpeter Hugh Masekela, and the seasoned, celebrated drummer Bernard Purdie. Before they arrived, however, locals were employed, including classical string musicians and a local glee club for backing vocals; horns came courtesy of the Jamaican army band. According to Purdie, plenty of time was given to these sessions, which did not end until everyone was satisfied. Some of the tapes were sent up to New York, where tracks from further musicians and backing vocals were added. After the glee club had been dispensed with, most of the backing vocals on the completed Kingston sessions came from Norman, his songwriting partner Al Pyfrom, Norman's wife, Dorothy, Johnny Nash, Rita Marley, and Peter Tosh.

Bob's music, Norman noted, 'was always entertaining, with great rhythm and exceptional melody. When thinking of Bob, here is a picture that always comes to mind: we would leave the studio for a break, Bob would always climb up the hill, find a large rock, lie down upon it, light up, commune with nature, and be at peace.' Among the many gorgeous songs that emerged from these sessions were 'What Goes Around Comes Around', a rock-steady update of 'Put It On', and a new 'Nice Time' on which Hugh Masekela played; there were fresh gems like the first try-out of a song called 'Soul Rebel', 'Rocksteady', and 'Chances Are'. Peter Tosh also recorded and released the first version of a song that would come to personify the gangly, tall youth, 'Stepping Razor' ('I'm a stepping razor / Don't you watch my sides / I'm dangerous'). In subsequent years inspiring many a newspaper headline about Tosh, 'Stepping Razor' was often assumed to have been written by him. In fact it was penned by his old, and continuing, mentor Joe Higgs. 'As well as the spliff and the chillum, these were some of the most inspiring months of my life,' said Jimmy Norman.

But he claimed that it was he who wrote 'Soon Come', which was somehow credited to Peter Tosh; similarly, that 'The World Is Changing', a socially conscious tune on which Peter sang lead vocals, and 'Treat You Right', both credited to Bob Marley, were written by himself and Al Pyfrom. Mostly collected later on the 1998 JAD release *The Complete Wailers* Part 1, the conversationally coherent songs from these sessions were as militant or magical, or conspicuously atmospheric or sensually abrasive, as anything recorded in the later Island years. Danny Sims was the first international music business figure who recognised and loved Bob's talents, long before any others did. Bob, moreover, respected Sims's connections, and the fact that he could get his records played on the radio.

Yet – if even further proof were needed that the Wailers were in a glorious 'Golden' phase of their career – the intrinsically unhurried recordings for Danny Sims were about to be surpassed by work of an even greater distinction, tantalisingly world-shaking in its scintillating essence.

First, however, Bob Marley yet again returned with his family to Nine Miles, to reacquaint himself with his creativity. Always pleased to pass on the baton of encouragement and inspiration, he found such an opportunity one morning late in January 1969. Living in the coastal town of St Ann's Bay, the birthplace of Marcus Garvey, also in the parish of St Ann, was Burning Spear, a vocal trio who had taken the favoured Jamaican form of the three-piece-harmony group to its most roots extreme. The group's leader was Winston Rodney, who by the early seventies would himself personally take on the Burning Spear title: his gravelly vocals sounded as though they contained every piece of truth the island of Jamaica had ever known – ultimately, he would become the undisputed elder statesman of reggae music.

As a youth, Spear had dug Bob and the Wailers' early tunes. 'Bob was Jamaican number-one star. Bob was the man. There was no other man. We have a lot of singers who were even in the business before Bob. But Bob ended up being the man.'

For whatever reason, that late-January morning, Spear found himself in the innermost reaches of St Ann, close to the area of Rhoden Hall. As he stepped out along a rough road, Spear came across Bob travelling in the opposite direction on Nimble, the family donkey. Bob was heading for his cultivation, and garlanded about Nimble were a whole heap of plants. Bob and Spear got to reasoning. Dismounting, Bob sat down on the grass verge with Spear and rolled a spliff. And for many hours the two men reasoned upon the matter of Rastafari and its roots, the culture, His Majesty, the music . . . For many, many hours.

'Then I remember saying to him, "Jah B," – I call him Jah B – "'ow can I get started in this business?" And Jah B would turn to I and say, "Check Studio One. Tell Mr Dodd I sent you."

'And we were talking like a Sunday, when we meet in the hills, and on the Monday I was back out of the hills and thinking about it. Until the time came when I checked Studio One. That was a Sunday too. I checked Studio One and they were doing an audition thing, listening to young singers. And I was one of the ones who they select my song. My first song was called "Door Peep".

'So the whole thing for Burning Spear started, because Bob told I to check Studio One. That was the first time we had really exchanged talk, and we could look at each other and talk and laugh. That was one of my biggest musical experiences. Before I even get started. Dealing with the main man.'

*   *   *

At the beginning of April 1969, the Wail'n Soul'm record store, alternatively known as the Soul Shack, moved yet again, farther down the street to 100 Orange Street. At both these Orange Street locations it was run whenever Rita was absent by a friend named Dudley, who was more commonly known as Icewater. Most days, Bunny Livingston would join Icewater in attending to business at the Wail'n' Soul'm store. Bunny's mother, who for the previous nine years had lived in London, working in a toy factory in the north-west suburb of Neasden, had temporarily returned to Jamaica, gifting her son with a brand-new stereo record-player, which he set up on the counter at 100 Orange Street, playing tunes at maximum volume in an endeavour to attract passers-by.

By springtime, Bob had decided it was time to visit his mother again in Wilmington, Delaware, accompanied this time by his family – Rita, her daughter Sharon, and their children, Cedella and Ziggy, the new baby son. Mrs Booker observed that, as soon as she met the two adults, both tired from a journey which had included a number of changes of planes, they were irritably snapping at each other, Bob saying he had felt embarrassed by Rita breast-feeding Ziggy during the flight, a prickly Rita grunting back that she had had no choice as Ziggy had been hungry; it seemed a long way from the days when Bob would woo his bride-to-be with a can of Cow & Gate baby formula. Soon Bob's mother was caring for the children much of the time, as her son and his wife took jobs, Bob once more labouring at the Chrysler car plant off South College Avenue in Newark, Delaware, twelve miles south-west of Wilmington.

Before he borrowed his mother's car and drove out to the automobile factory, he asked her to trim his budding dreadlocks, gathering the clippings into a paper-bag and burying them in the backyard, aware that if they were simply thrown away birds might use them to build nests, turning the person on whose head they had grown into a bird-brain; or that they might be used to work obeah on him. Although his hair was still quite long, he wore it brushed back.

At the Chrysler plant, Bob would generally work on the second shift, from 3:30 in the afternoon until half-past midnight, with a half-hour meal break, driving a fork-lift carrying parts for the rear sections of automobiles – the experience was described in his autobiographical song 'Night Shift'. Although he would affect a red, gold, and green semi-tam, otherwise he was dressed in jeans and work-shirts.

At her house, Mrs Booker would overhear arguments between Bob and Rita, which sometimes ended with Rita sobbing her eyes out. Although her son's wife took a job as a housekeeper, she was dismissed when the rich old white woman who had employed her was made nervous by the sight of Bob and his family waiting in a car for Rita outside her gate. Rita then took employment as a nurse's assistant, but was dismissed when her Rasta hair was deemed inappropriate for the post.

Rita wanted a different environment from Trench Town for the children to grow up in: 'Everyone was getting big, and I said that I couldn't wait around for records to sell. This was my decision, not Bob's.' Cedella and Ziggy started to go to American schools, Rita was employed as a nurse, and their third child, Steven, was born there.

Before he needed to head off to the automobile factory each day, Bob had a measure of time to himself, sitting down in the basement with his guitar. In his mother's backyard, hidden by a high wall, was an eight-feet-high hedge of herb plants, a horticultural innovation implemented by her son on his previous visit. Bob would set himself up for the day by grabbing a handful of leaves and boiling it up into tea, adding honey; then plucking another bunch, he would lay it out between newspaper pages, iron it dry on his mother's board and roll it up into a Jamaican-sized spliff cone. Suitably fortified, from time to time he would meander down into

Wilmington, where he had made a handful of new friends. Amongst these was Ibis Pitts, who ran an African crafts store, the Ibis Specialty and Gift Shop, on 24th and Market. It was Rita Marley whom the shopkeeper had first encountered, when she had wandered into his premises barefoot, casually dancing around the shop as she glanced at the jewellery on display. Falling into conversation, Rita introduced herself and mentioned the name of her husband, informing Ibis that they were musicians: she said that she would bring Bob down to the store to meet him.

When Bob eventually turned up at Ibis Pitts's store, he spoke quietly, keeping himself very much to himself: 'He was very humble, very meek, very quiet. He didn't say much, but he did a lot,' said Ibis. He expressed himself far more in his playing of a guitar in the shop, which Ibis Pitts accompanied on the several drums on display in the premises. Soon Bob invited Ibis up to his mother's home, giving him a copy of 'Nice Time', and sitting in the basement with him, reasoning and consuming the new herb crop. Discovering that Ibis Pitts and his friend Dion Wilson were keen soccer-players, he began joining in with them in impromptu games.

As they reasoned, both in Ibis's store and at Mrs Booker's home, Bob Marley would assist Ibis Pitts in constructing the wire-and-bead necklaces and bracelets that were a staple product at the Ibis Specialty and Gift Shop. One night they sat up until dawn making such jewellery. The next day, 15 August 1969, marked the beginning of the Woodstock Music & Art Fair – the famous Woodstock music festival – and Ibis was heading up to the site in upper New York state, intending to sell these products. He invited Bob to accompany him, but – more exhausted from this stint assembling necklaces than from nine hours on the Chrysler night shift – the Jamaican bowed out.

During one conversation, Bob made an apparently casual prediction to Ibis Pitts and Dion Wilson. 'Nesta told us about him not being on this earth many more years than Jesus Christ was,' said Ibis. 'I just kind of passed it off, but Dion remembered the details. And when he heard the news about Nesta passing, he said, "Nesta said he was going to be leaving at thirty-six. And when he went, he was thirty-six years old.'"

Whilst he was in Wilmington, the only postal correspondence with Jamaica that Bob was able to maintain was with Tartar, his old bredren from Trench Town. No one else replied to letters he sent them, specifically, Bunny and Peter. In one letter that Tartar received, Bob was complaining that he had written to both of his spars in the Wailers, asking them to come up and join him in the United States. Yet neither had bothered to respond: he had wanted Bunny Livingston to come up first, followed by Peter Tosh.

As a registered alien, Bob Marley was listed on official American files. With the authorities anxious to find fodder for the body-bags daily being returned from the war in Vietnam, he was ripe for conscription into the armed forces. When one day not long after the Woodstock festival his call-up papers arrived, Bob Marley took his only option: he boarded a plane back to Jamaica.

At the end of the 1960s, many of the decade's human-rights issues remained still unresolved. Amongst the more specific abuses to which man subjected his fellows was the new apartheid regime in Rhodesia in southern Africa; since that country's unilateral declaration of independence from Britain, it had emulated the racist regime of its neighbour South Africa, where black people had been treated as sub-human beings since 1948. In June of 1969, such egregious thinking became enshrined in the breakaway nation when race separation passed into law.

Back in Jamaica, baring his militant side, Bob Marley held discussions about this iniquity with Mortimer Planner. The pair contacted Prince Buster, who by now was leader of the Black Muslims in the Caribbean. 'They asked me to help with a demonstration that they were trying to get together. We said we'd meet at twelve o'clock the next day for a protest against Ian Smith, who had his hands on Rhodesia. I was at the place at twelve o'clock in King Street, but there was no Bob Marley: maybe he'd got wind of what was going to happen. When the demonstration starts the police come and jump on me. Some big inspector walking down the street with a big stick: "Come here, Prince Buster." I'd been set up. Peter Tosh was there with me: he went to jail with me, arrested by Joe Williams, who later was head of the police of Jamaica.

'I didn't think I was breaking the law, I was protesting. So when I ended there in the night time, I was there to help Peter Tosh. He thought he'd been taken too. To this day, I don't know exactly what went on.'

Although the pair only spent a night in the police cells, Peter Tosh had yet again been noted by Joe Williams as a militant troublemaker. As for Bob Marley? In typically Jamaican fashion, he had simply been late.

Although inspired by the then current mood for communal country living, the Wailers', and then Bob's, moves to Nine Miles also had been motivated by a perennial problem for young people in whatever economic or social circumstances they found themselves – a need to find somewhere to live apart from their relatives. Even the residence in Regent Street had not been especially appropriate. What they needed, they decided, was to buy a property in which they would all live, one that would also incorporate a rehearsal space.

Danny Sims did not have an exclusive deal with the Wailers, and they were free to record for whomever they liked in Jamaica. Accordingly, early in 1970, Bob found himself travelling back into Kingston from Nine Miles and pulling his car up in front of the shop and office of Leslie Kong, the producer with whom he had made his very first records. The previous year, Kong had produced 'Do the Reggay' by the Maytals, the unequivocal statement of existence of the new beat that had followed on from rock steady, another extremely significant shift for Jamaican music. Since Bob Marley had first worked with him in 1962 on 'Judge Not', his first ever record release, the fortunes of Leslie Kong had taken an exponential leap: the six million worldwide sales of Millie's 'My Boy Lollipop', on which he had been in partnership with Island Records' Chris Blackwell, and the global successes of '007' and 'It Mek' by Desmond Dekker, Bob Marley's former welding spar, had made him a millionaire.

Aware that their talents were the only tools they possessed with which to manage to buy a home, the Wailers had a discussion with the producer, by whose store they had briefly set up the Wail'n Soul'm shop at the beginning of 1969. It was Kong's successful experience with overseas markets that drew the Wailers to him. Conscious that the new international record market embraced albums rather than singles, a change that had initially occurred after the enormous success of the Beatles' *Sgt Pepper's Lonely Hearts Club Band* in 1967, the Wailers proposed that they also should make a record exclusively for this substantial emerging audience, one that would not feature any songs previously released at 45rpm.

The resulting ten-song album was recorded in Kingston at Dynamic Sound in May 1970. Employed as backing musicans were Leslie Kong's house-band, the Beverley's All Stars, who consistently created one of the distinctive sounds of the era, and on these sessions provided a constant uptown groove. Although they would work for other producers under different names, their line-up remained the same: pianist Gladstone Anderson, organist Winston Wright, bass player Jackie Jackson, drummer Winston Grennan, Rad Bryan on rhythm guitar, and Hux Brown on lead guitar.

The sessions from the Wailers would not, however, come anywhere near to emulating the success of Millie or Desmond Dekker, although many of the songs were strong and substantial and would be seen as classics in years to come – 'Caution', 'Cheer Up', 'Soul Shakedown Party', and 'Do It Twice' were amongst the numbers written by Bob. Peter Tosh, meanwhile, sang a fiery lead on the protest hymn 'Go Tell It on the Mountain' and his own hectoring 'Soon Come', and yet again reworked the 'Can't You See?' tune he had first recorded for Studio One in 1966; he also contributed the original version of 'Stop That Train'; 'Soul Captives' and 'Back Out' completed the album's songs.

When it came to Kong's choice of title for the album, there came a considerable controversy. Clearly seeking a marketing angle, Leslie Kong declared that he would name the record *The Best of the Wailers*. Bunny Livingston responded with fury. Only at the end of one's existence could an individual's best work be judged, he insisted. As all three of the Wailers were healthy and fit men, he declared, such a decision must mean that it was Kong who was near the end of his life.

Leslie Kong laughed at what he considered typical Rasta-reasoning double-think. As well as putting out the LP under the title he wanted, he released three singles from the sessions (thereby devaluing the Wailers' overriding intention in making the album): 'Soul Shakedown Party', 'Stop That Train', and 'Soon Come'. Although 'Stop That Train' had the song 'Caution' as its B-side, the other two 45s each contained a 'version' on the flip. In this, Kong was responding to a significant development in Jamaican music. The previous year, 1969, U-Roy, a DJ who had been working sound systems since the beginning of the decade, had had a success with 'Dynamic Fashion Way', which he recorded for Keith Hudson. But this was a small beginning. In 1970, U-Roy mashed up the charts, holding the top three slots for six weeks with such tunes as 'Wake the Town', 'Rule the Nation', and 'Wear You to the Ball', recorded with Duke Reid. Working with previously successful rhythm tracks, he toasted over the top of them in an utterly addictive manner. 'The thing was like an experiment, and it worked,' Bunny Livingston said later of the first hit U-Roy tune.

At the same time, Osbourne 'King Tubby' Ruddock, who had begun his career as a radio repairman, was working as a mixing engineer for Reid; in 1967, U-Roy had been Tubby's toaster on King Tubby's Home Town Hi Fi sound system. It was Tubby who devised the style of slicing out sections of vocal or instrumental parts of an already recorded track and playing with them, dropping them in and out of the tune, literally 'dubbing' them. With the addition of a multitude of special effects, notably reverb, King Tubby invented what became known as dub. The combination of Tubby and U-Roy revolutionised not only Jamaican music but eventually music around the world. Rap music itself, and the phenomenon of the dance remix, can be directly attributed to the work of these two men. 'I used to go and watch U-Roy play King Tubby's,' said Dennis Alcapone, who would himself become an internationally renowned DJ. 'In them days up until now I never hear a better sound. That was the sweetest sound in all the wide world. U-Roy had this echo thing. When introducing a music or advertising a dance, all his words would echo: it blow my mind. It was Tubby's that introduce reverb in the dance. I never hear a thing like that, because reverb was mostly in the studios. But he had the reverb on the sound system and the echo. It was just brilliant. And you'd have one big steel horn up in a tree, right at the front, two on the gateposts, and some heavy-duty speakers at the front. In the night when the wind is blowing and the music is playing it is out of sight.'

Although the full extent of their influence would take some time to be thoroughly appreciated, U-Roy's success in 1970 did have an immediate effect on the Jamaican music business: aware of the cost-saving reality of not needing to record a separate B-side, producers began to include what was literally a dub 'version' of the A-side song on a record's flip.

Artists therefore would lose the opportunity for the flat fee they would have earned for such a recording; the notion of losing songwriting royalties, of course, never came into the matter, Jamaican producers almost always considering that they bought the copyright of the song when they paid for the studio performance.

U-Roy was already friends with the Wailers. Whilst Bob was in America, Peter Tosh had enhanced his session-playing reputation. He had also worked, with a feeling of extreme religious honour, on Lee Perry's production of 'Rightful Ruler', an ardent and outright expression of Rastafarian belief. The existence of the record was in itself a statement of protest – official behaviour, especially from the police, towards followers of Rastafari had hardly shifted at all since the denouncements from high political quarters during the early part of the decade. All those who contributed to the record were devout followers of the faith: on drums was Count Ossie, who had come down from his eyrie in the Wareika Hills; U-Roy, who on the song toasted the first Psalm, was known for strict advocacy of the faith; there was no questioning the position of Peter Tosh; and even 'Scratch' Perry, who had not been averse to leading a flash lifestyle, was veering towards belief in the divinity of His Majesty.

But what about Leslie Kong and what some considered to be a curse placed upon him by Bunny Livingston? On 9 August 1971, Kong paid a visit to his accountant. At this meeting he was told, so legend has it, precisely how much money he would earn from *The Best of the Wailers*. When he returned home, he collapsed and died, from a heart attack.

DUPPY CONQUEROR

None of the Wailers' Leslie Kong records sold particularly well. Yet although their records were selling in far fewer quantities than they had when they were recording for Studio One, the Wailers were better off than they had ever been. With Coxsone Dodd they had had high sales but small pay; now, Danny Sims and his retainer, and the energising creative buzz from their long hours of studio work, significantly improved their incomes. Bob and his family had moved back to Trench Town, to First Street now. The mood in the area was settled, although the police might occasionally move in and mash up some unfortunate suspect's dwelling in the middle of the night.

The reputation of the area was such, however, that outsiders had been fearful to tread Trench Town's streets and lanes to buy discs at 18a Greenwich Park Road. At the beginning of 1969, another tiny record shop had been opened, at 135b Orange Street, on the corner of Beeston Street, close by Beverley's record store. Known both as Wail'n Soul'm and the Soul Shack, the business was mainly Rita's province: she needed an outlet for her abilities – the Soulettes had fallen apart. Moving to the hub of Kingston's downtown commercial area felt significant. 'When we got the shop downtown, it was a thrill,' said Rita. 'Even though there was more work to be done by getting up to go down and locking up and coming home.'

Despite the Danny Sims deal easing the pressure with their small-level business, life was relentless for Bob and Rita. 'You'd have to meet obligations to pay for the records to be pressed. You don't see any improvement in your living conditions in Trench Town.'

Plenty had been going on that Bob needed the time to mentally process: his drive for self-determination had been interlinked with his espousal of Rastafari, but its success so far was clearly very relative.

As opposed to the burst of creativity Bunny and Peter had enjoyed when Bob first went to the States in 1966, now they had been largely inactive as a creative unit whilst he was away. In Wilmington, Bob Marley had had time to reflect: might not it suit his work better, he pondered, if he were to leave his bredren to their own devices? A new tune he had written, 'Black Progress' – like the organisation of the anti-Rhodesian demonstration with Planner, a symptom of his growing militant thinking – he was considering producing himself. In the United States, black militancy was generally more formed in its thinking than in Jamaica, and Bob had come under its influence. 'Black Progress' borrowed heavily from James Brown's '(Say it Loud) I'm Black and I'm Proud' and also from Sam and Dave's 'Soul Man'. In the States, Bob had also outfitted himself with some flashy new clothes, of the style favoured by stylish young black Americans: big-collared shirts and jackets, vastly flared trousers.

Hanging out with other Jamaicans whilst in Wilmington, he had heard a hot new tune from the island, 'Watch This Sound' by the Uniques, a version of Buffalo Springfield's 'For What It's Worth'. Bob had been especially taken with the hard style of bass-playing on the record. If he was to record 'Black Progress', he decided he wanted that bass player for the song. Accordingly, he learned who he was – Aston 'Family Man' Barrett – and sought him out. When they met, Bob was allegedly surprised that Family Man was so young, having expected 'a more professional, older person,' as Barrett would recall.

Born on 22 November 1946 into a childhood of grinding poverty in downtown Kingston, Family Man, whose nickname came from the prodigious quantity of children he had fathered whilst still in his teens, had been unruly as a youth and been sent for eighteen months to a Jamaica Youth Corps camp in Manchester, in the centre of the island. Prior to this, Family Man had been unfocused and lacking any interest in education. Now, living in the cool mountain climate of the region, he felt for the first time the force of music.

Picking up the art of metalwork at the camp, Family Man worked as a welder, locksmith, and bike mechanic when he returned to Kingston. But where this new skill really benefited him was in giving him the ability to make his first bass guitar. Why the bass? 'I loved all the instruments. But the bass is the backbone of the thing. I love bass and I love music and I listen to it and feel I could take it to another stage, a higher stage. And I've worked on that over the years. When I am playing the bass it is like I am playing a bass harmony. I try to harmonise with the melody from the artist. So I come up with some kind of line they would call melodic.'

Family Man worked as a rhythm team with his younger brother, Carlton. 'Carly', born on 17 December 1950, had built a set of drums out of some empty paint tins, and been initially influenced by Lloyd Nibbs, the great drummer from the Skatalites. The combination of Family Man's melodically sonorous, authoritative bass and Carly's driving, percussive drums made them the toughest rhythm team in Jamaica.

It was with the Hippy Boys that they grew as musicians, initially standing in for the group's regular rhythm section when they failed to turn up for a show. The Hippy Boys' line-up from then on consisted of the Barrett brothers, guitarist Alva 'Reggie' Lewis, keyboards player Glen Adams, and vocalist Max Romeo, soon to have a very big hit in the UK with his rude 'Wet Dream' tune. Working for a friend of Family Man's called Tony Scott, the Hippy Boys made a number of records – a song written by Scott called 'What Am I to Do?', an instrumental with the title 'Dr No Go', and a version of the Staples Singers' 'I'll Take You There', which transmogrified into Harry J's 'Liquidator'. They became top session players.

Working, unusually, without his brother, Family Man had played on the 'Watch This Sound' tune with the Uniques, the vocal trio composed of Slim Smith, Lloyd Charmers, and Jim Riley. After that, he had recorded briefly with the very likable Bunny 'Striker' Lee, a former record plugger for Duke Reid who, in 1967, had set up his own label, Lee's; after hits from Pat Kelly, the Sensations, Derrick Morgan, and the Uniques, Striker had established himself as one of Jamaica's top producers. Family Man and the Hippy Boys soon met Striker's good friend Lee Perry, with whom the Wailers and Soulettes had already worked at Studio One; in 1968, the Hippy Boys began working with him.

Lee 'Scratch' Perry, who was born in Kendal in Manchester Parish on 20 March 1936, had graduated from being a 'selecter' on Coxsone Dodd's Downbeat sound system and a 'fetcher' – although a 'fetcher' grabbing any moment of available studio time to learn the craft of making records – at 13 Brentford Road to a far more formidable figure. Finally falling out with Coxsone Dodd in 1967, he was given a career break by a new producer, Joe Gibbs.

That year, when Gibbs installed a two-track recording machine in the rear of his Beeston Street television-repair shop, he brought in Lee Perry as his engineer. Their first success came the next year, with one of the earliest rock-steady tunes, Roy Shirley's 'Hold Them'; meanwhile, Scratch Perry wrote a number of local hits for the Pioneers for Gibbs before he left to set up his own label. Scratch's first release, 'People Funny Boy', was a viciously satirical attack on his former boss's business practices. (Almost inevitably, Gibbs released an answer record using the same rhythm, 'People Grudgeful'. Jamaican record producers are frequently more like film producers, coming up with the finances and facilities and letting others do the creative work. Gibbs almost created the mould. He replaced Perry with first Winston 'Niney' Holness and then, in 1970, with Errol Thompson – both becoming legendary engineers who brought him great and deserved success.)

On Charles Street, Lee 'Scratch' Perry now had his own shop, Upsetter Records, where he would sell the discs he produced. Before he left Jamaica on his second trip to Wilmington, Bob was already in the habit of going to check this extrovert figure who delighted in fascinating, witty word-play, often with a metaphysical twist, as befitted a man who had a reputation for working with obeah. Their mutual flight from Coxsone had bonded them with shared experience.

Some attributed the birth of reggae to Scratch alone – ultimately, he would reveal himself to be one of the finest artists the Caribbean has produced in any field – after he started dabbling with a musical pace that made you feel, he said, as though you were stepping in glue.

Family Man and the Hippy Boys would work with both Scratch and Bunny Lee: the two producers would book the same studio, and run their sessions back to back, using the same musicians. 'It's two different kinds of flavours, two different kinds of producers,' said Family Man. 'Lee Perry is more like an artist – he is a singer and a musician. Bunny Lee just listens to it and knows. Scratch is more likely to be involved in the percussion sections and arrangements too – although him don't play instruments, he was a musical genius.'

The first tune that the Hippy Boys recorded for Scratch was a cover of an instrumental by the Meters called 'Sophisticated Sissy'. With a Jamaican musical flavour added to it, the song was retitled 'Medical Operation'. The Hippy Boys were renamed the Upsetters, after another of Lee Perry's several nicknames – his task, he said, was to 'upset' Coxsone Dodd. As the Upsetters, they had a big hit with 'Return of Django', a reference to the Sergio Corbucci spaghetti western – its comic strip ultraviolence made it a huge favourite with those downtown rough-necks who enjoyed loosing off revolver shots at the screen of Kingston's Carib cinema. The tune crossed over to the UK, making the Top Five there in 1969, and the Upsetters toured Britain on the back of it; later they shared their touring experiences with the Wailers, telling them how they had been received.

For Family Man, whose sobriquet was commonly abbreviated to 'Fams', choosing to become a bass player turned out to have been a blessed decision. When he linked up with Lee Perry, the producer decided to make the bass the lead instrument of the new form, reggae, in which he was now working.

Family Man knew that there had long been a connection between Scratch and the Wailers. Both the Barrett brothers by this time were following the path of Rastafari, and were aware that the three-piece group from Trench Town was dealing with a spiritual message. 'So we have a special respect and love for the Wailers, and the whole concept of them, even the people them. It was good energy coming from the beginning.' For Family Man, in fact, who had loved the Wailers since he had first heard 'Simmer Down', it was like a 'miracle' that he should be playing with them.

So it was through Family Man that Bob Marley went over to see Lee Perry, to suggest that he work with him and with the Hippy Boys. At first Scratch claimed he was reluctant to work with any singers at all, largely because of the 'so stink and so rude' behaviour that he felt had characterised many of the vocalists he had recorded at Studio One and Joe Gibbs. Instead, he was happier working on instrumental material such as 'Return of Django'. But when Bob sang him the lyrics of a new song, 'My Cup', Scratch was taken with the idea of working with him. 'I tell him to let me hear what song him have to sing and him say he is overflowing and he don't know what to do,' he said, paraphrasing the tune's lyrics.

Persuaded, Scratch invited Bob over to his home at Cardiff Crescent in the Washington Gardens district in the west of Kingston. Bob moved in for a few days, as the pair worked on musical ideas. Despite the form into which the new songs would fit, the pair did not consider them reggae music but as 'revolutionary soul', a definition that could have derived from the 'Black Progress' song alone. In keeping with this specific vision, when the two albums emerged from the sessions, they would be titled *Soul Rebels* and *Soul Revolution*.

Lee Perry and Bob travelled out to Hanover Parish, on the far north-western tip of Jamaica, to check Scratch's mother, Miss Ina, and pick up some country vibes. It was here that Bob came up with the tune 'Kaya'; they had run out of herb, and realising it was about to rain, swiftly dispatched Scratch's brother Sonny on his bicycle to fetch some more – the lyrics on the finished song perfectly capture the tale. As anyone can attest who has heard his beautiful 'Dreadlocks in Moonlight' song, recorded in 1976, Scratch himself had a powerful, affecting voice, redolent with the timbre of the roots and earth of Jamaica. It has been suggested that as he worked with Lee Perry during these few days at his home and in the country, Bob Marley's own voice mutated, taking on a tone that was distinctly similar to that of the producer. If that is really what occurred, Scratch Perry could give name and number for why this happened. 'Bob Marley was temporarily lodged in the front room so that he, Perry and the spirits could work more closely together,' said Perry's biographer, David Katz.

'Bob was having my front room, and that's where I have my genie,' Scratch told David Katz. 'My genie's not in a bottle, it's the breeze, the bag of breeze. He was living in the genie room and absorbing the power of the genie to do the job because I didn't hear a singer, and he didn't have the personality and the looks and the complexion and the hair, even though it wasn't dread when he come. So after him gather the power and him get mighty strong I know it was real power, and he put on the dread and decided to take over.'

Scratch persuaded Bob Marley that he should give up his idea of working on his own and bring the other Wailers in on the project. 'Bob didn't want to go back with the Bunny and Peter thing,' Scratch told David Katz. 'I say, "Well, I think you should do it with this soul revolution for special reason, because the three of your voice blend very good like an angel, to manifest your work on this soul revolution . . . It was my idea to put them back together; he alone didn't want to do it. Bob wanted to sing with me alone without them, but I said, "No, you need them for special work like 'Sun Is Shining', you need the harmony."'

Bob Marley and Lee Perry had 'a chemistry', said Rita Marley. 'And that was lacking from the Wailers for a time: from Bunny and Peter . . . The chemistry after a time started to diminish, and Bob felt that something was lacking: he knew he wasn't able to be as creative as when he started out to be. So this is where Perry came in as a relief. If it was not happening with these two brothers, then there was someone else he could get some expression from. Scratch would be able to get things out of Bob in a jovial way, and go into the studio and make it a chemistry: put it on tape and make it work.'

So Scratch and all the Wailers linked up – although, interestingly, the 'Black Power' tune that had been the seed of this working relationship employed the Hippy Boys as musicians, but was self-produced by Bob, as he had always intended; Scratch did not work on the song. Bob persuaded Bunny and Peter that here was another opportunity to make enough money finally to buy that elusive property, with its own studio, they had hoped to fund by working with Leslie Kong: an ordinary, reliable, practical goal. The deal they had discussed with Scratch Perry was about as good as you could get in Jamaica, the profits split 50/50 between the producer and the group – or that was the Wailers' understanding. The Wailers were also aware of Scratch's ability at operating within the music business, with marketing and distribution, and with radio stations; unlike the Rasta Wailers, he had no problem with going to nightclubs to buy disc jockeys drinks and even girls to get his records played.

The recordings made by the Wailers with Scratch resulted in the finest work done by both parties, at any stage of their careers; around ten of these songs were re-recorded – part of the Jamaican musical tradition of the 'do-over' – during the next decade, for release by Bob Marley on the international label Island Records, to which he would sign. 'Though it may never be known who influenced whom,' said Steve Barrow, the English reggae expert known in Jamaica as 'The Professor', 'the recordings they made together constitute a significant turning point for the participants and for Jamaican music.'

To produce these recordings, in the back of his shop, Scratch Perry worked with the three members of the Wailers, rehearsing them, reconstructing them. In particular, he persuaded them to drop their doo-wop harmonising and follow the innate feel of the sound within their own heads, literally to find their own voices.

The songs were all recorded at Randy's, a four-track studio opened in late 1968 above Jamaica's most comprehensive and prestigious record store of the same name, at 17 North Parade, in the downtown square called Victoria Park but more familiarly known simply as 'Parade'. All the Wailers, as well as Scratch, had a good relationship with Vincent 'Randy' Chin, the owner of the store and studio, as well as with his son Clive, who took a production role. They managed to get free studio time from Clive – in the past, they had readily turned up to perform on numerous tracks Chin had been recording, and now they traded in these favours. Their access to this free time was integral to the Wailers being able to cut a deal with Scratch. Clive Chin loved good herb, something that the Wailers always had with them, and they were ever ready to roll him a king-sized spliff of 'goat shit', the finest weed of the era. Partially because its facilities appeared little used, Randy's seemed always available to them. It was not easy to find the studio. Access was obtained by a door just before the entrance into the record store itself. Along a corridor, up a steep, dark set of stairs, were the studio itself and the control room. The only permanent piece of musical equipment in the studio was an upright piano. (Eventually, assisted by his family, Vincent Chin set up VP Records in the United States. VP became the biggest reggae label in America, and in 1999 it was named *Billboard* magazine's number-one reggae label.)

The reconstituted Wailers made pragmatic use of their free time at Randy's, already having learned from working with Leslie Kong of the danger of putting all their eggs in one basket. Accordingly, at Randy's they would record for Scratch one day, employing him to engineer the session, then would use the next day's time, with Clive Chin at the mixing desk, to make a new song for their own label, which they had decided to reinvigorate.

This came about largely through Bob Marley and his close relationship with Allan 'Skill' Cole. Around this time, before Skill left Jamaica to play football for the Brazilian team Sport Recife, he was enlisted as the Wailers' business manager, after a discussion at Wail'n Soul'm/Soul Shack between himself, Bob, Bunny, and Peter. The Wailers were very specific that it was their business – as opposed to their music – he was to look after; and that they would split the profits four ways, one part to each of the Wailers, one part to Skill Cole. Skill's first act was to form a new record label for the Wailers, founding it with $10 of his own money; he gave 33 per cent of the company to Bunny, the same percentage to Peter, and 34 per cent to Bob.

With the splintering apart of the Soulettes, there no longer was any reason to continue using the Wail'n Soul'm tag. Now there was a new name, Tuff Gang, registered by Skill Cole at Companies House in Kingston. When it was pointed out to the three members that Tuff Gang carried the unavoidable tang of 'bad-boy business', it was changed and re-registered to become Tuff Gong, which they all felt carried a far greater symbolic resonance. Later, Bob Marley himself assumed the sobriquet of 'Tuff Gong' or 'Gong', but this was a nickname bestowed upon him retrospectively: the impetus for calling their label Tuff Gong – as implied and built into his myth to an extent – had nothing whatsoever to do with any statement about Bob Marley being some kind of street-fighter. He wasn't.

The first tune that the Wailers recorded with Scratch Perry was 'My Cup', the song that had seduced him into taking on the sessions when Bob had first played it to him. Like 'Black Progress', this also was a reworked James Brown tune, 'I've Got to Cry, Cry, Cry' in this particular case. (Both tunes bearing such influences gave a clear indication of what Bob had been listening to in the United States.) They also recorded a song for their Tuff Gong label: 'Duppy Conqueror', as it was titled, was a big Jamaican hit for the trio, the Wailers proclaiming that if any bad forces came along to test them, they could just mash them down with their spiritual strength and power. A 'bullbucka', the foe in the lyrics of the duppy conqueror, was a person who could literally buck bulls, a feature of every rodeo scene in Western films.

The Wailers could have done with some tough cowboy gunslinger in the studio. After they had recorded 'Duppy Conqueror', Randy's wanted money to release the tape, so convincing a hit did the song sound. This was unprecedented: the Wailers had worked consistently at Randy's without ever having to pay for their tapes to be released. Errol 'ET' Thompson, the engineer on the session, moonlighting from his work with Joe Gibbs, insisted he would hang on to the tape until payment – which the Wailers could not afford – was received. In response to this, Bunny swung a piece of wood at Thompson's ribs: the engineer slipped to one side, and the wood hit the door, breaking in two. A furious Bunny held the jagged edge of one of the pieces to Thompson's throat, explaining how the Wailers were hungry and desperate now, and if the record were a hit, everyone would benefit. Trembling, ET fetched the 'Duppy Conqueror' tape and handed it over.

'Small Axe' and 'Soul Rebel' followed for Scratch. Then Glen Adams came up with the majority of the lyrics for a song called 'Mr Brown', a spooky story that exemplifies the manner in which the whisper of a rumour can whip up into a hurricane force in Jamaica. This tale originated with a story that a John Crow, as vultures are known on the island, that somehow came to be called Mr Brown, had been seen riding through Kingston on a coffin on its way to a cemetery. Then Mr Brown was claimed to have been seen in a courtroom, dressed in a shirt and necktie; it was as though the power of obeah were being physically manifested, and people became afraid to leave their yards at night. The story's developments were even covered in the *Daily Gleaner*. 'Lee Perry had the ears as to what the street people were listening to,' said Rita. 'Any kinky thing happening, he would immediately know: "Mr Brown ride through town in a coffin." He and Bob would get together and laugh about it, and say, "What is this? What is going on there?" And then the two of them get together and *b-a-n-g*: it's a song, it's a hit, what's happening in the street.'

The subject matter of 'Mr Brown' made it an appropriate tale for work with Scratch, whose magical twists and mystical turns were naturally attracted to such fabulous narratives. 'Scratch felt that Bob would carry the message much better, and I didn't dispute it,' said Glen Adams of the song he had set in motion. He would observe lyrics being formed: 'Sometimes Bob and Scratch would sit down in a room and write lyrics after we had done the rhythm tracks. We would never interrupt that type of work going on. It takes total concentration.' The keyboard player thought highly of the way Scratch worked with the musicians: 'He's a good engineer, a very inspiring person. He can sing. He's a very good writer, lyrics and melody. Although he doesn't play an instrument, he can hum a line and tell you how to play.'

The Hammer horror sounds at the beginning of 'Mr Brown' were made by Bunny Livingston. The tune used the same rhythm as on the first cut of 'Duppy Conqueror' – but the Wailers were not satisfied with that version of 'Duppy' and did an adjusted version. In the minds of the trio there was always a connection between 'Duppy Conqueror' and 'Mr Brown'. There were several other songs by other artists about Mr Brown – Prince Buster had one, for example – but the Wailers were in the shops first. 'Mr Brown' sold around two thousand copies in Jamaica, hardly the sales of a big hit: 'Duppy Conqueror' itself had done fifteen thousand.

Although he eventually had a fight in the studio with Scratch, largely absenting himself thereafter, Glen Adams's perception of the Upsetter differed from the attitude of Bunny, who himself twice in the studio knocked down an over-feisty Scratch, condemning him as a 'joker', and that of the equally sceptical Peter. 'He get the job done: that's the important thing,' said Adams of Tosh's work on the sessions, his qualification revealing the criticism. Aware of the tight relationship between Bob and Scratch, and unaware that, without the insistence of Perry, the Wailers would no longer even have existed, both Peter and Bunny exhibited behaviour that certainly could be attributed to jealousy. Lee Perry was dismissed by them, for example, as a 'pure country boy' who didn't have a rebellious bone in his body. They were also nervous of his reputation as an obeahman. 'Peter and Bunny thought Scratch was a madman, and a battyman,' said Rita. 'There was a problem there. This was why Bob and Scratch became more of a team than the other two.'

'Duppy Conqueror', the tune recorded side by side with 'My Cup', was not the first Tuff Gong release. Backed by Lester Sterling's All Stars, Bob and Rita – performing like such vintage American R'n'B male-and-female duos as Shirley and Lee – had already put out a classic emulation of that US style, 'Hold On to This Feeling', shortly before Randy's sessions. A lovely song, 'Hold On to This Feeling' was the first tune that any of the Wailers had recorded after the opening of the Soul Shack record store at 100 Orange Street, near to Scratch's own shop. 'Trouble on the Road' and 'Comma Comma' were also recorded almost at the same time. (As was another more unexpected and arcane cover of a song: the Wailers' version of 'Sugar, Sugar', the international bubblegum smash by the Archies, an American cartoon group whose sound was entirely created by session-players. The idea to cover this song, giving it a reggae beat – which harks back to the Wailers' days at Brentford Road, covering the likes of Tom Jones and the Beatles – came from Vincent Chin at Randy's, and the disc was released only in the United States.)

Quickly needing to follow up 'Duppy Conqueror', the Wailers consciously tried to commercially structure a further hit. Bunny Livingston had been writing a tune called 'Scheme of Things'; the number had an especially affecting bass line and, one day, whilst Bunny was playing it, Bob Marley began to sing over it the lyrics from a song he was writing called 'Trench Town Rock' ('rock' in this case had nothing to do with any musical style, but was a name by which Trench Town was sometimes known – it meant, simply, tough). At the song's instrumental session, Bunny and Family Man conferred over the bass sound until it was precisely what Bunny had first heard in his head – and then Bunny played it, not Family Man. On 'Trench Town Rock', Peter Tosh played keyboards; Roddy Tenn played repeater drum; and, although Bob Marley was supported by a guitarist called Wally Williams on rhythm, it was Bob himself who played lead, introducing a significant, deceptively simple innovation: what Bunny later called his 'check-e, check-e' sound. 'No man's check-e sound like Bob's check-e,' he said. It was a guitar sound and feel that would be copied everywhere in reggae music, but it was Bob Marley who originated it, having assiduously practised the sound before the recording at the upstairs rehearsal studio on the corner of First Street and West Road, using it to drive the song along. (The 'check-e' sound was also used to great effect on the song 'Stir It Up' when later recorded for the *Catch a Fire* album.)

Also present in the studio for the making of 'Trench Town Rock' were Pipe, Bread, Fats, Garth, and Buddy from the Wailing Souls, the excellent Trench Town harmony group. Although only Bunny and Peter were harmonising on the 'Grooving in Kingston 12' lines, the Wailing Souls' fine voices were employed to the fullest to give more strength to the oft-repeated title line. The result was a masterpiece. When the single appeared, there was the added bonus of a U-Roy toast over the tune on the B-side.

(Bunny Wailer would later reprise his bass line, played by the rising star Robbie Shakespeare, to whom he had taught the part, when he included 'Scheme of Things' on his *Protest* album, released in 1977. Scratch, Bunny was prepared to acknowledge, had 'the ear for bass'. Although Lloyd Brevitt, the bass player with the Skatalites, had played the instrument in patterns, almost no other Jamaican bass players had understood his innovation. Now, however, Scratch ensured that Family Man's bass was being emphasised as a pattern, becoming round, full, and often the lead instrument.)

Other singles released on Tuff Gong by the Wailers as they continued working with Scratch in fits and starts for most of 1970 were 'Screwface' and 'Redder Than Red'.

The entire *Soul Rebels* album was 'voiced' in one day; eight of the instrumental tracks had been recorded twenty-four hours previously: 'Rebel's Hop', 'Cornerstone', '400 Years', 'No Water', 'Reaction', 'No Sympathy', 'Soul Almighty', and 'Soul Rebel' – the vocals for 'My Cup' and 'Try Me' had been recorded at a previous session. Also present at the studio that one day was Jimmy Riley, who had sung with the Uniques on the 'Watch This Sound' tune that had so impressed Bob. The vibes felt clean and high, the creative muse beaming down from the Oneness. There were three microphones, one for each of the Wailers, who were experimenting freely with their singing, lifting parts from Temptations and James Brown vocals, dropping in bird sounds or anything that seemed appropriate to give the music an extra notch of appeal. At the end of the day's session, everyone involved felt thrilled at what they had achieved. They believed something magical had taken place, as though Scratch's spirit friends had been aiding and assisting them. Some privileged witnesses felt that the Wailers were clearly the greatest group in the world. The songs were put on the *Soul Rebels* LP in the order they were recorded. It was the Wailers themselves who decided to call the album by this name; it was Scratch who decreed that the second of the two LPs they made should be called *Soul Revolution*.

Soul Revolution was released in Jamaica in 1971, with the track listing of 'Keep on Movin'', 'Don't Rock My Boat', 'Put It On', 'Fussing and Fighting', 'Duppy Conqueror', 'Memphis', 'Riding High', 'Kaya', 'African Herbsman', 'Stand Alone', 'Sun Is Shining', and 'Brain Washing'. So 'Keep On Movin'', the Curtis Mayfield–written Impressions tune that the Wailers had been playing for five years, its lyrics seeming to accord with the Wailers' lifestyle, finally made it into these Scratch sessions. With Bobby Aitken on acoustic guitar added to the Hippy Boys' line-up, the tune had Bob opening up on lead vocals, followed by Peter and then Bunny; Peter also applied a dangerous, affecting falsetto to his performance. 'Kaya', inspired by Bob and Scratch's visit to the producer's mother in Hanover, was a paean to herb, though at no point was there a specific reference to the plant. In fact, the word 'kaya' was not a known code for ganja: kaya was what mattresses were made from in rural Jamaica, fibre in the husks of dried coconuts beaten into a pulp.

Scratch loved this song, insisting they had to record it. On the record, Bob, Peter, and Bunny whisper 'wake up' over the song's introduction, highlighted by the echo added to it by Scratch. The entire song has had a trippy smidgin of echo delay added to the vocals, so that Bob's voice literally feels as if he is so high that he can almost touch that sky above the falling rain – reminding us, of course, that the imminent rainfall on that day in Hanover was what added urgency to his and Scratch's request for more herb.

On the recording of 'Kaya', Bobby Aitken played acoustic guitar, whilst Uziah 'Sticky' Thompson was on percussion. Alva 'Reggie' Lewis played electric guitar; unfortunately, within this ensemble, he was beginning to fall by the wayside, as a result of the innovations wrought by Bob Marley on the recording of 'Trench Town Rock', and also by the distinctive style increasingly rendered by Peter Tosh. 'Reggie' Lewis, who was fond of partying and chasing girls, would not respond well to the constant refrain from Bob Marley throughout these sessions at Randy's: *'Not good enough!'* From this point on, Bob Marley and Peter Tosh played all the guitar on the Wailers' Jamaican recordings, no longer bringing in hired guns.

'Don't Rock My Boat' had been written and released even before Bunny went to prison; there has often been contention about this partic-ular version, some claiming it was not a Scratch production at all but one that the Wailers had recorded and produced themselves at Randy's, Scratch appropriating it behind their backs. On the bluesy 'Riding High', Bunny wrote and sang lead vocals, sometimes in falsetto, with Peter singing sliding, high harmony. Peter was also on piano, with Glen Adams on B3 Hammond organ. 'Riding High' was like a return to the subject matter of Wailers' songs five years previously, Bunny complaining about how a girl doesn't treat him right when he greets her. Bunny also took lead vocals on his 'Brain Washing' song, an excoriation of various social iniquities. Although he distinguished himself with his melodica playing on the 'Memphis' instrumental, Peter has no lead vocals whatsoever on any song on this record.

There was one song on the album, 'Stand Alone', that unequivocally explained why Bob was now happy to spend nights at Scratch's home, and why he would equally vanish away to Danny Sims's Russell Heights house. On 'Stand Alone', Bob is pleading with Rita to behave herself – though his own behaviour with other women frequently left question marks over his right to accuse his spouse. The lyrics are precisely to the point: 'Days I wasted with you, child.' 'Stand Alone' had no guitar parts on it, but Peter on melodica and piano, and a new addition to the musicians, Tyrone Downie, on organ.

There were plenty of tunes recorded that did not end up on any of the albums. Bob's semi-rude song 'Guava Jelly', recorded at the same session as 'Trench Town Rock', was one. Again, Bob's yowling guitar-playing on the track is unmistakably his. Bunny again played bass, as he was the only musician who understood the complicated bass lines he'd written. (Bunny fulfilled the same task on the 'Midnight Ravers' tune when they came to record *Catch a Fire*.) Also playing on 'Guava Jelly' was Seeco, their percussionist friend who had taken the Wailers up to Studio One for their first audition.

When it came to the marketing of the first album, *Soul Rebels*, the Wailers were shocked and angry at the scantily clad girl Scratch had picked to appear on the front-cover artwork. On the rear of the sleeve, however, the three Wailers are pictured wearing stylish dashikis; they were made by Bunny's then girlfriend, Sister Jean, who at that period made most of the clothes worn by the trio. Bunny also had another girlfriend, Marlene, a 15-year-old cousin of Rita's who lived at her house. Jean was also only 15, though Bunny, oddly, would sometimes refer to her as his 'mother'.

Having been burnt once, they took control for the *Soul Revolution* sleeve. Glen Adams took the cover shot of the Wailers brandishing guns – which were actually water-pistols that belonged to Scratch's kids.

Eventually, after several inspirational sessions, enough material had been recorded for two albums. It was psychedelic reggae, and the inspirational influence of Jimi Hendrix and Sly Stone, two artists whom Bob had been listening to over and over again, was only too evident. As well as the two LPs, numerous singles emerged from these sessions. This time in the studio with the extrovert Scratch Perry had been of immense significance for the more introverted Bob Marley. The two of them had put the Wailers back on a creative course that was at the cutting edge of reggae. The rhythm section that would become part of the future Wailers had been unearthed; Family Man would prove an invaluable in-house arranger and second lieutenant; and in Lee 'Scratch' Perry, Bob Marley had found a foil with whom he would work in one way or another for almost the rest of his career. Although there was often an indefinable tension to their relationship, Bob respected Scratch as a musical genius; he was awed by the street suss through which this non-musician heard musical possibilities that would escape a trained player. Scratch even demonstrated his flair as a natural shuckster in the street-level PR he performed for the group: to explain away the erratic course taken by Bob's career in recent years and the time he had spent in the States and in Nine Miles, Scratch came up with the story, which was printed in *Swing*, the monthly Jamaican music magazine, that, after years in prison, Bob was back and on top.

Suddenly, at the end of the recording sessions with Lee Perry, there was more activity. In the spring of 1971, Danny Sims asked Bob if he would fly to Stockholm. Johnny Nash was in the Swedish capital, where he was starring with an actress called Christina Schollin in a film being made there, called *Vill så Gärna Tro*, known also as *Love Is Not a Game* or *Want So Much to Believe*. Could Bob write some songs for the sound-track?

Creatively, the trip was productive – although the movie flopped in Sweden and never opened anywhere else. Tucked away in a house in the outer Stockholm suburbs, Bob had a bedroom in which to write; sequestered away in it, he improved his focus with the ganja that had been obtained for him, working on new material, emerging to boil up fish-head soup in the kitchen – somewhat to the puzzlement of the Swedish girls who found their way to the residence, and invariably into his bed. Bob appeared briefly in a party scene in the film; and made a detour to a Stockholm studio to record the songs for the movie's sound-track. He provided Johnny Nash with a mixture of old and new mate-rial: 'Stir It Up', which he had written initially for Rita during his first absence in the United States; 'Cornerstone', which had already been recorded with Scratch Perry; and 'This Train', which dated back to the Wailers' days with Studio One. But there was also the sexy 'Guava Jelly', which Johnny Nash, Barbra Streisand, and the great Jamaican singer Owen Gray would all record; and 'Comma Comma', 'Dewdrops', and 'I'm Hurting Inside', another Bob Marley song detailing his internal pain.

The scenario in which he was living inspired this feeling. By a curious twist of fate, there was a close family witness to the torment Bob was undergoing in the supposedly liberated paradise of Sweden. Leroy Anderson, Rita's father, was a saxophone player who had left Jamaica in 1959, playing in Britain with a number of calypso groups; then a tour of Scandinavia concluded with Leroy settling in Stockholm with a Finnish girlfriend who bore him two daughters.

In between musical engagements, Leroy would drive the streets of Stockholm in his Mercedes taxi. On one of those Swedish summer nights of almost perpetual daylight, he met an old drummer friend. There's a guy in town called Bob Marley, he told Leroy. Leroy had never met his daughter Rita's husband, but he certainly knew of their marriage. The drummer had an address where he believed Bob was living.

Leroy found Bob living in a villa a little way out of the city. The others with him – Danny Sims, Johnny Nash, and a fellow Texan who played keyboards called Rabbit Bundrick – seemed to be living the high life in this rented accommodation.

Rabbit, who had never previously heard reggae music, was extremely impressed by the demeanour of Bob Marley: 'He wasn't afraid of anything or anybody, at least that was the image he projected. I loved the way he stood up for himself, no matter what. He was right, and everybody else was wrong. What confidence that guy had. Bob was down to earth, took no shit from anyone, and always stood his ground. For a small guy, he was as solid as a brick wall, not in his physical strength so much, but in his mind. He wouldn't budge, or take no for an answer, if he knew he was right. Like he said, "Stand up for your rights."'

(Rabbit would soon work again with Bob Marley. When that occurred, he was surprised to encounter Bunny Livingston and Peter Tosh: 'In all the time I lived with and worked with Bob, he never mentioned those two guys to me, not once.')

Down in his basement room, Bob Marley – when he wasn't trying to hit on Marlene, Rabbit's Swedish wife – had found himself in a state worse than misery. Somehow he had become mentally 'spooked', as Leroy noted; now his daughter's husband was having hallucinations, and seemed to be under great internal stress.

Bob was relieved to see his father-in-law, not the least because he got to eat some authentic Jamaican cooking, which brought a break from the chintzy smorgasbords Bob was offered everywhere in Sweden. It came as little surprise to Leroy when he later learned that Bob had simply upped stakes and left Sweden.

The strain Leroy had observed in Bob may well have been induced by sudden financial difficulties within the household in Sweden. In the way of many movie productions, the project had run out of cash; the wages of everyone involved had been cancelled. According to Rabbit Bundrick, Danny Sims resolved to save the situation by contacting Stockholm's top poker player and setting him up in a card game at their house; to give them an edge, he had imported a somewhat tricky individual from the United States, who, he guaranteed, would win all the hands, securing their money, and then some. Inevitably, the plan went awry, a gun allegedly even being pulled at one point. Unlike the terrified expressions that fell on the faces of the other parties, Bob's response at this critical juncture was merely to smile.

Bob Marley's solution to this financial disaster was to head for Stockholm's airport, transporting with him Johnny Nash's rented guitar and tape-recorder, which he considered to be some recompense for his missing payments.

There were, however, about to be more difficulties over cash. Whilst Bob Marley was in Sweden, Bunny Livingston and Peter Tosh had continued their association with Lee Perry. It was during this time that Peter Tosh recorded a pair of songs that would forever be associated with him: 'Downpressor', derived from 'Sinner Man', a spiritual that the Wailers had recorded at Studio One; and the poignant 'Brand New Second Hand', a tale of rejected love.

Unlike Scratch, however, the Wailers hadn't even got started in terms of exporting their records, although others had done it for them. They had had their records pirated by a local record-store owner. At first he only bought their records and sold them overseas, but then he started having stampers made from the records with which to press up further, illegal, copies to sell in 'fareign'. The Wailers were aware that, through their ignorance, they had lost much money.

What they didn't at first know was that Lee 'Scratch' Perry had sold the pair of albums, *Soul Rebels* and *Soul Revolution*, overseas, to Trojan in London, receiving an £18,000 advance for the twenty-six Wailers tracks. When they learned of this, the trio knew they had to ask him for some of the money they would be due under the terms of their 50/50 deal, even though they knew that it had never been formally acknowledged or put down on paper.

Each Friday night, the Wailers would go to the fashionable Sombrero Club, the hottest nightspot in town, on Molynes Road; they would listen to whichever upcoming band was onstage, be it the Fab Five, the Now

Generation, Inner Circle, Carlos Malcolm, or even Byron Lee. Other times, there might be a Derek Harriott promotion taking place with the Chosen Few and Scotty and Flames.

As much as anything, the Wailers would be at the Sombrero because they were celebrating their success. Each Friday night at 7:30, the hit-parade show came on the radio. As the Wailers were now selling records, the radio stations were playing them. They were also playing stage shows – but still they had no money.

So, one night when the Sombrero was full of Wailers supporters, rebel types such as Claudie Massop, Bob asked Scratch about their money. 'What money yuh talking 'bout?' demanded Scratch.

'The money for the record sales.'

'But how yuh see we a go do this money thing here and now?'

Bob reminded him of the 50/50 agreement he was convinced they had made. But Scratch said that this agreement had never existed and that he would only pay a royalty.

Bob and Bunny couldn't believe what they were hearing. Bob looked physically and mentally numbed. In a tremulous voice, he asked how much the royalty was. 'Ten cents a record,' said Scratch. When Bunny interjected, Scratch snapped, 'I wasn't talking to you – only to Bob.'

So Bunny attacked him, and started hitting him, mashing up the place and causing chairs and tables to go flying. The wreckage was so great that Bunny pulled himself back. Bob seemed to be in a state of shock. They also realised Scratch had been drinking, and thought maybe it was the liquor talking. And maybe it was telling the truth.

A few days later, when all three Wailers went to see him at his office at the back of Charles Street, Scratch now had a bodyguard with him. Bunny asked him for some money, but Scratch said he was trying to behave as he had at the Sombrero. Again, Bunny attacked him, and when the bodyguard came over, Bunny eased out his ratchet-knife and held it on him. The others in the room held Bunny back.

Scratch said he would work out how many records had been sold. A few days later, they had a formal meeting at the Charles Street office, with supposedly all the relevant receipts piled on the table. Scratch had asked Pauline Morrison, the Trench Town girl who had become his long-standing girlfriend, to fetch a bottle of yellow liquid from his car. When she brought it up, he put it in the middle of his desk, amidst the paperwork.

As Mr Touch, who had to touch everything, picked it up, Scratch straightaway commanded him to put it down. Peter attempted to remove the bottle's cork. But Scratch shouted at him not to do so. Later, Bunny Livingston was convinced that the bottle had contained acid, with which the producer had been prepared to attack them. But Scratch Perry laughed at this idea: 'That was just his suspicion, there was no acid there, that came out of his thoughts. They always think me have something to do them something, but it was only in their thoughts because they know I wasn't chicken.'

The meeting broke up inconclusively.

Perhaps the Wailers should not have been surprised to experience such difficulties with Lee 'Scratch' Perry over the vexed issue of money. Bunny 'Striker' Lee remembered an earlier incident: 'Bob and Peter and Bunny beat up Scratch one day. When John Holt's tune "Stick By Me" reached number one, they did have "Duppy Conqueror" out. And they ran into John down by Duke Reid, and him did tell them he could buy a good car from "Stick By Me". Him ask Bob what kind of car them car is. And same time Scratch drive in and them jump upon Scratch. They mash up Scratch bad. 'E end up in the hospital. John teased them, "Hey, only a Rastaman dare sing about duppy."'

Later that year, the Wailers recorded a further version of 'Mr Talkative', which they renamed 'Mr Chatterbox', for Bunny Lee. 'Niney did have out him record "Blood and Fire" which was selling well,' said the producer. 'Then Niney was saying that Bob and myself did break into him place and is stealing him records and is selling it. And Bob punch him. But is just Niney, because Niney and Rita and Bob is good friends. So we make the tune. We just go around to Randy's and rig up the tune quickly. Because it is one of them old-time tunes him did sing for Coxsone called "Mr Talkative". But we change it: at the front of the record it has Bob and myself talking, like we is talking about a session. And Bob seh: "See: the singer come." "'Oo? Niney? Well, a Mr Talkative dat. Bwai gone." And Bob gone.'

Did it sell?

'Yes, it did alright.'

THE ROD OF CORRECTION

As the 1960s progressed, Jamaican politics began to display elements that were almost anarchic. It also started to demonstrate an unhealthy symbiosis with the local music business. Political parties began to co-opt the gangs who served as protection for sound systems. In 1966, Edward Seaga, who had set up his West Indies Record Label before becoming a Jamaica Labour Party politician, employed the crew associated with Duke Reid; he was the first politician to do this. Michael Manley, the son of Norman Manley, and Seaga's People's National Party rival, soon linked up with the rude boys who performed a similar function for Coxsone Dodd. By the middle of the

1960s, guns were beginning to be smuggled into Jamaica, at first – so ran the legend – in children's teddy-bears.

The political tension on the island heightened after Walter Rodney, the Guyanese university professor and advocate of Black Power, was banned from Jamaica in October 1968. Across the island, the manner in which Hugh Shearer had suppressed the ensuing riots created great bitterness. From then on, political violence in Jamaica escalated until it reached devastating consequences in the murderous election of 1980.

Following the Rodney incident, the JLP became increasingly unpopular. Polls suggested that, at the next election, Hugh Shearer would be ousted from office by Michael Manley's PNP. Yet the PNP still needed to show a truly populist side; accordingly, Manley's media-savvy wife, Beverley, posited a concept that could show clearly how forward-thinking the PNP had become. The project was to be called the PNP Victory Bandwagon of Stars; it was essentially a package tour of top acts, whose performances around Jamaica would commence after a suitably tubthumping, rabble-rousing speech from the gifted orator into whom Michael Manley had developed.

Thanks to the zeal of Skill Cole, the Wailers had played several shows that summer in Jamaica, with the Barrett brothers as a permanent rhythm section: Family Man and Carly, smelling the wind, had moved away from Scratch Perry, which led to the break-up of the Upsetters, infuriating the producer. On 18 July, they played the Miss Jamaica 1971 Water Pageant Festival at the National Stadium swimming pool in Kingston, with Hopeton Lewis and Judy Mowatt; and later that month at the Red Stripe Award concert. In August there were a pair of concerts, one at Ferry Inn with the Fabulous Five and a re-formed Soulettes; and at the Sombrero Club for the Miss Chariot contest on the last day of the month.

The PNP Bandwagon shows, however, were truly big events. In charge of the evenings, working for no payment, was Clancy Eccles, who had helped promote the Christmas-morning shows the Wailers had performed in 1964 and 1965. Part promoter, part record-producer, part solo star, Eccles was a militant socialist who allied himself to Michael Manley's firebrand political style. During the 1970s, he had hits with songs celebrating the PNP, including 'Rod of Correction', 'Power for the People', and 'Generation Belly'. Manley, said Eccles, had requested he become involved in the project following a show he had performed in Kingston at the Ward Theatre entitled 'The Rod of Correction': during it, Manley had come onstage, presenting him with a wooden staff. It was as a consequence of this, claimed Eccles, that Michael Manley had reinvented himself, giving himself the name Joshua, as if he were a biblical figure treading through the wilderness brandishing a 'rod of correction' in chastisement of unbelievers. He began to dress in a bush jacket of the type favoured by Third World revolutionaries; it was an effective image that fitted his brand of left-wing politics.

Performing in their own right on the PNP Bandwagon shows and as backing band for the other artists was Inner Circle, a group of uptown musicians formed by Ian and Roger Lewis, who would come into their own right internationally by the end of the 1970s. This Inner Circle line-up included the keyboards player Ibo Cooper and the guitarist Stephen 'Cat' Core, who would later depart to form Third World, another Jamaican group who enjoyed a measure of international success. 'The Bandwagon,' said Roger Lewis, 'was really the beginning of a melting pot, a fusion of the earlier music and the new music, as well as a bridging of the Jamaican society and Rasta. The climate and the music were so free. The musicians weren't politically connected. It was not as though we were using the music to politically mastermind the people. It was just fun to be playing music, we never even thought about politics.'

The PNP Bandwagon played half a dozen shows around the island, in Port Antonio in the north-east; in Falmouth on the north coast; in

Morant Bay in the south-east; in Browns Town, on the way to Nine Miles; in Spanish Town, near Kingston; and in Port Maria, again on the north coast. The caravan was filmed by a local director, Perry Henzell, who also made television and cinema advertisements for the PNP. The artists' positions on the bill rotated. However, the Wailers had a certain prominence, thanks to the PNP's choice of their song 'Bad Card' as a campaign song – notwithstanding that the JLP was using the Wailers' 'Crucial' in its campaign. The Wailers played all the shows – among the tunes performed were 'Duppy Conqueror', 'Small Axe', 'Trench Town Rock', and 'Keep On Movin''. Other artists involved included Clancy Eccles (inevitably), Junior Byles, Marcia Griffiths, Brent Dowe of the Melodians, Max Romeo, and Ken Boothe. According to Bunny Livingston, the Wailers – non-believers in 'politricks', he insisted – played the PNP Bandwagon only because they were paid $150 a show: but also because Michael Manley had suggested he would 'free up herb', legalising ganja. The three musicians felt almost immediately let down by the incoming prime minister when he didn't follow through on this.

In Spanish Town, the island's original capital, eight miles from Kingston, the PNP Bandwagon played at Prison Oval, one of Jamaica's largest stadiums, on a playing field used for cricket, football, and stage shows. The dub poet Malachi Smith remembered that, at the show, Bob Marley was 'red', a local term for 'stoned', from consuming too much herb: 'Bunny and Peter hugged him every time he tried to skank away, and it appeared as if he would lose his balance and fall. It was a great concert, with the likes of Judy Mowatt, Heptones, Meditations, Derrick Harriott, Clancy Eccles, Max Romeo, and others. I think Bob and Peter Tosh definitely shared Manley's vision. Bob was very concerned about sufferation and oppression of the poor in the society, in Africa, and throughout the Third World. His music and interviews speak volumes about this.'

The Bandwagon event played at the University of the West Indies student union on 7, 8, and 9 October 1971. (There was an issue connected with those shows that can be seen as possessing lesser or greater significance, depending upon your point of view: for the first time the posters billed the act as 'Bob Marley and the Wailers', not as 'The Wailers'.) The Bandwagon returned to the same venue on 13 October and then again on 1 November for 'A Night of Togetherness', on which, it seems, Inner Circle did not appear. The *Daily Gleaner* – not known for its support of the PNP – reported that the show had 'the largest attendance of any of the promotions in the city on that night. This was expected with the team of promoters headed by footballer Allan 'Skill' Cole.'

The *Gleaner* also reported another positive development for the Wailers: that they were about to embark on their first US tour. It announced that they ('currently on the local charts with the popular "Screwface"') would be making live appearances in the New York area, playing with the Soulettes, who with a different line-up had been in the USA since August. If that was the case, then the Soulettes must have needed to return to Jamaica in mid-December for, according to Rita Marley, both groups then played a gig in Cuba.

Although the American shows were played to almost exclusively Jamaican audiences, they all the same marked the first attempt by the Wailers to make some kind of breakthrough in the US. The very first concert took place on 31 December 1971, a New Year's Eve show at the Concourse Plaza Hotel in the Bronx before a three-thousand-strong audience, backed by the Debonaires band. On the same bill was John Holt, Jamaica's leading vocalist, whose 'Stick By Me' had so upset the applecart with Scratch, Syd Joe and his Caribbean All Stars, and the Cinnamon Suns. On 7 January 1972, the Wailers played at the President Chateau, at 71 84th Street in Brooklyn. Glen Adams, who had moved up to New York following the demise of the Upsetters, went along to the event. Although the Debonaires were backing the Wailers, the organist was not playing as Bob Marley required. In the audience, he noticed Glen: 'Bob gave me a look to come up. We started playing "Soul Rebel".' When local Jamaican rude boys rowdily began exercising their muscle, however, the show was stopped by local police. 'It was very scary,' said Glen Adams. The next day they performed at the Manhattan Center, again with Glen Adams. Dates followed in Pennsylvania and Delaware, Bob's home from home.

Whilst they were in America, the Wailers' record shop on Beeston Street was broken into twice. The second time this happened the police caught the culprit, who confessed he had been sent by Coxsone to mash it up and take the turntable. When they returned to Jamaica, the Wailers continued to play PNP Bandwagon dates, including a show at the National Arena on 30 January. In retrospect, this particular performance carried considerable symbolic weight: on 5 February Parliament was dissolved and a general election was declared, scheduled for 29 February 1972.

At a meeting between the two Barrett brothers and Bob and Bunny at the Wailers' record shop, an agreement had been struck that, from now on, they would work together as a recording and live unit. As soon as that occurred, however, in the middle of February 1972, Bob left the island for London. Danny Sims had suggested he fly to the UK – he had a potential recording deal for Bob Marley with CBS Records' Epic label, to which Johnny Nash was now signed. One of the A&R men involved was Mike Smith, who had turned down the Beatles for Decca Records, redeeming himself by then signing the Rolling Stones to that label. Unity MacLean, a secretary in the A&R department whose husband took up a marketing post with Danny Sims, recalled visits to the office by the Jamaican: 'Bob used to sit around the office, and everyone was extremely rude to him. I liked him, although he did speak with an awfully weird patois.'

With Danny Sims footing the bill, Bob Marley moved, with his manager, Johnny Nash, and Rabbit Bundrick, into a flat at 34 Ridgmount Gardens. Bang in the centre of London, Bob Marley's first London address was a short distance from Goodge Street tube station on Tottenham Court Road. Later, they moved to Chelsea, to Old Church Street, off the then extremely fashionable King's Road. At the end of March, Bob found himself in the new state-of-the-art CBS studios off Soho Square, playing on Johnny Nash's *I Can See Clearly Now* album, which included Nash's version of Bob's 'Stir It Up', which the Wailers had first recorded in 1967, as well as 'Comma Comma', 'Guava Jelly', and 'You Poured Sugar on Me', a ballad which Bob Marley and Johnny Nash had written together. Among the musicians on the record were members of what soon became the Average White Band, a largely Scottish white-soul group then building a strong reputation who coped more than adequately with what was essentially a reggae record. Tucked away during the sessions, using the same musicians, Bob Marley also found time to record half a dozen of his own songs, including his one and only record release for CBS, 'Reggae on Broadway', which he had written – Nash's version of the song was included on later editions of the *I Can See Clearly Now* album.

'Stir It Up' was released in April 1972 in the UK and became Nash's first hit in three years, as well as Bob Marley's first international success. The record made the number thirteen slot in the UK, and twelve in the US, where it was released the following year. The album's title track, 'I Can See Clearly Now', was the follow-up to 'Stir It Up' in the UK, and a much bigger hit, number five in the UK and a number one in the States when it was released that November. 'There Are More Questions than Answers', the single released after that, was Nash's third UK hit of 1972, reaching number nine in the charts.

Handling public relations for Johnny Nash and introducing him to journalists was Paul Merry, who stressed how influential Nash was in helping to bring Bob Marley to the attention of the world: 'Johnny Nash took Bob Marley everywhere with him in London during the spring of 1972. He introduced Bob to rock journalists, radio DJs, fellow artists, and so on. Johnny really pushed Bob's barrow and has never had the recognition he deserves for this. If any one individual introduced Bob Marley to the world, it was Johnny Nash. Johnny brought him to England from Jamaica to promote Bob's career. Johnny Nash was an extremely nice man who championed Bob Marley's career unreservedly, with nothing in it for him.' As to the Afro-haired Bob Marley, Paul Merry could not help but feel that he and Johnny Nash were similar souls: 'I remember him as a quiet and polite guy, always well dressed. The dreadlocks would come later.'

When the A&R man Mike Smith turned down the Beatles, he had instead signed Brian Poole and the Tremeloes, from Dagenham in Essex. After Poole left the group, the Tremeloes had over a dozen worldwide hits for CBS Records with what came to be considered by 'serious' fans of 'underground' rock as 'bubblegum' pop. In 1970, however, the Tremeloes dismissed their fans as 'morons' and declared that henceforth they would only make 'intelligent' records. Understandably, their career nosedived – which only adds to the surreal vision of the 'Trems' sharing a railway compartment with Bob Marley, Johnny Nash, Danny Sims, and Paul Merry on 30 April 1972 on the final commemorative journey of the *Brighton Belle*, the luxury train that had ridden the sixty miles of track between London and the Sussex seaside town since 1933. 'Later that evening,' said Merry, 'a group of us, including Bob Marley, went as Danny Sims's guests to Mr B's, a club in Brixton, South London. We watched a reggae band perform, and it could well have been Bob Marley and the Wailers band, because I certainly saw him perform at Mr B's in the first half of 1972.'

The date of the *Brighton Belle*'s final journey and the possible memory of a Wailers performance was significant. Two days previously, Bob

Marley had moved into an address at 12a Queensborough Terrace, London W2, a property close to Kensington Gardens owned by Danny Sims; the accommodation was in the bustling section of Queensway, not far from the West Indian communities of Notting Hill and Shepherd's Bush. Here Bob had been joined by his musical allies from Back-a-Wall.

In Jamaica, in Bob Marley's absence, Family Man Barrett had been hired to form a new group to play at the Green Miss, a club that was opening on the edge of Vineyard Town in east Kingston. The group was called the Youth Professionals and featured Carl Dawkins on vocals, Tinleg the drummer, and a young pianist, still a schoolboy, whom Family Man had heard of called Tyrone Downie, who was a former lead singer with the Kingston College Chapel Choir. ('I got him into some session first, on the piano. Him did have a nice touch. So I show him a few tricks too,' said Family Man.) When Family Man was offered a better-paying job, however, he turned over the bass-playing position in the Youth Professionals to another up-and-coming young guy, Robbie Shakespeare.

The gig Family Man Barrett had opted for instead was in the house band of a Norwegian liner that ran between Miami, Jamaica, and Haiti; by the poolside, Family Man would play soca, meanwhile counting the cash he was saving. Every week the ship would dock in Ocho Rios, and the bass player would urgently attempt to contact his brother. 'Bob come yet?' he would demand of Carly. For almost three months, the reply came in the negative.

Then there was an unexpected twist. Danny Sims, Carlton Barrett told his brother, was arranging for plane tickets to carry Peter and Bunny and the Barretts up to London. The idea was that they would play support dates to Johnny Nash, on a UK tour.

*   *   *

In London, the Wailers were rehearsing diligently. Rondor, the music publisher associated with A&M Records to which Bob Marley would shortly assign his song-publishing rights, was based in Kilburn in north-west London. In the Rondor building were three rehearsal rooms. Whilst Johnny Nash rehearsed in one of these, with his group the Sons of the Jungle, the Wailers occupied another of the spaces. As well as Bob, Bunny, Peter, and Family Man and Carly Barrett, the line-up was aug-mented by three members of the Cimarons, the UK's first self-contained indigenous reggae band: Locksley 'Gishi' Gichie was on guitar, Carl Levy played organ and piano, and the Cimarons' drummer doubled up next to Carly.

When Johnny Nash's live dates began, the assorted Wailers musicians would travel with him on the tour bus, to study the show. At these concerts, Bob Marley would briefly perform as an opening act. Backed by Johnny's group, the Sons of the Jungle, which included the keyboards player Rabbit Bundrick and Alva 'Reggie' Lewis on guitar, he would sing a pair of songs, 'Reggae on Broadway', which had now been released as a single by Epic, and 'Oh Lord I'm Gonna Get You'. (In Jamaica it was released on the CoolSoul label.) It was a rocking tune whose funk drive could have come from the Temptations, a style that would be fully mani-fested five years later on the *Exodus* title track, and the lyrics of 'Reggae on Broadway' were hardly in the tone of Rastafari, in which the three Wailers' front-men now regularly proselytised: 'I'm gonna give you some love now . . . I go down, down, down, down, down . . . ehh, hmm . . . ! Give it to me, babe . . . Good God! Reggae is on Broadway . . .'

At the California Ballroom in the market-town of Dunstable in Bedfordshire, thirty miles north of London, Johnny Nash headlined on 3 June 1972, with Bob Marley briefly supporting him, in precisely this manner. Although Bob was not formally listed on the bill, Johnny Nash inquired of the DJ if his friend could sing a couple of numbers. It was the same routine at Shades club in Northampton on 25 June, Bob again singing the two sides of his current single, backed by the Sons of the Jungle. Northampton was only a short distance farther north up the M1 motorway from Dunstable, and the touring party was easily back in London by just after midnight. At the Speakeasy, a music-business night-club in Margaret Street, behind Oxford Circus, Bob Marley had been booked in for a show of his own, a promotion specifically set up to publicise 'Reggae on Broadway'. Again, Bob performed backed by the Sons of the Jungle. 'It was great fun,' said Rabbit Bundrick. 'It was like a family going out on the town together, to do a gig, have some fun, chase some women, get high, drunk, and so on. Just a night out. The gig went great. It was hot and sweaty, and the audience had a great time, judging by their applause.' On 22 July there was a similar gig, the Grand Midnight Dance at the Commonwealth Social Club in Croydon in south London, very much a Jamaican event. In addition, Bob Marley and Peter Tosh played a show at Alperton School in Wembley, in north-west London; the show was a benefit to raise funds for a new swimming-pool, and plenty of the older schoolgirls showed how happy they would be to jump in the water with the two Jamaicans. Bob also played guitar with the Sons of the Jungle when Johnny Nash himself played dates in assorted English secondary schools.

Meanwhile, Queensborough Terrace was practically an open house, especially where girls were concerned; and when a woman acquainted with Michael X arrived on the doorstep, matters took a further, unexpected twist. Until February 1971, when he had fled to his native Trinidad to evade extortion charges, Michael de Freitas, more commonly known as Michael X, had been a leading Black Power figure in London, a pet cause of the Beatle John Lennon. Bob entered into a Black Power reasoning with Michael X's friend and, inevitably, this led to them ending up in bed. When Bunny and Peter arrived from Jamaica they had brought with them $3,000 of the Wailers' money to cover expected expenses – a considerable amount of money, then; enough to buy, for example, two brand-new Volkswagen Beetles – but when Bob woke from his post-sex sleep, the money had vanished from its hiding-place in his room.

After the woman was sufficiently threatened, the money was returned, but Bunny and Peter were furious with Bob Marley over this incident: from then on, Bunny cared for the stash of cash. Moreover, all the Wailers agreed that the 'pure girls-girls-girls' atmosphere at 12a Queensborough Terrace was becoming less and less conducive to creative work; on 8 June they moved out. Danny Sims initially shifted the musicians into a nearby hotel, but then found them a house in which to live together in the blank suburban wasteland of Neasden, another area with a large West Indian population, close to the North Circular Road and where Bunny's mother worked in a toy factory.

Under the auspice of Danny Sims's Cayman Music, the entire Wailers ensemble then went into the CBS studio and recorded five tunes: 'Concrete Jungle', 'Stir It Up', 'Midnight Ravers', '400 Years', and 'Slave Driver', with its memorable 'Catch a fire' chorus-line.

Throughout this period, the entire Wailers ensemble played only one stage show, a cause of some simmering discontent amongst the rigor-ously rehearsed musicians during this sojourn in London. In either Bexhill on the east Sussex coast, or Bexleyheath, in the south-east London suburbs, the group supported Johnny Nash, who was touring under the tagline 'The King of Reggae', and the Sons of the Jungle. The collective appearance of the Wailers, personified by Peter Tosh's red, gold, and green militant style, replete with the leather Black Power fist he wore around his neck, caused a measure of consternation: when they walked into a restau-rant in which they hoped to eat a pre-show meal, locals walked out.

Before around five hundred people, including a sizable faction of reggae-loving white skinheads, the Wailers came on stage with towels wrapped round their heads in the colours of the Ethiopian flag. Bob, at centre stage, was wearing flared blue jeans; Carly drummed sporting a khaki army cap.

The crowd was already hot, as the Wailers were following a group that blended African and Latin rhythms and had brought the house down. When the Wailers kicked off their first number, 'Ringo', the old Skatalites tune, they discovered something that seemed suspiciously like sabotage: someone had de-tuned the bass and guitars. Bunny, on percussion, and Carly held the rhythm while the others tuned up. But Bob discovered that the strap on his guitar had been swapped for one that would not stay on. He had to put his guitar to one side, performing only as a vocalist. But, as their weeks of rehearsals were demonstrated in a super-tight set – consisting of 'Small Axe', 'Duppy Conqueror', 'Put It On', 'Rude Boy', 'Nice Time', 'Bend Down Low', 'Keep On Movin'', and 'Stir It Up' – the audience responded in a curious way: as though this were a giant office-party, or – more likely – an afternoon at the Notting Hill carnival, and a large segment of the crowd coiled around the venue in a seemingly ceaseless conga dance.

This party atmosphere turned momentarily ugly, however, when the Wailers left the stage and the audience, screaming for more songs, started to smash up chairs and tables. Even without such demonstrative behaviour, an encore was inevitable: 'Reggae on Broadway' had not yet been performed. The Wailers returned, playing Bob's single release, following it up with a pair of songs from their Studio One past, 'One Love' and 'Love and Affection'.

There were those who insisted that this success by the Wailers visibly dispirited Johnny Nash, 'the King of Reggae', who was watching from the wings, resplendent in his stack-heeled, patchwork-leather boots.

Back in Neasden, a serious problem soon occurred, one that could have had severely negative effects on the group's future in the United

Kingdom: the Wailers were all arrested, on suspicion of smuggling ganja.

Using the group's Neasden address, Jah Lloyd, a friend of Bob's from Trench Town, had sent his brother Archie in London a large quantity of herb, wrapped up in a bundle of *Daily Gleaners*. As soon as the weed arrived in London, it was detected by Customs. The next thing the Wailers knew was that their front door was being broken down in the early hours of the morning and all of them were being taken to the local police station and locked up in the cells. Although the house was only being used as an accommodation address for the weed, things looked extremely bad for the group members. Even if imprisonment was not the consequence, deportation looked almost certain – and it would have been nigh on impossible to get re-admission to Britain. In the end, however, an acquaintance of Bunny Lee's took the rap. According to Bunny Lee, it was Island Records which, hearing of the Wailers' plight – and in the absence of Danny Sims, who had flown to the United States with Johnny Nash – arranged for their bail.

Then matters took a further, surprising, negative twist. Before Danny Sims went to America, he had left instructions for the Wailers to add harmony vocals on Johnny Nash's as yet uncompleted *I Can See Clearly Now*. As they were about to go back into the CBS studio, the Jamaicans realised that, after the manager had taken their passports on arrival in the UK, the documents had not been returned to them. Danny Sims had supposedly delivered them to the Home Office, in order to secure work permits for the various musicians. Concerned, especially after Bob had recounted the problems over finances he had endured in Sweden, the Wailers contacted Sims's office, threatening not to do the harmony work on Nash's album until their passports were returned to them. Danny Sims was obliged to fly back to London from New York in order to return the travel documents.

This was the final straw. Bob was tired of the stop-start nature of his career: Sweden had been miserable; the support tour with Johnny Nash had failed to materialise (Bob backing Nash as he played dates in English secondary schools didn't count); CBS had singularly failed to promote 'Reggae on Broadway'; life as it was lived in Trench Town had come home to roost in suburban north London, almost landing the Tuff Gong in jail; and now it seemed there was some politrickery – or so some members of the group were convinced – from their long-standing manager.

Bob made a decision. There seemed to be, as far as he could make out, only one avenue of escape. He arranged for Brent Clarke, a record-company promotions man of Jamaican origin who did work for Sims, to effect an introduction with Chris Blackwell, the white Jamaican founder of Britain's most successful independent record company, Island Records.

CATCH A FIRE

Perry Henzell, the Jamaican director who had filmed and made advertisements for the PNP Bandwagon, had finally completed a film on which he had been working for some time. The movie was *The Harder They Come*, a rough-hewn classic, the first and the best home-grown Jamaican feature film. Based on the life of Ivanhoe 'Rhyging' Martin, a self-styled ghetto Robin Hood who died in a shoot-out with police in 1948, Henzell added an extra element by turning the gunman into an innocent country youth desperate to succeed in the cut-throat Kingston reggae world.

Having worked as a floor manager for the BBC in London, Perry Henzell had learned in 1959 that television was about to start up in his native Jamaica. It was in response to this that he returned to the island. There he set up Vista Productions, which over the next decade made hundreds of commercials, honing his directing skills. English commercials directors like Ridley Scott would use Vista's facilities.

By 1969, Henzell was ready to begin filming his first feature. Funded largely by relatives and shot at weekends or in one- or two-week bursts, *The Harder They Come* was not completed until 1972. During those three years, cast members died and were replaced by lookalikes. This method was employed when Jimmy Cliff, the reggae star who played the lead character, Bob Marley's friend from the early days of Beverley's Records, was unavailable for a re-shoot of the pivotal knife-fight scene.

In making *The Harder They Come*, Perry Henzell was influenced by such essays in realism as Gillo Pontecorvo's *The Battle of Algiers*. 'But I felt most realism was boring, very serious,' he said. 'I wanted to make realism lighter. I also realised I couldn't possibly write dialogue that was as good as what I heard people saying all around me. I was interested in capturing that poetry. That's sort of a cinema-verité technique.'

The Harder They Come, said the director, was 'two movies really: on one hand, it was for people who were well-educated and who wanted a glimpse into another side of life. But in the Caribbean and Africa and Brazil, it would be for the poor, for people living in slums. The impact of *The Harder They Come* on Jamaica was enormous.' When the film was first shown in Kingston in May 1972, it provoked riots by people unable to get into the sold-out Carib cinema.

It was, however, a different story when it opened later that year in London. 'It was a difficult sell,' said the director. 'The first night, the cinema was empty. Not one critic had gone down there to review it. I had to print up thousands of flyers and literally stand outside the underground station in Brixton and hand them out. That turned the tide. The film took off. Time and time again, everywhere, the film would just have died without a lot of hard work.' After a similar push in the United States, *The Harder They Come* ran as a midnight movie in Cambridge, Massachusetts, for seven years.

The global perception – and visual impressions – of a Jamaica far removed from the upmarket tourist resorts of the north coast was entirely due to the desperate but addictively attractive world of ganja, gangsters, and reggae runnings portrayed in *The Harder They Come*. Something else entirely, it showed, was going on.

Promoting the film and thereby both reggae music and Jamaica was one of the greatest soundtrack albums ever released. Perry Henzell had personally chosen the record's reggae gems, and *The Harder They Come* album became – before the success of Bob Marley – the gateway to introduce reggae music to the international audience it now enjoys.

In the early 1970s, new acts were largely broken in the rock market by how strongly their 'underground' status would lead to album sales. At the same time, that market was splintering: in the UK, glam rock, pub rock, and progressive rock rivalled each other – there was a clear thirst for something new.

When it was released, with the film, in 1972, the soundtrack became an invaluable primer for hip white kids wanting to find out about a new music. Amongst British whites, reggae suddenly made a thorough volte-face. After being the impossibly unfashionable music of skinhead football thugs, who had championed such sporadic hit singles as Max Romeo's risqué 'Wet Dream', it was now de rigueur at fashionable London dinner parties which ended with joints of Congolese bush or red Lebanese hash.

To an extent, the success of the *The Harder They Come* soundtrack album had already been test-marketed via Jimmy Cliff's own career. In 1963, Cliff had emerged as a successful ska singer, his songs 'King of Kings' and 'Dearest Beverley' hitting the Jamaican charts. After moving to London, he had been groomed by Island Records' boss Chris Black-well for the underground rock market. 'Wonderful World, Beautiful People', which Cliff had written, gave him a UK chart hit in 1969, which he followed up the next year with 'Vietnam', an acclaimed protest song which became a smaller hit. Later in 1970, Cliff's cover of Cat Stevens's 'Wild World' gave him his highest-ever chart placing.

Until the success of the film's soundtrack, however, sizeable album sales – largely the point of the exercise – had eluded him. But the sound-track suggested his finest talents had been waiting for the right moment. The album contained four of his best songs: although the iconic title track is certainly the best known, 'You Can Get It If You Really Want' – which sets out Ivan Martin's philosophy – is almost as celebrated; and it would be hard to choose between the poignant ballad 'Many Rivers to Cross' and the sumptuous 'Sitting in Limbo'. Chris Blackwell had no doubt that this was the singer's moment.

Chris Blackwell had founded Island Records in Jamaica in 1959, producing his records himself. An LP by Lance Hayward, a blind Bermu-dan jazz pianist, was his initial release. Blackwell's first big hit didn't come, however, until the following year, when Laurel Aitken's 'Boogie in My Bones' was a major smash in Jamaica. In 1962, he decided to move to London, having first acquired the rights to the recordings of the Jamaican sound-system giants Sir Coxsone Dodd, Duke Reid, and King Edwards, among others. Blackwell's releases were aimed at Britain's Jamaican immigrant community (ironically, one of the first records he put out was a tune from Leslie Kong, 'Judge Not' by Robert Marley aka Bobby Martell: the surname was misspelt as 'Morley' on the British release).

Unlike most white Jamaicans, Chris Blackwell had discovered the truth about the love in the heart of Rastafari. As a teenager in Jamaica, he had been on a boat that ran aground in shallow waters. After a long and exhausting swim to the shore, he collapsed on a beach, where he was picked up and carried to a Rastafarian encampment. Its inhabitants cared for his wounds, and fed him with both ital food and rhetoric from the philosophy of Rastafari. From now on, Chris Blackwell was not someone who feared the 'beardmen'.

In 1964, Millie Small, an act he was managing, had a huge worldwide hit with 'My Boy Lollipop'. Blackwell toured the world with her and when they returned to Jamaica for a show, the promoter was an American, Danny Sims. ('He's an interesting guy,' Blackwell said of Sims. 'He's got good taste and he's got good vision.') After that, Chris Blackwell was drawn into the world of pop and rock. He managed the Spencer Davis Group, which featured Steve Winwood, and launched Island as a rock label on the back of Winwood's group Traffic. Soon Island became the most sought-after label to record on for groups specialising in the 'underground' rock of the late 1960s.

By 1969, however, he was working again with Jamaican music, in particular with Jimmy Cliff. Blackwell had invested a small amount in *The Harder They Come*; now, in the sexy-rebel image sported by Jimmy Cliff in the movie, it looked as though Chris Blackwell had found what he'd been seeking: a way to take reggae into the rock-album market. And he would spearhead it, he had decided, with Cliff.

Then Jimmy Cliff told him he was going to leave Island. He could make more money with a major label, he told Blackwell, criticising the amount of time the label boss had spent on rock music. To no avail, a distressed Blackwell told him he believed his understanding of the rock market was crucial in trying to break reggae.

A week later, however, Bob Marley and the other two Wailers walked into his office. 'He came in right at the time when in my head there was the idea that this rebel type of character could really emerge. And that I could break such an artist. I was dealing with rock music, which was really rebel music. I felt that would really be the way to break Jamaican music.

But you needed somebody who could be that image. When Bob walked in, he really was that image, the real one that Jimmy had created in the movie.' (At the back of Blackwell's mind was the memory of Jimi Hendrix, another black act who had broken into the rock marketplace.)

Though he had released Marley's first single, and had sent Dickie Jobson down to check him out in 1967, Blackwell had hardly kept track of Bob's career. All he knew was that he had been warned about the Wailers, that these guys were 'trouble'. 'But in my experience when people are described like that, it usually just means that they know what they want.'

As they sat smoking a spliff on the roof of his converted church head-quarters in Basing Street, Notting Hill, a block from the West Indian 'front line' of All Saints Road, the three Wailers confessed to each other their initial wariness over dealing with Chris Blackwell. Aware that it was Island that had released the tunes they had recorded for Studio One, they also knew full well that they had never received any payment for these UK sales. When they had arrived at Basing Street and mentioned this to Black-well, he countered that he had sent thousands of pounds to Coxsone as royalty payments. But now, when he returned to the roof, he cut a deal with the Wailers. With no contract needing to be signed, he would give them £4,000 to return to Jamaica and make an LP. When he received the final tapes, they would get another £4,000. He also agreed to give Tuff Gong the rights to Wailers material in the Caribbean, which would provide them with a useful source of ready cash in the coming years.

'Everyone told me I was mad: they said I'd never see the money again.' Blackwell ignored these naysayers. And he proffered advice as to how he believed the career of the three singers should be pursued. The idea of a vocal trio with backing musicians was dated, he told them: they should take their favourite musicians and forge themselves into a tight road band, capable of touring and presenting several layers of identity in addition to the one that surrounded Bob Marley.

A deal had to be struck with Danny Sims. Accordingly, Bob Marley had a meeting with Sims at the hotel in which he was staying, Grosvenor House on Park Lane. Although Rabbit Bundrick overheard an extremely loud argument, a deal was struck, Chris Blackwell buying Bob Marley out of his contract with CBS for a further £4,000, and two percentage points to Danny Sims on every record sold. Danny Sims, meanwhile, kept Bob Marley's songwriting publishing. (Later, for their next album, Bob Marley wrote the song 'Burnin' and Lootin'' about that first meeting with Chris Blackwell at Basing Street; it included the line: 'So long it have to take for us to talk to the boss.') On their return to Jamaica, the group immediately went into rehearsals.

A new birth in a family can often prompt an impetus to improve the financial lot of the unit: a baby brings luck, as the saying goes. Was this behind Bob Marley's decision to seek a deal with Island Records? For while he had been in London, his wife, Rita, had given birth to Bob's second son, Stephen, on 20 April 1972. Not desiring to linger in Jamaica when her husband had departed for England, Rita Marley had taken her three children and flown up to Wilmington, Delaware, to stay with Mrs Booker. Putting the children into American schools ('We went to George Gray Elementary in Wilmington,' said Cedella), Rita then gave birth to Stephen in Wilmington, making him automatically an American citizen, something considered highly advantageous and desirable by many Jamaicans.

Yet there was a greater complexity about this new family addition than there appeared on the surface. For, within less than a month, two more sons had been born to Bob: on 16 May 1972, Robert 'Robbie' Marley was born to Pat Williams; and, three days later, on 19 May 1972, Rohan Marley was born to Janet Dunn (or Hunt – there is a discrepancy about her surname). Little is known about Janet, except that she was a dancer in a club. Pat Williams was a woman from Trench Town with whom Bob Marley had begun a relationship in 1970. After she allegedly had seduced Bob one night when she ran into him naked in a yard, the very next morning he wrote the song 'Midnight Ravers', which he would include on the next album by the Wailers, on the cover of a Kingston telephone directory.

As time progressed, Bob Marley would come almost to deny his marriage to Rita, even objecting to her continued, and clearly legally entitled, use of his surname. 'Me never believe in marriage that much,' he said. 'Marriage is a trap to control me. Woman is a coward. Man is stronger.' On occasion, he would insist that the sole reason he had married Rita was so that, due to his mother's green-card status, it would be easier for her to take his children into the United States; at other times he even referred to Rita as his sister. Events would, however, indubitably indicate that Rita had considerable justification for her complaints about the philandering of her husband. The next year, Bob Marley had another child, one born in England: this time it was a daughter, Karen, with whose mother, Janet Bowen, he had had a fling whilst in London.

In addition to the complexities of Bob Marley's personal life, when the Wailers returned from the UK to Jamaica at the end of September 1972, they discovered that their records were finally getting played on Jamaican radio, thanks to Allan 'Skill' Cole. Using his footballing celebrity, Cole would gain them entrance to the JBC and RJR radio stations, taking with him a pair of 'screwface' men. The records were always played.

Then there was a series of possibly apocryphal tales about financial mismanagement even closer to home for the Wailers. Bob Marley heard, to his surprise, that Lee Perry had allegedly been giving Rita boxes of the records they had made with him on consignment. Although Peter Tosh never addressed the principal individuals involved, he became deeply disillusioned by this series of revelations. Secretly, he blamed Bob Marley for these financial setbacks: despite the bitter feelings between them, Bob had somehow managed to maintain a friendship with Scratch Perry; Skill Cole was Bob's especial friend; and Rita was his wife. With regard to Rita, there was said always to have been an unstated subtext: it was Peter Tosh who was first sweet on Rita, and he always harboured a feeling that Bob had taken her away from him – it was Bob Marley who at first had delivered love-notes from Peter to Rita.

Another rumour then swept the camp. Peter Tosh had heard a whisper that Bob was going to run away to London with all the group's money. Wisely, Peter's way of confronting this issue was by telling Bob he had had a 'vision', or dream, in which this happened. Bob's response was to laugh at Peter: wouldn't it be stupid to do that, he said, when the group seemed to be starting to do so well?

As though to show Peter Tosh that he should not be too hard on Bob Marley, the tallest Wailer then learned a lesson of his own. The next time the Wailers went up 'a fareign', Peter placed his affairs in the hands of an acquaintance, who stole plenty of money. In response, until the funds were repaid, Peter Tosh confiscated the man's car. Occasionally, he would be seen in Kingston driving this man's vehicle – although more usually Peter was in his sedate Austin 1100. It was fortunate for this former aquaintance of Peter's that he received his automobile back in one piece: Peter Tosh was notorious as one of the worst and most dangerous drivers in Kingston – unlike Bob Marley, who was known for the safe way in which he drove his English Ford Capri along the potholed roads of Jamaica. (Although at the beginning of the 1970s, Bob, in another vehicle, had been involved in a serious accident, driving into the rear of a truck, the top of his head 'licked off'.)

Rehearsals prior to the recording of the Wailers' first album for Island Records took place at the upstairs studio they'd used before, at the corner of First Street and West Road; only, this time, neighbours complained about the noise.

The group then went into Harry J's, at 10 Roosevelt Avenue in New

Kingston, the best studio in town. Harry Johnson's Harry J's Allstars had of course had a Top Ten UK hit in 1969 with 'Liquidator', bankrolling his studio set-up. As well as the three Wailers and the Barrett brothers, other musicians on the sessions included the upcoming bass player Robbie Shakespeare, who had replaced Family Man in the Youth Professionals; and Tyrone Downie, the youthful Kingston College keyboards player Family Man had also enlisted in the Youth Professionals (dropping the 'Youth', the Professionals by the middle of the decade would become one of the hardest session outfits in Kingston). Marcia Griffiths, who with Bob Andy had the previous year had a big international success with 'Young, Gifted, and Black', another Harry J production, was on backing vocals, along with Rita Marley – proof that, personal differences aside, Bob and Rita could maintain a united professional front, a pointer to the course in which their relationship was evolving.

Although seven of the nine songs that eventually made it on to the resulting album were written by Bob Marley, the sessions were very much a group effort: the pair of Peter Tosh songs – '400 Years' and 'Stop That Train' – were of the same matchless standard. (Over time, Bunny Livingston's songwriting contributions to the group seemed to have lessened – although when he did turn his hand to songwriting, the results were never less than scintillating.) The fact that the group had already recorded and released half the songs on the record was of no matter, and part of an established tradition: in Jamaica, artists often release different versions of the same song – 'do-overs' – time and time again, until they finally hit.

Attending some of the Harry J's sessions was Richard Williams, in his role as assistant editor of *Melody Maker*, then the leading British music paper. His visit to Jamaica was part of Chris Blackwell's strategy to publicise the Wailers' music through the press. Within a year, Williams, who had a vast, extremely catholic knowledge of music, would become head

Bob Marley first met Peter Tosh and Bunny Livingston (later known as Bunny Wailer) in his hometown, Trench Town, a shanty in Kingston, Jamaica.

BELOW: The fledgling Wailers often had to practise on the streets around their homes. Poverty and violence were rife in Trench Town and would later become dominant themes in their music.

LEFT: It was during one of Joe Higgs's informal music lessons that Peter Tosh and Bunny Livingston met. Bob Marley credited Higgs as being one of his formative musical influences.

LEFT: Born Winston Hubert McIntosh, Peter Tosh stood out because of his 6'5" height. His short fuse and unveiled sarcasm earned him the nickname Steppin' Razor, after a song written by Joe Higgs.

LEFT: Jacob Miller with Bob Marley. As the vocalist with Inner Circle, Miller achieved some success before his untimely death, aged 27, in a car accident on Hope Road, Kingston.

RIGHT: Coxsone Dodd founded the first black-owned recording studio in Jamaica. He signed Bob Marley and the Wailers after they attended one of his regular Sunday auditions.

BELOW LEFT: Peter Tosh.

BELOW RIGHT: Tosh with Bunny Livingston (right).

FAR LEFT: Bob wearing the US jive-style outfit that he had picked up while visiting his mother in Delaware.

LEFT: Before Bob Marley's rise to fame, Desmond Dekker was one of the foremost singer-songwriters in, and out of, Jamaica.

Rita (far left) was introduced to Marley at Dodd's Studio One. Marley nurtured her career at the label as part of her group, the Soulettes. The pair married in 1966.

BELOW: Bob Marley relaxing at the mixing desk during a session for the *Survival* album at the Tuff Gong recording studio.

ABOVE: Mortimer Planner, the revered Rasta elder, leads HIM Haile Selassie, the Ethiopian emperor, from his plane at Kingston airport after his arrival in Jamaica on 21 April 1966.

The many faces of Bob Marley.

TOP RIGHT: Bob Marley reads the Bible. Especially during the later years of his life, Bob was driven and inspired by his belief in Rastafarianism.

LEFT: A shot of the classic Wailers line-up, with Rita Marley, who often worked with the three band members.

RIGHT: Bob and Rita with three of their children – Cedella, Ziggy and Stephen – as well as Sharon, Bob's step-daughter. Bob had a number of children, including seven from relationships outside his marriage.

Bob Marley and the touring band, still known as the Wailers, after their separation from Peter Tosh and Bunny Livingston.

ABOVE: Rita Marley.

BELOW: A shot of the Wailers during their time under the tutelage of Danny Sims.

ABOVE: Bob washing his locks at Cane River Falls, near Bull Bay, a regular feature of his early morning exercise routine.

The Wailers performing on BBC2's *The Old Grey Whistle Test,* their first national television exposure in the UK.

Bunny Livingston takes centre stage during a post-Wailers solo show.

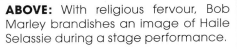

ABOVE: With religious fervour, Bob Marley brandishes an image of Haile Selassie during a stage performance.

BELOW: Bob Marley holds aloft the arms of Jamaican prime minister Michael Manley (left) and opposition leader Edward Seaga at the 1978 *One Love* Peace Concert in Kingston.

RIGHT: A poster for the Zimbabwean Independence Day concert at which Marley and the Wailers performed.

OPPOSITE TOP: Bob Marley, Mick Jagger and Peter Tosh at the Palladium in New York, 1978.

OPPOSITE CENTRE: Performing on stage at London's Crystal Palace Bowl in June 1980.

OPPOSITE BOTTOM: Bob Marley communing with the spirits during his transcendent five-night run at Hammersmith Odeon in June 1976, promoting *Rastaman Vibration*.

TOP RIGHT: Bob Marley makes his escape by car from the 1980 Crystal Palace Bowl gig.

ABOVE LEFT: June 1980, Marley receiving gold discs for *Babylon by Bus*.

BELOW: Crowds wade into the water as Bob Marley and the Wailers perform at the Crystal Palace Bowl.

ABOVE: Following the biggest funeral ever held in the Caribbean, many thousands followed the cortege to the wake at Bob's boyhood home of Nine Miles, his final resting place.

BELOW: Rita with her sons Ziggy and Stephen (left), and Bob's mother, Mrs Cedella Booker (right), at Bob Marley's funeral.

BOTTOM LEFT: The Bob Marley museum at 56 Hope Road, Kingston.

BOTTOM RIGHT: Ziggy Marley performs on stage with Mrs Booker.

of A&R at Island Records. 'I was prepared to find someone talented,' he recalled, 'because I knew the Studio One and Perry records, but it quickly became obvious that Bob simply was Marvin Gaye or Bob Dylan, or both.' He noted, however, that most of the songs were extremely long in their original recorded versions.

Chris Blackwell accompanied Williams to the studio, hearing the recorded songs for the first time – the record man was knocked out with what he heard. It was only now that he asked the Wailers to sign a contract. After listening to the tunes, it was Blackwell who came up with the album's title, *Catch a Fire*, taken from a line in the song 'Slave Driver'.

The decision was that *Catch a Fire* should be the first reggae album sold as though it were by a rock act. As Blackwell had always intended, the songs were then worked on further, at the studios at Island's then headquarters. 'The most important thing Chris Blackwell did at Island's studio in Basing Street was to edit and then sweeten,' said Richard Williams. 'The sweetening on that record was terrifically important, because there's absolutely no doubt that Blackwell was attempting to make it . . . not more palatable, but more attractive to the ears of progressive-rock fans.'

To this end, a pair of American musicians already associated with Island Records was brought in to add their abilities, one of them already known to Bob Marley: the keyboards player John 'Rabbit' Bundrick, who since he had last seen Bob during the summer had been playing as a member of the re-formed Free. 'I already knew Bob when Chris Blackwell asked me to work on *Catch a Fire*, so we were already friends. I didn't know the other guys, but Bob was the real reason I was there anyway. It was an exciting musical adventure doing that album. New sounds, new instruments.'

Bundrick claimed to have been the first person to use a clavinet on reggae tunes: 'The first time the wah-wah clavinet and synthesiser were ever used on reggae music was when I introduced them to the Wailers during the making of *Catch a Fire*. They loved it.'

Signed to Island Records was a group from Alabama called Smith, Perkins and Smith; it had been decided to break the group in Europe before tackling their home country. Their superlative guitarist, Wayne Perkins, who would later contribute his playing to the Rolling Stones' *Black and Blue* album and was even mooted as a replacement for Mick Taylor before Ron Wood took the job, was on his way up Basing Street's spiral staircase to the main Island studio when Chris Blackwell stopped him. 'He said there was a Wailers project he wanted me to play on. I said, "Who are the Wailers?" Chris said. "They play reggae," and I said, "That don't help me."' After a brief rundown on reggae, Blackwell told Perkins, 'Just get your Les Paul and your Fender amp, and come on down.'

'I was a twenty-year-old boy from Alabama confronted by these wild-looking Rastas from Jamaica. I had no idea what I was getting into,' said the guitarist. Asking Blackwell for advice on how to approach the Wailers' music, he was told, 'Don't listen to the bass, he's a melody-guy. The drums are on the 1 and 3, the guitars and keys are all on the upbeat, and that's pretty much it: best of luck.'

For Wayne Perkins to deny that he knew what reggae was would seem disingenuous. He was, after all, an Island Records recording artist, and it had been founded on Jamaican music. But the Wailers' sound was certainly very different from what he had previously heard: 'Desmond Dekker wasn't reggae to me, it was too much R'n'B, and I had been in the studio with Jimmy Cliff, but it was not the same as the real roots reggae sound that Bob Marley was known for. It was the strangest thing I'd ever heard: it was like nothing I'd ever heard, because I had nothing to compare it to.'

All the same, Wayne Perkins's distinct contribution to *Catch a Fire* and, ultimately, to the growth of Bob Marley's status and career would be impossible to disavow. Equally, it is impossible to underestimate the vision of Chris Blackwell in presenting Perkins with that eminent and historic role. (It is also worth noting the irony of Perkins coming from Alabama, that most notoriously racist of American states, the attitudes of whose people had ultimately contributed to the growth of the Civil Rights movement in the USA, which held great emotional, philosophical, and psychological resonance for all three Wailers.)

The first song on which Wayne Perkins was invited to add a guitar part was 'Concrete Jungle', the tune that would become the opening track on *Catch a Fire*. Already released as a single in Jamaica on Tuff Gong the previous year, that version had opened with swirls of organ, courtesy of Peter Tosh, whose bass voice sonorously intoned an evocation of Rastafari; meanwhile, on the Tuff Gong release, horns underpinned the choruslines. Now the organ was replaced with Rabbit Bundrick's gurgling, funky clavinet. But it was the meandering, yet supremely confident searing twirls from Perkins's Les Paul that defined a production of astonishing clarity, one of the greatest album openers ever, this tale of the grim reality of life in Arnett Gardens, west Kingston's new housing scheme. When Perkins nailed the solo on the third take, Bob Marley hurried from the control room into the studio, ecstatic, thrusting a spliff of gratitude into the mouth of the American guitarist.

The addition of such sweet guitar hooks and keyboard effects across *Catch a Fire* – on tunes like 'Rock It Baby', 'Kinky Reggae', and the closing 'Midnight Ravers' – confirmed its identity, counterpointed in perfect balance with the melodic rhythm of the Barrett brothers.

Present at the sessions was the journalist Jonh [sic] Ingham, who was working at the time in the press office of Island Records. Bob Marley, he insisted, was equally as ready as Chris Blackwell to add the extra musical elements. 'I do question this belief that Bob was somehow a pawn without a voice. I watched him doing overdub sessions with Rabbit

Bundrick, and he was directing every note. He paid Rabbit the highest compliment. It was a really weird progression, all offbeats against the melody line (I wish I could remember the song) and only four or eight bars – the kind of detail hardly anyone hears – and Rabbit was having a lot of trouble getting it down. Someone in the control room suggested they drop it, and Bob replied, "If I can hear it, he can play it." And he waited until Rabbit got it. What I am commenting on is the extraordinarily insulting view that all the sweetening on *Catch a Fire* is the work of Blackwell and Bob had no say or part in it.'

'Everything one needs to know about Bob Marley's conquest of Rock Babylon is really there in that first astonishing song on *Catch a Fire*,' said Barney Hoskyns, the English music writer. 'The opening seconds could almost be a snatch from some Grateful Dead jam. A clavinet gurgles into life over a heartbeat of a kick drum and ushers us towards the first verse. From the platform of the organ and the chicken-scratch bounce of the guitars emerges the raw, proud voice of the lead Wailer, lifted aloft by the lamenting tones of Peter Tosh and Bunny Livingston. The whole sound has a cohesion new to reggae, with the mix perfectly tailored to white ears.'

Yet the contributions of Rabbit Bundrick and Wayne Perkins on *Catch a Fire* went uncredited. Perhaps, a disappointed Bundrick believed, 'it wouldn't do for people to know that there were white rock musicians on the albums.'

Soon afterwards, the album cover was designed: an outsize cardboard replica of a Zippo cigarette lighter, an idea from an American art director. It hinged upwards, and the record was removed from the top of the sleeve; in fact, it often stuck within the packaging, but the desired effect was created all the same.

Danny Sims, eager to sell singles via American-radio airplay, had had no time whatsoever for Rastafarian subject matter. Chris Blackwell, however, positively welcomed it. As well as feeling sympathetic to the philosophy of the religion, he understood its strength as a marketing tool. To sell albums in the United Kingdom, the British music press had always been more important than the limited radio airplay that was at that time available.

'Danny Sims had thought in terms of singles. When he started working with Bob in the second half of the 1960s, albums hadn't really been selling in the American black record business: one of the first big black albums would have been Isaac Hayes's *Hot Buttered Soul*. So, to Danny Sims, to make records about Rastafarianism would make no sense at all.

'But from my point of view, I was in the album business, so to sing songs about something people didn't know about and that they could learn about was fascinating. From my point of view, Rastafarianism had an added commercial appeal, because I was looking at it from the English record-business point of view, whereas he was looking at it from the American black-business point of view. In the English record business, what made careers was more the press, rather than the radio.

'So what Bob Marley believed in and how he lived his life was something that had tremendous appeal for the press. The press had been dealing with the greatest time in the emergence of rock'n'roll, and it was starting to quieten down. Now, here was this Third World superstar emerging who had the same kind of point of view, an individual against the system with an incredible look: this was the first time you had seen anyone looking like that, other than Jimi Hendrix. And Bob had that power about him and incredible lyrics.'

'A lot of people in the music business thought we were crazy,' said Tim Clark, the then head of marketing at Island Records.

According to Bunny Wailer, he, Peter, and Bob continued to carry misgivings about their deal with Island Records. Specifically, this was over the company having released numerous Wailers' Coxsone 45s for which the group never received a penny of royalties – although under the terms of their deal with Coxsone Dodd it is by no means clear that they were entitled to further payments. Bunny claimed this was why the group all bore grim screwfaces on the record's cover picture: 'Because we were still like jumping out of the frying-pan and maybe jumping into the fire.'

The picture had been taken by Cookie Kinkead, a local photographer. It had taken her three days to organise, driving around Kingston picking up the various members, including the Barrett brothers, in her tiny Mini Moke; each time she thought she had pinned down the entire group, one of them would disappear. 'Most people thought I was crazy to be driving all over Kingston with these "weird radical musicians" but there was something about their energy that was very appealing to me,' she said. The criticisms of her acquaintances were themselves an indictment of the innate snobbery within Jamaica, a country that could sometimes feel like provincial Britain twenty years previously. The picture was eventually shot at the home of Dickie Jobson in Gordon Town, on a flight of steps which overlooked the Hope River, in the foothills of the Blue Mountains. 'After taking three days to get them all together, they only had enough time for about half an hour of shooting – more time was spent building the spliffs that were consumed before and during the photo shoot than on the shoot itself.'

At a meeting in Jamaica at a residence known as Strawberry Hill, three thousand feet above Kingston, in the Blue Mountains, Chris Blackwell played the Wailers the final mixes and their suspicions were mollified. 'So that day was a tense day,' said Bunny, 'but after we listened, and we all shared our views, we said that at least it had the international sound we were expecting it to have. The little additions that were done were pleasant, the little guitars, solos, and all that stuff, so it turned out everyone left in good spirits.'

DEPARTMENT OF EMPLOYMENT
Headquarters (EC B3)
Ebury Bridge House
Ebury Bridge Road
London SW1W 8PY

Telephone 01-730 9661 ext 229

Island Artists Ltd.,
8-10 Basing Street,
London W11

Your reference

Our reference
CLS/ 004332
Date
2 4 APR 1973

Dear Sir

IMMIGRATION ACT 1971

On .....9-4-73.......... you applied for a work permit to enable .Robert Nesta
....Marley..............., a Commonwealth citizen, to enter this country for
employment by you as .Lead Vocalist/Guitarist/Song Writer.

The issue of a work permit has been authorised but, in view of the impossibility of
issuing it to the Commonwealth citizen before he arrives, the Immigration Authorities
have been notified of the details of his arrival in advance.

When he reports to you for work you should forward immediately the completed
tear-off portion of this letter, to this Department in the enclosed envelope. An
Employment Certificate, which will incorporate the work permit, will then be prepared
and sent to you to hand to the Commonwealth citizen. He should be advised to keep
this in a safe place as he must produce it, with his passport, to the Home Office
if he wishes his stay in this country to be extended.

If he is still in your employment when an extension becomes necessary, the Home
Office will also require a letter from you confirming that you wish to continue to
employ him.

Yours faithfully

A Coward

When *Catch a Fire* was released in Britain, in December 1972, four
months before its American release, it was pitched at the very hippest
sections of the media. Immediately the Wailers were a critical success,
although a commercial breakthrough was still some way off, the record
initially only selling some fifteen thousand copies. Eventually these sales
multiplied by over a hundred times.

To further nurture *Catch a Fire* and build on the media interest generated
by the release of the album at the end of the previous year, Chris Blackwell deemed that a British tour should take place in the late spring of
1973. The task of setting up the UK dates for the Wailers fell to Mick

Cater. Cater was employed by the Island Artists management division of Island Records, working out of the company's premises at Basing Street.

Before *Catch a Fire* was released, Chris Blackwell had come into Cater's office and played him and his colleagues the tapes of the album. 'And we all sneered. As far as we were concerned, at that time the only people who were interested in reggae were skinheads.' Asked to book a tour, however, Cater went into overdrive. Following Blackwell's suggestion that the group should be treated as though it were a hip rock act, he sent a copy of *Catch a Fire* to the social secretary at every university and polytechnic in Britain – and before long he had set up a string of thirty-one dates, fifteen of which were in Jamaican reggae clubs. These were in distinct contrast to the principal London dates, however. The Wailers were slotted in for four nights at the Speakeasy, the long-fashionable, somewhat elitist club catering largely to musicians and the music business, at which Bob had played the previous year while promoting 'Reggae on Broadway'.

The Wailers were flown to London: in addition to the Barrett brothers, Seeco, their Trench Town percussionist friend who had introduced them to Studio One, came along, initially in the function of roadie; and so did Earl 'Wire' Lindo, a keyboards player and friend who had been a stalwart of Studio One sessions. The departure date on the airline tickets was 21 April 1973, the same date that HIM Haile Selassie had arrived in Jamaica seven years previously, a symbolism that appealed to the group. In fact, they left three days later, on 24 April, from Chris Blackwell's offices in Island House, the substantial Kingston townhouse, in an acre of its own land, that he owned at 56 Hope Road. Although such tardiness could be attributed to the traditionally anarchic approach to timekeeping associated with Jamaicans, there was a practical reason for the delay. Bunny Livingston wanted to take with him a new set of Nyabinghi drums which he had had made. As the drums' construction had been somewhat rushed, the new instruments had begun to stretch in the Jamaican heat, so they needed adjusting. At first Bunny said he would wait in Jamaica for the corrections to be made to his instruments, following the others to London, but then a decision was made that they would all travel together.

On King Street in Hammersmith in west London, near the new offices in St Peter's Square to which Island was about to relocate from Basing Street, the musicians were put up in a house which had a base-ment rehearsal room. Next door was an Indian restaurant from which was obtained almost every meal the musicians ate in London. A Ford Transit, the utility van which was then the staple transport of low-level acts, was provided, the driver none other than Dickie Jobson, whose fondness for fine herbs certainly accorded with that of the Wailers. Dickie's good-natured sister Diane was one of Bob's girlfriends in Jamaica; being a fully qualified lawyer, she would later work for him in this capacity.

Another of Bob's girlfriends was waiting for him in London. Esther Anderson was Jamaican, but had moved away from the island over ten years previously, establishing herself as an actress. When Esther Ander-son and Bob Marley met in New York at the beginning of 1973, she had just starred in *A Warm December* with Sidney Poitier; around the same time, she was also in a film called *The Touchable*. 'She was happening,' said Lee Jaffe, who introduced them. Only 22 years old, Jaffe had entered the world of film-making. Through certain friends, he had access to some of the best marijuana in New York City, which in turn gave him access to the world of Bob Marley, always anxious to secure the finest herb. Friends with both Marlon Brando – later another boyfriend of Esther Anderson, as Chris Blackwell already had been – and Maria Schneider, Lee Jaffe had been invited to the New York premiere of Bernardo Bertolucci's *Last Tango in Paris*, at which Bob Marley also happened to be present – possibly through the friendship Bob also had with Maria Schneider. It was here that Lee Jaffe met Bob Marley. The two men would become close friends. That evening Lee Jaffe watched the first meeting between Bob and Esther: 'There was definitely an immediate infatuation.'

Partially as a reward for having taken part in the PNP Bandwagon, Bob had been given government land at Bull Bay, ten miles to the east of Kingston on the Jamaican south coast: all that needed to be done was for the house to be built, which Rita Marley set about with a vengeance. 'Rita was this great matriarchal figure,' said Lee Jaffe, who almost immediately moved to live in Jamaica. 'I was very, very awed by Rita. I mean, she had all these kids with Bob, and they were building this little house, while they were living in it, out at Bull Bay, and she was physically constructing the house. She'd be carrying bags of cement, and yet she was always radiant, glowing with a calm elegance regardless of what tenseness or chaos might be surrounding. She was, and is, extremely beautiful.'

Bob, however, was rarely there. Chris Blackwell rented out much of Island House. Having effectively moved away from Rita and his legitimate children, Bob lived for much of the time at 56 Hope Road, in a front room, with Esther Anderson, who had flown down to Jamaica from New York. 'They looked to me like the most amazing couple,' said Jaffe. 'When you saw them together, the visual thing of it was so intense.' By now Jaffe too had moved into 56 Hope Road. Showing considerable panache and nerve, this white youth now began to play harmonica at Wailers rehearsal sessions. In other ways, Lee Jaffe was handy to have around: to Rita, Bob would cover up his relationship with Esther by saying that the actress was Jaffe's girlfriend. Another girl called Cindy Breakspeare, whom Bob had first met at Danny Sims's home, also lived in the house. Youth from Trench Town – some with shocking reputations, such as Frowser and Tek Life, whose sobriquet was self-explanatory – were also hanging out at 56 Hope Road: Bob would always claim he was trying to reform them. Sledger, Bob's cousin from St Ann, was around, acting as driver whenever Bob needed someone to take the wheel of his Ford Capri.

That February of 1973, Chris Blackwell had rented a DC-3 plane, with the intention of flying down the Caribbean to Trinidad for the three-day carnival, one of the finest and most extravagant of such events in the world. Lee Jaffe found himself going along on the plane, with Bob Marley, Chris Blackwell, Dickie Jobson, and Jim Capaldi from Traffic. In Trinidad, Bob was fed up – he couldn't find any herb. Yet you cannot help but notice that the life of Bob Marley was clearly changing. Although the celebrated Trinidad carnival was essentially of peasant origins, open to all, his method of arrival there would have been defined at the time as 'jet-set'. And he was no longer living in Trench Town, or even at Bull Bay, but in a substantial uptown Kingston house – even though it was owned by his record-company boss. Perhaps more significantly, in these tales of Bob Marley's altering existence, there is no evidence whatsoever of Bunny Livingston and Peter Tosh, his brothers in the family of the Wailers.

Shivering in the chilly London spring of May 1973, however, Bob found plenty of solace in the arms of Esther Anderson. He rarely spent a night at the group's King Street address, not unreasonably preferring his girlfriend's more upmarket, and more comfortable, apartment nearby.

When the Wailers arrived in London, they had immediately met Mick Cater. Cater's task hadn't ended with simply booking the dates for the tour – Chris Blackwell had asked him to travel with the Wailers to all their shows. But Cater was still unconvinced about the group's viability as a commercial act and he didn't at all want to go to the first date, at Lancaster University. 'I travelled in the van with the group, and couldn't understand a thing they were saying. I was also exhausted by the time I got there, because they wouldn't have the heater off.'

When the group began to perform, however, Cater rapidly changed his opinion: 'They were playing support act to a disco. I watched the show and was amazed. From then on, I wouldn't let anyone else work with them.' Mick Cater was to make it to every single show the group played on their first UK tour. As well as the profound experience of being with the Wailers and hearing their music, he also remembered that he ate thirty-one curries with them – on the road in Britain, it was the only food they would eat. By the time the last of those curries had been consumed, the Wailers had become a crack touring outfit, as tightly sprung as a ratchet knife.

At that time, Phil Cooper was promotions manager for the north of England for Island Records; it was natural that he also would make his way to that Lancaster show. Amongst the acts with whom Cooper had regularly worked were Mott the Hoople, Free, Traffic, Cat Stevens, and Roxy Music. But the Wailers were different in every possible way, and not only in their attitude. 'They were musically different, and visually different. Their presentation was hardly the European approach to rock-'n'roll. Instead, what came off them was the warmth of sunshine and friendliness, and they had lyrics that had an unbelievable meaning. Bob believed in every word he sang. All the lyrics were very specifically from his life. At that time people didn't necessarily understand this, how everything related to a particular time and moment.'

Cooper went backstage after the Lancaster show and met the Wailers for the first time. 'They were very friendly, but also almost shy. They'd arrived somewhere to perform and were really confused about where they were and why they were there. Bob didn't have locks when I first met him: only mini-locks.'

The only thing that puzzled the group when they left the stage were the loud shouts from the audience. Didn't they like them? Had they done something wrong, like at the Palace that Christmas morning in 1965?

There was no tradition of vociferous audience response in black clubs, either in Jamaica or – as the group would imminently discover – in Britain. Island employees pushed the group back onstage, for their baptism of fire in the Zen art of the encore. As Mick Cater perceived it, 'At first the United Kingdom was as confused by the Wailers as the Wailers were by the United Kingdom.'

At the end of that evening in Lancaster, Cooper had to drive Seeco, then still a roadie rather than a percussionist, to the local hospital – he was vomiting severely and his body was wracked with aches and pains. Seeco quickly recovered from the illness, but it was an omen of the sicknesses with which Peter Tosh would be plagued on the next UK tour – with dread consequences.

By the time they returned to London for the four shows at the Speakeasy, Cater was also beginning to note the differences in personalities among the three Wailers proper: 'It took a very long time for Bob to trust me. Peter and Bunny were integral to the group, but Bob had such charisma. He was the best live act there's ever been, both with Peter and Bunny and later without them. A complete powerhouse onstage, but off – nothing like that, just very quiet. There was the private Bob, and the public Bob.'

At the soundcheck for the first Speakeasy show, a Jamaican-born London schoolboy slipped through the stage door, clutching the precious camera that had become the wellspring of his existence. Dennis Morris, who was then only fourteen, had read about the Wailers in the British music press: 'They seemed to be a very underground thing; even reggae itself was really this new thing in Britain.'

Hesitantly, Dennis introduced himself to the Jamaican trio. 'They seemed really pleased to meet me: they'd never met a young black English person; but I'd never met a young Jamaican rebel. I found myself talking mainly with Peter and Bob – Bunny was a little blackheart man.

Peter was strutting, a wide boy, full of himself. But Bob was very positive of where he was going, very direct, with a lot more humour than Peter. Bob was softer, lighter, with that twinkle in his eyes.

'They told me that they were going on the road. The next morning I left to go to school and instead met up with them. My parents didn't know I was going to disappear. They just knew I was crazy about cameras, and was always saving up for them.'

Such was the buzz created by *Catch a Fire* and the Island publicity machine, led by Brian Blevins, that this set of London shows, for which the Wailers were being paid £250 a night, was a complete sell-out. More than that: on the first night, the small venue was host to the hippest cultural event London had experienced that year. Bianca Jagger, Bryan Ferry, Brian Eno, and assorted members of Traffic – as well, naturally, as Chris Blackwell – were all in an audience composed of London's top taste-makers. (Other nights drew even greater representatives of then rock royalty: Eric Clapton, Jeff Beck, and members of the Who and Deep Purple.) Unusually, these hipsters waited patiently in their seats; the fact that the Wailers were so resolutely unpunctual in arriving onstage at their appointed hour seemed part of the attraction: this Jamaican *soon-come* way of thinking was deemed by the radical chic to be definitively cool, and delineated a specific initial response towards the Wailers from some white, supposedly educated quarters: a delight in so-called primitivism that involved an exotic 'othering' of the Caribbean – which may or may not be a form of inverted racism – by those of bohemian bent.

When the Wailers appeared onstage, the contrast between their shuffling demeanour and the aura of decadent affluence about their audience couldn't have been more pronounced. Crammed onto the tiny stage, the group embodied humility in its manner but kicked with a revelatory power in the performance of its apocalyptic material. For those used to the self-importance at the core of most rock shows, such an approach was, literally, stunning. The strangely quiet, almost hushed performances of the Wailers at the Speakeasy on those nights in May 1973 were life-changing experiences, transformative, perfect moments.

For a start, at the beginning of the set there were no stage lights on the group – the lighting only gradually came up, revealing the musicians. And, as though stating their case, the concert began with only the sound of the Nyabinghi drums Bunny had brought from Jamaica; but it was 'Wire' Lindo playing them, and he was only emphasising the bass drum, as it brought in a new song, 'Rasta Man Chant'. After a few moments, Wire moved over to keyboards, as this extremely traditionally structured, deeply spiritual song permeated the alcohol-infused but now hushed atmosphere of the Speakeasy. After the audience's attention had been grabbed, the Wailers then confused the audience even more by playing the old Skatalites instrumental 'Ringo' (aka 'Ringo Rides'), which they had also played that night supporting Johnny Nash. Between songs, there was virtually no communication with the audience, tune following tune. It was as though there was a spirit hovering over the group that sprang direct from the heart of the Ark of the Covenant.

There was only one hint of a bad vibe: returning to their Ford Transit after one of the Speakeasy shows later in the week, the group found that someone had lobbed a brick into their windscreen, smashing it. Simple vandalism, or sinister racism? No one really cared too much – these live UK shows by the Wailers were working.

Dennis Morris travelled to Blackpool and to the Midlands industrial city of Birmingham with the Wailers. Birmingham, with its large West Indian community, provided an audience sympathetic to the Wailers' material. But in the north-western seaside town of Blackpool, they played a venue whose attractions alternated between chart acts and ballroom dancing; the group drew a crowd of no more than a hundred people, and it was almost exclusively white. Dennis Morris, however, was struck by the readiness with which a woman jumped onstage and began dancing with Bob. 'It was the white audience in Britain who took Bob up first – really, the Rastas got into him later. Chris Blackwell had put him into that crossover market, and white people were the first to pick up on it. Later, of course, Bob had a huge black audience. But they seemed to misinterpret what Bob personally was saying about Rasta, and read it as just being a black thing, a Black Power thing almost. But to me Bob always insisted, "It's the system we're against – it's not a black and white thing."'

'I don't have prejudice against miself,' said Bob Marley. 'My father was a white and my mother was black. Them call mi half-caste or whatever. Mi don't dip on nobody's side. Mi don't dip on the black man's side nor the white man's side. Mi dip on God's side, the one who create mi and cause mi to come from black and white.'

Island Records' promotion team had astutely booked the Wailers on *The Old Grey Whistle Test*, a weekly forty-minute programme on BBC2 that offered the only regular access in the UK to televised broadcasts for album artists. Due to the tastes of the producer and presenter, the avuncular but amiable Bob Harris, the music proffered was more likely to be Californian soft rock than the voice of potentially troublesome ghetto sufferahs. But the Wailers' performance, for which they had rehearsed rigorously all day, pre-recording the backing tracks but not the vocals, was a triumph. They played two songs, 'Stir It Up' and 'Concrete Jungle', in that order. Starting off with a close-up on Bob's Telecaster as he played (or mimed) the distinctive *chinga-chinga* guitar-chord intro to 'Stir It Up', which had the advantage of familiarity, thanks to the recent Johnny Nash hit, the show was a revelation when beamed into UK homes late on a Tuesday evening, the first televised presentation to the British nation of Bob Marley, Peter Tosh, and Bunny Livingston. Although Bob seemed to wear an unruly Afro hairstyle, there was not a hint of dreadlocks anywhere, and you could not help but note the 'whiteness' of the facial features of the light-skinned Bob Marley in contrast to the distinctly African 'blackness' of all the other musicians. However, wasn't this simply a matter of Bob Marley fulfilling his destiny? There's also the contrast between Bob's dressed-down pale-blue denim shirt and jeans – garb that could equally have attired such *Old Grey Whistle Test* favourites as Jackson Browne or Poco – and the rich fullness of the colours worn by the rest of the group, especially the regally purple top adorning the stately Peter Tosh. Bunny Livingston's moody black top hat, meanwhile, gave him the appearance of some bone-shaking New Orleans voodoo doctor – or, perhaps, Jamaican obeahman. The sound and appearance of the Wailers on *The Old Grey Whistle Test* cast a spell over those members of the British public who took the time to watch and listen.

As well as performing at London's elite Speakeasy club, the Wailers played another date in the British capital on that first tour. A steaming, smoky joint, the Greyhound, on Fulham Palace Road, Hammersmith, was a pub that had established itself as a free venue for groups who had got maybe a couple of rungs up the long ladder of their careers; it played host to plenty of Island acts as they started out.

At the Greyhound, the Wailers played to a house that could not get any fuller. In the audience was a young drama student. This man had an evening job in another pub and had already had to ask his boss if he could take an hour off to watch that edition of the BBC's *Old Grey Whistle Test* on which the Wailers had appeared. His name was David Rodigan, and later he was to become renowned and respected as the UK's most knowledgeable reggae-radio DJ. By 1973, Bob Marley was already a hero figure for Rodigan: 'I just thought that he was the man who'd followed on from Prince Buster, and he simply was reggae. From "Put It On" onwards, his songs had absolutely captivated me.'

After the epiphany-like experience of watching Bob onstage at the Greyhound, Rodigan had tried and failed to get backstage to meet his hero. Leaving the venue and walking down Fulham Palace Road with his girlfriend, however, he saw a cloud of smoke billowing out of a shop doorway. 'It was Bob, behind a huge spliff, with Wire Lindo. So I went up to him and told him how important his music was to me. He smiled at me and said, "One love. Thanks." And I watched as he climbed into a car that had pulled up, and he waved and called goodbye.'

(In 1980, when Bob was on his way back from playing at the Zimbabwe independence celebrations, he stopped in London for a few days and agreed to appear on Rodigan's Saturday-night reggae show on Capital Radio; Rodigan's entire programme that night was to be given over to a history of Bob Marley's music. 'I took him into a room at Capital,' said Rodigan, 'and I asked him if he minded not talking about politics and religion, but just talking about music. And Bob beamed and said, "At last." You know, Bob Marley was so amazing, so remarkable. He really was the original blueprint.')

Following the Speakeasy dates, Benjamin Foot was made tour manager for the Wailers. 'I had the advantage of having been brought up in Jamaica, so I spoke the patois.' His father, Sir Hugh Foot, had been Governor-General of the island, and Chris Blackwell had in his late teens been employed briefly as Sir Hugh's assistant. Later, Benjamin Foot worked for the Save the Children fund in Addis Ababa, an appropriately poetic destination.

'I was always frightened,' Foot said, 'that they were going to become unhappy or even angry when we went to play in these grotty venues that they were booked into: England was tough going the first time around – in the provinces, people didn't know what was going on. And the Wailers had to play on such tiny stages. But they were extremely professional and never objected at all. They were very positive towards me, always very keen that things should run smoothly. Peter and Bunny were certainly more difficult to please than Bob. There was some tension, but when they got up and played it always disappeared.

'Those early days with Peter and Bunny were unique: you had the three writers and therefore a spread of songs. You had the harmonies of Bunny's high voice and Peter's low voice; and it was those harmonies that really made it.'

As Foot worked more and more closely with Bob Marley, however, he began to note certain tensions within the musician himself. 'One has to be careful about a legend,' he considered, 'but I felt at this time that Bob was not secure in himself. I think he was perturbed that one of his parents was white, and he wanted to prove himself very much as being a black Rasta. He would behave in this way that was very tough and hard, which wasn't really him at all.

'On his own, we got on very well. But when he had his court around him, he'd behave in this very tough way with me. But it was a pose, it wasn't the real man. Bob's particular problem, I always felt, was that he was an up-and-coming black star, based on this entire Rasta philosophy; and he didn't quite feel the part.'

For the next few weeks, Benjamin Foot's on-the-road activities with the Wailers were of a purely local nature, ferrying equipment and then the group to Island's studios in Basing Street. Following that first major UK tour, in May and June 1973, the Wailers immediately set about over-dubbing parts on their second album for Island; not in Kingston, where at Harry J's in April they had already laid down the rhythm tracks, but in Notting Hill. When Chris Blackwell showed them the two studios, they opted for the smaller one, Studio 2, down in the basement of the building, which reminded Family Man of Treasure Isle. 'We say, "This is the one: feel the beat." You can really feel the bottom.'

By the time the Wailers' sessions began, the Rolling Stones were in Studio 1, finishing off the *Goats Head Soup* album they had recorded in Jamaica. (At one point, the sessions in Studio 2 were interrupted by Mick Jagger entering to inquire whether Chris Blackwell could pull any weight for Anita Pallenberg, who had been busted for drugs in Ocho Rios in Jamaica.)

The new album would kick off with 'Get Up, Stand Up', jointly written by Bob Marley and Peter Tosh, such a statement of militant intent that it would seem later to personify Peter Tosh; Bob Marley's role in its composition was somewhat overlooked. Even though here both Bob and Peter appeared on lead vocals, with Bob taking the lion's share, in time Peter Tosh's solo version of 'Get Up, Stand Up' – included in 1977 on his masterly *Equal Rights* album – somewhat overshadowed this original version. Rather than merely exhorting people to stand up for their civil rights, the lyrics of 'Get Up, Stand Up' tell a more complex tale of self-realisation: it is because they've seen the light through Rastafari, discovering that the Mighty God is a living man, that they are going to stand up for their rights.

In many ways, this second Island album, which would carry the title of *Burnin'*, offered a more traditional sound than *Catch a Fire*, the harmonies of the three Wailers interweaving and soaring as though they were being performed in the First Church of Rastafari. Nowhere was this more notable than on 'Rasta Man Chant', a traditional Nyabinghi hymn which would not have been out of place had it been performed live at Pinnacle, Leonard Howell's original Rastafarian encampment; 'Rasta Man Chant' would become the closing track of the album. Although the songs were credited to the name of Jean Watt, there was a pair of Bunny Livingston tunes on the record, 'Hallelujah Time' and 'Pass It On', which could have come straight from a similar hilltop ceremony – although the instrumental introduction to 'Pass It

On' seemed a direct lift from the then extremely popular 'Sitting in Limbo', the Jimmy Cliff tune that was a feature of the soundtrack of *The Harder They Come*. What had one to 'pass on'? The message that living for yourself was living in vain – 'Help your brothers' was an actual line from the song, and 'Be not selfish in your doings' was another. During the sessions, another Bunny Livingston song was recorded, 'Reincarnated Souls', which told how the Wailers were precisely that. The tune had already been released before these Basing Street sessions were finished, as the B-side of 'Concrete Jungle', taken from *Catch a Fire* as a further single to promote the first Island LP.

Amongst the more reflective songs recorded for the new album, there was also a pair of Bob Marley set-piece tunes of distinctive strength and artful merit: a reworking of 'Duppy Conqueror' (another 'do-over' was 'Small Axe', which suffered in comparison with the Scratch Perry production, missing its magical vitality), and a new tune, 'I Shot the Sheriff', a song that – as Bunny Livingston said – 'was supposed to have a cowboy ballad vibe, directly influenced by Marty Robbins'. Plunging to the core of the omnipresent cowboy imagery in Jamaica, where half the population sometimes seems to be living as though in a spaghetti western, Bob sang about how 'Sheriff John Brown' had always hated him – in the 1970s, 'John Brown' was a common Jamaican colloquial description of any Everyman figure who was a subject of interest; in the UK, it was a term in common use in the 1950s. (When Eric Clapton recorded 'I Shot the Sheriff' and released it as a single the following year, in 1974, the song became a global hit, confusing all those white rock fans of Clapton who claimed to hate reggae – and providing the career of Bob Marley with a quantum leap.)

Then there was the song from which the album title was ultimately taken, 'Burnin' and Lootin'', in which Bob Marley talked of how everything they had, they had lost, and how long it had taken them to meet the boss – that reference to Chris Blackwell. Therefore, from now on, this was a new time in which they would be burnin' and lootin', 'to survive'. The song seemed to look forward, to represent a move into a new life. On one hand, it was a general militant declaration of purpose; yet on the other, it was deeply personal. And taking the song in a universal sense left some of the lines not having any meaning: 'All those drugs will make you slow,' Bob wagged his finger. Who was he thinking about? Even on the apparently quintessentially combative 'Burnin' and Lootin'', Bob Marley adopted a softer pitch, making his point through understatement, as though he firmly believed that less was more.

He was to about to discover that one less Wailer could certainly be more. Island Records had set up a series of shows in the United States, with key dates in Boston and Manhattan. Bunny Livingston, however, had announced – in the exaggeratedly precise BBC English with which he would consider only the most important of issues – that he would not be partaking in this quest. The chemistry of musical combos is a complex matter: the actions and reactions within them are by no means pre-dictable. The official explanation given was Bunny's refusal to travel on an 'iron bird'. But this was essentially a metaphor for Bunny's distaste and, it seems, confusion at having found himself a man apart in the world of Babylon. Sometimes it feels as if something was being lost in transla-tion. When Bunny, for example, asked Chris Blackwell what kind of venues they would play in the US, the record-company boss had replied, 'freak clubs'; 'freaks', of course, being a term which had become affec-tionately synonymous with hippie-types. Yet Bunny interpreted this as meaning they would perform in clubs full of Babylonian degenerates. He decided he would take no part in such a venture. Perhaps this did not overly concern Chris Blackwell, for, working in the studio with Bob Marley, he had come to a revelatory conclusion: 'Bob had a voice that was very good for recording. It's to do with the frequencies: you can surround Bob's voice with instruments at a high level, but his voice is of such a frequency that it will always cut through.'

The US dates were set for July 1973. Bob Marley, Peter Tosh, Wire Lindo, and Family Man and Carly Barrett rehearsed rigorously at 56 Hope Road. To cover up the absence of Bunny's high-harmony parts, Bob and Peter agreed to bring in Joe Higgs, who back in Trench Town a decade or so previously had rigorously instructed the Wailers on how to sing harmony and overseen their early Studio One sessions. 'Joe Higgs helped me to understands that jazz music,' said Bob Marley. 'He taught me many things.'

Bureaucratic tardiness at the US embassy in Kingston meant that the Wailers' work permits had not come through by the time they were scheduled to depart Jamaica. Accordingly, with Benjamin Foot continuing in his role of tour manager, it was decided that the group would fly to Toronto in Canada, crossing into the United States at Niagara Falls, where there would be an immigration officer of their acquaintance. From there they drove to Boston, to a tiny jazz club called Paul's Mall. It was those Boston shows, Benjamin Foot believed, that first broke the Wailers in the United States. 'They played a week of three sets a night in Boston – it would terrify me having to go and get them out for a third set at one a.m.,' he admitted. 'All the same, it did them an incredible amount of good. Because that was where they really broke: after that they had an underground following in the States.'

'The first place we break the reggae was in Boston, at a basement club they call Paul's Mall, a jazz club.' Family Man recalled the dates slightly differently. 'We got two shows each night, and played it for two weeks straight. There is a jazz workshop next door, and every time the jazz guys take a five from there, they say, "You guys have everybody from the vibrations you are playing." After a while we went back there and played again, because we were shaking the roof down.'

The next venue on this American tour was Max's Kansas City in Manhattan, New York, located at 213 Park Avenue South, near Union Square, the sort of venue Chris Blackwell may have had in mind when he spoke of 'freak clubs'. At Max's, which basked in its own fashionable underground aura, the Wailers had a six-night residency which commenced on 16 July 1973, playing two sets a night with a hot new young singer from New Jersey called Bruce Springsteen – somewhat gauchely being promoted by his record company as 'the new Dylan'; the shows were as much Springsteen's New York launch as they were the Wailers'. (The manager of Max's had booked the Jamaican group after listening to *Catch a Fire* – 'the Drifters with a conscience' was what he heard.) Although the Wailers, who, like Springsteen, performed an hour-long set, had previously played in Manhattan, this was the first time there that their audience had not been made up of almost 100 per cent expatriate Jamaicans; indeed, the atmosphere of impenetrable 'cool' around Max's, part of the psycho-geography of the Andy Warhol Factory scene (as well as the fact that CBS, busily promoting Bruce Springsteen, had purchased almost all the tickets), was such that nary a single Jamaican made it to the event. Even this apparently negative element was significant. From now on, reggae music would no longer be localised to Jamaica and Jamaicans; with *Catch a Fire* and their shows in the UK and USA, the Wailers were introducing an entirely new flavour to Anglo-American popular music.

As with the Speakeasy shows in London, all of fashionable New York was there on the first night – quite a squeeze, as Max's had space for fewer than two hundred people. Playing a set akin to the one with which they had held the similarly snooty Speakeasy spellbound – 'Put It On', 'Slave Driver', 'Burnin' and Lootin'', 'Stop That Train', 'Kinky Reggae', and 'Stir It Up' amongst the tracks – the Wailers triumphed. 'Every rock critic in New York showed up for what would be their first exposure to live reggae, and yes, the Wailers' opening set was rapturously received by all,' said the journalist Steve Simels. 'Few bands have ever had two frontmen as charismatic as Bob Marley and Peter Tosh. After intermission, however, I realised that the aforementioned highly jaded press contingent, having already had their tiny minds blown by a bunch of Rastas turning the beat around, were not about to fall for any "new Dylan" hype and had beaten a hasty exit.'

Also present at Max's was Billy Mernit, a songwriter whose tunes had been covered by Carly Simon and Judy Collins, among others. 'You could smell the Jamaican homegrown in the room,' he remembered. 'Max's was literally and figuratively smoking that night. For a couple of hours, it was musically heavier in there than it was inside any other club in the city, and by the end of the weekend you'd have to be craned in through the chimney to see the show.' Mernit was good buddies with Lee Jaffe, who was travelling with the group and staying with them at the Chelsea Hotel on West 23rd Street – it was thought the management of the Chelsea was probably the only one in the city that would not object to the habitual herb-smoking of the group. Some of the Chelsea rooms had their own kitchens, allowing the Wailers – especially Carly Barrett – to cook their own ital food, Bob traipsing through the West Side corner markets for fruit to juice in a blender borrowed from Lee Jaffe's parents. Billy Mernit lived on Greene Street in SoHo, above the Blue Rock recording studio, which he unofficially kept an eye on for its owner. One night he was woken at two in the morning by a phone call from Lee Jaffe, who said he had a friend with him and wanted to come to the studio to jam. Accordingly, still high from that night's show at Max's, Bob Marley stepped into Blue Rock out of the steamy Manhattan summer night, a spliff dangling from the corner of his mouth. 'He had a guitar case in his hand and he was vibrating with herbal energy. There wasn't a lot of talking,' said Mernit. Setting up in the studio, with Mernit on piano, Bob jammed with him on 'Concrete Jungle' and 'Duppy Conqueror' for an hour or so. And then Bob Marley disappeared off into the night, as suddenly as he had arrived. Maybe he wanted to get back to Mooksie, the Danish beauty he had met who lived on the eleventh floor of the Chelsea, and who would guide him as they glided arm in arm through the havens of West Village pot dealers, searching to score Colombian gold, in that time when Colombian marijuana was considered some of the finest in the world.

Following the dates in New York, the Wailers returned home to Jamaica.

As his refusal to tour 'Babylon' would suggest, it was Bunny who of all the Wailers was the most combative in terms of black militancy. With Jean Watt, his beautiful girlfriend, Bunny had moved to live in a bamboo hut amongst the devoted Rasta community by the beach at Bull Bay, the address he had given on his work-permit application for the UK *Catch a Fire* tour. Attuned to the slightest nuances of symbolism and poetry in everyday life, these Rasta inhabitants set a certain store by the fact that the beach's sand was black. 'Capturing' – as squatting is termed in Jamaica – a stretch of unclaimed terrain on the nearby rocks, Bunny had built his home there himself, giving this essay in simplicity a touch of luxury with a floor of splendidly polished rare wood. ('It was small and primitive and sophisticated at the same time – quite exquisite,' recalled Lee Jaffe.)

Most mornings at around 5:30 Bob would get behind the wheel of his Ford Capri and drive out to Bull Bay to run with Skill Cole, ending their exercise with a headlong dive into the delicious azure ocean of the Caribbean – it was Bob's favourite swimming beach in Jamaica. Then, before the sun rose too high, they would jog up into the adjacent hills to bathe in the cascading waters of Cane River Falls; afterwards, they knew, in the Rasta encampment they were always certain of finding some peanut porridge or fish tea simmering in a pot, usually in the vessel owned by Gabby Dread. 'He was like an inspiration to them,' said Gilly, 'because he was the best man on the beach that have the steam chalice ready, and have the roastfish ready, and fish tea on Bull Bay beach.' Across this entire stretch of land, a myriad of red, gold, and green Ethiopian flags fluttered in a breeze as soft as parrot feathers as it rolled its way inland off the Caribbean.

Secure in his faith, Bunny was on more wobbly ground when it came to his finances. 'At one point, towards the end of the Wailers' period together, he had to go out and fish for a living because he had no money,' Lee Jaffe recalled of Bunny's life at this time. Although he now had marginalised himself away from the group, to an extent Bunny Livingston always had been marginalised as a group member: although he would strum guitar and play percussion, unlike Bob and, especially, Peter Tosh, he didn't really play any instrument to a virtuoso degree.

As if it were an augury, Peter had been seeing vampires everywhere, glimpsing them out of the corners of his eyes, the whites of which were permanently flecked red, an effect of his ceaseless herb-smoking – Peter even blamed his constant car crashes on vampires having grabbed his steering-wheel. And if Bunny Livingston felt uncomfortable about travelling to Babylon, Peter Tosh had recently felt the full force of Babylonian oppression in his own Jamaican backyard: the previous year, 1972, he had suffered the first of several beatings he would endure from members of the Jamaican police.

One evening, Peter Tosh had arrived at his home from the country, where he had gone on a mission to score some killer herb. He now lived in Spanish Town, the former capital, where he had rented a home for himself and Yvonne, his tiny 19-year-old girlfriend, hoping that there he would be unlikely to earn the scrutiny of prying members of the Jamaican constabulary. When Peter had arrived back from his herb-hunting expedition, a party was taking place within the communal yard that Peter shared; in the background he could hear the liquor-fuelled chatter and laughter of the revellers. Sitting at his kitchen table, firing up his exotic ganja, Peter went into a reverie: locked as he was into the creative impulses of the herb, he soon no longer paid any attention to the discordance created by his neighbours. Tapping a rhythm on the table, he simultaneously found a set of matching words running into his mind: 'I see the mark of the beast on their ugly faces / Me know them a wicked.' As he formulated these lyrics clearly for the first time, for the song that came to be titled 'Mark of the Beast', his trance was shattered by the sound of a gunshot. Yvonne told Peter that the bullet had been fired by a group of police outside the building – just the kind of visitors Peter had been hoping by this choice of location to avoid. Then a posse of cops charged through his own front entrance, heading for the yard where the party was being held, their specific targets. As they did so, one of them glanced through the door of the room in which Peter Tosh was sat, and saw the spliff in his hand. 'A ganja that y'have deh,' said the cop. 'Ganja is a bird in Australia,' replied Peter obliquely.

The policeman snatched the spliff from Peter, who grabbed it back, trying to stuff it into the top of his pants. The cop hurried outside to his comrades. 'One criminal inside yah!', Peter heard him utter, before half a dozen plainclothes cops rushed into his home, dragging him outside. With a pair of them holding on to each of his arms, the man who had first entered Peter's room proceeded to beat him in the stomach with the butt of his .38 revolver. Then he beat him in the same place with a fist. Seeming to tire of this, the cop then took a rifle from another policeman and slammed it into Peter Tosh's ribs, dislocating one of them. Taking up a thick piece of wood, the cop then smashed it down on the side of Peter's head, causing a wound that required seven stitches.

When Peter was taken to hospital for treatment to his damaged ribs, Bob Marley, arriving to visit his injured spar, was himself arrested in the hospital car-park on a trumped-up ganja charge by a Rasta-hating cop: it was Bob's turn to be dragged off to the cells. When Bunny told Peter what had taken place, Peter dragged himself from his hospital bed, dressed himself, and drove with Bunny towards the police station to rescue Bob. As they rounded a corner, however, they saw Bob driving back towards the hospital: the wisdom of senior cops had prevailed, and he had been released.

Was such vicious, aberrant behaviour on the part of the police a reflection of the growing confrontational mood in Jamaica? Highly likely: for since Michael Manley had become prime minister the previous winter, the country was beginning to seem increasingly polarised between its radical and reactionary citizens. It would not be long before a state of unofficial civil war existed in Jamaica. The incident only strengthened Peter Tosh in his resolve to continue smoking 'herb' in as public a manner as possible; the next year he released the 'Mark of the Beast' tune as a single.

On a personal level, Bob Marley now had further family preoccupations. In London, another child had been born to him, a daughter, Karen, whose mother was Janet Bowen, with whom he had had a fling whilst working on *Catch a Fire* at Basing Street. In December 1973, Bob Marley gave an answer in an interview that could hardly have delighted Rita, his wife: when asked if there was any special 'lady' in his life, Bob replied, 'No really a one lady yet . . . No, I don't really settle down with lady. Me not ready.' The irony here was that the 'special' lady to whom he had once pledged his troth was now pregnant again. But perhaps not by her husband.

29.xi.73

To whom it may concern:

    Peter McIntosh,
    c/o 436 Kings Road
    SW3

    This young Jamaican has influenza
and an upper respiratory tract infection
that prevents him from singing for four weeks.

    S. Kraemer

J.W.S. KRAEMER MB MRCP
J. W. S. KRAEMER

59 Brixton Water Lane
London   SW2 1PH
tel. 01-733 0752

*   *   *

Two and a half months after the Max's dates, the Wailers were again playing live in the United States. The group crossed to California on the West
Coast and on 19 October played the Matrix Club in San Francisco.

Burnin', the second Island album, had just been released and, following this Bay Area show, the Wailers had a support slot on a Sly and the
Family Stone tour. Sly and the Family Stone was at the time the biggest
black group in the country, one that had crossed over to the point where
the majority of its audience was made up of white 'underground-rock'
fans. What one might imagine would be an ideal series of concerts turned
into the complete reverse. After four dates, the Wailers were bumped
from the tour and left stranded in Las Vegas. 'Sly was really worried at
the effect they were having on his audiences,' Benjie Foot said.

Family Man was certain that Sly's audiences had been intrigued by the
Wailers. 'I was always quick to go to the exit doors to hear what the audiences were saying as they were leaving the theatre. They always talking
about the "opening group". "What kind of music is that?" they are saying.'
There are those, however, who assert there was no truth whatsoever
in the idea that the power of the Wailers was denting the impact of Sly
and the Family Stone. More accurately, Sly Stone's audience was baffled by the Wailers, unable to empathise in the least with the Jamaican
group – the real reason they were kicked off the dates.

For losing their tour, as what appeared at first to be a consolation prize,
the group was given what would later become known as a legendary
radio broadcast. Driving up to San Francisco, the Wailers played a further
couple of dates at the Matrix, on 29 and 30 October. On the morning
after the second of these shows, the group convened at the Record Plant,
the San Francisco recording studio, to record their entire set live for
KSAN, the hip Bay Area FM station; overseen by DJ Tom Donahue, the

group played in front of no more than five people. But the performance that resulted became renowned. The penultimate song was 'Lively Up Yourself', which they had recorded for Scratch Perry and which Bob was contemplating including on their next album. The performance ended with 'Walk the Proud Land', originally recorded in the mid-1960s, with the phrase 'skank quadrille' thrown in, almost as punctuation (it was later to appear on the *Bunny Wailer Sings the Wailers* album). The recording of the show became widely available as a coveted bootleg, an accolade in itself, and another subtle marketing tool from Chris Blackwell and Island Records; later it enjoyed an official release, as part of the *Talkin' Blues* music-and-interview album. The purity and perfection of the KSAN set almost made up for the stop-start nature of this short West Coast tour.

In November 1973 the Wailers – again without Bunny – returned to England for their second tour that year. As a warm-up to the concerts proper they performed three songs at the Sundown Edmonton, on the farthest fringe of north-eastern London, a benefit for the Ethiopian Famine Relief Fund: the tunes chosen were 'Get Up, Stand Up', 'Slave Driver', and 'Stop That Train'. Count Prince Miller, a singer of somewhat bawdy reggae songs as well as an actor in the black sitcom *Desmond's*, was the MC: 'Make the boys feel good,' he exhorted the audience.

The main UK tour consisted of a set of shows in colleges, mostly in the north of England, in the grimmest industrial cities, at a time of year when the inclement, unpredictable weather can cast a pall of depressing gloom over the entire region. The dates kicked off on 19 November in a bitterly cold Nottingham, followed by shows in Bradford, Birmingham, Stafford, and Blackpool.

However, the tour was never completed. After a performance at Leeds Polytechnic on 27 November 1973, the group set out to drive the two hundred miles back to London, where they were staying. By now, Mick Cater had grown to be wary of long journeys with the group in their cramped mini-bus – 'the Bibles would come out and the arguments would become very heated.' But on this occasion matters became far more serious. Cater was a great admirer of the statuesque though – notably since his beating by the police – increasingly moody Peter Tosh. With a black carved fist in red, gold, and green emblazoned on his stage sweatshirt, he resembled a biblical prophet; this was an effect only reinforced when Tosh kicked off the live sets with the portentous lines from 'Rastaman Chant': 'Hear the words of the Rastaman . . .' But now Cater saw a very different side of him. 'Peter went mad. In the middle of the motorway on the way back from Leeds, he threw a very strange tantrum. He had flu. But I remember thinking that there was more to it than just being ill: he really seemed to have gone mad.' The incident must have been disturbing for Yvonne, Peter's girlfriend, who had accompanied him on the tour.

The next show was in Northampton, on 30 November. The gig went ahead, despite a sick note, dated 29 November 1973, written by a doctor whose address was given as Brixton Water Lane, declaring that 'Peter McIntosh' was suffering from influenza and a throat infection and would be unable to perform for four weeks (see page 242). As they arrived at the venue, thick snow was falling. Peter, who argued violently with Bob, interpreted this as a clear sign that the tour was doomed. By abandoning the dates and boarding a flight back to Jamaica, he turned this perception into a self-fulfilling prophecy.

Although dispirited by the problems of touring with Peter and Bunny, Bob Marley retained his vision of how the future would unfold. 'I don't think he would allow anyone to crumble his ambitions,' said Rita Marley. 'Like he said in one interview, he could not sit at home idle and think of how when Ziggy and his children grew up they would ask why he didn't go to work to send them to school. So he was pushed because he felt he had a responsibility more than the other two guys – even though their decision was more, "Well, wha' 'appen, 'appen". I was always there with that wife talk – that something had to be done for the children.'

None of the musicians involved would ever tour Europe or the United States in winter again. The official reason offered by the Island Records office for the cancellation of the tour was that 'it snowed.' Although their fans were disappointed, this explanation had the advantage of making the Wailers seem even weirder than they were already imagined to be (though at this time no one knew that the trio from Trench Town was virtually over). 'I never try to come between Bob, Peter, and Bunny,' said Family Man, 'because I have a special respect for the man there, my favourite spiritual group singing about God and t'ing and Rastafari. One time I hear them say we finish with the tour. I think, "Finish with it? I think the tour just get started. Must be something I don't know about." The power of this thing with Rastafari and God . . . Well, I just accept that and go through. They have that saying, "Everything happen for a wise purpose."

'Now Bob have to get busy, not only as a singer, but also as a businessman. He see that if you have a product you have to go there to promote it.'

Bob and Bunny continued to maintain a good relationship. The most mystical of the Wailers simply wasn't prepared to make the sacrifices that life on the road as a new group entails. Bob was ready for this, however: he knew that it would not always be so uncomfortable. Peter, meanwhile, was receiving advice from those around him that he was as powerful a performer as Bob and could easily make it on his own. All three members of the group had outgrown each other; they needed space to work; but they didn't need the carry-go-bring-come people who gathered around them distorting how each felt about the other, causing tension.

NATTY DREAD

A new phase of their lives was being embarked upon by all three principal members of the original Wailers. Two years previously, Bunny Livingston had developed the idea of Peter and himself establishing their own labels, Bunny coming up with the concept of the Solomonic and Intel-Diplo imprints. When he had suggested to Peter that he choose one of them, he picked Intel-Diplo. Although often explained as being an abbreviation for 'Intelligent Diplomat for His Majesty', Bunny originally had taken the word-twist from a line in the Bible maintaining that Solomon had been an intelligent diplomat; both label names therefore were a reference to Solomon, the wise man. Bunny had designed each label with visual allusions to Egyptology: Solomonic had a six-point star with two eyes; Intel-Diplo had a five-point star with one eye. It was the label design that impelled Peter to choose Intel-Diplo. 'Mi love this one,' he said. Peter Tosh then moved fast; the first tune he had out on his own label was 'Maga Dog', followed by 'Dog Teeth', and then 'Ketchy Shubby'.

'Even from the very beginning, Peter was a powerful musician, a powerful artist,' said Danny Sims. 'He sang a lot, he made his own records. But Bob was the singer with the Wailers. Bunny was a very good singer, Peter a good singer, but Bob was the lead singer. Because Bob wrote all the songs.' ('They felt after the first two Island albums that they were not getting the chance to record enough of their own songs,' said Lee Jaffe of the predicament jointly experienced by Peter Tosh and Bunny Livingston.)

'Even in the break-up, I didn't see a break-up between Peter and Bob,' maintained Danny Sims. 'The concept of everybody giving Bob a hard time over the split was a problem of jealousy. Because when Chris Blackwell wanted to work with just Bob Marley . . . Well, Bob was a better businessman at that time: Bob Marley was a very good businessman. Bunny and Peter were only budding businessmen at that time.'

'Peter was always difficult,' said Chris Blackwell. 'I found Bunny easier than him, because Bunny was consistently no: he didn't want to tour overseas, he didn't want to do this, do that, didn't want to have anything to do with Babylon. Peter was yes and then no, yes and then no. And that was more difficult. So really I didn't work with Peter hardly at all after *Burnin'*. But I did continue to work with Bunny.'

'Mi really used to work hard, you know,' admitted Bob Marley. 'But if you in a group and you get tense . . . Mi no want say this but mi little bit tense with the Wailers we have first time, Bunny and Peter. Is like them don't want understand mi can't just play music fe Jamaica alone. Can't learn that way. Mi get the most of my learning when mi travel and talk to other people.'

As to explaining the cancellation of the UK *Burnin'* dates, Bob Marley was utterly to the point: 'Well, the thing was, some of the members of the group can't stand the cold.'

Back in Jamaica, Bob Marley busied himself with writing or improving new material. Amongst the tunes he was working on was one he had played to Benjamin Foot when he had arrived in London for the *Burnin'* tour. Appearing at Foot's home in west London early in the morning, direct from the overnight flight from Jamaica, Marley picked out a song for him on his acoustic guitar that he said he had written on the plane. 'It seemed to me to be a rather ordinary, semi-folk song. Which probably goes to show why I'm not still in the music business,' Foot remembered. The song was called 'No Woman, No Cry'. It contained a line referring back to Bob's time at Tartar's yard in Trench Town: 'Georgie will make the fire light.' As a mark of respect, the composing rights were given to Tartar, hence the V. Ford – for Vincent Ford, his real name – songwriting credit.

One day, Bob drove down to Trench Town to visit a girl he had been seeing. Georgie Robinson heard he was in the area, but didn't see the Tuff Gong anywhere. Then he heard Bob had gone up to Boys Town to play football. Finally, Bob came over to Tartar's yard to see both his longtime friends.

'Wha' 'appen, ol' Georgie?'

'Nothin' much.'

Bob leaned on the wall of the yard and asked Tartar to fetch him his old acoustic guitar. Then he started to perform 'No Woman, No Cry'. The song, with its deeply personal reminiscence of their impoverished life in the yards of Trench Town, moved Georgie to the edge of tears.

When he first heard the song, Family Man was similarly impressed: 'It was good, like a semi-chant with a little ballad feel. And not only did it play a tempo, but it played a riff within the tempos, to give that soulful feeling. We used a rhythm box to set the feeling.' To the bass player, 'No Woman, No Cry' sounded like a hit: 'It was good stuff. And when we play it we see the response from the audience. On the first live album it seemed to be the only music that seemed to be mixed to the standard of the time. The rest of it sound too tinny, like live stuff.'

Another new song had been written in Jamaica, a consequence of Bob being held up in a police night-time car check, and given the journalistic title of 'Rebel Music (3 O'Clock Roadblock)'. Still in love with Esther Anderson, Bob spent much of his time with her, often at Little Bay, a small fishing village with several beaches ten miles from the then hippie haven of Negril, in the far west of Jamaica, a five-hour drive from Kingston. With the original Wailers clearly no longer part of the contract, he had struck a new deal with Chris Blackwell; an important clause gave Bob Marley full rights to 56 Hope Road, so long as he remained with Island Records. With part of the proceeds of this new agreement, Bob Marley had purchased a brand-new BMW. It was in this vehicle, driven by his cousin Sledger, that Bob and his passengers, Esther Anderson and Lee Jaffe, were obliged to run a gauntlet of several police roadblocks on a journey from Little Bay, on each occasion Bob having to throw away his 'little herb-stalk' – as he sings in 'Rebel Music'. As this state of aggressive absurdity manifested itself during their drive, Bob Marley started throwing out appropriate lyric lines; meanwhile, Lee Jaffe, in the rear of the car, accompanied him on harmonica. 'Bob would work on writing songs nearly every day,' Jaffe recalled. 'Usually the process would begin with acoustic guitar. When I was around I'd be playing harmonica along with him. Sometimes Seeco Patterson, the Wailers' percussionist, would be banging on something. When he started to write he would often keep working on a song for days, weeks, or even longer, changing words or lines or altering a melody. When it would reach a certain stage of readiness he'd go into the studio and start to work with Family Man, who

August 20th, 1975

Bob Marley,
56 Hope Road,
Kingston 6,
Jamaica, W.I.

Dear Bob,

Have now done a mix of the recording we made at The
Lyceum of NO WOMAN NO CRY and KINKY REGGAE.

They have turned out great, everyone likes them and
we are releasing a single here with NO WOMAN NO CRY
as the A side and KINKY REGGAE as the B side.

Will let you have stampers and some samples incase
you want to release it in Jamaica.

Should be in Jamaica for a few days around September
9th so will see you then.

Best wishes,

Chris Blackwell.

would come up with bass lines and work with Bob on arrangements and record demos to start to get the feel of what a record might sound like. I really admired his work ethic and attention to detail.'

Lee Jaffe was of the opinion that both Peter and Bunny felt that all three original Wailers members eventually would reunite. Although they never would work together again in the recording studio, it was not long before they found themselves once more sharing the same stage.

Marvin Gaye, one of Tamla Motown's biggest pop acts during the sixties, and during the seventies a symbol of not only black consciousness but also of black sexuality, was scheduled to play at the Carib Theatre in Kingston on 28 May 1974; this show would be followed three days later by a larger event, at the city's National Arena.

The concerts were charity occasions, intended to raise money for the Trench Town Comprehensive Sports Centre – the aware Gaye had been eager to perform at them. Before he had even asked the Wailers, Tony Spaulding, the minister of housing, had put the group's name on the poster advertising the show. And it was made quite clear to the group that their services as support act were expected. As they rehearsed at 56 Hope Road, a rough-looking individual arrived at a session and let them know quite unequivocally that there would be severe penalties for non-appearance, threatening them with a trumped-up prison charge.

'Rebel Music (3 O'Clock Roadblock)' was one of the hits of the evening when debuted before the packed audience at the Carib Theatre. For this yard show as support to Marvin Gaye, who came onstage wearing a discreet tam, the three original members of the Wailers were augmented as per usual by the Barrett brothers, and by Tyrone Downie on keyboards.

Marvin Gaye had only recently returned to live work and – despite playing with a full orchestra – was below par at the Carib show. The

Wailers, moreover, were performing in Jamaica for the first time since they had recorded the Island albums and toured hard supporting them. They mashed Marvin down at the Carib, although the second, larger date was a more even match. (Throughout his career, even up to his penultimate dates with the Commodores in New York, Bob was accomplished at appearing as the opening act and irrevocably stealing the show: a guerrilla attack from the ghetto.)

Yet it still seemed almost miraculous that Bob, Peter, and Bunny managed to make it on to the same stage – although they would perform together again briefly, with two other Motown acts: the Jackson 5 and Stevie Wonder.

To all intents and purposes, the hit-making trio from Trench Town was a thing of the past. As though in confirmation of this, in the middle of the summer of 1974, Bob Marley received his greatest recognition as a composer of commercial music: Eric Clapton's version of 'I Shot the Sheriff' went to number one in the US singles charts, his only American number one. 'I want to say "I shot the police" but the government would have made a fuss, so I said "I shot the sheriff" instead. But it's the same idea: justice,' admitted Bob.

(According to Lee Jaffe, 'I Shot the Sheriff' was written soon after they had returned from the Trinidad carnival, during a visit to Hellshire Beach, about 45 minutes drive south-west from the capital. Hellshire would later become the main beach used by Kingstonians, but that was after a metalled road had been laid. In 1973, Bob had to carefully negotiate potholes along the dirt road so as to avoid damaging the suspension of his Ford Capri. Sitting out on the grainy sand, being sprinkled by ocean spray, Bob was playing the guitar, and Lee Jaffe was on the harmonica, when Bob suddenly threw out the line, 'I shot the sheriff,' to which Lee Jaffe riposted, 'But you didn't get the deputy.' The song developed from there. That day on the beach, Bob played with the tune on his guitar and

Lee Jaffe riffed on his harmonica. Soon a pair of fat, big-bottomed girls started to dance in front of them, before long joined by most of the people on the beach. This was when they knew that they had written a hit song.)

You might have imagined that such international acclaim would have spilled over, elevating Bob Marley's status in Jamaica. Instead, there were those in Jamaica who resented him for it, especially as he was nothing but a 'dutty Rasta bwai': as the seventies progressed, and the rootsical style of reggae developed into one of the nation's themes, so the attitude of upstanding Jamaicans towards Rastafari hardened rather than loosened.

Bob and the Wailers still received almost zero airplay on Jamaica's two radio stations. The large Jamaican record companies had long-standing 'arrangements' with the disc jockeys and programme directors which ensured independent labels such as Tuff Gong barely got a look-in. When 'Rebel Music (3 O'Clock Roadblock)', recorded for the new album, was released on Tuff Gong as a single, its controversial nature alone precluded it from their playlists. Although Bob's spar Skill Cole was no longer managing him, the man who had helped set up Tuff Gong was incensed by this lack of airtime. Accordingly, he would drive up to the RJR and JBC stations; wielding a baseball bat, accompanied by the diminutive but intimidating pair of Tek Life and Frowser, the strapping Skill Cole would demand that 'Rebel Music' be played immediately. Sitting outside in their vehicle, Bob Marley would hunker his slight frame down in his car seat and wait to hear the tune sail out of the radio.

'We go up there and have to beat boy,' said Skill Cole. 'We go and fight a system where they just have money power. We are on the street: we are street boy. We beat programme director, disc jockey. We no afraid of no guy. Puncture the man car supposed to get puncture. Box a bwai supposed to get box if he won't play them tune. Konk them up in them head and kick them batty. They was fighting us because we was Rastas.

'Bob Marley was the singer: he was a quiet little brethren. Can't do nothing more than be quiet and give you the best lyrics and the best music. So mi just deal with things the right and proper way.'

Working as tour manager for Marvin Gaye when he played in Kingston was a man called Don Taylor, a garrulous Jamaican based in the United States whose previous experience in the music business had included managing the American doo-wop group Little Anthony and the Imperials. Before he left Jamaica, Taylor had earned money by diving for coins thrown from tourist ships – he was said to have been the first such individual to own a suit, an indicator of his upward mobility. Having trekked up to 56 Hope Road early in the morning after the first show with Marvin Gaye, Taylor woke Bob and pitched him a plan for becoming his manager. Impressed with his initiative, Bob decided to try him out.

'Don Taylor,' said Chris Blackwell, 'was the person who Bob was able to turn to, to work with. He was able to get him on the road and bring to life what was not going to happen unless Bob toured. Bob broke from people seeing him and saying, "*Fuck: I can't believe this guy!*" and then going and buying the record.

'I realised I was in big trouble if I couldn't get Bob to tour, and there was nobody I had who could handle his management. And Bob had no use for the guys around in Jamaica. Don Taylor came in and hustled it together. In that respect he is an absolutely key man in Bob's success – no doubt of it. It wouldn't have happened if Bob had not gone out and gone touring, and Don got that together for him.'

In Don Taylor, a manager had been secured for Bob Marley and his group. But what group? Who would he play with? It was crisis time, and the dilemma required to be resolved straightaway.

Bob Marley was concerned about precisely who he should be sharing the stage with in the future. Clearly, the differences between himself and Peter Tosh and Bunny Wailer were insurmountable. The chance of any further collaboration with Peter Tosh had been irrevocably severed when Chris Blackwell declined to issue a contract for a solo album by the self-styled Stepping Razor; such a release, claimed the Island owner, would conflict with his marketing strategies for Bob Marley. Tosh departed in a huff to release a flurry of militant, powerful singles. Bunny's reluctance to tour, meanwhile, meant it was impossible to rely on him to be part of the worldwide strategy that Bob was envisaging for his music. To add to the complications, Wire Lindo had announced he was quitting the group, to work with Taj Mahal, the eclectic American blues artist.

So Bob sat down with Family Man and his brother Carly, all that was left of the group that had made and toured *Catch a Fire* and *Burnin'*. 'We have time to sort ourselves out and to close together,' said Family Man. 'Mi sit down in an armchair with Bob and say we can work it still: when we go up to UK as Upsetters in '69, nothing wrong if one man short. And Bob laugh and say 'im going to book some studio time at Harry J's. 'Im say 'im going for two horn men. And 'im want mi to bring two rhythm men. I say, "All right, I know who I'm going to bring." I went for Gladstone Anderson, who play piano, and Winston Wright to play organ.

'That was when we began to start the new series – *Natty Dread*. That is where everything get serious. No problem going forward, no matter what it is.'

Rehearsals for the new album, conducted with customary seriousness and diligence, took place at 56 Hope Road. At the rear of the property was a small garage-like storage room. Together, Bob and Family Man soundproofed the small building, taking care to use the most natural materials. Afterwards, Family Man ceremoniously planted a bamboo tree in front of the building, a seedling he had brought from his farm in the hills by Mount James. Then they were away, Bob's reel-to-reel tape machine, on which he would assiduously listen to every single run-through, rolling constantly.

Despite the soundproofing, the rehearsals would draw complaints from buildings all around. Only the Indian embassy, sited directly behind the rehearsal building, never made a murmur of complaint: clearly, they knew how to enjoy themselves. Miss Gough, an old English lady living on the premises, would occasionally mention that the music was very loud. More often than not, however, she would smile in appreciation at the musicians.

Following the rehearsals at '56', Bob and the group went into Harry J's once again. Harry J's studio was renowned for being equally good for bottom, top, and mid-range sounds; and from 1974 onwards also for having one of Jamaica's top engineers, Sylvan Morris, who had started out with Coxsone – his cousin – at Studio One, and moved to work with Harry Johnson at the time of the recording of *Natty Dread*. Morris was capable of empathising with the artists he was working with and bringing out the true feeling of the music in a way that was unparalleled in Jamaica. 'Some engineer who work for you, you don't even see them dancing,' said Family Man. 'Well, Sylvan Morris is not like that.'

Despite his lack of locks, Morris was an ardent believer in Rastafari. He actively encouraged Bob to bring his Rastafarian brethren to the studio, aware that they were essential in assisting the Tuff Gong to attain the right mood. If it required Gilly, the former national footballer who had become Bob's friend and juice-man, in the studio's kitchen blending June-plum juice or Bob's beloved Irish Moss (a seaweed blend), then surely this could only add to the recording's effectiveness, and Morris was sensitive enough to realise this. But he was also tough enough to stand up to any artistic arrogance he might encounter. 'I also determined when the artist I was recording was singing, like even with Bob Marley,

JOB CARD

HARRY **J** RECORDING STUDIO

№ 1276

10 ROOSEVELT AVE., KINGSTON, JAMAICA, W.I. TEL: 932-4956
937-9336

22 / 3 / 19 74

TERMS:

CONFIRMATION:

BILL TO: ISLAND RECORDS
BOB MARLEY

CLIENT'S SIGNATURE

JOB NO.			REF. NO.	DEPOSIT		
STUDIO TIME	16 TR	HOURS	RECORDING START 3.00 — Finish 12.30 = 9½ Hrs			
OVERDUBBING			Recording 3.000 To 9.00			
EDITING			Voice 9.00 — 12.30			710.00
			2 hours @ $75.00 per hour	150.00		
			7½ x $80.00		560.00	
TAPE	1	REELS	ONE 16 TR 2" TAPE			85.00
			Tapes @ 85 u.	85		
MASTERS						
ACETATES						
DUBS.						
INS.	ORGAN AT		For 6 Hrs @ 6.00	36.00		
	AT					36.00
MISC.						

ENGINEER S. Morris

CLIENT'S APPROVAL

TOTAL AMT $ 831.00

LESS DEPOSIT

BALANCE $ 831.00

871.00

I CERTIFY THAT THE ABOVE SERVICES AND MATERIALS HAS BEEN RECEIVED

RECEIVED BY:

whether they needed or not to change a lyric. I would always make sure they did it without any excuses.'

Natty Dread was the first record on which Morris worked with Bob Marley, a crucial, transitional album. 'His approach was very disciplined. They used to do a whole lot of rehearsals, and when they came by the studio, they would lay down four tracks: bass, guitar, drums, piano. Always just four tracks. But even from the laying down of the basic rhythm, you could hear that certain vibration. You could hear the discipline within. On all of the rhythms, you could hear that basic discipline, and I think it was really because of the rehearsals. Bob was a stickler for rehearsals.

'Family Man was the individual who you'd call the organiser. They relied on him to do a lot of the arranging. Because he also was very disciplined: for him the thing had to be right. So they relied on him a lot. It was a *total* effort. But Family Man was the main guy that Bob relied on.'

On the early sessions for *Natty Dread*, Bob himself would play much of the guitar. He always impressed Morris with what he could play, and with what Morris felt was a unique personal touch.

He also noted the way that Bob introduced the I-Threes to the recording. 'Again, the main theme always is discipline. Bob Marley was a very disciplined chap. And he commanded discipline within his music. So they had to conform. So probably this was one of the reasons why they became so good, the I-Threes.

'Bob had this air about him that he would just say something and it had to be right. They always know that, and because they know that, the discipline is there in the sound. And because all these girls were so professional. They were stars in their own right. They were just real good and they knew what they were doing. They weren't people you would have to train: they were just perfect soloists. And because they knew what they were doing, and because of the discipline, it came out well.'

By this stage Chris Blackwell had invested over half a million dollars in Bob Marley, a colossal figure for that time. 'I was always sure he was going to make it. Except at this time before Don Taylor turned up when suddenly I didn't feel I was going to get him out in front of the public.

'When *Natty Dread* was finished and the record sounded fantastic, I was really worried. Because if we couldn't get him to tour, what were we going to do with it? I was gearing it up. And also I was paying him royalties he hadn't earned. People read they are the greatest thing since sliced bread, but they haven't got any money actually coming in. So I would advance royalties to Bob that he hadn't really earned.'

By early October 1974, Bob's new LP, which had at first been titled *Knotty Dread*, was ready for release, for sale in the shops on 25 October. It had been recorded at Harry J's, with Bunny Livingston lending creative support, working on the harmonies; Bob Marley had then flown to London during the summer, where, under the auspices of Chris Blackwell, further production work had completed the record.

At Blackwell's suggestion, the pivotal recording that was *Natty Dread*, sparser and harder-sounding than the two previous Island LPs, was credited to 'Bob Marley and the Wailers'. The circumstances of the recording of *Natty Dread* meant that every song on the album had the luxurious advantage of being unified by Bob Marley's voice; on an early listen, it was almost confusing to hear a Wailers album without the distractions of the tones of Peter or Bunny emerging every track or so, or on harmonies. Untrammelled by the necessary compromise of working with Peter and Bunny, Bob Marley's spirit flowed freely, and he worked decisively as an auteur; from the album opener, 'Lively Up Yourself', the record ran perfectly, like a suite. At the same time, *Natty Dread* contained a number of virtuoso set-piece classics. 'No Woman, No Cry', the new song that Bob had played to Benjamin Foot, would – when released as a live version – become his first international hit single. And counterpointed against this more sentimental work was the hard militancy of both 'Them Belly Full (But We Hungry)' and 'Rebel Music (3 O'Clock Roadblock), as well as the self-explanatory 'Revolution'. The mellifluously floating 'So Jah Seh', meanwhile, contained one of Bob Marley's most memorable couplets: ''Cause puss and dog they get together / What's wrong with loving one another?' And the title track seemed like a statement of intent, the two words assuming the status of another of Bob Marley's sobriquets, a useful fallback for writers of newspaper headlines. There were, however, complaints from the Rasta high command in Jamaica about the cover image, a brooding representation of Bob Marley painted by Tony Wright, Island Records' London-based art director: for his own reasons, perhaps an effort at greater marketability, Wright had omitted to include Bob's wispy, straggly beard – making it appear as though Bob were contravening the Rasta code of not trimming body-hair.

Whilst in London for the final mixing and overdubbing of the record, Bob was introduced to an American guitarist called Al Anderson, who played some parts on 'Lively Up Yourself' and 'No Woman, No Cry'. Bob invited Anderson to come back with him to Jamaica when he returned to the island.

Other Americans were also interested in Bob Marley: the Grateful Dead revealed that they were big fans of the Wailers. They flew them out to San Francisco for a Dead gig at the Fillmore, taking Bob and Lee Jaffe to dinner, giving them the finest herb. They told Bob they would take him on tour with them as the support act. This would have seemed the perfect bill for the Wailers, as the Dead's stoned fans would certainly take to the Jamaican act – they were precisely the audience at which Chris Blackwell had been aiming – almost guaranteeing them a quantum leap in record sales. Moreover, there was a suggestion that Bill Graham, the San

Francisco promoter who had become one of the most powerful figures in the American music business and already cared for the affairs of the Grateful Dead, would become their manager too. But as a Rasta who did not believe in death, how could Bob Marley accept the offer of a group whose name – to him – certainly suggested that they did? Bob turned down the tour, citing also the fact that the Dead leader Jerry Garcia's junkie lifestyle surely meant that he already was in the ranks of the living dead. Yet Bob Marley gave careful consideration to Bill Graham's offer of management, though he finally decided against it.

There were complications everywhere in 1974 for Bob Marley in his dealings with his fellow men and women. When, late that year, Bob's mother, Mrs Booker, made her next visit to Jamaica, she found no one had come to pick her up at the airport, so she took a taxi the few miles out to Bull Bay, to the address she had been given for her son's new home. Shortly after she reached there, Bob arrived, annoyed no one had gone to collect her. It was then that Mrs Booker realised that Bob and Rita were no longer living together, that Rita was living in Bull Bay and Bob was at 56 Hope Road. She also saw that there was a new addition to the family, a baby girl called Stephanie, born on 17 August 1974 while Bob was away in England on business. In her book, *Bob Marley: My Son*, Mrs Booker writes, 'one look at her told me that she wasn't his. Her father turned out to be a friend of Nesta's, a man named Tacky who everyone called Ital.' Ital, a local truck-driver, openly admitted to Bob's mother that he had fathered the girl, and even helped the elderly woman out one day when she found herself financially strapped.

According to Mrs Booker, however, Rita never admitted that the child was not Bob's. 'Nesta fretted and fretted as though his heart would break. He kept pressing Rita: How could he be Stephanie's father? Who was the real father? Inside, it ate away at him. He was like a man tormented by a truth too terrible to face.'

Although she may not have admitted that Stephanie was not Bob's child, at home in Bull Bay, Rita equally never hid her relationship with Ital, even showing Mrs Booker a ring that the man had given her. With the intention of keeping the peace, Mrs Booker made sure she never told her son about this.

An element of Bob's anguish over the birth of Stephanie was a personal rule of life that once a woman he had been involved with went with another man, Bob would drop her for ever; he behaved similarly with Pat Williams, the mother of his son Robbie. Bearing in mind Bob's own behaviour with a considerable number of other women, several of whom bore him children, this could be seen as extremely hypocritical and surprisingly unevolved: but matters are rarely rational when it comes to ways of the heart. Besides, Bob knew only one pick-up line: 'Yuh wan' have my baby?'

But what was really going on at 56 Hope Road? Significantly, as 1974 progressed, Bob's relationship with Esther Anderson seemed finally to be fading away. And he was becoming increasingly attracted to a stunningly beautiful white Jamaican girl called Cindy Breakspeare who also was living in the property, having been rented space in another section of the substantial house by Chris Blackwell. This was the same girl whom some said had turned her nose up at Bob and Peter when they would visit Danny Sims and Johnny Nash at their house in Russell Heights.

At one point in 1974, Bob Marley had got in touch with Beverley Kelso, saying he needed her to sign some papers, perhaps part of legally tidying up his past during his contract renegotiations with Island. He asked her to come up to 56 Hope Road. She was distinctly unimpressed with what she found at the address: 'I went up there with a friend one evening. And that evening when I went up there, Cindy Breakspeare, she take over. It was all white people. I couldn't go inside to see Bob any more. And so I talked to her and I tell her who I was and Bob came out to me.

'When Bob came out to me, Bob didn't know who I was. He was just looking at me and gazing. He was just like in another world, looking at me and, "What your name? Who are you?" And I said, "What?" My girl-friend was just laughing and I start to cry. And I said, "What happened to Bob?" I start to cry. I was living at Forest Hill and I feel down and I actually walked home to Forest Hill that day.'

What sounds like a misunderstanding that could have been created from an excessive consumption of herb on the part of Bob Marley, linked to the everyday on-the-road norm of meeting more and more unrecognisable new faces each day, created a great sense of hurt for Beverley Kelso, a founding member of the Wailers. It must be said, however, that few expressed an equivalent negative view.

In London that summer, in what sounded like a joyous state of herb-assisted reverie, Bob Marley, accompanied by his friend Delroy Washington, had auditioned Candy Mackenzie, who was making her way as a backing singer in London, along with a sister, in an effort to see if they could fulfil his need for permanent backing singers. Bob was jamming along on a song that seemed to be entitled 'Hold Me Now'. Tapes exist of this session, and the atmosphere was clearly flirtatious, on all sides.

'Yuh talk 'bout inspiration: that's chat I like / Some of them keep their minds too shut / I'm talking to you, lady, how you feeling tonight?' sang Bob.

'Irie,' she giggled.

'She's feeling irie,' he sang, before starting a new song: 'If I tell you I wouldn't tame you, I wouldn't know.'

'I bet you wish you were from Ladbroke Grove,' said one of the girls.

'Not really,' Bob sang back.

'I'm from Wolverhampton,' she replied.

'I'm from Africa, baby. Hold me now. I'm loose,' whooped Bob Marley.

'You need gospel singers, don't you?' interjected a girl.

'I'm loose,' Bob wailed again, and then again.

'I bet you are. Which part, baby?' giggled one of the girls.

'*I'm loose!*'

Although Bob Marley decided against taking on the two girls, the problem over a lack of backing singers remained unresolved. At the end of 1974, Bob went out to stay for a few days with Lee Perry at his home in Cardiff Crescent, in the Washington Gardens section of Kingston. 'We were all of us talking, talking, and Bob said, "Bwai, mi not know what fe do,"' said Perry's wife Pauline, who as a girl would see Bob singing under that tree in Trench Town on her way home from school.

'So I said to him how American artists would all have a very identifiable set of people to work with. And if you have three girls with you, you will look representative of the way people are performing in foreign. Bob laugh and say, "Which three girls?"

'I say to him, "You have Marcia Griffiths, you have Judy Mowatt, and you have Rita, your wife." He said to me, "Them girls, deh?" Mi say, "Of course, because those are the three girls mi really see now could go fe back up a man like you."

'"Im say, "OK, mi see how it go."'

Marcia Griffiths was the diva of reggae, having had a stream of Studio One hits in the sixties before scoring a massive international success, 'Young, Gifted, and Black', with her husband, Bob Andy, also a seminal figure in Jamaican music. Judy Mowatt, meanwhile, who came from Gordon Town, in the foothills of the Blue Mountains, had joined a singing trio called the Gaylettes in 1967. When the group split she continued as a solo act. In 1972, Judy Mowatt had been asked to perform in a show at Kingston's Warwick Theatre in which the Wailers also were playing.

Rehearsing the Elvis Presley song 'Suspicious Minds', Judy heard some-one harmonising at least two octaves higher than her sweet voice was singing. She looked around to see who it was, certain that it was another woman: Judy was amazed when she saw that it was Bob Marley.

'I knew that he was a great songwriter and he was a man for whom I had great respect. So I said to him, "I want you to write me a song." And he said to me, "No, man, I have a reservoir of songs down at Trench Town." He said I should come down to Trench Town and I could get any amount of songs I wanted.'

From this time, Judy began regularly to visit Bob's home in the ghetto, becoming friends with Rita, whom she had already met. 'As a Rastawoman, she displayed a lot of qualities that I always wanted to emulate. She displayed the qualities of a perfect mother, and she was very knowledgeable about the faith.' Brought up as a Christian, it had not been hard for Judy to accept Rastafari. Initially she had difficulty in accepting that Haile Selassie was Christ incarnate. But as a Bible student, she found in Revelation 5 where it is written that Christ shall return in a new name: King of Kings, Lord of Lords, Conquering Lion of the Tribe of Judah. 'Then I discovered that His Majesty had that title and I realised His Majesty not only had that title, but His Imperial Majesty is the two hundredth and twenty-fifth king to be seated on King David's throne. So he's from the direct lineage of King David. And we learn that Christ shall come through that David lineage.'

They would sit and reason as they waited for Bob to return each evening from his regular games of soccer. Often Bob would be playing with Skill Cole, who eventually became Judy's 'kingsman' – she had three children with him.

Sitting on the doorstep of his yard, Bob would play the guitar and teach them new songs. Judy was particularly impressed with a tune Bob had called 'Down in the Valley', written about Patrice Lumumba, a great

African leader. Although the song was diligently rehearsed in these evening sessions, Bob never recorded it. When Judy made her *Black Woman* solo album in 1979, she made sure she included the song on it.

To Judy Mowatt, Bob Marley was clearly far more than a musical leader. 'He was like my father, my brother, my friend . . . everything. He was someone you could talk to: he had this fatherly aura; he was a young man, but he had a lot of authority; he had a lot of discipline – he was a very disciplined person. When we were on tour, Bob would be first on the bus, so we have to be on time, and often we are trailing after him.

'He is also a man with a lot of love and respect for all people. Bob cared for humanity. Bob said, "My life means nothing to me. My life is for the people." And he demonstrated that throughout his life.'

Judy Mowatt and Rita Marley first sang together when Marcia needed some harmony vocals on a song she was recording at Studio One with Bob Andy. That evening, Marcia had been due to perform at a club in New Kingston called House of Chen: she asked them to sing harmony vocals with her on a song by the Supremes called 'Remember Me'. The performance was received sensationally well by the audience, and Bob got to hear about it.

It was with the line-up suggested by Family Man, augmented by the I-Threes, that Bob Marley played with Bunny and Peter on 8 March 1975, supporting the Jackson 5 at National Heroes Stadium.

During the sixties, Martha Velez, who was of Puerto Rican background, had been a member of the New York–based folk group the Gaslight Singers. After appearing in the Manhattan production of *Hair*, she became one of the female singers in Van Morrison's Band and Street Choir, moving to the alternative musical power-point of Woodstock.

Signed to New York's feisty independent label Sire Records by Seymour Stein, the label owner, she recorded three albums, often with musicians from the British blues school, including Eric Clapton, and Jim Capaldi of Traffic, Island Records' flagship 'underground-rock' act. It seemed only a small step, therefore, to work with an artist who had grown up with the rather different 'blues' of a former British colony.

After a disco twelve-inch remix of a Velez tune called 'Aggravation' became a noted track on the New York underground disco scene, she had approached her label to suggest covering 'Stir It Up', the Bob Marley composition which she knew as a Johnny Nash song. Craig Leon, her A&R manager, had met Bob Marley through Alex Sadkin, a friend who worked as an engineer on recordings by Jamaican artists. Leon phoned Bob and suggested that he produce Martha Velez. Bob expressed vague interest, which was heightened after Seymour Stein contacted Don Taylor, with whom the label boss was acquainted.

It seems worth noting that, with her cascading dark-brunette hair and striking sultry looks, Martha Velez seems very much the same female 'type' as Cindy Breakspeare. And Bob Marley was certainly attracted to her rebellious lyrics on her earlier records. 'There was one song that particularly struck him which I had co-written called "Livin' Outside the Law". He mentioned that this song really spoke to him,' she said. After he had flown up to New York with his manager early in 1975, Bob agreed that Martha Velez should come to Kingston in May that year, for a three-week session with him at Harry J's studio. (Velez noted that at the meeting Bob was clad 'head to toe' in black leather, a rock-star-like new look – akin to being the Jim Morrison of reggae – he would adopt for most of the rest of his life.)

Checking into the Sheraton Hotel in New Kingston, a location that was becoming a fixture of the upmarket end of Kingston's reggae scene, Martha Velez quickly discovered that recording sessions would frequently be interrupted by trips to the beach and games of football. Sometimes those trips to the beach involved the five-hour drive to Negril: Bob, the Wailers, and Peter Tosh, in a gesture of conviviality, went out to the west end of the island to rehearse the songs before entering the studio. Caught in one of the frequent outbursts of torrential rain that are a feature of Jamaican weather, Seeco was unable to control their car, which spun round and round in circles, seemingly indefinitely. As others in the car screamed, Bob Marley laughed through the entire adventure, calling to Jah for assistance. When the car finally slurried to a halt in the roadside mud, Bob laughed and sang as he helped push the vehicle back on to the asphalt.

The album was created between these excursions, in flurries of creative energy. 'He was a very quiet man, unassuming in manner,' said Craig Leon. 'I recall Bob sitting around a lot, talking and getting high, and then going into an incredible rush of energy and productivity and doing the work very quickly.' Although Bob oversaw the project, permanently entrenched in the studio, he brought in Scratch Perry for his expertise at the production desk, with Sylvan Morris engineering the sessions – as he had those of *Natty Dread*. Bob Marley concentrated more on the integrity of the material, working with Velez on new songs. 'The way that Bob worked was through channelling inspiration,' she said. 'He would gather the Wailers and begin to jam on an idea of a song. Seeco, his percussionist, usually would play a tape recorder and capture the song and the ideas that were created spontaneously that session. It was very inspired. I got to witness this.' At Martha Velez's suggestion, she and Bob wrote a tune together for the LP, entitled 'Disco Night'. 'We did it in the American way of sitting down and hammering out ideas, lyrics, and music ideas, hooks, etc.' Because of complications over his publishing deal, Bob gave Rita the whole songwriting credit.

All the Wailers, along with the I-Threes, played on the record, as did the Zap Pow horn section; Earl 'Chinna' Smith, one of Jamaica's most sought-after guitarists, also contributed to the sessions. On the resulting album, *Escape from Babylon*, Bob Marley and Lee Perry were credited as the record's percussion players. 'The backing vocals of the I-Threes blend particularly well with Velez's deep timbre throughout,' said David Katz, 'and Chinna Smith's bluesy guitar lead also enhanced some of the beat numbers, but it was the percussion added by Marley and Perry that really gave the album its African-Caribbean flavour.' 'Get Up, Stand Up' and 'Bend Down Low' were among the Bob Marley originals included on the record, along with 'Hurting Inside' and 'Stand Alone', respectively retitled as 'Happiness' and 'There You Are'. Martha Velez's voice was perfectly suited to the material, and given a sophisticated reggae-pop edge by Scratch's studio work. 'Lots of Rastas were lying around the studio,' said Velez. 'I didn't quite know what they were doing there, but they were cool, and then I realised that they were providing energy, a cool energy, a comfortable sound space. The studio experience was a synthesis of cultures – American and Rasta musical styles. And there was a lot of male-female energy. Rasta women are less aggressive than American women, but they manage things in a more subtle way.'

As much as anything, the significance of *Escape from Babylon* lay in the collaboration of Bob Marley and Lee Perry, and their continuing creative relationship. This would not be the last time in 1975 that they would work together in the recording studio.

'My most vivid memory of the recordings,' said Craig Leon, 'was the size and quantity of the spliffs and the fact that everyone had their own for the duration of the session. None of this hippie social convention of passing around a skinny little joint amongst thirty people.'

By the early spring, the line-up that worked under the name of Bob Marley and the Wailers was even further expanded. As ever, the Barrett brothers were there holding down the rhythm section; Seeco Patterson, Bob's brethren from Trench Town, became the group's percussionist; and

Tyrone Downie joined to play piano and synthesiser, leaving the Caribs, the resident group at the Kingston Sheraton Hotel; Wire Lindo, meanwhile, returned to the fold on organ. Al Anderson had been asked to join as guitarist.

'I've meet Al in England while he was doing some overdub guitar,' said Bob Marley of his new guitarist. 'We talk a little and it's nice, ya know? So I ask him to come and play with the group. Him think about it for some time and then him decide he would do it. Boy, him great! Fuckin' good, mon.'

From certain purist quarters – specifically, elements of the UK music press – Bob earned considerable criticism for bringing an American into the group, which meant they knew nothing of Lee Jaffe's role on harmonica. As usual, Bob Marley had a larger point of view on this: 'We really not deal with people in categories like if you come from Jamaica you have the right. Regardless of where you are on earth you have the right. I can't deal with the passport thing. To me him prove himself not an outsider because if him can play with us then him no outsider.'

Natty Dread had been released to great critical acclaim in October 1974. The album, the first to be credited to Bob Marley and the Wailers, had also registered far higher sales figures than either of the Wailers' two previous Island albums. 'The *Natty Dread* album is like one step more forwards for reggae music,' said Bob Marley. 'Better music, better lyric, it have a better feelin'. *Catch a Fire* and *Burnin'* have a good feelin', but *Natty Dread* is improved.'

To continue the record's promotion, a twenty-seven-date American tour was set up, followed by a brief foray into the English market with two London shows, one in Birmingham, and one in Manchester. Under the direction of Don Taylor, Bob Marley and the Wailers were at first consistently booked into halls smaller than they could sell out, to increase the demand for tickets. In Boston, for example, Bob Marley again played Paul's Mall, for six nights this time, with two shows each day. But in Philadelphia, the ensemble performed at the theatre-sized Spectrum. There was a magical performance in Brooklyn, to an audience that consisted almost exclusively of expatriate Jamaicans. In Los Angeles, meanwhile, they sold out five nights at the prestigious Roxy on Sunset Strip.

Further recordings for Martha Velez's album took place while the band was in New York, although Bob and the group were kicked out of the snooty Manhattan hotel into which they had been booked for cooking their own food in the corridor outside their rooms. At Bob's insistence, as the tour continued across America, he was kept in touch with the progress of the mixing of *Escape from Babylon* by having each new version of the tapes couriered out to him; he would send back notes that contained his suggestions.

Whilst on this American tour, Bob paid a visit to his mother in Delaware for a couple of days. This time Bob had clearly decided to offer his mother instruction in Rastafari to the fullness. 'Before Bob was born I would go up to this Sunday school where I go and accept Jesus,' explained Cedella Booker. 'And I try to live up to that standard. But the strictness and the rules them give, afterwards Bob say to me that all that was hypocrisy, and it didn't make no sense: all the things you must wear to church – rules – these people only seek power, to rule other people. It have no Christianity in it or Godliness in it.

'But it take me some time to see it. Bob tell me that His Majesty is the Almighty God – it not Jesus no more. And me with my little thin sense doesn't even understand what's going on. Me say, "How you know that? He is a man." 'Im seh, "Yes, he is a man." I turn to him and I say, "I think he is a great man. But I don't think he is God." And 'im seh, "Oo yuh t'ink is God?"

'I never 'ave no answer: because I was looking that God is a white man like the picture I have on the wall. Then Bob tell me to take it off the wall. And he showed me the pictures that I should have on the wall.

'Up until then I had just put things as decoration. And Bob looked at the pictures I had on the wall and said to me, "Do you have any reason for these pictures here?"

'I said that I just hung them there to go with t'ing and t'ing. But he showed me how it represented an emblem or something. I had a bronze eagle up on top. I also had President Kennedy, Martin Luther King – just the pictures. He is telling me what is the significance of the eagle and the one president over there and the one over here. He reads out the whole symbolism. He said, "This picture you must take down; and this picture you must take down. And these are the pictures you are to let stay." And he showed me all these little things.

''Im said when we reason, "You know, Momma, why is it so hard for you to believe me when I say His Majesty is God? Because from the time you are a little girl growing up, you hear them talking about Jesus Christ: you go to church and you're into it.

'"But today 'im come in a new name: no Jesus Christ no more. And 'im said 'is name shall be terrible amongst the heathen – which is the unbelievers. If you wasn't my mother, him seh, me wouldn't even bother to talk to you. But, anyway, you is a Rasta from the day you is born. And as time goes on you will see. And as time goes on mi see everything just like how him never have to tell me no heap o' nothing no more."

'That night we sit down and me and him reason in my kitchen. From about nine o'clock we sit down at the table and just start to reason. When me look upon the time again, it was three o'clock in the morning.

'Bob and I sat and talked for all those hours, and it never happened again. It happened that we spent hours together, but not in that intense manner.

'Whatever it was, it was given to me that night, and I fully received it, and my blessing is there going on now.'

Leaving Los Angeles on 14 July, the musicians flew straight to London.

The buoyant mood of the US tour was more than maintained in London. For the pair of dates in June at London's Lyceum ballroom, Mick Cater had personally sold every ticket in less than a day: the venue didn't have a box office of its own. ('We could have sold out five nights,' reflected Cater later, as though confirming Don Taylor's policy of turning the scarcity of tickets for Bob Marley shows into a virtue.) *Natty Dread* had not only appealed to a hip white audience, but for the first time British-resident Jamaicans had gone for Bob's music en masse. As a consequence, on the first hot night of the two London dates, the Metropolitan Police's notorious Special Patrol Group was sent into action to clear the streets around the venue of over three thousand people, mainly Jamaicans, trying to get in to see Bob Marley without tickets. A pair of fire doors was demolished, and Tyrone Downie found himself locked out of the venue, almost not making it back inside in time to perform.

The shows were as extraordinary as the build-up had predicted. Bob Marley and the Wailers tore the Lyceum apart. The road crew had struggled to get good power and sound – a notorious problem at this venue but particularly so as the shows were being recorded for a possible live album – and their painstaking efforts were enhanced a thousand-fold by the electrifying performances produced by Bob and his group. Quite simply, they were fantastic.

Bob held the audience as though they were part of his collective soul; he could have told them to go out into the street and to burn and loot and they would have obeyed his every word. 'From that gig,' Dennis

Morris remembered, 'every person who was there decided they were a Rasta, and it snowballed. The whole movement just spread.'

The Lyceum shows were recorded on the Island mobile studio, for what became the memorable album *Bob Marley and the Wailers: Live!* *Natty Dread* had already briefly been a Top Ten album in Britain, Bob Marley's first sniff of a hit and, in September, the live record followed it into the charts, climbing higher. Most important, it spawned a first hit single, in the live version of 'No Woman, No Cry', a song whose status would grow until it was irrevocably intertwined with the existence of Bob Marley. He had set out on his own, without Bunny and Peter, only a little over eighteen months previously. If he had had time for a moment's thought to himself, mustn't he have felt considerable justification at the subsequent arc of his career?

Island Records

invite you to a reception in honour of

BOB MARLEY & THE WAILERS

following their performance at the Lyceum
on Thursday July 17th, 1975.

It's at midnight, the venue:

Columbo's Club.
50 Carnaby Street.
London W.1.

Only admits one.

island records

island records ltd

BOB MARLEY & THE WAILERS

Thursday, July 17th, 75.	The Lyceum, The Strand, London W.C.2. Tel. 836 3715 Show starts 7.30 p.m.	
Friday, July 18th, 75.	The Lyceum, The Strand, London W.C.2. Tel. 836 3715 Show starts 7.30 p.m.	
Saturday, July 19th, 75	The Odeon, New Street, Birmingham 2. Tel. 021 643 6101 Show starts 7.30 p.m.	Birmingham Centre Hotel, New Street, Birmingham B2 4RX Tel. 021 643 2747
Sunday, July 20th, 75.	The Hard Rock, Great Stone Road, Stretford, Manchester. Tel. 061 865 3227 Show starts 7.30 p.m.	Post House Hotel, Palatine Road, Northenden, Manchester 22. Tel. 061 998 7090

NOTES   Shows start at 7.30 p.m. each night.

4 rooms booked at hotels in Birmingham and Manchester for use during the evenings and everyone returning to London after the shows each night.

Road crew stay in Birmingham and Manchester

island records ltd
22 St. Peters Square, London W6 9NW. Telephone 01-741 1511. Cables: ACKEE Telex : 934541
Directors: David Betteridge John Leftly Tim Clark Tom Hayes Eric Edwards
Regd. No. 723336 England Regd. Office: 124 Finchley Road London NW3 5HT

RASTAMAN VIBRATION

Back home in Jamaica after the tour, Bob Marley discovered that his recently bestowed and hard-earned title of 'King of Reggae' was in danger of being usurped by an up-and-coming vocalist. The name of the supremely accomplished Dennis Brown, who had started out at Studio One in 1969, was such a guaranteed brand of vocal and recording quality during the seventies that his nickname, 'The Crown Prince of Reggae', was truly deserved. Although second only to Bob Marley in the Jamaican nation's cultural consciousness, Dennis Brown's audience remained almost entirely within his native community; his great talent was accepted as a given and it was somehow always assumed that it was just a matter of time before he crossed over to a wider audience. However, despite hitting the UK pop charts in 1979 with Joe Gibbs's 'Money in My Pocket', Brown never greatly broadened his market. Almost because of this, he gained a reputation as being something like the purest personification of reggae.

When Bob had returned to Jamaica after the Lyceum show, he heard that, on the radio airwaves, it was pure Dennis Brown; in the dancehall, it was pure Dennis Brown; in the rum bar, it was pure Dennis Brown. Not only did Brown have a great voice and tunes to match, working with Winston 'Niney' Holness and Joe Gibbs, he had developed a crack recording outfit. 'A which guitarist that?' demanded Bob Marley on hearing Brown's recent material. At Bob's request, Skill Cole went and searched out who was playing the instrument on these Dennis Brown hits. When he learned it was Chinna Smith, who had recently worked with Bob on the Martha Velez project, he hired him to play on the next album Bob was setting in motion, *Rastaman Vibration*. At some of these sessions, again at Harry J's, Scratch Perry was present, offering creative contributions towards the final structure of both the songs and the entire record. A pair of tunes were 'do-overs', originally having been recorded with Scratch: 'Night Shift' was a new version of 'It's Alright', a track on the *Soul Rebels* album; and 'Man to Man' had originally been the title of what would now be called 'Who the Cap Fit'. Scratch also was said to have arranged the song 'Rat Race'.

Although he had been taken to Jamaica by Bob Marley, Al Anderson had fallen out of favour. Donald Kinsey came on board for the *Rastaman Vibration* sessions. Donald was the son of Big Daddy Kinsey, a Chicago bluesman; as a guitarist, Donald had been a child prodigy, playing onstage with B.B. King at the age of twelve, and at sixteen becoming Albert King's bandleader.

By the time *Rastaman Vibration* was recorded, a larger, riper sound was being worked with. 'Maybe something in the scene was changing,' thought Sylvan Morris. 'But I didn't look on it that way at that time. I just deal with music as such. But certainly the consciousness had started to settle within the whole scene: where the Rasta thing was sort of blossoming. So in the lyrical content, that is starting to be expressed as well: the maturing within the Rasta scene. I think now they start to establish themselves in the Rasta cult to the fullness.'

Morris particularly recalled the recording of the tune 'War', using as lyrics the text of a speech by Haile Selassie to the United Nations. Skill Cole had urged Bob to record the song: he had bought from a dread in Parade a pamphlet which contained the words of His Imperial Majesty, and these became the song's lyrics. 'It hit me very strong with that particular tune,' said Skill Cole, 'because of Haile Selassie's statement within it. It was the first time I was hearing statements like that. By this time the whole scene was a passionate scene: "I'm a Rastaman, this is me, I'm going to put out as much as I can in terms of how I feel." They handled everything in that vein. Religiously so. My personal remembrance of Bob is that he wasn't a very laughing character. If he smiled, he would smile very briefly. He always seemed to be so disciplined. If someone made a joke he would just laugh briefly.'

Do you think he was a happy person? 'Yes. I would say that. Because he was probably getting what he wanted musically. His message in music, he was getting what he wanted. So I think he was happy.

'After a while, when they went away and did *Kaya*, I definitely think they started to change their sound then. Very commercial. As a matter of fact, I remember getting a vision [dream]: I was in the States and saw when they were going to release that album. We were all in the vision: Chris Blackwell, everyone. I remember all of us seemed to like the album. But I made a statement: "What happened to the drive?" Which, in truth, was something that I heard in life.

'At the beginning when they first started, whenever they came into the studio and laid the rhythms, there was that pulsating, disciplined vibration. Which probably I heard which perhaps other people didn't hear. The earlier albums seemed to have more drive.'

On 27 August 1975, following the receipt of the shocking information, much of Jamaica fell into a state of distress: His Imperial Majesty Haile Selassie I, King of Kings, Conquering Lion of the Tribe of Judah, had passed away in Ethiopia; there was a possibility that this royal ruler had been murdered. As well as being tragic news, the death created a predicament of almost metaphysical dimensions, placing complex demands on Rasta theology: how, after all, could God die, even if he was a living man?

August 27 was, remembered Judy Mowatt, a very sad, cold day in Jamaica. Some immediately lost their faith. But many more clung on, aware from reading the Bible that news might come from afar and set the careless Ethiopians afraid and astray.

'We were not afraid. We knew that it was not true. We knew that He had the power to disappear.'

Initially, Bob Marley responded by interrupting the recording sessions at the beginning of September. But he had his own beliefs about this grim information, replete with an intricate resolution of the dilemma. One day Rita's daughter Sharon ran up to Bob: 'Is it true? Jah is dead?' Bob denied it. Anxious to make a statement about this, and aware of the despair into which many Rastafarians had been thrust, Bob resolved to record a song to this effect, which would be titled 'Jah Live'. 'So Bob wrote this song "Jah Live", and went into the studio, and he invited us to do the back-up singing,' said Judy Mowatt. 'Immediately after, he started to do the album *Rastaman Vibration*, and we were invited to do the back-up vocals on that. We felt highly privileged to be asked to do the back-up for such a great performer. I was excited. I saw it as divine intervention. Because Bob is a messenger of the Lord, and God has chosen me to work with that messenger. I felt really elated.'

And when he wanted someone who could fire some creative juice into the song, he contacted Scratch Perry and brought him down to Harry J's. Released on the Tuff Gong label, the highly significant 'Jah Live' was in Jamaican shops within days, to great national acclaim.

Prior to the *Rastaman Vibration* sessions, Bob and Scratch had worked on a tune called 'Rainbow Country', which was pressed on extremely limited dub-plates for Jack Ruby's Ocho Rios sound system. Some of the lyrical subject matter of 'Rainbow Country' was repeated in 'Roots Rock Reggae' on *Rastaman Vibration*. Around this time, Bob also recorded a further new song, 'Natural Mystic', at the Black Ark studio Lee Perry had set up at the rear of his Cardiff Crescent home. The song's harmonies were overdubbed later by the Meditations, a male vocal backing group, as opposed to the I-Threes. Soon afterwards at Black Ark, Bob worked with Scratch on the beautiful statement of love for his nation that was 'Smile Jamaica', on an uptempo, rootsy version of the song.

Again, what seemed most important was how close Bob Marley and Lee 'Scratch' Perry were. 'The one person I would say I met who Bob was wary of, or had a lot of respect for, was Scratch,' said Chris Blackwell. 'Bob was like a master in the studio, but not as far as Scratch was concerned. Scratch would push him a lot more. I think the best tracks of Bob are the ones that Lee Perry produced. He was always important. But certainly when I was working with Bob, he and Bob never really got on that well.

'Scratch produced some tracks on *Rastaman Vibration* – the good ones, the groove ones, but Bob didn't give him any credit. I don't know if it was a rivalry or what. There was some unease about the relationship.'

Yet Bob had a continuing and much tighter history with his two blood-brethren from the Wailers, Bunny and Peter. And on 4 October 1975, they played the Wonder Dream Concert at the National Stadium, in Kingston, supporting Stevie Wonder, the final show the original three members would perform as any form of ensemble. Wonder's set included a version of 'I Shot the Sheriff', on which he was joined onstage by the three original Wailers. (Later, Stevie Wonder, who is claimed to be psychic, said that when he met Bob Marley at that show, he knew he would die young.) The Wailers' set included a controversial hit of the summer, Peter Tosh's 'Legalize It'. It was Bob Marley who had personally financed Peter's going into Duke Reid's Treasure Isle studio, where he had recorded a number of songs for a potential solo album to be titled after the single. Lee Jaffe, who felt he had been edged out of the Bob Marley camp by Don Taylor, had begun working with Peter, encouraging him to record, helping him find appropriate musicians. By now, Peter Tosh had become famous in Jamaica for his verbal agility and love of wordplay. 'You felt like he must have just spent all of his time thinking up this stuff,' thought Lee Jaffe. 'Phrases just appeared, fluently, as if you were watching an actor in a movie. And he didn't need a second take. He was really prepared with all his lines all the time.' Jaffe watched as Peter employed a similar manner in his work in the recording studio, on all the songs for *Legalize It*, a method of great precision and exactness – knowing what he wanted when he went into the studio, achieving it quickly, and then leaving. 'I figured all those songs had been in him for so long that he had all the finished versions in his mind, or at least ninety per cent. And also we were broke, we didn't have a budget to do that record.'

When the 'Legalize It' song was inevitably banned by Jamaican radio, Tosh took a quarter-page advertisement in the *Daily Gleaner*, printing the lyrics of the pro-ganja song, one that would lead to Peter Tosh giving himself the title of 'Minister of Herb'. 'Legalize It' immediately soared into the Jamaican charts, bolstered by constant jukebox play.

Although the radio stations would not play 'Legalize It', they were still prepared to interview Peter Tosh about the record, which he understood as a useful means of getting out his increasingly militant and controversial message. When he arrived for just such an event at JBC, where only the previous year Skill Cole, Frowser, and Tek Life had threatened the ranking disc jockey, Peter was ushered into the studio. Drawing heavily on a pipe of ganja throughout the interview, Peter dedicated much of his time on air to delivering an attack on Bob Marley. 'After twelve years working together, Bob Marley desert us to go and work with Chris White-hell!' was just part of what sounded a very bitter rant.

Leaving the studio with Yvonne, his girlfriend, Peter headed towards his home in Spanish Town. Clearly emotionally fraught, he was driving perilously fast, just missing other vehicles. Although concerned about Peter's driving, Yvonne felt there was a larger issue to discuss. In the radio interview, she told him, he had been far too hard on Bob: 'Bob Marley yuh brother, yuh know.'

Hitting on his herb-pipe, Peter nodded in agreement: 'Yuh right, Yvonne: mi gwan tek Bob some of this killer herb,' he declared, indicating the ganja pipe he held in the palm of a hand. As he headed up a newly opened flyover over the Spanish Town Road, a preoccupied – and certainly stoned – Peter spun his car around: straight into the path of another vehicle, which slammed into him in a head-on crash.

Whilst he lay in a hospital bed in a squalid ward, his cracked skull taped and bandaged up, Peter asked after Yvonne; and received a devastating reply. 'Dat the girl wit' you in de smash? She in a coma: she dead soon.' A look of utter despondency descended upon Peter's face as tears coursed down it. Yvonne died three weeks later. Understandably, it was often said in Jamaica that, following that car accident, Peter Tosh was a changed man. A contrary view on this, however, came from Danny Sims: 'That didn't change Peter. Peter was gonna change. Society changed Peter. Peter was a product of his time and society. I just think that because of the time, Peter became tough.'

Released finally from hospital, in a state of utter grief over the death of Yvonne, Peter Tosh still needed to complete the *Legalize It* album. Further financing was obtained from a major Florida herb-smuggler, and the record was completed in Miami. When informed of the title of the album he was bankrolling, the dealer was gnomic in his response: 'You realise that if this record works, it's going to put me out of business.'

The Stevie Wonder concert in Kingston effectively marked a formal ending of the professional relationship between the three Wailers. According to Bunny Livingston, however, Don Taylor fouled a promised opportunity for all three members to do a deal with Island Records, under which they would have continued to record for the label as solo acts; this deal would finally have given them the money they had always sought to build their studio. Moreover, built into this structure was a clause ensuring that the three founder members would reunite after releasing these albums. Don Taylor, Bunny felt, deliberately fluffed this deal.

As a settlement from Island, Bunny and Peter were each offered either $JA54,000 or $US45,000. A patriotic man at heart, Bunny insisted on receiving his money in Jamaican currency, in cash, paid out in $20 bills, at the Sheraton Hotel. With this money stashed in his new Land Rover, Bunny Livingston drove around Jamaica for the next three weeks, searching for land to buy. Finally, he discovered a farm plot of 142 acres in the hilly Portland countryside, sixty or so miles by road from Kingston, where he built a house.

To all intents and purposes, Bunny Livingston seemed to have vanished into that hilltop eyrie. But in the summer of 1976, he released his first solo LP, *Blackheart Man*, an album of ital vitality, for which he was paid a further $US45,000, on Island Records. He was re-marketed, probably sensibly, as Bunny Wailer, which was thought by Chris Blackwell to be a more identifiable brand-name – such as it was – than Bunny Livingston. Bunny, who had stepped away from the Wailers almost the moment there was a hint of international success, had clearly been saving up songs for a long time.

Blackheart Man was an absolutely fabulous record: profoundly sincere, deeply poetic, absolutely heartfelt, a beautiful work of art. Famously, Bunny refused to play live dates to support his work. (His *Protest* album, released the next year, proved equally strong.) As suspected, left to his own devices, Bunny proved to be the most sentimental hippie of all the Wailers, as he revealed on *Blackheart Man's* nursery-rhyme-like 'Fig Tree'. The engaging, distant, warbling flute that introduced the entire album, on the title track, could have come from one of Traffic's more pastoral folk-rock albums, marking this out as an LP amply suited for the partic- ular label on which it appeared. The second song on *Blackheart Man* altered the mood, however: the moody, dark, and memorable 'Fighting Against Conviction' (previously released as 'Battering Down Sentence') was a tune about his trumped-up jail term. And on 'Armagideon', Bunny Wailer addressed the issue of little children having their own little chil- dren. There were a number of 'do-overs': 'Dreamland', 'Reincarnated Souls' from the *Burnin'* sessions, 'This Train', originally recorded for Studio One, with lyrics direct from the age in which it was first made: 'It's the Age of Aquarius / Can't you see it dawning?' It indubitably was the Age of the Aquarian that was Bob Marley.

When it was released in May 1976, *Rastaman Vibration* rocked into the British and US Top Ten album charts. Suddenly, Bob Marley and the Wailers were internationally serious contenders. The success of the record simply confirmed what had been abundantly clear since those dates in London at the Speakeasy promoting *Catch a Fire*: that Bob Marley was an unparalleled artist, working in a precise and unique musi- cal field. Amongst more reactionary rock fans, especially those who associated reggae with skinhead violence, there had been many who had initially scorned the buzz that built around the first Wailers Island releases. Now they were being converted. (*Rastaman Vibration*'s mock-burlap sleeve contained some useful advice: 'This album jacket is great for cleaning herb.' More Island marketing aimed at the target audience.)

The success of the new album was even more marked in the United States. '*Rastaman Vibration* came out after we'd done a big marketing campaign,' said Chris Blackwell. 'There was a lot of press on Bob. It was breaking out in *Rolling Stone* – a moment when there was some real interest. There was some good momentum in America. It went to number eight in the charts. It sold well.'

A major American and European tour was set up to promote the album, beginning in June 1976. As did much of Bob's live work, the *Rastaman Vibration* dates began in Miami, just an airplane jump away from Jamaica. '*Coming rootically all the way from Trench Town, Jamaica, the proverbial, the prophetic Bob Marley!*' was the onstage introduction by Tony G, Bob's effervescent road manager.

The tour then swung up to the Tower Theatre, Philadelphia, for a show with deep personal meaning for Bob: his mother had driven the hour-long journey from Wilmington to see her son perform for the first time ever. She was almost beside herself with excitement. 'When I sit and view him onstage, it is as though I'm looking at a different person. It's not Bob I'm seeing now, I'm seeing somebody else. The glory that I see in this man here made me sweat – and when they turn on the light it look like blood running down.

'And mi look and see he is singing from the depths of his heart. And when he is putting his sounds and his words out, the personality is a different one, because he was under such a glorious sensation of the spirit that you could see it just flowing. And it make me feel so good, such a thrill.

'When I see all the crowd of people, I say, "Is this God? Is this me?" I couldn't believe it. But I know God is glorious, he is great, and everything he does is well done. Rastafari lives. Just give thanks.'

Bob Marley and the Wailers then moved on to Boston and afterwards to New York, where the group played the Beacon Theatre. In New York, Bob was interviewed by *High Times* magazine, which supplied him with fresh buds of Thai grass. 'Do you think herb will be legalised?' the interviewer asked him. 'I don' know if dis government will,' Bob replied, 'but I know Christ's government will.'

When the *High Times* reporter asked the question: 'Who sets the system?', Bob enjoyed a lengthy peroration: 'De system been set! Manley come, comes ta someone. Dat someone, dere was someone before dat, someone comin' from where it was comin' from in England. It comin' down from England now. I don't know how financial dem set up, how much money Jamaica borrow from England, or what kinda plan Jamaica an' England 'ave, but I know Jamaica owes money to certain people. And if de politician run for politics an jus wanna run for politics and don't unnerstand de runnings a all de t'ings a' gonna face him, den he gonna run away from de system, an' if ya run from de system, de people kill you! Y'unerstan'?

'Dat is when ya dare to go up 'gainst God, fight 'gainst God. If ya come to do somet'ing, ya do it. But if ya come to do something an' ya don' do it, ya fighting 'gainst God. And all de people ya trick all de while. So where's system getting from? I don' know de business deal dem have, but dey can't just look upon Jamaica an' say, "All right Jamaica, we give ya some a dis and some a dat. All right Jamaica, we're withdrawin' from ya," or whatever. Because either you swing wit' capitalism, or ya go wit de other "ism" – socialism. Tell 'em 'bout some more "isms". See, ya govern by dis "ism" or dat "ism". We gotta trim it in right dere; no middle way. Even if ya go upon dis "ism", him don' wanna lose friendship wit' America. Let me tell ya something – de same situation dat put de people in gonna catch 'em. Devil trick devil. I find now people want Africa. But if America help Africa, I don't even want dat neither. But what de people want is Africa.'

After playing Chicago, Bob and the group moved on to Los Angeles. On Sunset Boulevard, where they played to a rapturous audience at the Roxy club, there was an enormous billboard advertising *Rastaman Vibration*, along the street from one for the Rolling Stones' *Black and Blue* album that had been defaced by feminists. The Tuff Gong empathised with the pace and warmth of Los Angeles, and the group did a mini-tour of southern California, taking in dates in Santa Monica, San Diego, Long Beach, and Santa Barbara.

The tour then crossed the Atlantic into mainland Europe, for five dates, in Düsseldorf, Hamburg, Stockholm, Amsterdam, and Paris; as yet, movement in Europe was somewhat slow: at a German open-air festival, Bob followed the 'progressive' rockers Jethro Tull onstage, only to find almost all the audience had gone home. In Britain, an extensive nationwide tour of theatre-sized venues had been booked. When Don Taylor was setting up the British dates, it had quickly become clear that there were those who had not yet been caught by the Marley infection. One established London promoter suggested that Bob was not capable of selling out more than one show at the 4,000-seater Hammersmith Odeon.

Mick Cater knew better, however. He booked Bob Marley and the Wailers into the venue for five successive nights; he knew – as did Don Taylor – that the Lyceum could easily have sold out that number of times. Such a run was almost unprecedented at the Hammersmith Odeon, and gave a suggestion of the superstar status Bob was very soon to earn – Bob was already being billed as 'the first Third World superstar', with no apologies to Bruce Lee, the rightful possessor of that title. 'Rather like the Rolling Stones,' said Cater, 'Bob never really sold colossal amounts of records. But he sold concert tickets by the wheelbarrow-load.'

Cater advised the Hammersmith Odeon management that he thought they would need to hire extra security for when the advance tickets went on sale. The venue's management ignored his suggestion, and were surprised when a thousand people turned up on the morning that tickets were released.

Pandemonium reigned around the shows themselves. Tensions were high between the black community and 'Babylon', in the form of white officialdom. Three months later, there would be running street battles two miles away from Hammersmith between black youths and the police at the Notting Hill carnival. Since the Lyceum shows, many of London's blacks had begun growing their locks; they had a new attitude towards Bob: '*He's ours . . .*'

The Hammersmith Odeon was rammed with the kind of bass bins that bring out feelings of grandeur when the bottom ends of the notes hit your gut and your brain. Nobody sat in their allocated seat. When Bob and the group came onstage, the event simply went *off.* It was just like Bob always knew it was going to happen: he was *rocking . . .*

But there was a downside. In the opening ten minutes of the first night at the venue, eighty people were mugged in the stalls, as half a dozen teams of sticksmen prowled the show. At the end of the evening, twenty boxes were filled with handbags that had been looted and dumped on the floor of the auditorium.

Sometimes this out-on-the-edge stuff lost its threatening feel and simply became surreal; on the third night, a guy stood at the front door: 'Tickets,' he said, holding his hand out, taking dozens from innocent white liberals before he disappeared to sell them again around the corner from the venue.

(Also in 1976, CBS Records put out the *Birth of a Legend* album, on its subsidiary Calla label, containing much of the early Coxsone Wailers material. Coxsone Dodd was the Caribbean licensee for material on the

Roulette label, owned by Morris Levy. When Nate McCalla, a Jamaican who was associated with Roulette, went to the island to lease product for American release, he did the deal for CBS. According to Coxsone Dodd, Nate McCalla was later found in Miami, in his bathtub with his throat slit. Other sources say he was found in a lounge chair with his head blown off.)

On the long road-treks in Europe and America between shows, it was always Bob who would be the first on to the group bus each morning. Hunkering down on his personal bunk, he would pull out a worn pocket-size cash book, in which he would jot down the previous evening's earnings. As the rest of the group settled down for the journey, spliffs would be rolled, Bibles produced, and reasonings would commence on arcane interpretations of biblical symbolism, various members of the group pacing back and forth along the central aisle of the bus as they lectured their brethren. On the road, Bob Marley and the Wailers were a compact, tight unit, with no extraneous personnel. Family Man and Carlton Barrett were the only musicians who were guaranteed to be members of the group: all the rest – even loyal spars from Back-a-Wall such as Wire Lindo – blew in and out of the line-up.

But what about such Babylonian problems as drug laws? Police and customs border patrols were a hazard on European tours as the group crossed the various frontiers back and forth. Holland's liberal marijuana legislation inevitably entailed a thorough cleaning out of the bus before the country's border was left behind, the vehicle travelling for the last half-hour with all available windows and doors open. Driving into Germany, the group was especially wary: body searches were often carried out on various Wailers by German border police. At the Düsseldorf show, Bob was questioned for twenty minutes by police whilst he palmed a spliff.

Bob and the Wailers brought the ghetto on the road with them. Wherever they went they'd take over the top floors of hotels, the sites of the most luxurious suites. Down the stairwells and lift-shafts would drift the sweet aroma of ganja, until a diluted version of that musty smell which wafted thickly about each of the group members permeated the entire building.

Gilly, Bob's spar and cook, would set up shop in the floor's house-keeping kitchen, where the stove would be filled with boiling pots of ground provisions, rice and peas, and fish tea. After the shows ended, the group members would rarely go out: it was back to the hotel and up to the suites for ital food. Bob and the Wailers would keep very much to themselves, although every black model within fifty miles was likely to be helping out in their interacting.

'Wherever he was staying,' remembered the writer Vivien Goldman, 'Bob would pick up his battered Ovation guitar and start to strum, singing fragments of songs he was developing – for example, the song 'Guilti-ness', which I remember later listening to and thinking, "Oh, didn't I hear that in that nice suite overlooking the park in Munich?"'

Ultimately, Bob Marley and the Wailers were far more popular in Europe than in the United States or even in Britain. Everywhere, however, the tours enjoyed what became a familiar pattern. 'On the first tour,' recalled Mick Cater, 'there would be, say, fifteen hundred people in the venue. On the next dates there would be five thousand to ten thou-sand in the audience. And the next time round, Bob would be playing huge outdoor venues.'

In Sweden, for example, Bob Marley was a huge star. On every tour he would play one of Stockholm's major venues, set outdoors in a fair-ground. The first time he played there, in 1977, he drew a respectable audience of seven thousand. Only three years later, in 1980, the last time he played in Stockholm, at the Gröna Lund, the gates had to be closed for the first time ever when it was filled to capacity with more than thirty thousand people.

'Two weeks after the end of each tour,' said Mick Cater, 'I'd give Don Taylor a breakdown of the final financial settlement. And about another two weeks later, Bob would show up with someone else – always a different person – to see the same figures. For example, he came with Diane Jobson, his Jamaican lawyer, at one time. Bob was unquestionably the boss, and he'd play people off against each other – to see what happened.'

From that very first tour of England with Bunny and Peter, Mick Cater said, there had been no doubt whatsoever as to who was in charge. On the road, Bob was 'ruthlessly professional'; after every show he would listen to a tape of the performance. 'He ran the group with a rod of iron, and if they caused problems they ran the risk of getting a slap. I remember on one show, Junior Marvin was really showboating, showing off, and he got slapped afterwards.'

Bob Marley split the money from live work right down the middle between himself and the rest of the group – 50 per cent to him, 50 per cent to the Wailers, who became for a time moderately rich people, certainly by Jamaican standards. 'I live a long time before me see any money,' said Bob, 'but my work here is not to become a "star" or anything like that, and my life no go toward material vanity. I find myself doing this music t'ing and me have to do it. Really, I am just a man of the heart.'

Promoted from promotions man in northern Britain to head up the Island Records international division, Phil Cooper had the task of spreading the word on Bob Marley, not at first an easy one: 'Everybody had heard of ska and bluebeat, but it hadn't received major attention. At first it was an uphill struggle with the people who distributed Island overseas. But I just used to grit my teeth and keep banging my head on their doors.

'It was easier with DJs and journalists, although you still had to go and seek out the right ones, the ones who understood. Because Bob and the Wailers became a major success with students in the UK, they crossed over to the right audiences in Europe. Right from the start, they'd pack out the Paradiso in Amsterdam, for example. If you were a journalist who had any suss, you'd be into them.

'It was funny, really: in every major city Bob played, you'd have these press conferences with about ten journalists there, and none of them would understand a word: everything Bob would be saying would be in patois. But they couldn't believe they had this access and opportunity, and they'd go away and write what they thought he'd said.'

One of Cooper's tasks was to arrange Bob's overseas interviews, everywhere except for the UK and USA. 'Whenever I turned up, Bob would turn to Don Taylor and tell him, "Promoter-man is here." I'd take him round the European radio stations. It was a chore for him, but he'd always have a smile on his face, because he knew it was important for getting his message across.'

Persuading tour managers such as the redoubtable Tommy Cowan, himself a former Jamaican star, that Bob's routine must be broken for a press interview was a harder battle. Bob would have to be woken even earlier than usual, so the journalists would be taken to his hotel. There were those members of the press who were confused by what Bob Marley said. 'The first thing you must know about mi is that I always stand for what I stand for. Good? The second thing you must know about yourself listening to mi is that words are tricky. So when you know what mi a stand for, when mi explain a thing to you, you must never try to look 'pon it in a different way from what mi a stand for.'

In October 1976, posters appeared around Kingston announcing a free performance the following Christmas Day by Bob Marley and the Wailers, the 'Smile Jamaica' concert, on the prime minister's spacious lawn at his official home of Jamaica House. When, as a consequence, Bob paid a visit to the prime minister's residence, adjacent to 56 Hope Road, he complained to Michael Manley that the poster suggested he was officially supporting the Jamaican leader's PNP party. In response to this, Manley asked Bob – desiring a gesture of national solidarity from the island's ranking superstar – to instead play a show at Kingston's National Heroes Circle, one that he said would have no political undertones. Bob was assured by the prime minister that a political connection between the singer and the PNP was the last thing he desired; Bob was being invited by the government of Jamaica and therefore would be performing for the entire nation: the 'Smile Jamaica' poster was to contain the words: 'Concert presented by Bob Marley in association with the Cultural Department of the Government of Jamaica.'

A week after press releases went out about the concert, which was to take place on 5 December, Michael Manley announced that a snap election would be held on 15 December. Such a tricky sleight of hand played by the Jamaican prime minister again made it appear as though Bob and the Wailers were personally sanctioning the actions of the PNP. Certainly JLP supporters interpreted it in this manner.

To some extent, Bob had had his arm twisted: he was repaying a debt to Tony Spaulding, the PNP Minister of Housing, for setting Bob's family up in their new home in Bull Bay. As he had already bought Spaulding a BMW, you might feel that the debt had been settled. Through Spaulding, Bob Marley had met Tony Welch, an 'efficient enforcer' – as Don Taylor euphemistically described him – for the PNP; the charismatic Claudie Massop, a close associate of the Tivoli Gardens don Jim Brown, held a similar position for the JLP. In an effort to dilute the day-to-day political violence in Kingston, Bob Marley welcomed both Welch and Massop to 56 Hope Road, where they became almost permanent daily fixtures. This led to some confusion for onlookers: they would see one or the other of these ranking gunmen entering or leaving '56' and draw their own conclusions.

During rehearsals at 56 Hope Road, a 'white bwai', as Bob described him, came to the property and advised the singer to tone down his lyrics, and to stop aiming at a white audience in the USA; if he didn't, he would find his visa to enter America had been taken away. Then the man left, as suddenly as he had arrived. Whoever this was would appear to have been acting under instructions from the US embassy, if not from the CIA. Don Taylor was convinced it was a message from the CIA, who at that time had a close relationship with the JLP; this was part of a strategy of relentlessly undermining Michael Manley's policy of allying with other Third World nations, notably Communist Cuba. Effectively, Jamaica was in a state of covert civil war, to such an extent that, on 19 June 1976, a nationwide State of Emergency had been called by the Governor-General, the formidably named Sir Florizel Glasspole: the PNP charged that the JLP and CIA were plotting to destabilise Jamaica.

There were, noted Judy Mowatt, 'some eerie feelings in the air'. On the Jamaican radio airwaves, however, everything sounded irie: massive play was being given to 'Smile Jamaica', a musical celebration of the island's virtues which Bob and the Wailers had recorded after the concert was announced – this was the slower version of the tune recorded at Harry J's, without Scratch's assistance. The night before the song was recorded, however, Judy Mowatt had had a 'vision'. She dreamt she was being shown a headline in a newspaper: 'Bob Got Shot,' it read, 'for a Song.'

Troubled, Judy went to Harry J's later that day for the session to record the track. Now she noticed something about the song that hadn't been previously apparent: it contained a line which ran, 'Under heavy manners'. This phrase, meaning under strict discipline, was the PNP's principal political slogan. Bob had until recently been off the island, on the *Rastaman Vibration* tour, and seemed unaware of the political implications of such words. Clearly, realised Judy, they would mark Bob out as a PNP supporter. Anxiously, she expressed her worries to Marcia Griffiths, telling her about the content of her dream. 'Go and tell him now,' exhorted Marcia.

In the control room at Harry J's, Bob was surrounded by his brethren from the Twelve Tribes sect of Rastafari, one with which the musician empathised. The air was thick and grey with herb smoke as they listened to various playbacks. All the same, Judy told him she must talk to him. 'Yeah, mon,' he said, and went out on the steps with her. She told him how the 'under heavy manners' line would label him as a PNP supporter. Bob agreed.

Returning to the studio control room, he spoke to his brethren: 'Gentlemen, wha' yuh think 'pon the line "Under heavy manners"? And everyone say, "Bwai, mi not think about it." Then one say, "Bwai, it nuh right, because they use it fe them slogan."'

Now everyone was taking it upon themselves to advise Bob against using the words – though, noted Judy, none of them previously had bothered to say anything against them.

Early on the morning of Friday 3 December, Bob, Skill Cole, Seeco Patterson, Carly Barrett, and Neville Garrick, the Tuff Gong art director, drove out to jog a mile or so along the beach at Bull Bay; 'a lickle eye-opener', as Bob referred to these regular morning athletic expeditions. 'Man, I had some weird dream last night,' a puzzled Bob told Neville. 'I couldn't make out if it were gunfire or firecrackers, but it sound like I'm in a war.' Immediately afterwards, one of those out-of-the-blue incidents that so characterise Jamaica occurred: police arrested Garrick at gunpoint as he rolled a spliff in his car, and he was taken to the Bull Bay police station. Bob followed him down there and, using his influence, took him back with him to 56 Hope Road.

The night before, Judy Mowatt had had another disturbing dream. In it she saw a rooster and three chickens. Someone shot at the rooster, and the bullet hit one of the chickens; from the side of the wounded chicken protruded its intestines. This dream scared Judy: 'I looked at Bob as being represented by the rooster, and we were the back-up chickens.'

Arriving at 56 Hope Road to rehearse for the 'Smile Jamaica' concert, she told Marcia and Rita about this dream. Marcia admitted she had also felt premonitions; she decided to leave 56 Hope Road and go home. But Rita and Judy stayed on and rehearsed. Later that evening, Rita was booked to take part in rehearsals for a pantomime, *Queenie's Daughter*, at the Ward Theatre. The two women singers said they would leave the rehearsal at the same time, Rita to the Ward Theatre and Judy to her Bull Bay home.

The rehearsal was held in the upstairs room that was sometimes used. Judy, who was seven months pregnant, continued to feel edgy. At the end of each song they ran through, she found herself wandering over to the doorway and looking out down the corridor. 'Subconsciously, I knew something was going to happen.'

When the rehearsal was finished, she asked Bob if he could drive her home. Bob said he was waiting for someone and instead he asked Neville to drive Judy in Bob's BMW. Neville was not particularly pleased. Notwithstanding his experience with the police that morning, he was awaiting with pleasure the arrival of Up-Sweet, who would be bringing with him some herb fit for connoisseurs. Neville knew that, by the time he came back from Bull Bay, the best herb would have all gone.

Later Judy realised that she and Neville, who were accompanied for the ride by Sticko, a former 'sticksman' employed as gateman, had left in the nick of time. 'Because if they saw Bob's BMW leaving, they would have shot it up with Neville and myself.' As they drove out, Judy passed her cousin, who was also pregnant, walking through the gate. Later her cousin told her she had only walked a few yards up Hope Road when she heard shooting – she had kept on walking.

Leaving the rehearsal room, Bob had wandered down to the kitchen. Peeling a grapefruit, he looked up as Don Taylor came into the room. Bob's manager walked straight into the line of fire of a gunman who had appeared in the doorway and was loosing off shots indiscriminately in the direction of Bob. Taylor took four shots in the groin – the gunman was firing from one of the lower steps leading into the kitchen – and a bullet that missed him ricocheted off a wall and whizzed across Bob's chest into his arm. If he had been inhaling instead of exhaling, the bullet would have gone into his heart. Then Taylor fell on him. 'Selassie I Jah Rastafari,' uttered Bob.

Rita, meanwhile, had been sitting in her yellow Volkswagen Beetle, starting up the engine, with a pair of youths occupying the rear seat. Five shots were fired at her through the vehicle's rear window as she screamed at the boys to get flat on the floor. Putting her VW into gear, she raced off around the corner of the house, heading for the gate. But a pair of gunmen ran after her: a bullet was blasted through the door, and a final bullet went through the front windscreen. Although at least one bullet hit her in the head, the glass seemed to have slowed it down, and it slid over her skull, not fully penetrating it. As she neared the lion-encrusted wrought-iron gate of the property, Rita braked the car to a halt, feeling blood dribbling down her neck. As she did so, one of the gunmen ran up, pointing his weapon at her head; Rita played dead, and the gunman, apparently having been distracted, ran off.

Still up in the rehearsal room, Family Man heard the shots. Realising this was a 'serious business', he ran down the passageway into the bathroom, leaping into the metal tub. He was followed by the three horn players, Glen Da Costa, Dave Madden, and Vin Gordon, who bundled up on top of him, followed by Tyrone Downie. On top of them suddenly jumped Bob. As he tried to hide himself as low down in the bath as he could get, he somehow knocked a tap, and water began to pour in on Family Man's head.

At this stage, however, Family Man was not aware that Bob had been hit. Only when they all stood up, Family Man somewhat damper than when he'd dived into the bath, did he notice that Bob was squeezing and rubbing his left arm.

That evening, Chris Blackwell had gone out to Scratch Perry's yard off Washington Boulevard. Scratch played Blackwell an extraordinary tune – lazy, sticky, languorous – called 'Dreadlocks in Moonlight'. He told Blackwell he had written it for Bob to record. But the Island boss said that he loved the demo vocal Scratch had put on it and that he should release it himself on Island. How long would it take him to mix it? he asked. About half an hour, came Scratch's optimistic reply. Blackwell decided to wait. Perry, who didn't have a phone (he had been waiting for one for five years), eventually finished the mix some two and a half hours later. Chris Blackwell had been scheduled to meet a documentary crew at 56 Hope Road to discuss filming the 'Smile Jamaica' concert. Had not Scratch's tune been so good, he might have arrived at Hope Road at exactly the time the bullets were flying.

The cops came to Bull Bay that evening looking for Cedella, Sharon, Ziggy, and Steve. The experience was frightening in the extreme. Their father had been whisked away from hospital after his wounds, which were found to be superficial, had been bandaged up. Then he'd been driven up the road of 365 curves that leads to Chris Blackwell's home of Strawberry Hill in the Blue Mountains, overlooking Kingston. A police guard was mounted around the premises. They would have found, however, that after the shooting, Bob Marley was not frightened: he was furious.

Fifty-six bullets – the number of the address, of course – had been fired at Bob. Yet he was only grazed. As the night-time mists swirled around Strawberry Hill, perched three thousand feet above Kingston,

Bob Marley prophesied that the person who did this would die from the same number of bullets. Fifty-six was the number of bullets that Claudie Massop's body allegedly contained when he was shot dead by eleven policemen in February 1979, on the corner of Industrial Terrace and Marcus Garvey Drive, when he was heading home after watching a football match in Spanish Town. Yet no one really believed that Claudie Massop, Bob Marley's good friend, would have involved himself in such a treacherous move. But Jim Brown, don of the JLP stronghold of Tivoli Gardens, and alleged godfather of the multimillion-dollar drug-dealing Shower Posse, might have done it, to show Edward Seaga that he could be a trusted assassin.

Such was the talk of the time. For his part, Don Taylor was left with a bullet in his spine. A private plane, paid for by Chris Blackwell, flew him to Miami and a hospital operation that saved him from paralysis.

Bob and Rita's children were taken up to Strawberry Hill but, with characteristic insensitivity, none of the police bothered to say why they were going there. Chris Blackwell discovered that he would have to explain their parents' condition. All the kids had been told was that their parents had been shot. And although they had heard that their father was okay, Cedella was told that their mother had been shot in the head. 'So I said, "She's dead, right?" Because if somebody gets shot in the head you don't expect them to live. There was a lot of panic: we were looking at each other and wondering where we were going. "Are we gonna be okay?" After that we just got really militant. We never trusted anybody after that. I didn't like any of my dad's friends any more. You come to discover that sometimes the bad men are the nicest people. But they are nice people who would kill at the blink of an eye. I wouldn't wish anybody to go through having their parents shot.'

Rita Marley, who had passed out when the bullet sliced her skull, was still in hospital. The shooting had confirmed for her that evil was a tangible reality. 'When that happened, it was a confirmation for me that evil does exist. There was no reason to put this plot together. Whoever did it, I don't know. But it still feels like it was politically motivated. It's too big to be some ordinary gangster thing.'

The big question was whether the 'Smile Jamaica' concert would still feature a performance by Bob Marley and the Wailers. Family Man was nowhere to be found: he had stashed himself away at a Nyabinghi grounation that was taking place on the beach at Bull Bay: 'With the fishermen, burning fire and playing drums, singing chant music, giving joy to the father.' Marcia Griffiths also had gone into hiding. Amongst the rest of the Wailers, however, the expectation was that they would be playing the show. But it was up to Bob: what did he feel?

No one knew. Just in case, however, Judy went to the hospital to look for Rita. As soon as she saw her fellow member of the I-Threes, Rita told the doctor she wanted to be discharged. Still wearing her hospital 'duster', she was driven home to Bull Bay.

At her house was Tony Spaulding, speaking on a walkie-talkie to Bob at Strawberry Hill. 'He was telling him he has to do the concert; the people were waiting on him; he had to show them he had overcome this,' said Judy. 'Bob was kind of iffy . . . But I knew in the back of his head, his mind was made up, because of the people: if it meant his life, he would do it. Still, Bob was asking everybody's opinion. He asked me: "Judy, wha' ya t'ink?"

'I said, "If you're going to do it then I'm there with you." Rita said the same thing. "We don't want you to do it. But if you feel in your heart you should, then we're here with you, to support you one hundred per cent."'

Rita and Judy were driven the hour-long journey to Strawberry Hill. 'When the hour came to do it,' said Judy, 'police cars came and Bob went in the lead police car. His friend Dr Fraser – Pee Wee – had a VW and so Rita and myself went in that behind the police car. The road from

Strawberry Hill has about a million corners, and the police car was driving at about 120mph around these bends. And Pee Wee was following in the little VW. We got to a square and a JLP meeting was going on. We were so frightened: we said, "Jesus, this is an ambush." The police siren was going and the lights flashing. But the people cheered and in a couple of minutes we get to Heroes Circle.

'I don't see Bob because people had him and they lift him up and pass him from man to man until they put him onstage. Before we even get to the stage we hear Bob singing "Curfew". We just take the mic – Rita in her hospital bedclothes. That night I thought Rita was in the spirit, because she sang the loudest I have ever heard her sing.

'While the show was going on there was a helicopter flying over. I myself started wondering if they had a gun with telescopic sights that could just shoot us on the stage.'

Although Bob had not been expected to perform, by 5 p.m. there were fifty thousand people at the venue: three hours later, there were eighty thousand in the audience. Also on the bill, working their way through their sets, were Third World, Ras Michael, Kiddus-I, and Bunny Rugs. When Bob Marley arrived, Cat Coore from Third World played bass until Family Man arrived; Donald Kinsey was on guitar, and Seeco was also playing.

Bob Marley played a full set, ninety minutes long, surrounded by over two hundred people on the stage around him, so many that Bob could hardly move. These people were onstage to protect him – if the gunmen came back, they would have to shoot a lot of people, including the chief of police.

Bob Marley's long-sleeved denim shirt hid his wound. But at one point Bob pulled up his sleeve, brandished his wounded arm, and announced, 'Bang-bang – I'm okay.' The 'Smile Jamaica' concert was one of the very few times Bob Marley performed *Natty Dread*'s 'So Jah Seh'. Towards the end of the tune he went into an a cappella moment, put his hand out as though still holding an invisible grapefruit, and sang, 'If puss and dog can get together / What's wrong with loving one another?' Quite simply, it marked one of the greatest moments in the cultural history of the twentieth century.

The event was filmed, by a crew brought down from New York under the auspices of Perry Henzell. When it transpired that the cameraman was Carl Colby Jr, whose father, Bill Colby, had been head of the CIA until January that year, the conspiracy theorists went into overdrive. Although Colby had been at Strawberry Hill all that Saturday, filming the wounded Bob Marley and his entourage, the film, directed by Jeff Walker, never was given an official release.

Immediately after the 'Smile Jamaica' show, Bob and Neville Garrick sneaked out of the island on a chartered Lear jet to Nassau, in the Bahamas, to stay at a house owned by Chris Blackwell. Three days later, Bob's worried mother flew down from Wilmington. She joined Neville Garrick, Carly Barrett, and other band members, as well as a convalescing Rita: Cindy Breakspeare was imminently to arrive. It was to be almost fifteen eventful months before Bob Marley returned to Jamaica.

Perhaps in an effort to divert attention from the murderous political hell into which Jamaica had descended, some gave a separate explanation for the attempt on the life of Bob Marley. Caymanas Park, the horse-racing track to the west of Kingston, had long been a hotbed of corruption, with jockeys, grooms, and trainers frequently bribed, and horses drugged. Skill Cole was no stranger to organising such scams. Earlier in 1976, Skill had allegedly set up the fixing of a race, persuading a number of Kingston's ranking badmen to participate. The plan was botched, however, the supposedly doped horses not finishing in the positions they were needed to in order for the conspirators to clean up. Instead, the men all lost sizable stakes. Because Bob Marley was such a close friend of Skill Cole, and because the plan had been hatched during a reasoning at 56 Hope Road, he became linked with the financial thrashing they had all taken. After money had been extorted at gunpoint, Bob for a time was being forced to hand over some $2,000 a day. (In a separate dealing with some of these badmen's associates exiled in Miami, Bob Marley was said to have handed over a cheque for $40,000, which was cashed by a known arms-dealer.) Skill Cole's life was in danger; he effectively fled Jamaica, first for America, and then to Ethiopia. As time progressed, it became thoroughly apparent that the true cause of the shooting was political.

In socialist, politically correct Jamaica, beauty contests were considered beyond the pale. This was especially the case for black women, who were surfing on the wave of newly activated black consciousness. As Cindy Breakspeare was white, she could escape such stereotyping: she was already the reigning Miss Jamaica Bikini and Miss Universe Bikini. And as Bob Marley was smitten with her – she was always said to be the subject of the song 'Waiting in Vain', which would appear on his next album – she could effectively do what she liked. Although living in separate sections of 56 Hope Road, their paths inevitably would cross – and Bob Marley had several times made passes at her, which were always rejected. Yet he still made many visits, often accompanied by Skill Cole, to the Dizzi Disco, two miles up Hope Road in the suburb of Papine, where Cindy worked; his outings to the club were specifically to try and obtain some form of connection with her.

Don Taylor felt that her interest in Bob Marley did not become manifest until he effectively owned 56 Hope Road, becoming her landlord in the process. Taylor was surprised one evening when he went to see a film; when he dropped by to pick up Bob to take him with him, Bob brought Cindy Breakspeare along, which seemed significant: 'Bob did not take women to movies,' considered Bob's manager. He was even more surprised when Bob Marley asked him to provide the funds for Cindy to travel to London, to take part in the Miss World contest. On Friday, 19 November 1976, with her campaign financed by Bob, Cindy was crowned Miss World, two weeks to the day before her mentor was nearly assassinated. When Cindy gained the Miss World title, she told press interviewers that Bob Marley was her boyfriend; she needed to get back to Jamaica to her Rasta, she said.

Almost as soon as she had returned home, however, Miss World was obliged to catch a plane to Nassau, following Bob Marley into his exile.

EXODUS

In the first week of 1977, Bob Marley and the Wailers flew to London, taking up residence in a house rented for them at 42 Oakley Street in Chelsea. The location had been especially chosen, as it was the approach road to Albert Bridge, which led across the Thames to Battersea Park and its assorted playing-fields and exercise facilities: Bob Marley was keen to have a football pitch and running areas close by. His life in Chelsea was lived almost precisely as it would have been in Kingston. 'In the morning,' said Gilly, his footballing friend and cook, who alternated in this regard with 'Lucky' Gordon (the former lover of Christine Keeler, sexual scourge of 'Babylon' in the early 1960s), 'Bob loved bush tea: circe tea, mint tea, fever grass – a blend of two or three. He'd drink tea first, and then eat fruit, like suck two orange. And then we go jog, 'cause you can't jog with full belly. Then after, he have good Irish moss and good porridge. And then we cook down the good vegetables. We always have things stirring. The fire always keep burning with food, bowl of fish tea, big pot of Irish moss. We cook down steam fish, or fry down some fish, or cook down the good ital stew. In that we'd put the best in vegetables, red bean, coconut milk, carrot, turnip, pumpkin. Whatever was in season.'

Bob Marley's presence in London palpably added to the collective creative energy in a city whose artistic thinking was undergoing a profound shift through the catalyst of punk. At first, however, Bob was deeply resistant to this revolutionary musical form, perceiving it as simply another manifestation of Babylon.

After the Lyceum shows in 1975, a young dread named Don Letts, who had been deeply inspired by Marley's music, had followed Bob and the Wailers back to the apartment they were staying at in Harrington Gardens, Earls Court. Slipping behind the musicians and other assorted London dreads into the living-room, Letts sat in a corner listening to the various reasonings that were going on. As daylight was breaking, however, the inevitable occurred: Bob ran out of herb. Letts proffered his own small, humble supply and entered into a long discussion with his hero about Rastafari.

So began a relationship of sorts. Whenever Bob was in London, he would come and check Don Letts at Acme Attractions, the cutting-edge clothing store he ran on the Kings Road; Letts, after all, could always turn him on to the best source of sinsemilla in town.

By the beginning of 1977, Don Letts had started to learn to become a film director. After having been DJ at the Roxy Club, turning the punk masses on to reggae, he was shooting as much as he could of the emergent punk groups, and he was only too aware of their spiritual connection as outsiders with followers of Rastafari like himself.

But when Don Letts turned up in Oakley Street wearing a pair of bondage trousers to see Bob, the Gong was shocked. 'What yuh wan' look like all them nasty punk people feh?' he demanded, puzzled.

Letts told Bob he was wrong: that punk was a positive, creative spirit that was confronting the system and should be respected. They had a small argument, and agreed to differ.

By the time he had been in London for a few months, however, Bob Marley had changed his mind. He saw the importance of the punk movement. When the Clash played their *White Riot* tour dates at London's Rainbow Theatre, Bob Marley stood in the wings, watching. With Lee Perry producing, and Aswad, a young London reggae group, as backing musicians, that summer Bob recorded 'Punky Reggae Party'; this became the definitive celebration of the punk-reggae fusion that was taking place in 1977, the year when the two sevens clashed – 'Two Sevens Clash' was the title of a big-selling Jamaican hit by the vocal trio Culture, in which they celebrated in song this pivotal time of change, long predicted by numerologists.

As soon as they arrived in London, Bob and the group had locked themselves away in the basement rehearsal room at the headquarters of Island Records in St Peter's Square, west London. Company employees were sworn to secrecy: there were fears that further attempts could be made on Bob's life. It wasn't until the end of March, when Neville Garrick and Carly Barrett ran into Vivien Goldman, the journalist who specialised in reggae music, in Shepherd's Bush market, that there was any media awareness at all that Bob Marley was living in London.

Bob had hit another level in the public consciousness. The attempted shooting of the 'first Third World superstar' undeniably created a frisson of outlaw romance. But it was a romance of the heart that was garnering as much media interest for Bob Marley. His affair with Cindy Breakspeare, the beautiful Jamaican woman who had been crowned Miss World the previous November, provided ample material for front-page features in the European popular press.

Cindy Breakspeare had joined Bob Marley in Nassau over Christmas. Was she aware that, whilst she had been in London winning the Miss World title, bankrolled by Bob, he had been assiduously hunting further females? Did she know that Bob had slept with her friends, the sisters Nancy and Virginia Burke? (Like Cindy, the Burkes were Kingston uptown girls.) She joined Bob in London but, meanwhile, Bob was having a further affair, with Princess Yashi, the daughter of the oil minister of Libya. Wearing a suit and tie, Bob took the princess on a date to Tramps, a prestigious, very upmarket nightclub in Jermyn Street which was a haunt of the likes of the Rolling Stones Keith Richards and Ron Wood, and drank four bottles of Dom Perignon champagne, having a great time. Don Taylor felt that Bob Marley was very happy in London, away from all the hassles associated with the ghetto scene uptown at 56 Hope Road.

If he needed some family tenderness, Bob could always slip round late at night to see Rita, lodged with the other two members of the I-Threes in their service apartment in Harrington Gardens provided by Island Records. For Bob's relationship with Rita had taken on some of those almost arcane complexities that are characteristic of certain marriages. Despite his open relationships with other women, it would be to Rita that Bob went when he needed thoughtful care to be given to his perpetually extending dreadlocks; Rita would massage his head, shampoo his locks, and comb, dry, and oil them, a process that could take up to a day. Clearly convenient for keeping Rita out of the way of Bob Marley's various liaisons, the separate living quarters sprang from one very real situation. On the German leg of the last European tour, Janet Bowen, the mother of Bob's daughter Karen, had come to see Bob. When she had left, Rita allegedly complained about the money her husband had spent on his former mistress and their daughter. Bob beat his wife around the hotel suite, and a very large bill was presented to Don Taylor for repairs to assorted fixtures and fittings. After this isolated incident – from then on Bob controlled his temper towards Rita – Don Taylor always separated the men and the women by at least a hotel floor; even so, from time to time, Bob would sneak into Rita's room at night, seeking solace of one sort or another. Despite confiding in those close to him that Cindy Breakspeare was the only woman he had ever loved, in Jamaica, Bob Marley continued to keep his clothes at the new house he had bought for Rita and the kids in Kingston's exclusive Barbican section, and would turn up there whenever he wanted. The location was a compromise: Rita had shown him the home she really wanted, a mansion on sumptuous Skyline Drive on Jack's Hill, perhaps the ritziest Kingston suburb of all with its scintillating views of city and sea.

Although there seem to have been a not inconsiderable amount of plus signs in Bob's relationship with Rita, there were also two very specific negatives. First, there was 'Auntie', who had raised Rita and exercised considerable sway in their getting married, an influence which Bob always put down to her being an obeahwoman. Brought over to London at one point, Auntie managed to make her presence felt even before the plane had arrived in the UK. Seated in first class, Auntie was offered hors d'oeuvres by the flight attendant. 'A what dat foolishness dem a serve?' she grunted, reaching under her seat to produce a sealed pan of doctor fish – which effectively stank out the cabin for the rest of the trip. And secondly, of course, there was Stephanie, the daughter that Cedella was convinced belonged not to Bob but to Ital.

But there were other children he was obliged to acknowledge. Two more sons had been born to Bob Marley in the previous two years: Julian, on 4 June 1975, to the Barbadian Lucy Pounder; and Ky-Mani, on 26 February 1976, to Anita Belnavis, the Bermudan table-tennis champion of the Caribbean. By the end of the year, Cindy Breakspeare would also be pregnant, bearing her son Damian on 21 July 1978.

Those who knew Bob well were only too aware of the emotional insecurity within him. 'The fears that went through Bob's mind as a child were terrible,' said Rita. 'Bob went through a terrible lot of sadness for much of his life, more so than joy. His children was what he was really looking forward to coming and enjoying. Maybe that's why he had so many so fast.'

Marriage to Bob Marley was not easy for Rita. It seems simplistic to say that her husband simply began to play away from home as soon as he was able, an irony, considering he had virtually begged Rita to marry him. The statistics, moreover, seem to confirm an extreme version of that cliché: thirteen children by eight different women.

Understandably, there are those who judge Bob harshly over this, specifically over such public romancing in front of Rita. But who knows what emotional and psychological complications, and indeed patterns of fate or karma, were involved? Acclaim and adulation contain their own traps. Whatever the case, Bob Marley was hardly the first celebrity to enjoy the company of an array of increasingly exotic girlfriends.

Rita would pluckily play the part of Earth Mother, at which she was certainly skilled, to their children. But how did she really feel about Bob's behaviour? 'It is something you learn to live with over a period of time. I think Bob had such a lack of love when he was growing up. He seemed to be trying to prove to himself whether someone loved him and how much they loved him. There came a time when I had to say to him, "If that's what you want, then I'll have to learn to live with it." But there were certain things I would have to draw a line at.

'There was a lot of experience. A lot of different experience for me: what became personal and what became something you learnt to live with. Because you have to please someone. And I would always still try to please Bob. I felt the respect I had for him was more than just being a wife, because of what I saw him doing for the world. And in himself not even knowing how powerful he was becoming.'

Working away in Island's rudimentary basement rehearsal space, however, Bob appeared oblivious to everything else. As though the shooting had only strengthened his resolve, he was on a creative high, with songs pouring out of him; Bob was working closely with Tyrone Downie, who was becoming more prominent as the group arranger than had been Family Man. By the end of February, Bob was ready to lay the tracks down, and the group moved to Basing Street to record. Songs had flown out of the sessions, many of them inspired by events around the shooting. The new album was to be called *Exodus*, decreed Bob, even though that was one of the only songs he hadn't yet written. When the epic work that was the 'Exodus' track finally appeared, there were those who criticised it for sounding like a song belonging to the new form of disco – which precisely missed the point, for Bob Marley's intention all along was that it should be a disco tune. Unsurprisingly, an extended version of 'Exodus' saw release as a 'Disco 45', a twelve-inch version of the single, a form at the time extremely coveted by specialist collectors of Jamaican music.

At this time, there was one problem within the Wailers: they no longer had a guitarist. Al Anderson, briefly returned to favour, had gone off once again with Peter Tosh. Now his replacement, Donald Kinsey, had also joined Tosh's group. Junior Marvin, a guitarist friend of the group Traffic, was introduced to Bob, and they jammed in Chelsea at Oakley Street on 14 February 1977. 'We kinda clicked right on the spot, and to my amazement Bob said to me, "Welcome to the Wailers." They were my favourite group: I was delighted that I even had the chance to meet them, much less play with them.'

8th June 1977.

MEDIA AIDES LTD.
Tortola,
British Virgin Islands.

Island Records/Artists Ltd.,
22 St. Peters Square,
London W.6.

Dear Sirs,

I hereby acknowledge receipt of the sum of £1,800 (eighteen hundred pounds only) paid to me in cash. FOR SALARIES TO D.HARPER + A. McSTRAVICK.

This figure is understood to be a payment by you in respect of a recoupable tour support advance for Bob Marley in Europe 1977.

Should the album "Exodus" ILPS 9498 be certified gold as per RIAA standards in the United States of America you will charge the above figure to us as an advance against all and any royalties to accrue to us as per our agreement with Island Records Inc. dated August 6th, 1975.

Yours faithfully,
For and on behalf of
MEDIA AIDES LTD.

Don Taylor.

'Bob and Junior got on well: they liked each other,' said Chris Blackwell. 'And Junior was very good for Bob: he was a very good communicator in the outside world, whereas Bob was very quiet. Junior and Tyrone were very valuable in that respect.'

Bob, noted Junior Marvin, was in a very happy mood. 'I guess he was happy to be alive. He was writing a lot, writing every day. He seemed to be having a great time.' The guitarist saw straightaway one of the reasons why Bob was so gifted a songwriter: 'He worked so hard at it. He tried to write a song every day. Out of every hundred songs he wrote, he would end up with just ten to fifteen, the ones that had a certain magic.'

Marvin's own magic came from several years of paying his dues. Born in 1947 as Donald Richards, he had left Jamaica for England with his parents when he was nine. Like countless other British teenagers, he had been inspired by the bespectacled Hank Marvin, lead guitarist with the hugely successful instrumental group the Shadows and the source of Junior's stage name: Junior and a friend went out and bought guitars and formed a group. Later, he moved to the States and played with Billy Preston, Ike and Tina Turner, and T-Bone Walker. In 1972, ironically, he had spent time hanging out with Al Anderson; he was playing with the revered soul-jazz organist Larry Young, who came from the same town in New Jersey as Anderson.

The fact that Junior Marvin moved around a lot onstage would give Bob a chance to cool out during his performance. Junior's joining the group was a contentious matter for purists, however. When *Exodus* was released, the reviews criticised his rock-style guitar-playing – although his Hendrix-like approach was one of the reasons he'd been chosen. 'There were a few people who wanted the music to be strictly one style, but Bob said to me, "How can I be free if they want it to be strict – music has got to have some kind of freedom."'

Junior Marvin started working on the new songs immediately. Things had hardly changed from the days when the Soulettes would be drilled by Bob at Studio One. 'It was very intense and disciplined. There wasn't much fooling around. They gave me a whole load of old Wailers albums to listen to. And I jammed on some of the new songs with Bob and Tyrone, just the three of us.'

There was only one, unfortunate, break in the routine of recording. On 6 April 1977, Bob was fined £50 at Marylebone Magistrates Court in west London for possession of cannabis. 'I know this is almost legal in your country,' said the magistrate, 'but as you know it is not legal in this country.' Family Man was fined £20 for a similar offence. The pair had been stopped by Notting Hill police as they drove from Basing Street recording studio late one chilly night in their Ford Cortina estate, with Neville Garrick at the wheel. Driving past Notting Dale police station, by the junction of Ladbroke Grove and Holland Park Avenue, they were pulled over by a police car. To the police searching them, discovering a pair of Thai sticks on each of the men, at first they were just another pair of local dreads. It was only when they were taken into the police station that Bob's identity was revealed.

During his time in London, Bob Marley was interviewed on camera by the film director Jeremy Marre for the documentary that became *Roots Rock Reggae*. Don Taylor had agreed to Bob appearing in the movie but, when editing was completed, Taylor played a fast card: now he was demanding $1 million, in cash, for the rights to show Bob in *Roots Rock Reggae* – or he would take out an injunction prohibiting the film's release. Marre phoned Chris Blackwell, who advised the director to expect a visit at the cutting-room. 'The next day in walked Bob with an entourage of ganja-puffing brethren,' said the director. 'They watched the film and then disappeared in a cloud of smoke. Next day I got a call from Don Taylor apologising for his errors and dropping all objections.'

By the end of March, all the songs for *Exodus* seemed to have been recorded, but the group worked on in the studio, completing a total of twenty-four tunes. Quickly these were weighed up – the tone of ten of them was perfect for *Exodus*, whose first side was given over to five songs about the shooting: 'Natural Mystic', 'So Much Things to Say', 'Guiltiness', 'The Heathen' (with its lines 'He who live to fight and run away / Live to fight another day'), and concluding with the title track, its lyrics a metaphor for Bob Marley's own flight from Jamaica. By contrast, the remaining tracks contained three love songs – 'Waiting in Vain', 'Turn Your Lights Down Low', and 'Three Little Birds'; the pop Rasta-reggae of 'Jammin''; and, to close the record, a 'do-over', 'One Love/People Get Ready', that old Studio One staple, now opulent with I-Threes harmonies and the dynamic lethargy of Carly Barrett's drive. In 1999, this material, which had been released in a distinctive all-gold sleeve, the colour of the earth's life-force, was voted Album of the Century by *Time* magazine.

The remaining songs, lighter and more mystical in vein, were put aside for the next album, *Kaya*; *Kaya* was mixed at Criteria Sound in Miami, a conscious and successful effort to give the record a different feel and sound.

Exodus was rush-released, in the shops on 3 June 1977 – but not in time for the start of an already booked fifteen-date European tour; this began on 10 May 1977, in Paris.

The day before the first date of the *Exodus* tour, at the Pavillon Baltard in Paris, which would be on a Sunday, Bob Marley, the Wailers, and a number of local journalists played an evening game of football on a pitch of synthetic turf between the Hilton Hotel, where the group were staying, and the Eiffel Tower. 'Football is music,' Bob had said. The opposing squad was known as the Polymuscles, a side made up of French veterans of showbusiness, television, and cinema, with the addition of Francis Borrel, the then president of the Paris Saint-Germain team.

ISLAND RECORDS INC.

MEDIA AIDES LTD.

Statement of recording costs in respect of "EXODUS" Album ILPS 9498'

Bills to hand as at June 8th 1977.

	£	US $
Hammersmith Studio	6638.61	11411.77
Basing Street Studio	19500.26	33520.95
Equipment freight to UK	1177.83	2024.69
Polymoog purchase	2152.69	3676.80
Snare Drum purchase	186.42	318.40
Junior Kerr session fees	5000.00	8595.00
Rita Marley session fees	2914.60	5000.00
Marcia Griffiths session fees	2914.60	5000.00
Aston Barrett session fee	800.00	1375.20
Carlton Barrett session fee	800.00	1375.20
Seeco session fee	800.00	1375.20
G. Da Costa session fee	500.00	859.50
G. Da Costa air fare	398.00	684.16
V. Gordon session fee	500.00	859.50
V. Gordon air fare	398.00	684.16
D. Madden session fee	500.00	859.50
D. Madden air fare	398.00	684.16
Saxophone repair	55.00	94.55
Equipment hire	1603.00	2755.55
Equipment repair	63.86	109.77
Polymoog case	130.84	224.91
K. Pitterson air fare	256.80	441.43
K. Pitterson hours Hammersmith	1655.03	2835.00
K. Pitterson hours Basing Street	4185.08	7162.50
	£ 53528.62	US$ 91927.90
less credit for 3 weeks studio mixing time	£ 6041.00	. US$ 10384.48
	£ 47487.62	US$ 81543.42

Before the match, Bob was interviewed by a reporter from Antenne 2, a French television channel.

'Mr Marley, isn't it strange that you play music for poor people but you are so rich?' asked the journalist.

'I am what I am,' replied Bob.

In the football game, played in a light rain, Bob was tackled hard; a French player stamped on his right foot, and it was badly hurt and the nail torn off the big toe. It was the same foot he had damaged twice as a youth, and almost cut in half with a hoe in 1967 when living out at Nine Miles. And if the body of the foot had already suffered grievous injury on assorted occasions, that toe was also already vulnerable. Bob had, of course, again injured it in 1975, when it was slashed near the nail by another player's pair of rusty running spikes whilst Bob was playing football on the Boys Town recreation ground in Trench Town. Although he had tried to clean up that wound with cotton and antiseptic, Bob never went to a doctor for an anti-tetanus shot. The wound never fully healed: Cedella, his daughter, would dress it for him in the evenings. When he was with his mother, she would sprinkle Golden Seal powder on it. But apparently to no avail.

The doctor Bob saw in Paris injected the toe and removed its nail, then told Bob he must stay off his feet. But he didn't heed this advice. The only compromise he made was to wear sandals for some time, which revealed a large bandage on his right foot. The Tuff Gong even played some shows wearing sandals and the bandage. Even dressed like this, he would still play soccer every day, wincing when the ball banged his foot. Bob's brethren Gilly could even recall the injury with the running spike in Trench Town, and for how long the Gong had had it: 'For a couple of years at least he had a bloodshot toenail that he never did anything about. Until he was stepped on he never limped or anything like that. It was the guy stepping on him that aggravated it. Then he toured for about six weeks.

He was hopping and skipping and doing his thing with his bandaged toe during the '77 European tour. He was like a raging lion.

'They gave him a cap to put on it if he was going to play soccer, like a sponge thing. He played after, he played hard soccer.'

Skill Cole flew up from Ethiopia for the Paris shows. 'Bob is an inspired youth. A messenger: he come to sing and make the children of Israel dem learn. Him a truthful brethren. Him seh when I come to his hotel room in Paris, you going to find everyone on a trip: everyone turn superstar. When mi come back from Africa people call Bob prophet and all dem t'ing. And the people around him is saying they are prophets because they know him.'

Judy Mowatt, Skill Cole's queen-woman, had a more reverential perception of the tour. The on-the-road discipline had intensified – this was how she assessed the mood. It was, she noted, like taking a church on tour. 'It was a crusade, a mission. We were like sentinels, like lights. On tour, the shows were like church: Bob delivering his sermon. There were mixed emotions in the audience: you see people literally crying, people in a frenzy, on a spiritual high. I remember one night in Canada a woman gave birth in the audience. Those concerts were highly powerful and spiritual. There was a power that pulled you there. It was a clean feeling: you leave a concert as though you have learned something, you have gained something. For months and maybe years it stays with you.'

Although there would always be one suite in every hotel set aside for hanging out, serious partying rarely took place. Bob was more interested in sitting down with the group members and listening to the previous show than in going to any nightclubs. 'If you went to Bob's room at midnight, one o'clock, three o'clock, Bob would be playing a song,' said Judy Mowatt. 'As the great philosopher said, "Height of great men were not attained by sudden flight, but while their companions slept they were toiling through the night."

'Most of those songs of Bob that we hear and make us feel so joyful in our hearts, he wrote late, late at night. Sometimes you'd be passing his room and you'd hear the guitar playing. You would hear him singing quietly in the still of the night.'

In his review of the Paris concert in *Melody Maker*, Ray Coleman clearly did not discern that Bob was suffering from any physical injury. 'Marley says he's added Junior Marvin so that he can be freer to move around the stage as a singer. Nowhere was this more in evidence than during his exotic, dervish-like dances on "Lively Up Yourself".

'We know Marley to be an athlete – a strong footballer, he gets up at home in Jamaica every day at 5 a.m. to go running – but his energy and surprisingly inventive dancing here was a joyful sight, perfectly in the mood of the song. Arms and dreadlocks flailing, he was a magical picture.' Following the performance, Coleman interviewed Bob Marley. 'People want to listen to a message, word from Jah,' the singer told the journalist. 'This could be passed through me or anybody. I am not a leader. Messenger. The words of the songs, not the person, is what attracts people.' The British tabloid press was more interested in running shots of Bob dancing in a Paris nightclub with Miss World, Cindy Breakspeare. The headline in the mass-selling *Daily Mirror*? 'The Beauty and the Beast'.

Attending the date at Munich's Circus Krone, Vivien Goldman, who through synchronicity had discovered that Bob Marley was in exile in London, wrote about the show for *Sounds*: 'It throbbed and burned forward, as natural and irresistible as the moon tugging the sea. It's a natural mystic flowing through the air. Let Jah be praised. And when he sings, "Forget your sorrows and dance," your heart swells so much you're hardly aware that you're dancing, feet and soul.'

At another German date, in Berlin, Bob and the Wailers clearly felt very relaxed. Before they went onstage they had been given a bundle of their beloved Thai sticks. These presented Bob with a different perception of the evening's performance. On the second encore, he stopped the show and started the set again from 'Positive Vibration', which fell roughly a third of the way into the set. The group didn't come offstage until 2 a.m.

In Heidelberg in Germany on 16 May, Bob and the Wailers played in a former aircraft hangar that had been converted into a factory that made artificial limbs. The photographer Kate Simon took a sequence of pictures of Bob Marley gazing at the bottom half of a leg that stands on a table, as though seeing a vision of his potential future.

Despite his injury, Bob was determined to get through the tour. After the chaos of the Hammersmith Odeon dates, the Rainbow in Finsbury Park had been the only venue in London willing to put on a series of Bob Marley shows – four, beginning on 1 June 1977. It was only six months since the shooting in Jamaica – it was to be another ten months before he was to return home – and there was maximum security at the London concerts. Both Bob and Don Taylor were worried that some brethren of the Kingston gunmen might emerge out of the shadows of London's large Jamaican community. All backstage passes included a photograph of the holder, and the only people permitted in the backstage area were members of the group – Mick Cater and Don Taylor would stand at the stage door vetting everyone entering the building.

Each day, Bob would arrive at the venue at 4 p.m. in a black London taxi. As he was coming through the stage door on the second day at the Rainbow, a burly West Indian tried to follow him into the building. Taylor and Cater went to hold the man back, but he pulled out a gun and fired four shots in their direction. All those standing around the door fell back like dominoes, and the gunman ran off.

That evening, however, it was discovered that the incident had been something of a false alarm: the shots were only blanks, the weapon a starting-pistol. The man doing the shooting had tickets to that night's performance. But because Cater had been fearful that some potential atrocity could take place, he had had metal detectors installed at the main entrance to the Rainbow, and the starting-pistol was immediately detected.

Sometimes, following a show, as after one of the London dates at the Rainbow Theatre, Bob Marley would find his boot filled with blood. Those around him noticed that Bob had to keep changing the bandage; clearly the wound was not healing. Accompanied for moral support by Junior Marvin, Bob went to see a Harley Street specialist in London. The doctor told him the toe was infected with melanoma cancer and should be cut off; he also warned that if it was found to have spread further than the toe, he might need to amputate his entire foot. 'Mamma, I never do nobody no evil. I never do nobody no wrong. Why would Jah give me cancer?' Bob asked, perplexed, of his mother.

While Bob was in London that extremely hot summer of 1977, Michael Manley, who had won the Jamaican election he had called after announcing the 'Smile Jamaica' concert, visited the city. On a warm Saturday morning, Bob Marley and Don Taylor were summoned to the Jamaican embassy on Kensington Gore. Manley told Bob he must come back to Jamaica, for the sake of his career. But he also claimed to know for certain that responsibility for the shooting lay directly with the CIA. It was around this time that Chris Blackwell was summoned to the US Embassy in Kingston, where he was informed with no uncertainty that the American government was keeping an eye on Bob Marley. Bob Marley also found himself involved in the 'politricks' of another nation close to his heart: Asfa Wossen, the Crown Prince of Ethiopia, met Bob in London, and asked for assistance in getting the family of Haile Selassie out of Ethiopia – Bob immediately gave him $50,000.

A tour of the United States was scheduled to begin in August. But on

20 July 1977, Don Taylor announced to the US promoters that the tour was being postponed until the autumn. Everyone around Bob began to offer an opinion about his illness. For example, Gad Man, the leader of the Twelve Tribes of Israel in Jamaica, told Bob Marley that it was impossible for a Rasta to suffer from cancer. Bob also was advised that having his toe removed could ruin his career, as it would necessitate the cancellation of the next leg of the tour, in the United States – it was suggested that he get a second opinion. So, accompanied by Denise Mills, Chris Blackwell's ranking assistant, Bob visited another Harley Street specialist. The doctor hardly beat about the bush: 'the toe or the tour' was the verdict he delivered after examining Bob's foot. Immediate amputation was the only course of treatment, he insisted.

A Dr Bacon in Miami, who had operated on Don Taylor's spine following the shooting before the 'Smile Jamaica' concert, was recommended for a second opinion. When Bob flew to Miami to see Dr Bacon, the specialist discovered that Bob Marley was indeed suffering from melanoma. Like the doctor in London, Dr Bacon insisted that removal of the cancerous material was the only solution; after close scrutiny, he decided that if he were to cut away all the infected areas of the toe – a sizable proportion – the problem could be healed with a skin graft. Accordingly, Bob Marley underwent such an operation, remaining in hospital in Miami for a week as his body healed.

As a gesture of sympathy towards Bob, Princess Yashi flew out to Miami to spend time with him, Cindy Breakspeare being safely out of the way on Miss World ambassadorial duties. Bob took Yashi, along with Don Taylor, out for a meal at the Forge on 79th Street. The Princess asked if she could order her favourite wine, a 1953 Château Lafite Rothschild. When the bill was presented, it was for $35,000.

As Mrs Booker suffered from arthritis, which was exacerbated by the cold, Bob suggested to his mother that she move south from Wilmington, Delaware, chilly in winter, to the endlessly warm climes of Miami in Florida, almost next door to Jamaica. Don Taylor, at whose home Bob was convalescing, put a local Realtor to work to find a property for Bob's mother. The house that was eventually located, on Vista Lane in south Miami, would become Bob's home when he was in Florida. It was a substantial, six-bedroom property with a pool, set within almost two acres of garden – its only disadvantage the occasional hostility Mrs B. experienced in this all-white neighbourhood after moving there at the beginning of October 1977. 'Bob was recuperating from the toe,' said his mother. 'Then he decide that the toe start to feel a little better. Because they cut some out and grafted some on. I remember him say, "Every time I'm to do a tour here in the US something happens."'

But Bob scarcely had time to enjoy living with his mother before he had to return to hospital: an infection had developed in the toe from which the cancer had been removed. When the infection had cleared, Bob Marley received reassuring news – one of his doctors told him she was certain that all the cancer had gone from his body.

Bob came to his mother with an idea: if she sold 'dis yah house', he advised, she could buy three equally well-appointed homes in Jamaica. Although she had not been in the property for more than three months, Cedella Booker went along with this plan of her son's, and the Miami house was put on the market. But with Bob away in London, confusion reigned and Mrs B. ended up buying another home in Miami, in the Cuban neighbourhood of Tamiami Trail. When her son returned to Miami, he expressed surprise that his mother and her children should be living in such a poky property. Seizing control, and learning that the house on Vista Lane out of which his mother had moved was not yet legally sold, he insisted she move back to it. Although, due to his not having left any will, there would be difficult, contentious times after Bob had passed on, Cedella Booker lived there for the rest of her life.

The final, necessary cancellation of the US leg of the *Exodus* tour had a bad effect on the sales of the album, which had been bubbling in the American charts, awaiting the major promotion that a tour would give it. Island Records' efforts for the album to follow *Rastaman Vibration* into the US Top Ten were thwarted – *Exodus* only edged into the US Top Twenty albums. Although there was no way this cancellation could have been avoided, Bob's reputation with US promoters was harmed. 'It affects people a lot when tours get cancelled,' said Chris Blackwell. 'If it's an English rock act, that's one thing: it does you a lot of harm. But when it's a Jamaican act then it's much worse: people say that there's no point in booking it because you know these Jamaicans: they are never going to turn up. So you get a credibility gap you have to get over – which is very hard.'

Bob spent close to five months in Miami. Here he lived a life hardly dissimilar to that he would pursue in Jamaica. Rising at five or six in the morning, he would brew up some bush tea and then wander out to sit on the stoop in the backyard. There he would play around with tunes and sing until around eight or so. Much of the time, Neville Garrick was with him. 'Him used to like sing in the morning, because him voice sound more hoarse, throaty. I never saw him record then, though. I remember him writing 'Misty Morning' in Delaware after the *Natty Dread* tour. We wake up one morning. Everywhere she live Mrs Booker always plant a big garden: she even have a breadfruit tree in Delaware. We are out there: cloudy, cloudy morning. 'Im say, "It so dark up here." Then him just sing: 'Misty morning, don't see no sun / I know you're out there somewhere / Having fun.' And him work on it for next two hours: it just come like that.'

Whilst living temporarily in Miami, Bob Marley had been obliged to return to London. Island Records had asked for his involvement in a new promotional form, a video, which they wanted to film for a song called 'Is This Love?', which would be a single taken off the next album, *Kaya*. The location for the filming was the Keskidee Centre, off Caledonian

Road in north London, close to Pentonville Prison. A former church, this building had played an inestimable role in the lives of London's Caribbean and African immigrants, and as Britain's principal black arts centre at that time, it was the country's main repository of African culture, as well as being the home of black theatre in Britain.

The Keskidee Centre also played host to the Caribbean Artists Movement, in which many of the leading artists from the region had involved themselves. Exhibitions of paintings by prominent artists, as well as prose and poetry readings, were held at the centre, which boasted an extensive library, the largest collection of black cultural reading matter in the United Kingdom. In 1977, its librarian was a young black poet by the name of Linton Kwesi Johnson.

Linton was present when the video shoot for 'Is This Love?' was set up at the Keskidee Centre. The video was to be shaped around a children's party, in which Bob played the part of a kind of Rastafarian Pied Piper, even leading the children out of the building and away down the street; this party was entirely contrived, but a delight all the same for the underprivileged 3- to 12-year-olds who were invited, one of whom bore the name Naomi Campbell. They remained nonplussed by their famous host, but one and all were fascinated by Bob's dreadlocks.

Linton Kwesi Johnson was introduced to Bob Marley. 'He knew who I was, because I'd left a book of my poetry at Island for him. He wanted to know why I wasn't a Rasta. I said I wasn't religious. He asked why I was so angry. I said I was just expressing reality. He was a little, ordinary kind of guy, very affable, but very private.'

Later, Bob was to acquire the Jamaican rights to Linton's records – as he also did for those of Steel Pulse – for Tuff Gong; however, in the end, the records were never released.

The video shoot was thoroughly documented by the photographer Adrian Boot, although the true importance of this photographic session was not understood until years later: 1984, to be precise, when the Island Records art department was searching for a suitable cover shot for the *Legend* compilation LP. It was a shot from the Keskidee session, of Bob wearing the ring that had formerly belonged to His Imperial Majesty Haile Selassie, that was eventually chosen.

The video, ironically, was never shown at the time of the single's release: it was felt to conflict with the more militant image of Bob that was then being put forward, and it was aired only much later, in 1984, when a compilation of Bob Marley videos was released by Island. Footage shot at the event, however, was integrated into the video of 'One Love/People Get Ready', made in that same year by Don Letts, the young dread who had followed Bob back to his residence after the Lyceum show and who by now was known as the 'Rastafarian film director'.

This Keskidee Centre video shoot had one more important outcome: present were the ranking JLP gunman Claudie Massop and, for the PNP, Bucky Marshall, and that other shock-troop commander, Tony Welch, having come to ask Bob if he would return to Jamaica to perform a peace concert to help bring an end to the murderous political rivalry on the island. Life seemed to be imitating art, specifically that of Bob Marley's latest work, the marvellous *Exodus*. As Linton Kwesi Johnson said of the record: '*Exodus* moves from despondency to hope: a reflection of his personal experience at the time.'

Island Inc

REGISTERED MAIL
to media

Media Aider Ltd
c/o 12401 VISTA LANE
MIAMI
Florida 33156

Dear Sirs,

        We hereby inform you that as per
the terms of our agreement dated August 6th 1975
we accept the album entitled 'KAYA', index no ILPS
9517 delivered totally comprising recordings by Bob Marley — as
defined, with a release scheduled for the early part of
March 1978

        Our cheque in the amount of US$ 29129·73
(Letters   US dollars), which represents
the sum payable as per the attached schedule of
advances & payments &c is enclosed.

        Please note that it is our intention
to release a single from the album entitled
" Is this love / Crisis" on February 3rd 1978
          Easy Skanking.

        Kindly acknowledge receipt of this letter
& enclosure.

                Yours very truly,

cc JES.
① Don T. Miami & NY.
② Bob Marley Miami
③ Zell + Harris NY   for Island Records Inc.
④ Charlie Nuovo NY
⑤ Chris Blackwell NY + London   T. HAYES.

ISLAND *Inc*

David Steinberg

[handwritten annotations]

Dear David

Re: ~~Bob Marley~~ *Media Aides Ltd.* *Telex N° 1295 9517*

We hereby inform you that as per the terms of our agreement with the above
artist we accept the album entitled "KAYA" as delivered and have scheduled
a release for the beginging of March 1978. Accordingly please find enclosed
~~our~~ chque ~~for the sum of _____ being ~~our~~xforxxthisxalbum~~
~~payable for this labum~~ less the sum of £ *[handwritten]* expended (a breakdown
of which is attached hereto) *[handwritten]*

Please note that ~~we also intend~~ to release a single from the album entitled
"Is This Live#Crisis" on 3rd February 1978.

Telex N° WIP

[handwritten] Bob Marley man.
c.c. Don Taylor, Miami. *[handwritten]*
[handwritten lines]

T**ony.**

Very rough draft. Please let me have figures
& also inform if being paid by Inc &
not us.

Ellie

ISLAND RECORDS LTD. 22 St. PETERS SQUARE LONDON W6 9NW TEL. 01-741 1511 CABLES: ACKEE TELEX: 934541
Directors: Tim Clark Tom Hayes Tony Pye John Leftly Dave Domleo Martin Humphrey
Reg. No. 723336 England Reg. Office: 124 Finchley Road London NW3 5HT

PEACE CONCERT

At the beginning of 1978, in Kingston, there were only two real topics of conversation: ceaseless complaints about the increasing shortage of goods on sale in the island's stores, the consequence of Washington's efforts to bankrupt the Manley government; and the imminent rumoured homecoming to Jamaica of Bob Marley, a hero returned from the self-imposed exile into which he had gone following the attempt on his life on 3 December 1976.

Bob's flight touched down at Kingston's Norman Manley Airport on Sunday 26 February 1978; as the plane coasted to a halt, he was aware that this return to his home country would be viable and valid only if it contained a direct effort to end the escalating violent hatred that was tearing Jamaica apart and terrifying its population.

Picking up his luggage from the rickety baggage carousel, Bob immediately had it rigorously searched by an officious customs officer. It was as though the man was putting the Gong in his place. Bob's anger firing up, he snatched his bags back – 'Bwai, gimme dis bloodclaat!' – and stormed out of the airport. The next day, Don Taylor received a call from the head of customs, asking him not to let Bob again embarrass his officers in such a way. Bob clearly carried greater weight than his Wailer brethren Peter Tosh. Returning to Jamaica earlier that month, Peter had been obliged to endure a customs officer leaning across towards his ear. 'I am looking for a reason to shoot you,' the man had whispered.

This was precisely the thinking that Bob Marley was hoping to alter. Since the meeting with Claudie Massop, Bucky Marshall, and Tony Welch at the Keskidee Centre in London, it had been privately agreed – though not yet publicly announced – that the 'One Love Peace Concert' would be held in Kingston on 22 April 1978, under the auspices of the Twelve Tribes of Israel. Bob Marley was bankrolling the event, to the tune of $50,000. Profits from ticket sales would go to assorted community projects.

The political parameters that exist in Jamaica are hardly the same as those of the United States or Western Europe – they are more like those of an archetypal, mythical banana republic. Jamaicans often seem to have severely misunderstood the dividing line between reality and art, allowing it to become blurred and indistinct: life in the ghetto area of west Kingston can seem as though it is being lived in a Sergio Leone film, with the body count equally as high. Suddenly, as the sluggish heat hangs torpidly, violence of an extraordinarily desperate and vicious degree can erupt, only to evaporate utterly within minutes.

Someone who had certainly experienced the whims of the spirits, hobgoblins, and duppies that drift sometimes maliciously through the

Jamaican psychic ether was Peter Tosh. Since recording his *Legalize It* album, he had established the beginning of what was a successful solo career. Assisted by Lee Jaffe, he had found an excellent manager in Gary Kurfirst, a young New York music-world whiz kid whom Chris Blackwell later described as 'one of the first managers who basically built the rock business'. Kurfirst, who also managed Toots and the Maytals, had secured Peter a good deal with CBS Records in New York, and Virgin Records in London, for the release of *Legalize It*. Although a man of a liberal, creative persuasion, even Kurfirst had been a little surprised when Peter Tosh had demanded that the manager bring him his advance to Jamaica in cash – which Peter, who sometimes seemed wilfully eccentric, promptly took and buried in a hole in the bush. Early copies of *Legalize It*, released in late 1976, contained a scratch-and-sniff sticker which gave off the scent of the most potent lambs-bread herb; the cover, shot by Lee Jaffe in a herb field up in the hills behind Bluefields, Peter's Westmoreland birthplace, depicted Tosh garlanded by marijuana plants, holding his treasured herb pipe. Inevitably, the title track became the potheads' anthem. Sitting on the album, next to a strong set of other songs – 'Whatcha Gonna Do?', 'No Sympathy', 'Why Must I Cry?', 'Igziabeher', 'Ketchy Shubby', 'Till Your Well Runs Dry', and a 'do-over' of 'Brand New Second Hand' – the 'Legalize It' song came to personify the character into whom Peter Tosh had metamorphosed as a solo act. He was, as he would declare to all and sundry, Jamaica's Minister of Herb. Putting together Word, Sound, and Power, a hot, tight group that included the drummer Sly Dunbar, the bass player Robbie Shakespeare – the rhythm section's recruitment was expensive, as they needed to be persuaded there was another life outside of their lucrative session work – and both the American former Wailers guitarists Al Anderson and Donald Kinsey, as well as the multi-instrumentalist Mikey Chung, Peter Tosh seemed on the cusp of becoming a considerable star. *Legalize It* was a strong global seller, notching up half a million copies, far more than any other record Peter Tosh had hitherto released. These figures were more than replicated on his next album, *Equal Rights*, released in 1977. An unalloyed masterpiece, *Equal Rights* is one of the most influential and powerful reggae records ever released. As the title suggests, Peter was making an angry album that was a militant demand for human egalitarianism. 'Equal rights and justice!' was Peter's plea in the title song. The material and its delivery on this record would firmly mark out the position of Peter Tosh as the Malcolm X of reggae – in contrast with Bob Marley's Martin Luther King–like posture. The *Equal Rights* album concluded with an excoriating attack on racist South Africa in the song 'Apartheid'. Every song on the record was a classic, rebellious, on the edge. Kicking off with a 'do-over' of 'Get Up, Stand Up', to which his sonorous tones seemed to bring ownership, the record ran through the prophetic 'Downpressor Man', the bare, open 'I Am That I Am', before hitting another 'do-over' in 'Stepping Razor', which Joe Higgs had written for him a decade previously. Following the title track, the 'African' song presented a gorgeous, evolved sense of identity; 'Jah Guide', meanwhile, was like a soothing soul hymn. The songs' subject matters were caressed by intricate, sophisticated musical patterns that only enhanced the accessibility of the entire album. Bunny Livingston and Rita Marley both contributed to this record, produced with visionary clarity, which managed simultaneously to be a definitive Jamaican reggae release and the definition of a crossover hit. *Equal Rights* sold even better than *Legalize It*, establishing irrefutably Peter Tosh's international position as a Jamaican solo star.

On 21 April, beneath a rising full moon, as dusk gave way to night, Bob Marley and his entire group played an extensive sound check, readying themselves for the next day, at the National Stadium, empty apart from various functionaries; it was the first time they had played on the island since the 'Smile Jamaica' concert. Present was Mark Rowland, an American writer: 'There on the bandstand before us, framed by stage lights and gels, stood Bob Marley and the Wailers, and the I-Threes too, seamlessly rehearsing songs for the following evening's historic occasion. The music resonated from the stage into the crisp night air, and a creamier, more lustrous sound I never heard, or may ever hear again. It was the sound of emotional rapture.'

Planeloads of assorted members of the media had descended upon Jamaica, to the delight of every pickpocket and gunman in Kingston. Seizing the moment with unerring pragmatism, Island Records cleverly had managed to spin this historic event into being simultaneously both a great humanitarian act and a kind of enormous ghetto launch-party for the release of *Kaya*, Bob Marley's new album, a collection of love songs and, of course, homages to the power of ganja (the album was also to provide a pair of chart singles, 'Satisfy My Soul' and the beautiful 'Is This Love?'). In effect, the One Love Peace Concert was the first date of the *Kaya* world tour.

Flying in the face of most predictions, the concert on Saturday, 22 April, was a resounding success, a focus for the media of the Western world. Sixteen of the island's most significant reggae acts, including Jacob Miller and Inner Circle, Beres Hammond, the Mighty Diamonds, Trinity, Dennis Brown, Culture, Dillinger, Big Youth, Peter Tosh, and Ras Michael and the Sons of Negus appeared. The 12-year-old singer Junior Tucker was the opening act.

In a controversial section of the show, fired by a typical selfless arrogance, Peter Tosh harangued Michael Manley and Edward Seaga for persecuting ghetto sufferahs for their fondness for herb, and lit up a spliff onstage. Bob Marley's action of raising together the arms of Michael

Manley and Edward Seaga above his head is the one defining image of the One Love Peace Concert, yet in their own way, the actions of Bob's compatriot Peter Tosh were every bit as memorable. However, only an audio record remains of them, Peter – who was introduced as 'Peter Touch' – having refused to have his section of the concert filmed. 'Yuh have a some lickle pirates a come from America with camera and their TV business fe get rich off I and I,' declaimed the Minister of Herb from the stage. 'But hear mi nuh, man: if a man come to talk to I-man, a lightning flash anywhere in the ends of the earth. I-man flash lightning, so mek sure them a come give me good argument about my rights.'

In fact, Peter Tosh had been reluctant to play at the One Love Peace Concert, though he eventually gave in to Bob Marley's entreaties. Everyone who played there, Peter insisted, would end up dead. Of course everyone would, given the fullness of time, but this is not precisely what Peter meant. He was discussing a theme of his 'Equal Rights' song: 'Everyone is calling out for peace / But no one is calling out for justice.' 'This concert here, them say is a Peace Concert,' he declared in a lengthy peroration over an instrumental passage during his performance – appropriately – of the song 'Funeral'. 'And I wonder how many people know what the word 'peace' means. You see, most intellectual people in society think the word 'peace' means coming together.

'Peace is the diploma you get in the cemetery. On top of your grave that is marked, "Here lies the body of John Strokes that rests in peace." Seen?'

Peter Tosh also had a distinct vision of the source of Jamaica's egregious violent turmoil. 'Learn this,' he decreed, part of a seven-minute harangue from the stage, before kicking into his final song, 'when Columbus and Henry Morgan and Francis Drake come on, and dem call dem pirates. And put dem in a reading-book and give us observation that we must look at and live the life and the principle of pirates to the youth: dem now fire up dem gun like Henry Morgan, same way. Yuh nuh see it?'

What really brought the fury of Jamaican officialdom down upon Peter Tosh were his words later in the same tirade. Directly addressing Prime Minister Michael Manley and Edward Seaga, leader of the opposition JLP, both of whom were in the audience, he ranted against the ganja laws, and the manner in which they were abused by the police: 'I am one of those who happen to be in the underprivileged sector, seen, hassled by police brutality times and times again, and have to run up and down fe wha'? Fe have a lickle spliff in my pocket or have a round of herb or if yuh buy a draw, yuh have to be tense and cork yuh batty until yuh come back because police will lock yuh with a roadblock down the road.'

To the rage of the watching forces of law and order, Peter Tosh then lit up his giant spliff onstage, before launching into 'Legalize It'. 'We never knew Peter was going to talk the way he did,' said Sly Dunbar, drumming behind Peter during his performance. 'We were surprised when he began to talk: a lotta people said Peter was the star of that show.' It was certainly Peter Tosh's finest hour.

Unlike Peter, however, Bob Marley seemed in a state of transcendental bliss. Instead of attacking the prime minister and the leader of the opposition, he attempted to bring them together. How did Bob Marley do this? By spelling out the truisms that many people had vaguely felt or thought. Using the structure of the mythology of Rastafari, he articulated the unconscious rumblings of the soul of global alternative thinking. This was his job, his purpose in life, of which he was fully aware: as he declared in 'Rebel Music (3 O'Clock Roadblock)', 'Check my life if I'm in doubt'.

During 'Jammin'' his dancing delivery and scat extemporising on the lyrics were those of someone taken over by the spirit, close to speaking in tongues, channelling Jah Rastafari:

To make everything come true, we've got to be together, yeah, yeah. And to the spirit of the most high, His

Imperial Majesty Emperor Haile Selassie I, run lightning, leading the people of the slaves to shake hands . . . To show the people that you love them right, to show the people that you gonna unite, show the people that you're over bright, show the people that everything is all right. Watch, watch, watch what you're doing, because . . . I'm not so good at talking but I hope you understand what I'm trying to say. I'm trying to say, could we have, could we have, up here onstage here the presence of Mr Michael Manley and Mr Edward Seaga. I just want to shake hands and show the people that we're gonna unite . . . we're gonna unite . . . we've got to unite . . . The moon is high over my head, and I give my love instead. The moon is high over my head, and I give my love instead.

As ghetto gunmen hovered on the edge of the stage, Bob brought together the hands of Michael Manley and Edward Seaga above his head. And held them firmly linked. Both politicians looked uncomfortable in the other's company. Yet despite the desperate bloodbath into which Jamaica would dissolve by the turn of the decade, this instant remains one of the key civilising moments of the twentieth century.

'Yes, the Peace,' Bob Marley said later, 'is really the Youth of Jamaica started it. Asked me to help and get it together, y'know, knowing that I was one of the victims during the time of the politics. This peace work . . . it don't stop . . . it never stop . . . We know it never stop. That mean, we the youth got a work to do.'

Peter Tosh's tour de force performance earned him a record deal from Rolling Stones Records, one of whose owners, Mick Jagger, was in the audience. As though tremendously excited at being at an event that was the quintessence of outlaw cool, Mick 'Jaguar' – as he was known in Jamaica – ran around the One Love Peace Concert, hither and thither, on his own, without a bodyguard, which says much about the egalitarian nature of the event and also about Jagger. 'Maybe we should kidnap him,' considered Bucky Marshall. When, the day before, Vivien Goldman had asked Marshall why he thought the Peace Concert was taking place at that time, the PNP man had replied, matter-of-factly, 'Because we shoot harder.'

On a Wednesday afternoon shortly after the Peace Concert, Bob Marley and Don Taylor were taken by Tek Life to McGregor Gully in Kingston. There they found three men tied and bound. Leggo Beast, whom Taylor had previously met, confessed that he and three others had been trained by the CIA, and given guns and unlimited cocaine to attack Bob Marley at 56 Hope Road on 3 December 1976. At McGregor Gully, two of the men were hanged on the spot; the other was shot in the head – the gun for this was offered to Bob. 'Bob refused,' said Taylor, 'showing no emotion whatsoever, and I realised that he was entering a different phase.' The men screamed as they were led away. A fourth man involved had already died of a cocaine overdose.

The 'peace' brought about by the One Love Peace Concert was somewhat illusory: in 1978, almost four hundred people were killed in Jamaica. Two of the ranking gunmen who had organised the One Love Peace Concert were dead within twenty-four months: Claudie Massop was gunned down by police and Bucky Marshall was shot to death in a Brooklyn nightclub in March 1980.

In an endeavour to seclude himself away from Kingston's gun business, Bob Marley bought a sizable property, a total of seventeen acres, on a headland on the Jamaican north coast in the tiny picture-postcard town of Oracabessa in the parish of St Mary. The residence was one with a legendary reputation: Goldeneye, as it was known, was hard to beat as a creative power-point. In the previous twenty years, the property had become a by-word for glamour, sensuality, and artistic endeavour, a location permanently overhung by the knowledge that this was where the writer Ian Fleming had penned his apparently immortal tales of the superspy James Bond; the first Bond book, *Casino Royale*, was written at Goldeneye in the winter of 1952. Goldeneye's endless retinue of famous visitors included not only Noël Coward, a neighbour, but also the painters Cecil Beaton and Lucien Freud, the writers Truman Capote, Graham Greene, and Evelyn Waugh, and the former British prime minister and his wife, Sir Anthony and Lady Eden. That it had been purchased by Bob Marley, a country boy who had moved to the Kingston ghetto, and eventually made his fortune, was a tremendous tribute to his capacities. Unfortunately, the reason that Bob had wanted to buy Goldeneye – its distance and therefore apparent security from the lifestyle of Kingston – was why after only a few months he decided that he was not comfortable living there. Eventually, he sold the house to Chris Blackwell.

Largely, there seemed little domestic peace for Bob Marley. During the *Kaya* tour, on the California leg, Rita Marley confessed to her husband that Ital was Stephanie's father. According to Mrs Booker, the news broke Bob's heart. In what seemed clearly an act of revenge, one evening, Bob, accompanied by Seeco, drove Rita out to Kingston Harbour, where he threw her wedding ring into the sea. Had there been a measure of vengeance on Rita's part in telling her husband the truth about Stephanie's father? On 21 July 1978, the night that Bob Marley and the Wailers played at the Starlight Bowl in Burbank, California, a show on which Peter Tosh appeared as special guest, Cindy Breakspeare gave birth to Damian Marley, another son for the Tuff Gong, a son who in time would be given the sobriquet of 'Junior Gong'. Bob already had bought Cindy a house in Kingston, in uptown Cherry Gardens, for $49,000. Soon after, he gave her an additional $100,000 as start-up funding for the Ital Craft store that she established.

His own art moved forward. In a promotional interview for *Kaya* in California, Bob Marley bared his thoughts. 'People don't understand that we live on this earth too,' said Bob of the album. 'We don't sing these songs and live in the sky. I don't have an army behind me. If I did, I wouldn't care, I'd just get more militant. Because I'd know, well, I have fifty thousand armed youth, and when I talk, I talk from strength. But you have to know how you're dealing. Maybe if I'd tried to make a heavier tune than *Kaya* they would have tried to assassinate me because I would have come too hard. I have to know how to run my life, because that's what I have, and nobody can tell me to put it on the line, you dig? Because no one understands these things. These things are heavier than anyone can understand. People that aren't involved don't know it, it's my work, and I know it outside in. I know when I am in danger and what to do to get out. I know when everything is cool, and I know when I tremble, do you understand? Because music is something that everyone follows, so it's a force, a terrible force.'

The American leg of the *Kaya* tour was scheduled to begin in Miami, Florida, on 5 May 1978. But it ran into difficulties: Junior Marvin initially was refused a US visa, his 'numerous drug convictions' cited as the reason. The Miami concert was cancelled four hours before showtime, leaving a local promoter furious. The Florida date and others in the American south were re-scheduled, and the tour kicked off at the Hill Auditorium in Ann Arbor, Michigan, on 18 May. After a date at the Music Hall in Cleveland, Ohio, the following night, the tour moved on to Columbus and then to Chicago. In the Windy City, Bob, whose reading matter was usually restricted to the Bible and music publications, visited a number of black bookshops. A large quantity of black-consciousness literature was bought, including various biographies of Malcolm X, as well as work by Angela Davis, who had been a professor and friend of Neville Garrick. For the rest of the tour Garrick would see Bob devouring these volumes at every opportunity. 'You can see how his lyrics matured in terms of clarity over the next records. From *Natty Dread* to *Survival* is a big leap.'

The tour continued through Milwaukee, and Minneapolis, and in June hit Pittsburgh, Rochester, Detroit, Philadelphia, Boston, and Montreal, arriving at Toronto Maple Leaf Gardens on Friday the ninth. After two more shows, in Buffalo and Washington, DC, Bob Marley and the Wailers arrived in New York City; they played a Saturday-night show at Madison Square Garden, where they were supported by Stanley Clarke and drew a sell-out, racially diverse crowd of over eighteen thousand people. As befitted these larger venues that Bob and the group were now playing, the shows were an exaggeration of their past, heavy with rock guitar from Junior Marvin, and almost histrionic in their presentation. The Wailers were now exhibiting what was possibly the first example of twin lead guitars in reggae. Al Anderson had come to Bob and told him he'd like to play again with the group. Bob had said to Junior, 'What shall we do about Al?'

'I said, "If you want to get him back it will be a good thing, because you can get the same sounds on the tracks he plays on records, and the same thing on the ones I play on." So Al came back and it was really cool – it made the group stronger.

'Bob would say, "We'll have a guitar night tonight." Sometimes he would make a joke, "Tonight the guitar player dem take the stage." We felt very secure musically, everyone played to their best abilities. There were two keyboard players that were really good – Tyrone and Wire, and they would try and push each other to do better. The same thing happened with myself and Al. We both wanted to sound as good as we could. So competitively it was good. So Bob got the best of everyone.'

Larger than life, the message came across to an audience that was often more used to the melodrama of big rock shows. A conscious decision had been taken by Bob and Chris Blackwell that this was the way to communicate on an even greater scale.

In *The New York Times*, John Rockwell reviewed the Madison Square Garden show: 'The concert was a triumph . . . for reggae in general but for Mr Marley in particular. There were plenty of non-West Indians on hand, for one thing. And for another, after a slightly slow start, the concert built to a climax that was really wonderful in its fervor and exultation . . . By the final number, "Jammin'", and especially in the encores of "Get Up, Stand Up", "War", and "Exodus", Mr Marley was extraordinary. Who would have believed Madison Square Garden would have swayed en masse to a speech by Haile Selassie, the words of which Mr Marley incorporates verbatim into "War"?' Rockwell expressed a quibble or two: 'To a casual listener, the steadily rocking, offbeat accents of the music could seem too unvarying, especially with the minimal pauses between numbers and the frequent running together of one song into the next . . . But the band members overlay the pulse with solos in the traditional jazz and rock manner, and the order is determined with an ear for variety.'

In the edition of the *Black American* published after the Madison Square Garden concert, there was a further review of the same performance: 'The crowd was near peaceful hysteria when Marley put down his guitar and did his patented herky-jerky dance across the stage as the Wailers ran through three rhythmic breaks that would have made the best of the disco groups envious.

'Marley finally danced into the wings while the Wailers kept "Jammin'" onstage. By now, however, Marley's crowd was too far gone to stop dancing. Cries of "More, more," began to rise until the noise became deafening. Then a thunderous train-like sound grew as people began stomping their feet in delight. It was really breathtaking.'

After a final East Coast date in Lenox, Massachusetts, the tour headed off across the Atlantic for shows in Paris, Ibiza, Stockholm, Copenhagen,

Oslo, Rotterdam, Amsterdam, Brussels, and Bingley in Staffordshire – slap-bang in the middle of England. 'Marley has now taken the best of his material to the absolute limits of interpetation,' wrote Eric Fuller in *Sounds* of the Staffordshire show, 'and the Wailers are much concerned with showy and extended instrumental workouts within the framework of each song to give them some feeling of freshness and supply the extra thrills demanded by live performance. Given that Marley's melodies are his finest moment, the value of this style of execution is a matter of debate – but certainly lead guitarist Junior Marvin's exaggerated stage showmanship and US-soul-revue fashion histrionics seem headed in precisely the wrong direction.'

After faulty planning led to three bus-loads of media people arriving long after Bob's set had begun, the reviewer in *New Musical Express* assessed the British concert under the headline of 'Babylon By Bus'. When it was brought to Neville Garrick's attention, this became the title of the double live album of the tour which Chris Blackwell put together.

The tour then swung over to the American West Coast. Bob Marley and the Wailers played in Vancouver, Seattle, Portland, San Francisco, Los Angeles, and Santa Barbara. Then they wheeled through the dates in the US south that had been cancelled at the beginning of the tour. And, finally, the Bob Marley posse returned to Jamaica.

But Bob was not there for long. Almost immediately, he took off again, on a flight to Ethiopia. His old friend Skill Cole was still living there. Skill was employed coaching a local football team, and Bob seized the time to visit him in this Holy Land. Although he was there for only four days, during which time he wrote the song 'Zimbabwe', Bob didn't mind leaving: he knew he would be going back there very soon. Although he would often be surrounded by companions, Bob Marley was very rarely accompanied by an official bodyguard. In Ethiopia, however, he was escorted by a Kingston youth named Lips, later killed in a ghetto shoot-out.

Back in Jamaica, Bob Marley spent time with his old spar Scratch Perry. After having linked up again with the increasingly eccentric producer in London the previous year to record 'Punky Reggae Party', their relationship had been revived. Now, in one day, Bob cut four tunes out at Black Ark: two recordings that were never released, 'Who Colt the Game' and 'I Know a Place Where We Can Go'; and 'Black Man Redemption' and 'Rastaman Live Up', both of which came out as singles on Tuff Gong, and which were a marked departure from the softer subjects of *Kaya*. The militancy of this pair of new tunes pointed the way ahead to Bob's next two albums. All four songs were mixed at Tuff Gong. 'You can't show aggression all the while,' said Bob Marley. 'To make music is a life that I have to live. Sometimes you have to fight with music. So it's not just someone who studies and chats, it's a whole development. Right now is a more militant time on earth, because it's Jah Jah time. But mi always militant, you know. Mi too militant. That's why mi did things like *Kaya*, to cool off the pace.'

Someone who might have heeded Bob Marley's words was Peter Tosh. In September, he was badly beaten by police; he had been arrested in Half Way Tree by a plainclothes cop whilst holding a roach, but it was widely believed that this arrest was in revenge for his pro-herb tirade from the stage of the Peace Concert. Taken to the police station, Peter was locked in a cell with what he described as eight to ten plainclothes men. Wielding wooden batons, they beat him for ninety minutes, fracturing his skull, breaking his right hand, only stopping their vicious assault when Peter feigned death. Hearing what had taken place, Bob Marley rushed to the police station, bailing Peter and getting him to hospital. When he arrived at the station and saw Peter's pitiful state, Bob burst into tears. Bunny Lee heard the whole story:

'Bob come and go to the police and make them drop the charge. But Peter was kind of big-headed too. Bob said he was going to take it to court. But the policeman said to him, "Bob, you can take it to court. But remember when they call your and Peter's name they are going to hear, "Deceased, your honour." But eventually they decide to withdraw the charges.' Many felt that, following this beating, Peter Tosh never fully recovered.

Within weeks, however, Peter Tosh was driving a London-based record-company executive at terrifying speed up the endlessly winding narrow road from Kingston into Jamaica's Blue Mountains. Racing past a truck, he found another lorry heading straight for him, a head-on collision seemingly inevitable. The record company man screamed. Peter floored the accelerator and – as though by a miracle – slid his Cortina GT between the two vehicles.

When he arrived at his destination, that same mountain-top location of Strawberry Hill to which Bob Marley had fled following the attempt on his life in December 1976, it was clear that Peter was the star of a video-shoot that was about to take place; the filming was for 'Don't Look Back', Peter's first tune on Rolling Stones Records. Peter was in very good spirits: it was clear his life was taking – even if only momentarily – an upturn. Mick Jagger was present, greeting him with great cordiality. During the course of the shoot, in which Mick Jagger co-starred with him, Peter arranged for the master-tapes of the song to be stolen by an accomplice. The tapes were slipped back the next morning, and later that afternoon 'Don't Look Back' was available in record shacks in Kingston, on Peter's own Intel-Diplo label.

In the autumn, Bob and the Wailers headed across the Pacific to Australia and New Zealand. From all over the country, Maoris had journeyed into the New Zealand city of Auckland. At a ceremony of greeting, they awarded Bob Marley a name which, translated into English, means 'the Redeemer'. Bob made sure he spent time at a couple of Maori youth centres.

The most memorable of the shows on this leg of the tour was at Western Springs, a natural amphitheatre to the west of Auckland. This scenario was assisted by the Island label in New Zealand being run by Victor Stent, an enormous fan of reggae: in a competition among the various Island outlets to boost sales of reggae, Stent had easily outstripped everyone else.

In Japan, where he played four shows, Bob Marley met an extraordinary reception. At the concerts, the audience would show they knew every song, and would sing every word of the lyrics.

In subsequent years, reggae has enjoyed an immense popularity in Japan, and this may be directly traced back to Bob's only visit. But how did the Japanese perceive Bob? A little girl, for example, came up to him and bowed down reverentially. 'No, no: that's not for me – that's for the almighty God,' Bob felt obliged to say.

'Japan was memorable,' said Rita Marley. 'We had a lot of press there saying how well they thought it would be doing there in ten years' time: how it would be taking over Japan. And we said that it never would! They loved Bob, and Bob played a big part in them absorbing reggae as they have done.'

There was one problem, however: the almost zero availability of herb in this notoriously drug-intolerant nation. To alleviate this problem, it was necessary for a member of the touring party to travel to Japan ahead of the group. Such matters were always the responsibility of the local promoters, although this proved not to be understood in Japan. Alternative arrangements were made, however, and when Bob and the Wailers arrived in Tokyo, they were presented with fifty Thai sticks. The group retired to their hotel, surprised at the minute proportions of their rooms. As a security measure, the floors directly above and below them in their hotel had also been booked.

As was their wont, the group had consumed virtually all the Thai sticks by the time they went onstage. The next morning, they asked their Japanese fixers to bring them some more. The Japanese were amazed – they had believed that such a lifetime's supply of Thai sticks would certainly last Bob and the Wailers for the duration of the entire tour.

UPRISING

By ten in the morning the permanent hustle that was rarely absent from the yard at 56 Hope Road would be under way. Ghetto rankins and junior rankins would be coming up to check Bob or to hustle him for money, or just to cool out: 56 Hope Road was about the only uptown place where a ghetto youth could hang without experiencing the wrath of the police. During the time of the Peace Concert, even Michael Manley would be seen passing by to idle away an hour or so. Bob was always extremely welcoming to the 'mad' people – a feature of Jamaican life – who would peer through the white fence, pouring out their stream-of-consciousness rants. 'It a mad man,' Bob would say, always eager to hear an extreme point of view, 'send him in for a reasoning.'

Bob used to like to hold court in the shade of the awning over the front steps. Serious football, meanwhile, would go on in the grass-covered front yard. Sometimes a man would come up with a whole heap of fish or fruit to give Bob. If there was enough of the fish, they'd wrap it in foil, put it out on a sheet of corrugated zinc, and light a fire underneath.

As the voice of the ghetto, Bob could not help attracting gangsters and gunmen, who are always fond of mingling with entertainers. Skill Cole's position as a sports superstar held a similar appeal. Those around Bob believe that he was also turned on by hanging out with notorious characters. But Bob could be ruthlessly tough himself. On one occasion he was seen whipping a man tied to a tree after he had been caught stealing money from a visitor.

After the Peace Concert, many of these gunmen felt such a debt of gratitude to Bob that they would be even more in evidence at 56 Hope Road, to the point where their presence became a problem, even sometimes a threat. Who could tell what nefarious deals were taking place away in some corner under the shade of a mango tree?

'But as a Rasta you can't dismiss people,' pointed out Neville Garrick. 'Him only shield him could wear was him noted screwface: the screwface alone would turn people away. But then Bob love people and always want to help them. Him can empathise with everything. Bob don't have no easier life than any of them. Him kinda raised on the streets.'

'He grew up with a lot of these guys,' said Junior Marvin, 'and he wanted to straighten out a lot of them. He was trying to help them. He was trying to say, "Look, you don't really need violence; if you've got that kind of power, you don't have to use it: you can divert it into another kind of positive energy."'

In the evenings, however, a different life would go on. Round the back of the house, Bob would sit with his close brethren. Strumming his guitar, he would pick away at new or sometimes old songs. At these, the finest times, a peace of almost visible proportions would descend over the entire property. And, protected by Jah, Bob would be in touch with the deepest source of his creativity.

Early in July 1979, Bob Marley and the Wailers played their first show in Jamaica since the Peace Concert fourteen months previously. It was early in the morning when they went onstage at Jarrett Park in Montego Bay, the headliners on the Tuff Gong evening of Reggae Sunsplash II, a large outdoor festival. It was a reasoning at 56 Hope Road between Bob, Family Man, and the event's promoters that had led to the first Sunsplash. Away on tour and unable to perform there that year, Bob was determined the group should play now to give a shove to the event.

Their performance was more like a mudsplash than a sunsplash. It had been raining so hard before the group went on that there was mud all over the stage: Junior Marvin's shoes filled up with it, and the audience assumed his slipping and sliding was part of the act.

'I got *war* in *my* shoes!' cried Bob, turning this onstage problem around, in between verses of 'Lively Up Yourself', before debuting a new tune, 'Ambush in the Night', from the about-to-be-released *Survival* LP. The venue was crammed, not just with Jamaicans but with the Americans and Europeans who were now pouring into Jamaica. A potent consequence of Bob's ambassadorship was that the Island of Springs had joined India, Morocco, and Bali as a spiritual tourist spot for the counterculture. Bob had consciously played Reggae Sunsplash II to help it become a recognised event in the reggae calendar; his altruistic thinking paid off, for the festival was considered a serious fixture from then on.

Early the next afternoon, at a fenced-off part of the main beach in Jamaica's principal resort town, the very sand was skanking with the force of the dub shaking out of sets of massive speakers. Bob was presiding over his court at the regular party held to celebrate the event. All the Wailers were present, as well as Burning Spear, Bunny Wailer, Jacob Miller, and a host of local luminaries – some five hundred people when the party was kicking at its peak. It was a fabulous daytime rave, bright and breezy, and the group stayed on the beach for the whole of the day. Jamaica adored Bob. Reggae was really growing outernational, gaining international respect; there was a feeling of growth, a mood that this was the time to seize and not let slip the opportunities. It all seemed fused together by the mellow, upful vibe of spliffs and rum punch on the beach.

At the end of October 1979, Bob Marley and the Wailers began a seven-week tour of the United States – they were set to play a gruelling forty-seven shows in forty-nine days. The performances began with 'Natural Mystic', a tune that was almost a celebration of Bob's very existence. And they ended with an intensely militant trio of songs, like a three-act story of the reality of this iwah – 'Get Up, Stand Up', 'War', and 'Exodus'. On the road, Bob was playing with the structure of a new number he was writing called 'Redemption Song'.

These US dates kicked off at Harvard University in Boston, before a date at Madison Square Garden in New York previewed a short season at the legendary Apollo Theatre in Harlem. Here, in the venue where Marcus Garvey had preached, Bob and the group played seven concerts in four days. Backstage on the first night, Bob was introduced by Chris Blackwell to his friend the British journalist Anna Wintour, later to become the redoubtable editor of American *Vogue*. Anna Wintour disappeared into the night with 'the King of Reggae', and was at his side every night of the Apollo dates.

The intention of the tour was to promote the new album by Bob Marley and the Wailers, the resolutely confrontational LP *Survival*, released in October that year. Listening to it, it was immediately apparent how the shows in Harlem at the Apollo were clearly part of a larger plan. Originally titled 'Black Survival', the album's artwork was designed by Neville Garrick; its front cover displayed only the flags of the independent African nations – slashed across the top third was a shocking image, a line-drawing for the shipboard stowage of slaves.

Survival's material echoed its artwork. There wasn't a single love song on this militant masterpiece, but hard-hitting tunes that were gritty commentaries on social evils. As well as the title track they included 'Africa Unite', a paean to pan-Africanism; 'Babylon System', an attack on the iniquities of world capitalism; 'Ambush in the Night', about the assassination attempt on Bob's life by Kingston gunmen; the self-explanatory 'So Much Trouble in the World'; 'One Drop', with its urging to fight 'against ism and schism' (on an alternate take of 'One Drop', Marley revealingly scat-sings, 'I'm black-I'm black-I'm black-I'm black-I'm black-I'm black'); 'Wake Up and Live', a broader call for self-awareness (the title taken from a Jamaican advertising copy-line for a hangover cure); and 'Zimbabwe', the song he had written during his pilgrimage to Ethiopia in 1978 – in the lyrics he had expressed his unswerving support for the freedom movement in the country still then known as Rhodesia, with its trenchant opening verse:

So arm in arms, with arms, we'll fight this little struggle,
'Cause that's the only way we can overcome our little trouble.

To all intents and purposes, the *Survival* tour had kicked off on 24 September 1979, when Bob and the Wailers had played a benefit concert for Rasta children in the National Heroes Arena in Kingston (1979 was the United Nations International Year of the Child).

Interviewed by Neil Spencer for the *NME* during the Apollo dates, Bob was asked, 'What do you feel happiest about what you've achieved so far? That you've maybe woken people up?' 'Yeah, mi feel good that plenty people is aware that there is something happening,' Bob replied. 'Man can check it out cos I know Rasta grow. I don't see it deteriorate, I watch them and they grow more and more. It might not be in the headlines every day but dem grow.'

Spencer asked Bob Marley if a question of race hovered over the notion of Rastafari. 'No,' he replied, 'it's not really a race thing in that sense because a whole heap of people from all nation, kindred and tongue follow the Rasta movement. Is dat the Bible seh. But is really a black man organisation cos the white man nah know about it in that sense, the black man have the knowledge to hold that thing there while the white man him study fe mek all things a go to space. 'Im study too much, 'im get lost . . . but today there's no turning back, come too far and turn back now, it just mus' have fe go . . . But some people a go save still and all these people are one people who believe in something, believe in God, fear of true conscience and the works of Ras Tafari.'

The dates at the Harlem Apollo had been specifically requested by Bob Marley. He was concerned, even distressed, that the black American audience remained elusive. Many black radio-programme directors considered that reggae was 'jungle music' and that it didn't fit into their formats. *Kaya* had deliberately been a commercial album, in order that albums such as *Survival* could follow. In the United States, however, getting the message across was a battle that did not seem easy to win.

Still, Bob relentlessly plugged the Wailers on every local radio station he could get to visit. He was also disguising the fact that for much of the time he was operating in a state of sheer exhaustion, so much so that the keyboards player Tyrone Downie would accompany him to press interviews to answer the more mundane questions on Bob's behalf. By the end of this tour, many of those travelling with Bob were extremely worried about his health. Earlier that year in Kingston, I had seen for myself that Bob looked terribly tired and strained.

In one filmed press conference on that American tour, he expounded on matters Rastafari. Although looking drawn and thin, he all the same glowed as he expounded on the truth about Haile Selassie, Emperor of Ethiopia, as he reminded his listeners that Marcus Garvey, the great Jamaican prophet of black consciousness, had said that we must look for a king from the east, not long before His Majesty was crowned in 1930. 'It's just the truth, you know,' smiled Bob. 'Christ is always a lion, a lionheart.' The articulate Tyrone Downie offers an explanation of why it was that white people rather than black in the United States had been attracted to Rastafari: he claimed that this was because their higher standard of living permitted them the time to pursue such matters. But Bob bemoaned the fact that black people were not working together; they had wisdom, knowledge, and 'overstanding', he emphasised, but they must unite, which was part of Bob's intention behind playing this tour.

Bob Marley had first played the beautiful amphitheatre, ninety miles north of Los Angeles, of the Santa Barbara County Bowl in the late spring of 1976. Then he was promoting his *Rastaman Vibration* album, the Tuff Gong's breakthrough record in the United States, a Top Ten hit, and a record that was almost as militant as 'Survival', the song with which on 25 November 1979 Bob Marley and the Wailers began their second ever date at the Santa Barbara County Bowl.

Beneath the backdrop posters of Haile Selassie and Marcus Garvey, Bob and the Wailers peformed a bunch of tunes from the new record: 'Ambush in the Night', 'Africa Unite', 'One Drop', 'Zimbabwe', 'Wake Up and Live', and 'Ride Natty Ride'. There was also 'Is This Love?', 'Concrete Jungle', 'Them Belly Full', 'So Much Things to Say', and a version of 'War' which segued into 'No More Trouble'. As the show began in bright southern California sunlight, it was revealed that there were a dozen musicians onstage. And the complexity of their chemistry was apparent; there were such longtime stalwarts as Seeco Patterson, the percussionist from Trench Town who had helped instruct Bob in the art of music-making as a youth coming up; in contrast to his traditional burru-drum sound were the rock guitars of Junior Marvin and Al Anderson, heard to especially fine effect on 'Crazy Baldheads'; meanwhile, the whole was driven along by the loping rock-steady beat of the bass player, Family Man, and his brother Carly Barrett's drumming. Every song was received rapturously, but the show took a quantum leap as night fell and Bob and the Wailers burst into the masterfulness of 'Exodus', his work of epic poetry, replete with suitable lock-swirling from the Gong. By the time the show was concluding, with the militant 'Get Up, Stand Up', the entire auditorium was swaying along and mouthing the repeated lines of ''Cause I never give up the fight,' a defiant statement of intent, which brought this inspirational concert to a close.

A couple of days later, Bob and the Wailers played a benefit concert at the Roxy in Los Angeles, ninety miles to the south of Santa Barbara. The show was in aid of the foundation run by Sugar Ray Robinson, the former heavyweight boxing champion, which gave grants to assist sporting and artistic endeavours in schools in deprived sections of LA. 'This is the most positive spiritual message on this planet,' said one black girl in the audience, and it was a message that would live on.

As though emphasising the manner in which the United States so often seemed to consider the Caribbean basin as its backyard, Bob

Marley included a pair of dates in Trinidad in the last week of the US tour. From a Dallas, Texas, concert on 7 December 1979, the team flew down to Port of Spain, the Trinidadian capital, for two shows on 8 and 9 December, at the city's Public Services Association Grounds. The security at the shows was shockingly bad. A riot broke out when hundreds of ticketless fans rushed into the stadium and almost immediately tear gas was fired at them by the police, as Bob Marley continued to lead his group onstage. In an interview that Bob gave in Port of Spain to Keith Smith, a local journalist, he admitted he did not always eat a strictly ital diet, confessing to regularly eating meat – though not, of course, pork. (Bob was also partial, as his son Ziggy revealed, to that traditional Jamaican staple, cowfoot.) What he clearly did not feel inclined to add was that he had been advised to eat liver every day, as some sort of optimistic antidote to the cancer he was fully aware was still coursing through his body. But he did hand Keith Smith a piece of simple but life-changing information that is sometimes far too easy to forget, something clearly at the core of Bob's thinking: 'We are all in this together.'

Flying back to New Orleans first thing the next morning, Bob Marley and the Wailers played a show in the city that night. After concerts in Atlanta, Tampa, and Birmingham, Alabama, the heart of the old racist South, the tour wound up in Nassau in the Bahamas at the Queen Elizabeth Sports Centre on 15 December, a charity event for underprivileged children. Bob did not return to Jamaica, but went up to Florida to stay with his mother, at the house on Vista Lane in South Miami. There were practical reasons for being in Miami: despite Bob's best efforts with the One Love Peace Concert, his home country was in a state of virtual warfare, a lethal jostling for power exacerbated by the knowledge that a general election was imminent. For Bob Marley to return to Jamaica was simply too dangerous.

*   *   *

One day at the end of 1979 whilst Bob was staying in Miami with his mother, Don Taylor came to see him. They stood talking in the drawing-room; then, to the amazement of Mrs B., her son punched his manager, knocking him flat on his back. 'Wha' happen, Bob? Where dis yah come from?' cried a startled Taylor. Yet Bob's mother never found out the cause of this outburst of violence, except that it was because of 'some money quarrel'.

This incident, however, turned out to be merely the start of a much larger confrontation between the two men. The year 1980 began with Bob and the Wailers playing live again; this time in Africa, for the very first time. On 1 January, the group had flown to London and then on to Gabon in west Africa, for two shows in the capital, Libreville, at the Gymnase Omnisport Bongo, named after the ruling Bongo family, on 4 and 6 January. These shows formed part of the birthday celebrations for President Omar Bongo. Although this seemed an untypical event for the group to be performing, Bob was delighted at last to have been asked to play in Africa. In fact, he had offered to play for free, but Don Taylor told him that they had been offered a $40,000 fee, which they should take, as it would cover their expenses.

After the group had played their two shows – disappointingly, to small audiences of Gabonese high society – they remained in Gabon for a further two weeks. They stayed in a graceful hotel on the beach, and all-night reasonings would be held with the local youth on matters of spiritual importance.

As was his habit, Bob Marley would rise early. Then he would stroll along the water's edge of the Gabon Estuary. Always awaiting him would be some of the local youth, already familiar with and fans of his music. According to Gilly, 'They looked upon Bob like a king. Bob was so happy to be with his people and spreading the word through his music and through the image of Rasta livity.' Bob and his crew would wander down to the local market, giving away tapes, records, and posters.

One afternoon, Bob was invited to meet the president's son in the palace. Gilly remembered two enormous doors opening to reveal the young man on his throne, in his robe and ornaments. 'He talked to Bob about his music and his life, his country and his people.' Meanwhile, Bob Marley began a less formal relationship with Pascaline Bongo, the president's daughter, the pair becoming lovers.

At the end of the two-week stay, as they were about to leave Gabon, what was initially a small dispute emerged over Bob's fee. The problem escalated, however, and in the discussions that took place, the dirt came out: it was revealed that Don Taylor was receiving $60,000 and not $40,000 – the manager was defrauding Bob Marley. Bob was furious, beside himself with anger and distress at this betrayal – he and the group had been humiliated in Africa the first time they had travelled there to perform. In a three-hour confrontation in front of the entire touring party, Taylor was made to confess how for years he had held back large amounts from concert fees, and how he had played around with Bob's money on the Jamaican black market. Beside himself, Bob attacked Taylor, kicking and beating him.

'That was an exposure, the pinnacle of all that Don had been doing over the years,' said Rita Marley. 'Bob was the kind of man who doesn't really look into documents and contracts, which was very trusting of him. So Don was having a ball. For example, he set up a travel agency with his wife, April, and she would take care of all the tickets that we would need to do tours. So we'd be flying to Miami via California and Australia, because they could do better on the tickets that way. He was making big bucks out of it. He was very dangerous.'

'Bob tried to keep it as covered up as he could, but we knew what was going on,' remembered Judy Mowatt. 'Don got a licking and a kicking from Bob that day, man. For stealing money.'

'We were in the next door room, Gilly, Neville Garrick, and myself,' said Family Man. 'After a while we hear some hard talking, so Neville go outside to see what is happening. Then I see Neville coming back looking for a baseball bat. He can't find it, so he is looking for a pickaxe stick, and I hide the stick. So Gilly and I decide to walk over there and listen. So we hear Bob and Don Taylor talking. Then we hear some money business mentioned, and some feisty chat. Then we hear the whole thing. That wasn't really my department.'

After returning to Kingston and working on the sessions for the new *Uprising* album, Bob went to his mother's home in Miami during February. He needed a rest. But whilst in Florida he also had discussions with Danny Sims, his former manager, about the future of his career: Sims was about to resume the management role with Bob that had come to a halt in 1974. Bob Marley was still enraged by the discovery of Don Taylor's fraud, and one day he sent for him to come to the house on Vista Lane. With Skill Cole, Bob ushered him into a back room, where he demanded that Taylor sign a document in which he resigned from all his dealings with Bob Marley. When Taylor initially hesitated, both Bob Marley and Skill Cole pulled guns on him. 'If yuh nuh sign the bloodclaat paper mi a go shoot yuh,' threatened Skill Cole.

From the back room Mrs Booker heard cries from Taylor: 'Lawd, murder! Murder! Help! Murder!' Hurrying into the room, 'Mrs B.' – as she was habitually known – found Don Taylor flat on his back on the floor as Bob hovered threateningly over him. Respecting his mother's entreaties, and those of Ziggy, who had overheard the confrontation, Bob Marley let Taylor leave. A little later, when Bob and Skill had also departed the house, a policewoman arrived, demanding to see 'Robert Marley', and leaving when she was told that Bob was no longer there. When Bob returned, Mrs Booker told him of this police visit. Bob got on the phone to Danny Sims: no more was heard from the police. 'Personally,' thought Mrs Booker, 'I always thought my son was far too lenient with Don Taylor. Nesta was not a hard man to deal with. As far as I'm concerned, whatever chastisement he gave to Don Taylor was richly deserved.'

In March, Bob flew down to Rio de Janeiro for five days with Junior Marvin and Jacob Miller, as well as Chris Blackwell. Bob was in great shape on this trip, writing almost nonstop with Junior and Jacob, and playing football with Brazilians eager to display their abilities.

The visit to Brazil was a promotional trip, at the request of the local division of Ariola Records, which licensed Island material for Brazilian release. Bob Marley was there to pre-sell a South American tour following the dates already scheduled for the summer and autumn in Europe and the United States. Miller's Inner Circle was to support the Wailers. The day after the group arrived, the record company had arranged a press conference in the lobby of the Copacabana Palace Hotel. As though a karmic lesson were being handed out over the habitual lateness of many Jamaicans, Bob discovered that Brazilians could be even more tardy: blaming a rainfall, only one of the journalists arrived on time, and Bob huffily walked out, returning to his room.

A football match had been planned for that afternoon, at a place called Chico's Field. Unusually, Bob – who was wearing a number-ten shirt from the renowned Santos team – played badly. (Later this was offered as an indication of the extent to which his body by then was ravaged by cancer.) Playing with Bob was the legendary Paulo César Lima, more generally known as Caju, who as a striker had helped Brazil win the World Cup in 1970. Watching a television interview with Bob as he arrived in Rio, Caju saw Bob Marley saying what a fan he was of the famous dark-skinned footballer. Accordingly, Caju, a big fan of reggae, contacted Bob, hanging with him for most of his stay in Brazil. He watched as Bob, insisting he wanted to eat sushi – unknown at that time in Rio – in a restaurant they visited, made the chef cut slices of raw fish for him, to the bafflement of all concerned. And went with him to the 'Hippie Fair' in Ipanema's General Osório Square, where he noticed that Bob Marley loved the myriad juice-bars, requesting juice made from every fruit available. Bob and Caju came to an agreement that the Brazilian football ace would set up a soccer school for Jamaican youth; Bob's illness meant that this never came to pass. Later, up at Bob's hotel suite, a reporter watched Bob jamming on an untuned mandolin with Traffic's Jim Capaldi, who accompanied the Gong with hand-claps.

Two days after they returned to Jamaica, the charismatic Jacob Miller was tragically killed in a car accident on Hope Road near Half Way Tree. Tired from the trip to Brazil, he lost his concentration as he tried to care for his children, who were seated in the rear of the vehicle. Chewing on a piece of sugarcane, driving, and looking after the two kids was too much for him, and Jacob drove into a lamp-post, breaking his neck, killing himself instantly. 'He was a very kind man,' said Junior Marvin. 'I've seen him give hundreds of dollars to hungry kids, and then just laugh when he realised he had no more money left to buy his own food. He was a really jolly person.'

ZIMBABWE

As the stinging fog of tear-gas swirled about him, a shocked Bob
Marley stood alone, frozen inside his customary onstage marijuana trance.

It was 17 April 1980, the night of the Zimbabwean independence celebrations. Stunned, his eyes smarting, the Jamaican musical king gazed
in anguish at the bloody carnage playing out before him in Harare's
Rufaro Stadium. He had been oblivious that, at the first whiff of gas, the
entire Wailers group had fled from the stage behind him. In his
transcendent performing state, Bob Marley had not seen the horror
unfolding before him: his eyes had been shut, and at first the gas hadn't
seemed to have any effect on him.

Stepping out from the wings, a uniformed soldier of the new Zimbab-wean army pressed a water-soaked flannel to the delicately featured face of the slight Jamaican. Then he led Marley through the vicious mist to the comparative backstage safety of a locked trailer.

Following the raising of the new nation's flag at this evening cere-mony, the first official words uttered in Zimbabwe had been: 'Ladies and gentlemen, Bob Marley and the Wailers.' But the audience was not what Bob Marley had expected when he had personally shelled out over £100,000 to fly his group to the Rhodesian capital of Salisbury which, minutes before his set, had transformed into Harare in Zimbabwe. Rather than playing for those once oppressed by the former white supremacist prime minister Ian Smith, he had found himself performing before the replacement elite: amongst those present were the new president, Robert Mugabe, Britain's Prince Charles, India's Indira Gandhi, and assorted global political dignitaries. The audience was composed largely of former members of Mugabe's ZANU freedom fighters. (A Maori prince invited to the event was perhaps the most alert to the Jamaican's needs, send-ing him a sackful of marijuana.)

The reggae rhythms of 'Positive Vibration' had opened Marley's set. As they pulsed through the tropical night, outside the stadium the dense forest of fans and freedom fighters from the rival ZAPU party, led by Joshua Nkomo, made their protest at having been excluded from the cele-brations: seizing the moment, they forced their way into the national sports ground – through the gates, over the walls – and surged towards the stage.

Armed to the teeth, police and soldiers steamed in, batons and butts of M-16 rifles thudding brutally down on the intruders – so reminiscent to Bob Marley of scenes he had witnessed in Kingston, incidents he had always characterised as legacies of colonial oppression. These victims had retaliated by tearing apart the outdoor venue, hurling the resulting debris at the uniformed thugs before tear-gas was unleashed to stamp down the authority of the new politically privileged.

The infant state of Zimbabwe was only minutes old. Like one of those psychic visions to which Bob Marley always had been prone, its future descent into state violence and corruption seemed to stretch out in front of it and him, leading directly to an awful plight.

Ever since the extraordinary event of the One Love Peace Concert in Kingston in April 1978, aimed at helping quell Jamaica's murderous unofficial civil war, Bob Marley had been transmogrified into the role of a global, alternative political dignitary. Two months later at the United Nations building in New York, in a ceremony of such histrionic adoration, overseen by Senegal's Johnny Seka, that Bob almost burst into laughter, he was presented with the UN's Peace Medal of the Third World. Notwithstanding the event's comic melodrama, Marley was deeply touched by the honour, which had intensified his desire to create music of a more militant hue.

No doubt there was an inner need for Bob Marley to leave his life justified and complete. For he knew he was dying. Eleven years previously, in Wilmington, Delaware, the then American home of his Jamaican mother, he – this man who as a young boy would read the palms of rural folk – had prophesied to friends that his life would end when he was thirty-six. He had long borne knowledge of his coming death: is that why the cancer coursing through a foot that he had severely injured on at least four separate occasions had gone untreated? Did he simply believe he just had to get on with it and fulfil his mission? Although it has been suggested that 'dismantling' his body went against his Rasta beliefs, isn't such a pragmatic decision equally likely? He knew there simply wasn't time for lengthy medical treatment: he had to live out his book.

In his last years, aware that he had largely been marketed to white audiences (the source of his substantial record sales and concert attendances), Bob Marley was on a mission to expand his appeal to the black race. As the global figurehead of Rastafari, a rapidly enlarging sect of black Jamaicans who had created their own apocalyptic religion, with their own black God in the Ethiopian emperor Haile Selassie, and their own language, he could have had no other course. Increasingly, Marley would declare himself to be 'African' rather than Jamaican, which accorded with his Rastafarian beliefs and carried a more militant stamp.

On 21 July 1979, in 38-degree heat, Bob Marley and the Wailers had appeared with Dick Gregory, Patti LaBelle, and Eddie Palmieri at the Amandla Festival of Unity in Boston, Massachusetts: 'amandla' is a Xhosa and Zulu word meaning 'power', and the outdoor concert was a benefit for freedom fighters in the racist states of South Africa and Rhodesia. Marley was nailing his colours to the mast. The 'Zimbabwe' song on *Survival* cemented them there.

Onstage at that Harare concert, the Wailers had viewed the pandemonium breaking loose in the enormous crowd with great concern. Then they had observed large swathes of the audience on the pitch below them falling to the ground, covering their heads. Baffled by this at first, the group members quickly tasted their first whiffs of tear-gas and hurriedly quit the stage. 'All of a sudden,' said Judy Mowatt, 'you smell this thing taking over your whole body, going in your throat until you want to choke, burning your eyes. I looked at Rita and Marcia and they were feeling the same thing.' 'I feel my eyes and nose,' remembered Family Man Barrett, 'and think, from when I was born, I have to come all the way to Africa to experience tear-gas.' (Clearly, he had no memory of the tear-gassing of parts of the crowd in Trinidad four months previously.)

Backstage, holding wet cloths to their faces, the group hid in a truck adjacent to the trailer to which Bob Marley was led a minute later. All around them they could see small children fainting and women collapsing. It looked like death personified to Judy Mowatt, who briefly wondered whether they had been brought to Zimbabwe to meet their ends. She persuaded someone to drive her and the other I-Threes back to where they were staying, only to discover from the television that the show had resumed. After about half an hour, Bob Marley and the Wailers had gone back on stage. They ended their set with 'Zimbabwe'.

Bob had been just coming offstage as Judy Mowatt and her fellow women singers returned to the stadium. 'Hah' – he looked at them with a half-grin, before throwing their way a deliberately misquoted line from 'Zimbabwe' – 'now I know who the real revolutionaries are.'

But was Bob Marley surprised at what he had beheld that night in 1980? His own efforts to visit or work in Africa had been stymied or unsatisfying. On his 1978 visit to Ethiopia, he had been shocked by the disrespect shown to Haile Selassie: his body had been tossed into an unmarked grave. A proposed tour, in January 1979, under the auspices of Johnny Seka, of such francophone African nations as Senegal and Mali had fallen through at the last moment; and in Gabon, in January 1980, a disappointed Bob Marley had found he was only playing to the president's family and dignitaries.

Yet when two emissaries of the imminent Zimbabwean government showed up at 56 Hope Road four days before the independence celebrations, on 14 April 1980, Bob Marley had immediately gone along with honouring their request that he and the Wailers perform there. He had swung into action, volunteering to cover all the costs out of his own pocket. Personally making all necessary phone calls, within two hours, PA equipment, lighting and a sound crew, as well as a Boeing 707, had been booked to fly down to Africa from London. In charge of this advance party was Mick Cater, Marley's UK agent. At Salisbury Airport his arrival was met with consternation by customs officials, who were suitably mollified by gifts of Bob Marley T-shirts. Cater's *Exodus* tour jacket was 'my passport to everything.' The event was being promoted by Job Kadengu, a second-hand-car dealer and member of the ZANU party faithful. Kadengu passed Cater on to Edgar Tekere, the minister for planning and development in the new government. At 3:30 a.m. Cater was driven to Tekere's bungalow fo wake him and receive instructions. A bleary-eyed minister directed Cater to the Rufaro Stadium on the edge of Harare, where the independence ceremony was to be held. When he and his crew arrived there, a team of nightwatchmen loomed out of the darkness, trying to chase them off.

Meanwhile, Bob Marley and the Wailers had flown from Kingston to London, catching a commercial flight to Nairobi. As he waited in the transit lounge for his plane to Salisbury, Bob received an unexpected message from a royal equerry: Prince Charles was waiting in the VIP suite; would the Jamaican singer care to come and join him and pay his respects? Marley's reply was immediate: if Prince Charles wanted to meet him, he should come out there and check him with all the people. Needless to say, the singer's invitation to the British heir to the throne was not accepted. Some time later, as Bob and the Wailers sat by the window of the transit lounge, they saw the royal party crossing the tarmac in the direction of the royal jet. When Prince Charles had walked only a few yards, however, he turned and looked up at the window where Marley was sitting. Looking directly into Bob Marley's eyes, Prince Charles smiled broadly. Then he continued on his way.

Bob Marley and the Wailers arrived at Salisbury Airport at lunchtime on 16 April, shortly after the British royal jet bearing Prince Charles had arrowed down to the airport. Disgorging from their plane onto the hot tarmac, the Jamaican party found themselves falling into a lavish diplomatic ceremony, a red carpet having been laid out. Lined up to greet them – a function performed only minutes before for the Prince of Wales – was Joshua Nkomo, who had been made minister of home affairs in Robert Mugabe's new government, as well as assorted cabinet officials, and Job Kadengu, the promoter. Ritually, handshakes were exchanged between them and all twenty-six members of the arriving Marley party, which included Bob's sons Ziggy and Stephen, each side seemingly baffled as to whom they were actually meeting.

At Bob Marley's request, the entire team then drove straight to Rufaro Stadium. They learned that much of the wood provided for the stage was rotten: when Bob Marley and the Wailers performed, they were ever alert to the chalk marks on the covering tarpaulin, indicating holes that had appeared almost as soon as the stage had been constructed. Promised generators had not arrived and the lack of electrical power had been overcome by a method familiar to Jamaican sound-system followers – tapping into a cable, the road-crew watched as lights went out in a nearby village.

As they checked out the venue, the sound of beautiful a cappella chanting floated through the air. Suddenly a party of women hove into view, clad in military costume, singing as they marched. When he discovered that they were former freedom fighters, Bob Marley fell into a stunned silence. Those around him watched as tears formed in his eyes, trickling down his cheeks.

There was a problem, however: no hotel rooms had been booked for the Marley party. Everywhere was full, booked up weeks before, by visitors coming from all over the world for the independence ceremony. Bob and the Wailers were taken to the home of Job Kadengu, twelve miles out of Harare; yet there was little room and Bob shared with Neville Garrick, Family Man, Gilly, and Dennis Thompson, the sound engineer. To prevent the Jamaicans running up bills calling home, all phones had been removed – which also had the effect of not letting them call anyone involved with the concert. Bob Marley was pissed off.

Independence from colonial rule was granted to Zimbabwe as the stroke of midnight ushered in 18 April 1980. The independence celebrations which built up to this took place therefore on the evening of 17 April. Bob Marley and the Wailers' contingent was taken to the event in the back of a truck, which appealed to the militant in the singer. Following their fractured performance, they were scheduled to depart at around three in the morning in the same vehicle. Job Kadengu, however, had already left, to attend further celebrations, as had the truck's driver.

It was only when another driver was procured that it was realised that no one knew how to get back to Kadengu's house. Accordingly, on the epic day of Zimbabwean independence, for which Bob Marley had written an anthemic song and travelled 10,000 miles at his own expense, he found himself being driven round and round Harare, hopelessly lost. At first growing more furious with each passing minute, his legendary 'screwface' dominating the entire vehicle, Marley finally collapsed into helpless laughter, abandoning himself to his fate. It was daylight, seven in the morning, before they found their way back to Kadengu's residence, to find there was no food in the house. No one had any local currency, except for Dera Tompkins, a militant black American woman who had known the group in Jamaica – arriving two weeks previously in Zimbabwe for the celebrations, she had found herself becoming Bob Marley's guide. At a local market, she bought eggs and bread, and cooked them all breakfast.

Over the meal it was decided a further show should be played that evening at Rufaro Stadium, so the ordinary people of Zimbabwe could see Bob Marley. It was decided to make the event free. That night over a hundred thousand people, certainly the largest black audience before whom he had played, watched the show. Bob Marley and the Wailers performed for an hour and a half, the musicians fired up to a point of ecstasy. But Bob, who, uncharacteristically, hadn't turned up for the soundcheck, was strangely lacklustre in his performance; a mood of disillusionment had set in around him following the tear-gassing. No doubt he was also exhausted – as in a more general way he had been for some considerable time. Unaware of the convention of Western acts returning for lengthy encores, the Zimbabwean audience headed quickly for the exit immediately the group had quit the stage following 'Zimbabwe'. Before the musicians returned, most of the crowd had left the stadium, and it became one of the only Bob Marley shows at which an encore was not played.

With the departure of foreign visitors, hotel rooms became available. The Marley party moved into the St James Hotel in the centre of Harare. Although the I-Threes left to participate in a scheduled Twelve Tribes ceremony in Jamaica, Bob Marley and his entourage remained there until after the following weekend. At the hotel, his door was always open, to encourage locals to enter and reason with him. In the hotel restaurant, on 20 April, they celebrated Bob's son Stephen's eighth birthday – aware that he had not spent sufficient time with them, Bob had been especially keen that his two sons by Rita accompany him to Zimbabwe. 'Bob would sit with them for hours and Ziggy had to recite the Rasta prayers,' remembered Dera Tompkins.

In Harare, Bob Marley specifically went out to clubs, not to party but to meet the local people. He would be armed with handfuls of red, gold, and green badges to give away, as well as a special edition of the 'Zimbabwe' single, backed with 'Survival'; the sleeve displayed a picture of Robert Mugabe, with the tagline 'Majority Rules'. ('Zimbabwe' already was the number-one single in the country; at number two was Eddy Grant's 'Living on the Frontline'.) 'People didn't have the cult of celebrity, so they were very polite,' said Dera Tompkins. Job Kadengu himself owned a nightspot, which they went to after the second Rufaro Stadium show, for their first restaurant meal in the country: 'They had pork there on the table with the other foods,' recalled Tompkins. 'No one in Zimbabwe was aware of the Rasta restrictions on pork. As you can imagine, it was quickly whisked away.'

That weekend, Bob Marley and Neville Garrick made the papers when they went to watch a football match as Rufaro Stadium resumed its usual role in local life. 'He loved Africa and Africans,' said Tompkins. 'They sent a limo to take him to a township and he asked for a truck instead. He insisted on being very accessible in Zimbabwe.'

What Bob Marley really wanted was to go to the bush and see lions. When he did, they were unable to find any, the species being extremely rare in that part of Africa. Instead he had to content himself with a bottle of the local Lion beer – contrary to the myth of him being teetotal, Bob Marley was never averse to a refreshing glass of cold ale.

Already, unfortunately, there were glimpes of a darker side behind the new independent regime of Zimbabwe. Invited to tea at the presidential palace with Robert Mugabe, Bob Marley and the Wailers found the new ruler surrounded by drunken soldiers. 'It was so English and colonial: cucumber sandwiches and lemonade – all considered a bit off by the Wailers,' the late Denise Mills, Island Records' head of artist liaison, told me in 1994. 'However, Bob sang 'No Woman, No Cry' at the piano for the president's family.'

On another occasion, the Bob Marley team was invited to spend the evening at the home of Edgar Tekere. This also was not the most relaxed of social occasions. As Tekere's henchmen strutted around with their Kalashnikovs, Denise Mills was informed by the minister that he wanted Bob to stay in Zimbabwe and tour the country. 'Bob told me to say he wasn't going to, but the guy didn't want to hear me.'

While Bob Marley remained in the house, Rob Partridge, Island's late head of public relations, and Phil Cooper, the company's head of international affairs, sat out in the garden. 'I could hear,' said Cooper, 'Tekere saying to Bob, "I want this man Cooper. He's been going around putting your image everywhere. He's trying to portray you as a bigger man than our president."

'Then Bob came out and said to us, in hushed, perfect Queen's English, "I think it's a good idea for you to leave."

'Partridge and I went and packed, and took the first international flight out, which was to Nairobi. About five months later Tekere was arrested and put in jail; he had been involved in the murder of some white settler.'

The next day, Mick Cater found himself being cajoled in the way Denise Mills had been: 'Job Kadengu told me that there was a show in Bulawayo we had to do. I was to sign for trucks on behalf of the minister of development – Tekere, in other words. So we drove out to the airport with all the gear, loaded up the plane we'd chartered and left the country.'

This was the last time Bob Marley visited Africa: within thirteen months he was dead.

Returning to England from Zimbabwe, Bob was photographed with the entire group for the sleeve of the next album. The shot was taken by photographer Adrian Boot in the lift of the Royal Gardens Hotel in Kensington, west London. In the picture, Bob looks exhausted, his face lined and drawn. This has often been cited as proof of precisely how ill the Tuff Gong was becoming. Junior Marvin, however, gave another explanation: 'The reason Bob looks so tired and I'm looking to the left, to disguise my tired face, is because on the way back from Zimbabwe we'd stopped off in Paris for a couple of days. We'd been up all night talking to people about Zimbabwe on the first night; and on the second night we'd hung out with some people from Gabon – the president's family – making music and talking. Neither of us had slept – that's the only reason we look so tired. Bob had asked me to hang out with him, just writing songs and rapping to people. Both of us paid a penalty for it: by the time we got to London and the pictures were taken we looked really haggard.'

Uprising, as the album would be titled, had not even been completed at the time that Boot took the picture for the rear cover shot. When the French journalist Paul Alessandrini visited 56 Hope Road after Bob Marley had returned there following the trip to Zimbabwe, he found him recording in the now completed Tuff Gong studio on the premises, working on a song called 'Could You Be Loved?', an upbeat tune that contained the admonition, 'While you point a finger, someone else is judging you' – a clear link to Bob's first recorded tune, 'Judge Not'. Alessandrini watched Bob play football in the yard, untrammelled by the apparent physical deficiences that had held back his game in Brazil. 'Football is music,' declared Bob Marley to the Frenchman.

'Could You Be Loved?', a hit when also released as a single, was tucked away down the track listing of the *Uprising* album when it was released on 10 June 1980. *Uprising* was an extension of the militant subject matter on *Survival*. Bob Marley saw it as the second part of a trilogy, having already decided the title of the third part. It would be called *Confrontation*, he decreed, as it indeed was. The front-cover art, again by Neville Garrick, displayed a sketch of the Gong, ascending, beneath a rising sun, like an image of a mythological figure. In contrast to the downbeat feel and perceptions of the lyrics, the sound of *Uprising* was uplifting and bright, right from the start with the album opener, 'Coming in from the Cold'.

Although the song 'Real Situation' was an indictment of Babylon, in its title alone 'Forever Loving Jah' provided the antidote. 'Bad Card', meanwhile, was a poke at the neighbours around 56 Hope Road who complained about the presence of Bob, his fellow musicians, and the ghetto uptown; certain of those who lived in the area had endeavoured to have Bob Marley evicted from the premises, on the grounds that he was using a domestic residence for commercial purposes. 'Pimper's Paradise' – 'Every need got an ego to feed,' sang Bob – described an on-the-road world with which Bob Marley had become all too familiar, aware of the pitfalls and potential strife that could come from apparently glamorous girls. Yet the tour de force was a song that had not been included in the songs Bob had played to Chris Blackwell in late April. 'I feel there's something else you have to give,' the record-company boss had said to Bob Marley. The next day the musician played Blackwell a tape of 'Redemption Song', the song he had been working on sporadically for over a year. A folk ballad, played on an acoustic guitar, the song had a crystalline beauty that was like a summation of the entire philosophy of Bob Marley, an elegiac work whose haunting qualities came to dominate the album when positioned as its closing track.

Released on 10 June 1980, and a Top Ten album in the United Kingdom, *Uprising* only got to number 45 in the United States; chart positions in America are not only based on sales, but on such intangibles as the effects of touring on the promotion of a record, and it was expected that *Uprising* would head higher up the US charts when Bob and the Wailers toured America in the autumn.

In fact, the Tuff Gong *Uprising* tour began several days before the record was released, at the Zürich Hallenstadion on 30 May 1980. It continued at a gruelling, breakneck pace: in six weeks, the group was to play to more than one million fans in twelve countries. It was to be the largest-grossing tour of Europe up to that time. As the bus left 56 Hope Road for Kingston's airport at the beginning of the journey to Europe, Mortimer Planner was standing by the gates, bidding farewell and good

luck to his brethren. As the vehicle pulled past him, Bob's eyes momentarily caught Planner's. From nowhere a thought ran through the dread
elder's mind: 'I won't see you again.'

'I can recall myself, Tyrone, and Neville walking through these strange
towns to look for magazines,' recalled Family Man. 'And every one we
pick up has a promotional piece on Bob Marley and the Wailers. It really
looked as though we were the most popular group in Europe.' The highest point was when they drew a hundred thousand fans to Milan's San
Siro soccer stadium, the venue shared by the teams AC Milan and Inter-
nazionale. A stupendous performance, it presented Bob Marley at the
peak and height of his power. Considering the history of Italy earlier in
the twentieth century, it was ironic that so many Ethiopian flags should
have been flying in the audience that day. The previous week, the Pope
had addressed a congregation shoehorned into the San Siro. But Bob
Marley and the Wailers drew an even larger audience. 'The only thing
that I can do,' said Bob whilst in Milan, 'is sing about the problems and
the troubles, to tell the people the truth and to invite them to fight.'

Backstage, a pair of Italian youths approached Bob: 'We are not
responsible for what Mussolini did to the Ethiopians. But we want you to
know that we are friends of the Rastafarians, and that God has accepted us.'

This magical show was followed the next day, as though it were a
reprise, by one with a slightly smaller audience, at the grounds of the
Juventus football team in Turin.

After the Paris date at Le Bourget, Phonogram, Island's French
licensees, held a party on a boat travelling down the Seine. As a chic way
of showing their respect to Bob, it had been arranged for all the lights to
be lit on the buildings along the banks of the river. This spectacular light
show had cost over £10,000. But Bob never noticed it: all he did was
slump in the back of the boat and smoke a giant spliff.

On the boat, Paul Alessandrini screened a cut of *Rasta and the Ball*, a film about Bob Marley seen through the prism of football, which he had filmed in Jamaica only weeks previously. Bob seemed to thoroughly enjoy it. Later, Chris Blackwell called the French journalist to say that Bob would like him to film one of his shows, projected for later in the year, at the Maracanã Stadium in Rio de Janeiro, a date that would follow his next US tour.

On the tour bus between shows, an endless game of dominoes was in progress, the players slapping down their hands with the ferocity frequent in this fiery Jamaican version of the game. Many of the shows on the tour were opened by a set from the I-Threes; in Germany, Marcia Griffiths would introduce the group in that country's language – she had worked there frequently in the past. On many nights after the show, the I-Threes would find themselves back in Bob's hotel room, working out the harmonies on a new song he had written called 'Leah and Rachel', based on the biblical story about Jacob's concubine and his wife, Rachel. Many times, Judy Mowatt would be yawning, wanting to go to her bed. 'But Bob would insist that we learn this song: he is always a perfectionist. It was *not* fun sometimes. But when you go onstage you feel as though you are in your backyard: you are so comfortable with what you are doing, because you know what you're doing.'

After playing to a hundred thousand people in an open-air show in Dublin, the entourage moved on to London for another outdoor concert, at the Crystal Palace Bowl in south London. Separated from their audience by a small lake, Bob and the Wailers performed a show of sterling, uplifting professionalism which climaxed with Bob's solo acoustic version of 'Redemption Song'. '"Redemption Song" is one of the most profound and important statements Bob ever uttered,' said Neville Garrick. 'One of the most celebrated things Marcus Garvey ever said was "Uplift ye mighty race: you can accomplish what you will." To me, "Redemption

Song" is an update of that: it really lives with you; you have to make the move; you have to free your mind first, before you can attain anything.' Yet at that Crystal Palace show you could not help notice the exhaustion and pain that hovered like an aura about the Tuff Gong.

'We played at this place called Crystal Palace, where there was like a pool in front of the stage,' remembered Family Man. 'And I tell you, when the music get started, I don't see no pool. People in them suit is in the water to the waist.

'I tell you that show was a show, man. There was a lot of colours: I never see so much red, gold, and green. Each of us have three sweat-suit on that tour: a red and a gold and a green sweat-suit, and a red, gold, and green jacket and scarf and tams. The whole scene was colourful, I tell you.'

'I remember being slightly disappointed by the actual gig,' recalled the photographer David Corio. 'As it was the only time I'd photographed him, and I'd so long looked forward to photographing him, it seemed a shame.

'I was doing it for *NME*. I was twenty – it was one of the first big gigs I'd done. I was on the side of the stage and I thought the only thing to do was to wade into the lake. I got a plastic carrier bag and put one camera and some film into it.

'There was me and one other photographer in the water. It was up to my chest. And there was a muddy bank in front of the stage and I kept slipping back.

'The shot with the flailing locks was the last one on the film, the thirty-seventh or thirty-eighth exposure. I was holding out for that shot. I knew I'd got it when I took it. You can't make out his face, but everyone knows it's Bob.

'After I came out of the lake I went backstage. Bob was still onstage. But the cars were set up for his departure. I went round there, and prepared myself for him coming offstage. There were a lot of dreads hanging around. But Bob came off and was whisked away. Shapewise, that was the closest to a portrait that I got. It gives a nice shape, the way the lines lead. Considering how ill we later discovered he was, he looked very well.

'I went home on the tube, covered in green slime, shivering. But I was so up from the gig, really charged up, that I went off to see U2 in a pub, which was where Chris Blackwell was, watching them for the first time.

'In some of the pictures it's depressing to look at him – [Bob] seems so tortured. I wish I could have photographed him in more intimate surroundings.'

There was an early evening curfew on shows at Crystal Palace, and it was still daylight as Bob and the group rushed from the venue, hurrying to catch a flight to Munich for their next date. At Munich Airport, however, they found themselves trapped all night when no transport turned up to take the tired musicians to their hotel. For the next day's performance they were playing a festival in which they were jointly topping the bill with Fleetwood Mac. A major argument took place between the production crews of the two groups: Mick Fleetwood's drum riser, the Jamaicans were told, was out of bounds to Carlton Barrett – reason did, however, eventually prevail. But when Bob and the group went onstage, rain was pouring down on the 50,000-strong audience; instead of being daunted by it, the fans turned it into a virtue, luxuriating sensuously in the downpour as though it were a tropical thunderstorm Back-a-Yard. After the Wailers show the audience shrank to twenty thousand; it was as though Fleetwood Mac were being taught a lesson for their belligerence towards Jah people.

Returning to London at the end of the six-week tour, Bob plumped not to do any interviews at all – just to play football matches with assorted teams from the media. Accordingly, a succession of matches was arranged at an indoor sports stadium next to the Fulham football ground in west London. Amongst the five-a-side teams played against by Bob and his crew were representatives of *Record Mirror* and Ice Records, captained by the Guyanan star Eddy Grant.

'I was football-fixtures secretary,' remembered Rob Partridge. 'Every day, I picked Bob up from his apartment at Carlos Place and drove him down to Fulham.'

One day, however, Bob Marley called Mick Cater to his apartment in Harrington Gardens in South Kensington. He told him that he wanted the tour profits, which came to over a million pounds, in cash. It took a week for Cater to get this amount from his bank. When he had the money, he took it over to Harrington Gardens. Bob looked at it, and counted it. Then he said. "OK, put it back in the bank."'

In London, Bob considered his next moves. A tour of the United States was scheduled to begin in the middle of September, and the Wailers were flying back to Jamaica until it was time to head north again. But Bob Marley was warned off any return to the Island of Springs. Jamaica was riven by pre-election civil war and Bob was given the whisper that the attempt on his life in December 1976 would seem as nothing compared to what might happen if he returned home now. Instead, he flew to Miami and tried to rest up for the beginning of the US tour. To all those around him, Bob seemed to be very tired.

In the summer of 1980, Bob Marley visited a bar in downtown Manhattan, an unlikely scenario for the Rastafarian. But the drinking joint was the headquarters of Paul Castellano, the Mafia god-father, the so-called 'Boss of Bosses', head of the Gambino crime family, who co-owned Cayman Music with Danny Sims, who was once again firmly ensconced as manager of Bob Marley. 'Why have you come down to see me?' said the don. 'I would have come to your hotel.'

'I just wanted to check you out and see how you lived,' said Bob Marley.

The fact was that Paul Castellano was about to underwrite Marley's projected expansion into the US market. His son was a huge fan and had recommended the investment, but the idea had been floated by members of New York's leading black criminal syndicate: Chris Blackwell had so far bankrolled Bob Marley on his enormous global expansion, but the already legendary Jamaican singer was aware that a further push was required to take him to the top of the US charts; accordingly, he had received advice and introductions from certain acquaintances. Marley was considering leaving Island Records. His contract was due to terminate shortly, and Polydor Records had made him an extremely substantial offer. But, as it turned out, Bob Marley would never benefit from a substantial financial injection from the Mafia. Instead, the funds would be used to underwrite the career of Peter Tosh.

The American tour began – as Bob Marley's US tours often seemed to do – in Boston, on Sunday, 14 September 1980. Then the Wailers touring party drove south to New York City, where they were scheduled to play a pair of shows that weekend, on 19 and 20 September, at Madison Square Garden, sharing the bill with the Commodores, at the time featuring Lionel Ritchie as vocalist – this was in an effort to broaden Bob's American audience. For the Commodores' Madison Square Garden shows, the organisers didn't even bother to print Bob Marley's name on the tickets. Nevertheless, nine thousand people walked out after Bob Marley had finished his first-night support set in the 20,000-capacity arena. In New York, Bob was asked what audience he was trying to reach in the United States. 'To tell you the truth, people. Plain people. All people. Black people, Chinese. All people,' he replied.

Bob checked into the Essex House on Central Park South, the hotel he customarily stayed at in Manhattan; with him were Skill Cole and assorted members of his inner circle. The Wailers, along with Rita Marley and the I-Threes, however, were lodged farther downtown, at the

Gramercy Park. There they were removed from a mood of decadence that had not previously been seen on Wailers tours.

At the Essex House, champagne and fine wines were being ordered up on room service. Pascaline Bongo, the daughter of the Gabonese president, was ensconced in Bob's suite with him, a complication as Cindy Breakspeare had flown up from Jamaica. Limousines would follow the tour bus wherever it went, like some anti-Exodus. New York–based Jamaicans flooded into the various suites; cocaine freebasing was openly practised; goodtime girls sprawled about the rooms; at one point, Bob was photographed with members of the Shower Posse, the notorious Jamaican criminal gang, many of whom had moved to the United States. It was as though everything was disintegrating, everything was falling apart. Bob tucked himself away in his bedroom, often aghast at the bedlam taking place outside his door. As he himself would have described it, it was too much mix-up, mix-up.

Subsequently, those who were lodged at the Gramercy Park have voiced their theories as to why the band was separated from Bob in this way. Some saw it as a conscious attempt to isolate Bob from those who had always been around him. Danny Sims was advising Bob about his business affairs, and some thought they detected some kind of conspiracy between Sims and Skill Cole.

Although he doesn't go as far as this, Junior Marvin was surprised that they were not all staying at the same hotel. 'I started to feel a bit isolated, as though we were losing that sense of security when all of the band were together. When we were all together, people wouldn't come in on us so fast: you could tell that it was definitely a group. When we were apart it was definitely much easier for people to infiltrate it. It was easier for people to get to Bob, whether it be fans or hustlers.'

Skill Cole has a simple explanation as to why the rest of the group weren't checked in to the Essex House: the hotel was full, and only enough rooms for Bob and those immediately around him could be booked.

On the Saturday afternoon, Bob paid a surprise visit to the West Indian American Day Carnival at the Brooklyn Museum, appearing onstage briefly with the Wailers. He also posed for pictures with the finalists of the Miss West Indian American Beauty Pageant. In the carnival parade was a Bob Marley float, with a fifty-foot-high version of the *Uprising* logo; Bob had intended to parade through the streets of Brooklyn on the float, but when he realised how near he would be to the huge crowd, he changed his mind and returned to the Essex House.

As expected, the Madison Square Garden shows were a colossal success. Although Bob and the Wailers weren't given a full soundcheck, the performances were tremendous, as was the audience response. From the first note everything fell into place, Al Anderson in particular showing superb authority in his musicianship. 'We were *ready* for that tour,' said Family Man. 'We and Stevie Wonder were supposed to tour the US. We were going to break reggae big-big in the States just like in Europe. Then out of the blue something came up.'

The dates seemed to be taking an unexpected toll on the Tuff Gong: on the Saturday morning after the first concert he was almost beside himself with exhaustion. He managed to recover his energies for the evening's performance, but afterwards left the Negril reggae club early and went back to the Essex House.

The following morning, Rita called Bob's suite, to invite him to accompany her to a service at the Ethiopian Orthodox Church, as was their custom when they were in New York. The man she spoke to didn't sound like the Bob she knew. 'What happened?' she asked him. 'You didn't sleep last night?' Bob told his wife he didn't feel well and wouldn't be going to church with her, but that he would send a car to pick her up from the Gramercy Park Hotel. When the vehicle arrived, Rita told the driver not to take her to church but to the Essex House. 'When I got there he wasn't looking his normal self. I thought he must be out partying with girls and the usual hang-on things that happens sometimes after a concert.'

Rita left the hotel and took the car on to church. Bob felt nauseated and wanted some fresh air. Attempting to kickstart his life force with some light running, Bob and Skill Cole and a few friends jogged into Central Park, opposite their hotel. Before they had gone far, however, Bob started to collapse, calling out for Cole, who caught him before he slumped to the ground. 'Bob's body seemed to be freezing rigid, and he couldn't move his neck. It hurt him terribly and frightened him.' Helped back to the hotel, he recovered after a couple of hours, but the incident had shaken him to his core, and he still felt great pain in his neck.

A security blanket was thrown around news of Bob's illness. Family Man expected to see Bob come by the Gramercy to eat at their mobile ital kitchen. 'When I don't see him come for his food, I think maybe he's gone to do some TV or radio interviews. But then this youth called Ian Winter carried the food for Bob up to the Essex House. Him say when him reach the door, them just take the food from him and lock up the door. I said, "If you told me, I would have personally carried the food." A separation go on. We were always close: mi check with Bob before show, after show. Before soundcheck, after soundcheck. Before bedtime.'

So successful was the secrecy surrounding the incident that, the following day, the Wailers, still staying downtown at the Gramercy Park, left Manhattan and travelled to Pittsburgh for the next show. 'After Bob collapsed,' said Junior Marvin, 'it was more evident that things were getting a bit weird: we weren't even in the same hotel to find out how he was. We didn't know if he was okay or not.'

Bob didn't accompany them on the tour bus to Pittsburgh; instead, he was taken to see a neurologist, who rapidly diagnosed the problem: Bob Marley was suffering from a terminal cancerous brain tumour.

Rita Marley wasn't even aware that her husband had collapsed. It was only on the bus to Pittsburgh that she discovered what had happened to Bob the previous day. However, the general opinion seemed to be that it was a consequence of exhaustion. Yet the vibes on the bus were strange – Rita hadn't even been told where he was and why he hadn't accompanied them. 'I said something is not right. I kept saying it, and I'm still saying it.'

'I would say that Bob gave his life for his people,' said Judy Mowatt. 'Because it was when he was working that he got sick. I don't think he gave any thought to his toe. He never hopped, he never limped. And when you look at the shoes Bob used to wear onstage, it was boots up to here. So there was no air at all given to the toe. And he worked and he worked and he worked relentlessly, and nobody knew until it got out of control.'

For a long time, Chris Blackwell had kept an apartment on the top floor of the Essex House. Late on the Monday morning, his doorbell rang. It was Bob; even the sense of quiet sadness and physical pain about him could not wither his kingly nature as he told Blackwell the news: that he was suffering from what was apparently an incurable brain tumour and had been given no more than three weeks to live.

This grim news shocked Blackwell. Terrible remorse, even self-recrimination, momentarily took him over. He remembered how Bob had been told by the doctor he saw in 1977 that he should have a check-up every three months. 'Everybody kind of forgot about that. But when something like that happens, it rushes back. I felt I should have reminded him. I should have insisted he had the check-ups. If only he had, they could have caught it a lot earlier: if he'd had his toe amputated in the first place, it probably would have saved his life.'

But what has to be has to be. Before he departed for Pittsburgh, Bob suggested that he and Blackwell have their picture taken together. Blackwell had always disliked the clichéd schmooze picture of the record-company man with his arm around his artist: he felt it was anti-thetical to the spirit of a rebellious music; and he was also wary of any suggestion of racial condescension that might be implied by a picture of himself with Bob in such a pose. Accordingly, he didn't possess a single picture of himself with his most valued and loved artist. When this situation had been rectified, Bob left for Pittsburgh, arriving at the group's hotel that evening. 'What happened?' asked Rita.

Bob gave her a half-explanation: that he hadn't known what was happening; how people were doing cocaine all around him; so he had gone for a run. 'And 'im feel like somebody hit him in the back. And he turned around and couldn't find him speech. He said he didn't know what happened.

'Then I was totally confused. So I insisted on hearing what this doctor said.'

Rita had a dream that night: Bob was wearing a hospital robe and talking to her through a fence, all his hair cut off. The dream deeply worried her. At the soundcheck at the Stanley Theater in Pittsburgh the next afternoon, Bob seemed distant, not present in either his body or mind.

At the group's hotel earlier in the day, there had been a dramatic confrontation between Rita and Skill Cole. 'Why don't you stop the tour?' she had demanded. 'If Bob has a brain tumour, why are we even having a show tonight? *Stop the show!*'

'Cool it, man: I feel all right,' Bob had told his wife. But Rita could see that her husband seemed almost literally in another world.

When they got to the venue, Rita called his mother in Miami. 'I don't like what's happening with Bob here,' she told her. 'It doesn't feel right. I think we're going to come straight home.'

When Rita put the phone down, she ran into Bob's dressing-room. '*Stop the fucking tour now!*' she begged him, becoming almost hysterical when she heard that the neurologist had advised Skill Cole that Bob might as well complete the tour: he was going to die anyway, the doctor had told Bob's friend. When Rita learned that the doctor was a specialist recommended by Danny Sims, she felt she was beginning to unearth a plot. She called Sims and cursed him out on the phone. Then she telephoned those group members who were still at the hotel. 'They are telling me Bob is this sick, but we should go on with the tour . . .'

Instead of the usual four songs that would be tried out at a sound-check, Bob only performed a long-long version of the old Wailers ska tune, 'Keep On Movin'', sitting for much of the time on the drum-riser beside Carly. Although it involved only one tune, it was the longest sound-check any of the group remembered. Most of them felt very sad indeed.

That night's gig was extraordinary: Bob came onstage unannounced and the group played a ninety-minute version of their show that exploded into a succession of encores: 'Redemption Song', 'Coming in from the Cold', 'Could You Be Loved?', 'Is This Love?', and 'Work'. This was literally what he was doing. 'Work' was the last song Bob Marley ever performed onstage, as he gave his absolute best. 'That show had to be great,' said Junior Marvin. 'Everyone was aware that Bob wasn't at all well and that it could be the last show. We were just hoping that it wouldn't be.'

'Now I realise what he went through,' said Judy Mowatt. 'Alone, because it had to be alone. We did not know how he was hurting. We did not know the pain he was going through. We did not know if he was afraid. We did not know if he was wondering if he could do the show or not. He didn't say anything to anybody. But he did do the show. And then they said that that was the last one, because he couldn't go on any more. It was very, very, very sad.'

Later that night, at Rita Marley's instigation, a press release was put out. Bob Marley and the Wailers Tuff Gong International tour of the United States was cancelled. The reason? Bob Marley was suffering from 'exhaustion'. The group returned to Miami, and then dispersed.

LEGEND

Pee Wee, Bob's Rasta friend who was a qualified doctor, had recommended treatment by Dr Issels, and at his clinic in Bad Wiessee in Bavaria Bob Marley's health had initially seemed to improve considerably. Bob was extremely positive: he even began to play football again, and was strong enough to take long hikes in the mountains. Dr Issels's treatment was as much psychological as physical, and he considered the first step towards healing was for the patient to register a sense of forgiveness against all and any injustices they felt had been perpetrated on them. Cleansing the mind, and then the body, was an important step in giving the patient's 'inner physician' a chance to work at healing; such psychological assistance was served up with a detoxifying diet, homeopathic remedies, vitamins, and assorted mysterious injections. Mrs Booker recalled watching as Issels pushed a needle deep into her son's navel, removing it as Bob writhed in pain. 'As the months of dying dragged past, the suffering was etched all over his face. He would fall into fits of shaking, when he would lose all control and shiver from head to toe like a coconut leaf in a breeze. His eyes would turn in his head, rolling in their sockets until even the white jelly was quivering,' she said. Dr Issels never made any secret of his former membership of the SS. But when assorted dreads made their research, they heard rumours that he had been involved in 'medical experiments' in the concentration camp of Auschwitz.

As though confirming his legacy, even in death Bob Marley acquired a new child. On 30 May 1981, almost three weeks after Bob had passed on, his burial the largest funeral a Caribbean nation had ever known, Makeda Jahnesta Marley was born to Yvette Crichton. A radio DJ in Berkeley, a former girlfriend of Johnny Nash, Yvette, Mrs Booker recalled, was a 'fair-skinned' woman from Philadelphia, 'very fidgety and with nuff mouth'. Although Bob had fallen out with Yvette Crichton some time previously, Mrs B. had enlisted her assistance in running the Movement of Jah People fan club. When Bob was ill in New York, Yvette Crichton revealed to Mrs Booker that she was pregnant with Bob's child: she said she had conceived on a day she had taken Bob to see her new apartment. Although Makeda was born at the end of May, it was a late birth, the predicted date of her delivery having been 11 May, the day that Bob Marley passed on.

In 1980, reggae in Jamaica was beginning to change dramatically, as the upcoming generation made its mark with a new sound that made Bob Marley seem rather out of date. Rapidly, Bob Marley's style had found itself far removed from the hot new trends of Kingston's funkier studios. By the end of the year, the Jamaica Labour Party had overwhelmingly won an election, under Edward Seaga, which would keep them in power for the next nine years. It was under Seaga's predecessor Michael Manley's PNP that the rootsical style of reggae associated with Rastafari had flourished. Yet in the months preceding the election Jamaica had become dominated by the 'dancehall' style of producer Henry 'Junjo' Lawes. Dancehall was a rough, immensely catchy 'street' style of reggae. Such names as Yellowman, Eek-A-Mouse, Barrington Levy, and Josey Wales all owed their careers to Lawes. More established acts such as John Holt, the Wailing Souls, Alton Ellis, and Ken Boothe also enjoyed revivals after recording over his rhythm tracks for his Volcano label; with his pairing of the DJs Clint Eastwood and General Saint, favourites of the same UK college circuit on which Bob Marley first had built an audience, Lawes even reached the British charts.

Junjo Lawes's ghetto credentials were impeccable. Born in 1960 in Olympic Way in the slums of west Kingston, he spent much of his youth in McKoy Lane in nearby Whitfield Town – 'badman territory', as one person who knew him described it – where he had been a teenager during the civil war of the 1970s. The neighbourhood was the fiefdom of Jack Massop, the father of the by now late Claudie Massop, the 'ranking' PNP gunman of One Love Peace Concert fame. Due to the efforts of the legendary record producer Bunny 'Striker' Lee, always keen to discourage local youth from a potentially lethal existence, Lawes veered away from following a similar career and in 1978 began singing with the Grooving Locks trio. The same year, he began to produce records, working first with Linval Thompson.

Within twelve months, he had booked a series of sessions at Channel One studio, employing the Roots Radics group as backing band, which were to alter the sound of Jamaican music. The tough sound of the

Radics, who often employed old Studio One rhythms, was slower and more penetrating than the 'rockers' style of the Revolutionaries, Kingston's other dominant studio house-band. Thanks to his street-corner connections, Lawes was adept at sizing and signing up the newest talent, and for these studio dates he used the mixing-desk skills of Hopeton Brown, a young engineer who became famous under the name of 'Scientist' ('science' being another term for obeah in Jamaica): as a result, Barrington Levy's *Bounty Hunter* album, which emerged from these Channel One sessions, came to be considered a classic.

Success came fast. Soon Lawes was producing hits such as Michigan and Smiley's 'Diseases' (a warning of the dangers of unrestrained sexuality), Frankie Paul's 'Pass the Tushenpeng', and John Holt's 'Police in Helicopter'. The astonishingly prodigious Yellowman, who released sixteen albums between 1982 and 1983, recorded several of them for Lawes, including the classic *Mr Yellowman*. (The prolific Yellowman was even briefly – and ludicrously – considered some kind of local superstar successor to Bob Marley. Theses were produced delineating the swing from the 'conscious' subject matter of Bob Marley and the roots artists of the mid-1970s to the 'slack' subject matter of the early 1980s – that Bob Marley had always included a 'slack' element, in the shape of songs like 'Kinky Reggae' and 'Guava Jelly', in his body of work was temporarily overlooked.)

Playing the part of benevolent despot which is the stance of every ghetto youth striving for what in Jamaica is known as 'donship', Junjo Lawes was known for the uncharacteristic financial respect with which he treated his artists. 'I no really check fe money,' he said. 'Every man gwan 'ave a equal share, an artist, a producer, instrument player, and everybody. The set-up now is unlevelled.'

Though these words might have come from the mouth of Bob Marley, the localised coarseness of Junjo Lawes's sound was clearly far removed from the smooth international rock-reggae of the Tuff Gong. At the time of his passing, Bob Marley had lost popular ground in his native land. Although, at home, his tide had temporarily gone out, it was only a matter of a few short years before such an iconic status rolled back in for Bob Marley in Jamaica that he became one-third of a holy triumvirate of omnipresent images completed by HIM Haile Selassie I and Marcus Garvey.

In his last active months, Bob Marley had been looking to change his own sound substantially. By 1980, Bob was increasingly dissatisfied with the rigidity of the Barrett brothers. Family Man was not so regular a presence in the studio at 56 Hope Road as formerly. Bob also was considering replacing the I-Threes with a male chorus. On a tune written that year entitled 'Good Times', recorded in 1991 by the Melody Makers, the group formed by his children, he employed a driving reggae-funk rhythm, perhaps a pointer to the direction in which he wanted his music to develop.

At Mrs Booker's house in Vista Lane in Miami, Bob Marley would leave behind plenty of cassettes of rough material he had been playing around with. Unfortunately, as Mrs Booker explained, 'Most of it is gone. Dem stole it. The tapes walk right out of the house, even while we was burying him.'

However, on a surviving pair of tapes unearthed in a drawer at the house by the reggae archivist Roger Steffens, there are rough demos of eight songs. Steffens and Stephen Davis, whose biography of Bob Marley was published in 1984, have given the tunes titles derived from the lyrics. From the bossa-nova rhythm of 'Pray for Me', a feel Bob was known to have been playing around with between November 1979 and January 1980, they deduce that this was when these songs were recorded at Vista Lane.

Built around a pair of simply strummed chords, the song 'Jailbreaker' refers incessantly to the Hot Steppers, a vicious Kingston street gang also referenced in the song 'Here Comes the Hotstepper' by Ini Kamoze, a number-one record in the United States in 1994, a sign of how, by then, the American reggae market had evolved. 'The jury found I guilty / And I found them guilty too / 'Cause I'm a jailbreaker / A hot stepper' run some of Bob's lyrics, which seem to share certain themes with 'I Shot the Sheriff'. The song, said Davis, is 'a long meditation on crime and punishment'.

'Place of Peace', meanwhile, is a three-chord tune with essentially indecipherable lyrics. After a meandering beginning, 'Record a New Song' ultimately becomes a fully resolved version of 'We and Dem', which appeared on *Uprising*. At the end of the song, Bob Marley can be heard in tears – why? Is it, as Stephen Davis wrote, because 'one can feel the grief of the cancer patient who has realised that his battle against the disease is not one that he is fated to win.'

Following the lovely tune called 'Vexation', Bob returns to some of the themes of 'Jailbreaker' in 'Jump Them Outta Babylon', a song almost twenty minutes long – 'rambling, stream-of-ganjaness prison orientation', as Stephen Davis describes it. Bob speaks of others' perceptions of him, those who see him as an 'escaped prisoner', an 'extortioner', as 'armed and dangerous'; but instead Bob simply advises 'don't get nervous,' and you can see his characteristic twinkling grin, his head angled and chin raised.

On the second tape, the bossa-nova feel of 'Pray for Me' is achieved with the use of a drum machine; unlike the previous tunes, which employ only an acoustic guitar, this also features bass and lead guitar, with lyrics that reference the murderous December 1980 election, also included on 'Can't Take Your Slogans No More', which additionally features bongos and a keyboard. Meanwhile, the final song, 'Right On', is driven by a gospel-style melody, but doesn't finally come together.

By the time Bob Marley's cancer was diagnosed, it was already at a tertiary stage. Yet as these two tapes clearly illustrate, despite this very serious and ceaseless illness, Bob Marley never allowed it to stymie his creativity.

Bob Marley died without leaving a will. In legal terms he was 'intestate' (for many years, his mother, Mrs Booker, believed that this meant 'inter-state', on account of her son's death having effectively taken place whilst he was in transit to Jamaica). Under Jamaican law, dying intestate meant that 45 per cent of Bob's wealth should have been divided among all his children but, days after his death, an alleged conspiracy gutted the multi-million-dollar estate of almost all its money, some $13.4 million going missing. Some of Bob's baby-mothers, who until this time had been receiving regular money from him, were now penniless, drawing welfare payments in those countries that provided it – not in Jamaica, however, where such a system had never been established. In late 1986, it was learned that Bob Marley's former lawyer, David Steinberg, and his former accountant, Marvin Zolt, had persuaded Rita Marley to sign certain back-dated stock-transfer documents, which had the effect of diverting assets from the estate. In other words, Rita Marley, whose skill at replicating her late husband's signature had always concerned him, had forged several documents, which had been backdated to before the death of Bob Marley. These documents transferred record and songwriting royalties and publishing rights to various bank accounts in tax havens in the British Virgin Islands. Although Rita's hand had clearly held the pen, it was ruled that she was not part of this major-league financial scam. To recover the money from Steinberg and Zolt, the Marley family was obliged to sue them.

Rita Marley resigned as an administrator of the Bob Marley estate, and the Jamaican High Court ruled that a Jamaican bank be brought in to adminster it. In March 1989, Chris Blackwell bought the entire Bob

Marley estate, put up for sale by the Jamaican government, for the bargain-basement price of $8.6 million. For this, Blackwell purchased the rights to all of Bob's recordings, his song catalogue, and all future royalties. However, he then turned all income from this over to Bob's children.

On 11 May 1983, the second anniversary of Bob's death, Tuff Gong, through Island Records, released a new Bob Marley album, *Confrontation*. Some of the songs were out-takes from the *Survival* and *Uprising* sessions, others had been worked up from demo tapes, with the Wailers and the I-Threes adding overdubs. 'Mix Up, Mix Up' was built up from a two-track that had Bob's voice on one track and his own scratchy ska-like guitar and a drum machine on the other – edited down from an original eight minutes, it had a rhythm uncannily close to that of Marvin Gaye's 'Sexual Healing'; 'Give Thanks & Praises', close in rhythm and melody to 'If the Cap Fits' on *Rastaman Vibration*, had been written at the same time as that song; similarly, 'I Know' was a *Rastaman Vibration* out-take; 'Jump Nyabinghi' was again from a two-track demo, a master having been lost; 'Blackman Redemption' and 'Rastaman Live Up' had both been released as singles on Tuff Gong in 1979, signs of Bob's new militancy after the softer *Kaya*; 'Chant Down Babylon' and 'Stiff Necked Fools' balanced out the set; 'Trench Town' was a Tuff Gong single; 'Buffalo Soldier', another single, had as its subject the Native Americans who fought on the side of the Union in the American Civil War. Chris Blackwell, who produced *Confrontation*, pointed out that 'Buffalo Soldier' was a particularly meaningful song. As reggae proclaimed self-determination, so Native Americans had found a soul brother in Bob Marley. Many young Apaches considered him to have been a kind of re-born Native American chief – Marley's cry at the beginning of 'Crazy Baldhead' was identical to that of an Apache war-whoop. In Arizona, there was a cult of reverence towards Bob Marley amongst the Hopi.

As a fierce tropical rainstorm suddenly enshrouded in thick cloud his house high in the Blue Mountains, Blackwell emphasised to me quite how extraordinary had been Bob Marley's success. 'Before Bob,' he stressed, 'the only thing that anyone with Rasta hair could succeed at was being a carpenter or a fisherman. But Bob just had it naturally. He was a really exceptional person. When I first met him, I immediately trusted him. People at first would say to me, "Those guys, the Wailers, are real trouble." Which usually means that the people in question want to be treated like human beings.'

It was Bob Marley's simple, clear perception of life, believed Blackwell, that allowed the musician to realise the greatness he was destined to attain. In the hamlet of Nine Miles, deep amidst the steep valleys of the rural interior of Jamaica, his upbringing indelibly stamped basic country truths on Bob Marley, such as the time it takes for things to grow; in his career, he would always let time run its course, hardly typical of many hustling, would-be reggae stars.

In Jamaica in 1983, it seemed accepted as a matter of course that Bob Marley's myth and influence were as yet in their infancy. Even so, Jah Lloyd – 'elected by the elders of Haile Selassie's theocratic government to represent the divine structure to the secular powers of Jamaica' – already placed him alongside such Jamaican national heroes as the nineteenth-century rebels Sam Sharpe and Paul Bogle.

As well as the *Confrontation* record, Tuff Gong had another major release scheduled for that spring, *The Trip* by the Melody Makers. The Melody Makers were four of Bob's children: the then 14-year-old David 'Ziggy' Marley sang and played rhythm guitar; 9-year-old Steve played drums and even wrote some of the songs; 17-year-old Sharon and 15-year-old Cedella also sang. The Wailers provided most of the musical backing. When the Melody Makers' excellent 'What a Plot' single was released at the end of 1982 on Tuff Gong, the uncanny similarity between

Ziggy's vocals and those of his father was immediately apparent. *The Trip* was produced by Ricky Walters, Grub Cooper, and Steve Golding, who had provided the same service for Rita Marley's fine *Harambe* LP, a big Jamaican seller at the end of 1982.

Also in production at Tuff Gong was an I-Threes album, with the Wailers again providing the backing. It was being produced by the stately figure of Mrs Cedella Booker, Bob Marley's mother.

Out at Bull Bay, ten miles to the east of Kingston, the sun was setting, its last rays of the day finally cracking wide open a previously overcast sky. On the delicious Caribbean waters, the fishing boats bobbed peacefully up and down, as they must have done in the days of the Arawak. Twenty yards back from this black-sanded beach – Bob Marley's favourite when he wanted to swim and where he loved to run – Bongo, a 76-year-old dread who joined the Rastafarian faith in 1929, stood framed in the doorway of his shack.

He listened as a young-buck dread from Grenada poured out a variant on the conspiracy theory of Bob Marley's death. 'Every one of us came here to do a portion of Jah's work. Bob rise up as a songster. He died because Babylon killed him. He went innocently into their hands. He was mixing with the wrong sort of people. They began to call him the King of Reggae, when there is only one King: His Majesty Haile Selassie I . . . His blood is spattered all over Europe. Europe is responsible for his death . . . They gave him cocaine,' he asserted, as though privy to secret information. 'They can cut into that cancer germ . . . and his death is on the shoulders of that harlot in Britain!'

At the end of this harangue, Bongo smiled, waited a moment, then offered his own thoughtful interpretation. 'They try to seduce Bob Marley. But he is well alive. Death is not in our language. I and I deal with rest.'

Late one evening, by the front porch of the Tuff Gong house at 56 Hope Road, a white dread, a former American DJ who – inspired by the *Natty Dread* LP – had moved to Jamaica to become a Rastafarian, was standing and reasoning with the gathered brethren. He had heard from Rita Marley, he said, that there were sufficient Bob Marley songs remaining for at least one, possibly two more LPs. With the solemnity of a biblical prophet, he reeled off the titles of Bob Marley's albums, his tone drawing out the significance in which they were strung together: '*Catch a Fire! Burnin'! Natty Dread! . . . Rastaman Vibration! . . . Kaya! . . . Survival! . . . Uprising! . . . And now: Con-fron-tay-shun!*

'Yes-I!' he exclaimed. 'So the next LP, it must be given the title – *JUDGEMENT!!!*'

The release of *Confrontation* was only one of many creative interludes from the seemingly ceaseless legal brouhaha. But *Confrontation*'s success was nothing compared to what would come with the next posthumous album release from Bob Marley: *Legend*, a greatest-hits package, that in itself would become a legend amongst such compilations. 'I wasn't terribly keen on putting together a Best of Bob,' recalled Chris Blackwell. 'We didn't put anything together after he died. In 1984, Dave Robinson was running Island Records. He thought we should do it. I said I thought I didn't really want to get involved in it. He said he would do it himself. He worked a lot with Trevor Wyatt [Island Records' reggae A&R guru] in putting together the compilation.

'He approached the whole thing very, very professionally and very well. He did some market research on it, for example. Not the sort of thing I would have done: I was too close to it, I think. He researched what the general public in England thought about reggae. Did they know about Bob Marley? What did they think about him? Did they like him?

'Through all that research, he finally came up with what should be the album cover, and the album title. He learned that you should keep the word "reggae" out of it. Reggae had a mixed reaction: some people liked reggae, some people hated it. A lot of what people didn't like about Bob Marley was the threatening aspect of him, the revolutionary side.

'So the picture chosen was one of the softest pictures of Bob. It was a very well-conceived, thought-out package. And a very well put together record. It's an undeniable success. It was number one in Britain for nineteen weeks. And it's one of the Top Three catalogue records of all time.'

As Dave Robinson had astutely observed, what the mass public wanted was a record that was essentially Bob Marley Lite. But *Legend* was, all the same, a masterly piece of programming. The tracks ran as follows: 'Is This Love?', 'No Woman, No Cry', 'Could You Be Loved?', 'Three Little Birds', 'Buffalo Soldier', 'Get Up, Stand Up,' 'Stir It Up,' 'One Love/People Get Ready', 'I Shot the Sheriff', 'Waiting in Vain', 'Satisfy My Soul', 'Exodus', and 'Jammin''. When he took over at Island, Dave Robinson had been surprised that the sales of all Bob Marley records were comparatively low – even the biggest seller, *Exodus*, had only just passed 180,000 copies. But *Legend* went on to sell over twenty million records.

By 1988, one of Bob Marley's children seemed about to emulate him. That year, Ziggy Marley released his *Conscious Party* album. His *Hey World* LP had been released two years previously, to less fanfare. But *Conscious Party* was an exceptionally achieved work. Produced by Talking Heads' rhythm section, at Compass Point, Chris Blackwell's studio in Nassau, the record, as the *Rolling Stone* reviewer pointed out, 'may also be the best-sounding reggae album you'll ever hear; the producers, Chris Frantz and Tina Weymouth of Talking Heads, have given Ziggy and the band an aural punch that is both pleasantly high-tech and appropriately rootsy.' Keith Richards added guitar parts to the record; even Mrs Booker added backing vocals. Spawning the hit singles 'Tumblin' Down' and 'Tomorrow People', *Conscious Party* won the Grammy Award for Best

Reggae Album in 1989. Although Ziggy continued to release records, his stage shows featured such a large amount of his father's material that it sometimes seemed his own individuality could be in danger of being subsumed within the identity of Bob Marley. You could also feel the same two decades later about the shows of Damian Marley, Bob's son by Cindy Breakspeare. However, Damian's 2005 release, *Welcome to Jamrock*, was a masterful blend of hip-hop and reggae, direct from the Jamaican cultural zeitgeist, but with higher production values. *Welcome to Jamrock* deservedly won Damian Marley a Grammy in 2006.

Cedella Marley, Bob's first child with Rita, also felt the presence of her father one grim day in 1993. Living by now at the address to which Rita had always aspired, in a sizable house on Skyline Drive on Jack's Hill, with its sweeping views of the Blue Mountains, Kingston, and the Caribbean Sea beyond, next to the home of her mother, Cedella was unsurprised when a battered-looking automobile rammed with what appeared to be ghetto youth pulled into her driveway. Stepping outside to greet these presumed acquaintances, she was stunned when the vehicle's six occupants pulled guns on her, ushering her into the house, tying her up. Fully aware of how such matters often develop in Jamaica, Cedella kept her mouth shut as the men rummaged through the many rooms of her home. 'All the while I just kept thinking of Daddy,' she said. 'He was telling me to stay calm: I could feel him hovering over me.' After almost two hours, as suddenly as they had arrived, the men disappeared. They took nothing with them, but left an awareness of the perils Cedella's father had faced in his efforts to bring the ghetto uptown, to 56 Hope Road.

In August 1981, Peter Tosh played four shows at the Roxy on Sunset Strip in Los Angeles. In the Roxy dressing-room he told Roger Steffens, the

Californian reggae authority, how Haile Selassie had appeared in 1935 before the League of Nations. When he did so, diplomats from other nations had pulled out guns and shot at him, the bullets bouncing off his clothing. When His Majesty gazed at them with his full ferocity, these assailants fell to the ground, dead. When Roger Steffens questioned Peter Tosh as to the veracity of this tale, Peter became furious. Sticking a finger in Steffens's chest, he declared, 'This is history, I tell yuh. You nuh understand history.'

After having released three increasingly weak records on the Rolling Stones label, Peter Tosh arrived in 1984 at a Manhattan recording studio where Mick Jagger was essaying a solo album. Ignoring the assembled participants, the Minister of Herb dismissed them as 'battymen'.

Mick Jagger told Peter Tosh that he had read newspaper headlines in which Peter, claiming he had never been paid by Rolling Stones Records, had declared: 'I AM GOING TO KILL MICK JAGGER.' Mick knelt down in front of him: 'Then kill me now, Peter.' The others present swiftly departed the studio. When they returned, however, Peter Tosh and Mick Jagger were jamming on some tunes. Mick had told Peter he didn't know he hadn't received any royalties, and personally had written him a cheque for $100,000.

Peter's complex relationship with the Rolling Stones extended to Keith Richards. The Stones guitarist owned a clifftop property in the north-coast resort of Ocho Rios called Point-of-View. Whilst Keith was living in New York, Peter decided he would 'capture' the house, moving in like a squatter. When Keith learned of this, he finally flew down to Montego Bay, from where he phoned Point-of-View. 'I'm coming home now, Peter,' said the Stone, 'you'd better not be there when I arrive.' 'I am waiting for you with a machine-gun,' was Peter's response. 'Well, I'll be there in ninety minutes, so you'd better be sure you've put in the magazine,' said Keith.

When Keith arrived at his Ocho Rios home, Peter was nowhere to be seen. 'See,' said Keith, 'I always said all these Jamaican so-called hard-men are just pussies.'

In October 1986, Dennis 'Leppo' Lobban, a friend of Peter Tosh from their days as youths in Trench Town, was released from prison, where he had served a twelve-year sentence for robbery and attempted murder. During the course of his time in custody in Spanish Town prison, he had never ceased to denounce Peter for failing to visit him or support his family.

Out of jail, Leppo paid several visits to Peter, hustling money from him. On Monday, 7 September 1987, he once again made the trek to Peter's uptown home – since the previous month Peter had been complaining to Marlene, his girlfriend, that their Barbican house 'smelled of death'. Peter let Leppo know that he had arrived back in Jamaica from New York the day before. The ghetto badman complained that he was destitute, that he didn't even have a bed of his own. Marlene unleashed a stream of vitriol in Leppo's direction, but Peter immediately gave him a brand-new bed, as well as money.

Yet Leppo was hardly mollified. In subsequent days he also approached Bunny Wailer and Gregory Isaacs, among others, demanding money from them in a semi-menacing manner.

On Friday, 11 September 1987, Peter was holding a small social gathering at his home, to which he had invited a number of close brethren. At around 7:30 p.m., his friend Michael Robinson, a local craftsman, Doc Brown, a bush doctor, and Santa Davis, the drummer and percussionist who played with him in his group, were already there, along with Marlene. The JBC radio DJ Jeff 'Free-I' Dixon and his wife, Joy, were expected at any moment. When the sound of knocking came from the front gate, Michael Robinson was despatched to answer it.

At the gate was Leppo, who immediately admitted himself to the yard, followed by two other shadowy figures. As soon as Michael Robinson led them into the house's entrance hall, the three men produced 9 mm auto-matic pistols and pointed them at his head. Pushing Robinson up the stairs to the living-room, Leppo ordered everyone to 'get flat'.

Leppo was certain that Peter Tosh would have brought back cash from New York – although this was not the case. In the living-room's gloomy half-light the trio of gunmen moved edgily around the figures prone on the floor. 'Where the money? Where the silver? Where the gold?' demanded one.

'We don't have any money here!' screamed out Marlene, who was lying on the floor next to Peter.

Leppo cursed her as an obeahwoman, saying it was her alleged magic powers that had held back Peter from his customary generosity. 'Yuh dead tonight,' he vowed.

'No wait,' said Peter. 'We can sort this out.'

He looked up and into the face of the tallest gunman. As Peter lay there, this man leant down and yanked a gold chain from his neck. As he stooped over Peter to pistol-whip him, the musician spontaneously parried the blow with a karate move.

At this point, 'Free-I' Dixon and his wife arrived at the gate of Peter's home. Realising who was knocking at the gate, Marlene asked Leppo to leave them alone. But one of the other gunmen admitted them to the house, immediately thrusting a gun in their faces. 'Lie down 'pon the ground,' he ordered.

Meanwhile, the tall gunman stormed into the kitchen, returning with a machete, vowing to cut off Peter's head if he didn't reveal where money was hidden.

Leppo scurried about the house, searching for cash. Peter attempted to reason with him, saying he could draw money out of the bank for him when it opened the following Monday morning.

But then the tall gunman snapped at Leppo: 'Do what yuh come for!'

Leppo fired off a shot at Marlene. It skimmed across her scalp and ricocheted into Joy Dixon's mouth, shattering teeth and exiting through her cheek. Both women played dead.

Then he pressed his pistol up against Peter Tosh's forehead and fired twice. Peter's body arched, and he collapsed.

The three gunmen began to shoot indiscriminately around the room: Doc Brown was shot in the head and died instantly. Two shots slammed into Free-I behind his ear; he slipped into a coma and died three days later. Michael Robinson was shot twice, but survived. A bullet creased Santa's shoulder; another penetrated his back, never to be removed.

The gunmen were soon apprehended. Dennis 'Leppo' Lobban was sentenced to life in prison. Peter Tosh was the second member of the Wailers to be shot dead that year; in April, Carly Barrett had been gunned down, murdered as a result of a conspiracy between his wife and her lover. Ten years later, Junior Braithwaite, who had returned from Chicago to Kingston, also died by the gun.

In the time just before the death of Bob Marley, Bunny Wailer had allied his songwriting and recording to the ragamuffin dancehall style popularised by Junjo Lawes. But shortly before Bob finally passed on, Bunny worked at Harry J's and Dynamic Sound re-recording a number of classic tunes written by his former musical spar; these included 'I Shot the Sheriff', 'War', 'Slave Driver', 'Redemption Song', and 'No Woman, No Cry'. They were intended for an album which, when released in Jamaica on his own Solomonic label under the title of *Tribute to the Late Hon. Robert Nester* [sic] *Marley, OM*, immediately became the biggest record in Jamaica. Inspired, Chris Blackwell signed Bunny to Island Records once again, and Bunny recorded *Bunny Wailer Sings the Wailers* for him, a record of much earlier, relatively unknown Wailers material – among the tracks were 'Dancing Shoes', 'Walk the Proud Land', 'Mellow Mood', and 'I'm the Toughest'. Released towards the end of 1981, the record sold well around the world.

Later, Bunny Wailer flirted with the new digital style of dancehall that dominated Jamaican music from the middle of the 1980s. Finally touring America, he headlined in Manhattan at Madison Square Garden, coming close to selling out the venue – to the amazement of its management. But his refusal to promote his tour – he turned down an appearance on the nationally influential *David Letterman Show* – led to attendances going downhill from New York onwards. Eventually, the concert dates simply dwindled away.

All the same, his raised public profile had repositioned Bunny Wailer. Fittingly for a man who found himself developing into one of reggae's elder statesmen (although always second to the more congenial Burning Spear), Bunny Wailer was three times awarded a Grammy for Best Reggae Album – in 1990, 1994, and 1996.

In the time up to Peter Tosh's death, relations between him and Bunny Wailer had been frosty. In a fraternal spirit, Bunny had offered Peter the support slot when he had played Madison Square Garden the previous year. But, disappointingly, Peter had regarded the suggestion as a 'bumba-cla'at insult'.

Although Bunny had sufficient contact with Bob Marley in his 'visions', Peter Tosh resolutely failed to appear in them after his murder. But then Bunny had a dream in which he saw both the former Wailers. In the dream, Bob Marley addressed Peter Tosh as 'Perks', the nickname given to him by Bob, and used only by Bob, especially when wanting to dissolve any fractious mood between them. To Bunny, this was proof that this was Bob genuinely communicating with him; in the dream he experienced how the mutual laughter of all three of the Wailers turned to tears of joy.

* * *